MUIRHEAD LIBRARY OF PHILOSOPHY

An admirable statement of the aims of the Library of Philosophy was provided by the first editor, the late Professor H. J. Muirhead, in his desscription of the original programme printed in Erdmann's *History of Philosophy* under the date 1890. This was slightly modified in subsequent volumes to take the form of the following statement:

The Muirhead Library of Philosophy was designed as a contribution to the History of Modern Philosophy under the heads: first of different Schools of Thought—Sensationalist, Realist, Idealist, Intuitivist; secondly of different Subjects—Psychology, Ethics, Aesthetics, Political Philosophy, Theology. While much had been done in England in tracing the course of evolution in nature, history, economics, morals and religion, little had been done in tracing the development of thought on these subjects. Yet 'the evolution of opinion is part of the whole evolution'.

By the co-operation of different writers in carrying out this plan it was hoped that a thoroughness and completeness of treatment, otherwise unattainable, might be secured. It was believed also that from writers mainly British and American fuller consideration of English Philosophy than it had hitherto received might be looked for. In the earlier series of books containing, among others, Bosanquet's *History of Aesthetics*, Pfleiderer's *Rational Theology since Kant*. Albee's *History of English Utilitarianism*, Bonar's *Philosophy and Political Economy*, Brett's *History of Psychology*, Ritchie's *Natural Rights*, these objects were to a large extent effected.

In the meantime original work of a high order was being produced both in England and America by such writers as Bradley, Stout, Bertrand Russell, Baldwin, Urban, Montague and others, and a new interest in foreign works, German, French and Italian, which had either become classical or were attracting public attention, had developed. The scope of the Library thus became extended into something more international, and it is entering on the fifth decade of its existence in the hope that it may contribute to that mutual understanding between countries which is so pressing a need of the present time.

The need which Professor Muirhead stressed is no less pressing today, and few will deny that philosophy has much to do with enabling us to meet it, although no one, least of all Muirhead himself, would regard that as the sole, or even the main, object of philosophy. As Professor Muirhead continues to lend the distinction of his name to the Library of Philosophy, it seemed not inappropriate to allow him to recall us to these aims in his own words. The emphasis on the history of thought seemed to me also very timely; and the number of important works promised for the Library in the near future augur well for the continued fulfilment, in this and in other ways, of the expectations of the original editor.

H. D. LEWIS

THE MUIRHEAD LIBRARY OF PHILOSOPHY

General Editor: H. D. Lewis

Professor of History and Philosophy of Religion in the University of London

THE MUIRHEAD LIBRARY OF PHILOSOPHY—*contd.*

The Muirhead Library of Philosophy

EDITED BY H. D. LEWIS

THE NATURE OF THOUGHT

THE NATURE OF THOUGHT

By

BRAND BLANSHARD

Professor of Philosophy, Yale University

IN TWO VOLUMES

VOLUME TWO

LONDON: GEORGE ALLEN & UNWIN LTD
NEW YORK: HUMANITIES PRESS INC

FIRST PUBLISHED IN 1939
SECOND IMPRESSION 1948
THIRD IMPRESSION 1955
FOURTH IMPRESSION 1964
FIFTH IMPRESSION 1969

Reprinted in 1978 in the United States
of America by Humanities Press and in
England by Harvester Press by arrangement
with George Allen & Unwin Ltd.

USA ISBN 0-391-00923-0
ENGLAND ISBN 0-85527-545-6

Printed in the United States of America

CONTENTS OF VOLUME TWO

BOOK III

THE MOVEMENT OF REFLECTION

CHAPTER XX

SPECIFYING THE PROBLEM

CHAPTER XXI

OBSERVATION

CHAPTER XXII

INVENTION AND ASSOCIATION

CHAPTER XXIII

THE NATURE OF INVENTION

CHAPTER XXIV

THE SUBCONSCIOUS IN INVENTION

CHAPTER XXV

THE TESTS OF TRUTH

CONTENTS 13

CHAPTER XXVI

COHERENCE AS THE NATURE OF TRUTH

CONTENTS

BOOK IV

THE GOAL OF THOUGHT

CHAPTER XXX

LOGICAL POSITIVISM AND NECESSITY

CHAPTER XXXI

CONCRETE NECESSITY AND EXTERNAL RELATIONS

CHAPTER XXXII

CONCRETE NECESSITY AND INTERNAL RELATIONS

BOOK THREE

THE MOVEMENT OF REFLECTION

CHAPTER XVIII

THE GENERAL NATURE OF UNDERSTANDING

1. The account of reflection that follows is the complement of the theory of ideas presented in the preceding book. We have held that an idea is a purpose which only the object would fulfil, and is itself a partial realization of that object. The theoretic impulse expressed in the idea is an effort to get the object as it really is within experience. But the immanent end of thought forbids us to say that we have reached the object as it really is so long as that object remains unintelligible. In the present book we shall study the process by which thought seeks to render it intelligible. In Book IV we shall try to see what intelligibility means.

In some ways it would have been more natural to take the last point first. If all ideas, judgements, and processes of reflection, are directed toward the goal of intelligibility, it would seem that the path which thought must travel would be plainer were the goal in sight from the beginning. But for good or ill we have elected to follow another order, and to let the character of the end emerge gradually, as it does in experience itself. That such an end is gradually emerging will now, no doubt, be clear. We found traces of it even in the tied ideas of perception, though its workings there were dim. As the earlier free ideas gave place to ideas that were more explicit and more general, the character of the end came little by little into evidence. In the process of reflection it will become far clearer, rising where the rational control is firmest to richness and dominance. But the best and purest of human thinking is a broken and fragmentary affair compared with what it would be if its immanent end were working fully and freely through it. What thought of this kind would be like we shall try to see at the end of our course.

Meanwhile it is imperative that we should not proceed in the dark. If the movement of reflection is governed, however brokenly, by an end, it is necessary to know, at least in general, what this is; otherwise we cannot even be sure we are dealing with reflection at all. The present chapter will try to meet this need. Without attempting to set out the ultimate end of thought, it will sketch that end in the rough and provisional character in which it operates in common reflection. We shall hold that the movement of reflection is always more or less dominated by an ideal of understanding, and that what understanding means is apprehending something in a system which renders it necessary. The degree to which reflection is really reasoning, or on the other hand mere random association, is determined by the extent to which the immanent ideal of system has assumed control of the process. The direction the reasoning takes, its lapses into irrelevance and returns into the groove of necessity, the fact that it starts at all or ever comes to an end, its tentativeness in early stages or feeble intelligences, its acceleration in swiftness and ease as it goes up the scale—all these and indeed nearly everything else of real importance about the process of reflection are to be explained by the relative dominance of this end in minds differently placed.

2. The complaint is often made that in the account of inference in the logic books no light is thrown upon the way thought actually works. The point, in a sense, is inept. It is not the business of the logician to study the vagaries of actual thinking, but to define what ideal demonstration consists in. At the same time the light thrown by logic on actual thinking would be far greater if the ideal of cogency were recognized, not as an iron paradigm to which reasoning must conform either wholly or not at all, but as an end attainable in degree, a spirit or ideal that animates in some measure all thinking, but is never fully realized even in the best. It is a main contention of this work that unless thought is recognized as the pursuit of such an ideal, and the ideal itself is defined, neither logic nor the psychology of thinking can do its work.

Consider for a moment the task of logic. In this study, inference has been traditionally taken as the final stage, and inference seems to be any sort of thinking that can be made to conform to any one of a set of heterogeneous patterns, syllogistic, mathematical, inductive, and so on. These patterns have among themselves no discernible unity. As against this we maintain that inference is everywhere and always directed to one end, intelligibility, that this means essentially the same in all regions of experience, and that it is a principal business of logic to give unity to the types of inference by relating them to this end. But to do so it must of course define the end. If we found a work on aesthetics instructing us in detail about the technique of the arts, but supplying no sort of suggestion as to what that beauty is which all the techniques of all the arts are attempting to achieve, we should say that, however useful in practice it might be, it fell short of the full purpose of a work on aesthetics. If we found a treatise on ethics that enumerated rules of good conduct, but forgot the *summum bonum*, we should feel that as a work on ethics it left something to be desired. Why should we not feel the same about works on logic that discuss in disconnection the various forms of thought, and neglect the end which thought in its every variety and at every level is seeking to realize? Surely the account should not abruptly close when descriptions have been given of Aristotelian deduction, of the postulates and theorems of the author's favourite symbolic system, and of some revision of Mill's canons. For the question still remains, When matter *has* been arranged in these patterns, is it then fully intelligible? Does such arrangement bring the kind of insight that means complete understanding? If it does not, then it is idle to say that the task of logic has been done, for it is the task of logic precisely to describe the conditions under which the theoretic sense would arrive at ultimate satisfaction. And we shall see in our final book that neither conformity to the rules of the formal logician nor adherence to the fixed conjunctions of the empiricist will fulfil the demand of that impulse. It is seeking a further and different goal.[1]

[1] The above strictures on books of logic are of course not meant to apply indiscriminately. A large exception would have to be made for the writings of Bradley, Bosanquet, and Joseph, which seem to me

If a clear view of that goal is important for logic, it is almost equally important for an adequate psychology of thinking. Actual reflection is commonly punctuated by lapses into irrelevancy, followed by recalls into the path of the argument; and it is about as hard to see how such a process, with its baffled but incessantly resurgent attempts at rationality, is to be explained without reference to the implicit ideal toward which it keeps veering, as to explain the movements of iron filings on a paper without reference to the powerful magnet that is moving about underneath. At any rate our own account of the process of reflection, from the first shock that sets it off to its final verification through appeal to knowledge as a whole, will be a study of the operation in thought of this implicit ideal. There can be no psychology of reasoning worth the name that is not informed throughout by logic. Nor is there the slightest need to confuse the two. Logic is a study of the ideal of thought, that is, of the structure required of any object in which the theoretic impulse can rest; the psychology of reasoning is a study of the vicissitudes of thought in its attempt to attain that ideal. It follows that the relative emphasis on logic and on psychology must vary in different portions of our account. In this book, after a brief provisional statement of the ideal, we shall turn to psychology. As our account of reflection nears its end, and we find thought demanding verification by reference to its ultimate ideal, we shall turn more and more to logic.

3. Reference to the end is thus indispensable for both logic and psychology. But if we were to say without further ado that ordinary acts of thinking were attempts at realizing in experience a concrete systematic necessity, it would probably be set down as neither true nor illuminating. We believe it to be both; but

to be governed by a sound conception of logic, and to be far more helpful to the student interested in what we should call understanding than the writings of the formalists, whether Aristotelian or symbolic, or of those critics of formalism who write about 'logic for use'.

we do not expect to convince anyone of that except by detailed argument later. Meanwhile it is obvious that common reflection is governed by some end, if only a first approximation to this remote and ultimate end. Let us see if we can extract this from some typical cases of thinking. It is important that the cases should be really typical; for by taking thought in undeveloped or peripheral forms, as it appears, for example, in perception, in the train of ideas of a day-dream, or even in the syllogisms of the logic books, we could easily misconceive its purpose and start ourselves on the wrong track. Where are we to look for instances of reflective thought that will be typical and unchallengeable? We cannot do better than to look at any attempt to answer explicitly the question Why? All explicit thinking is the attempt to answer questions; but some questions are more obvious signals for reflection than others—Why? for example, than Who? or What? or Where? or When? Not that we should get a different answer in the end if we took these latter as typical; we shall see in a moment that this is not true; but the question Why? is the one that most indisputably calls for a reflective answer. If this is accepted, we have next to ask, Is there any end that is uniformly sought as an answer to this question? The reply seems easy: the *explanation* of something. But when is anything explained? Presumably when it is understood. But when is it understood? What character or arrangement must the matter possess if the question Why? is to be answered, and we can say, Now I understand? This stage is reached, we reply, only when some hypothesis regarding the point that was in doubt is apprehended as part of a system which is taken to render it necessary. Let us look at some examples.

4. A schoolboy is reading of Lindbergh's flight to Paris. He notes that at nightfall the flier was seen over Newfoundland, disappearing eastward, and a question crops up in his mind. Why in the world should a flier headed for Europe turn up in Newfoundland? He was aiming at the Irish coast, wasn't he?

And that is east of New York, isn't it? Well then, why didn't he fly straight across? If he wanted the shortest route to the east, why should he start by going a thousand miles to the north? The boy is undoubtedly reflecting. What has started the process in this case is the perception that two apparent facts do not fit together. A flier crossing the ocean would follow a straight line; but this flier flew far out of a straight line; and the two facts do not square with each other. Now what does thinking in such a case attempt to do? It attempts to find coherence in the facts either by showing that the two ill-assorted pieces do fit into a single picture after all, or that one of them can be dropped as a mere mistake. That this really is the aim is shown by what brings the process to rest. The boy asks himself, perhaps, Am I right about my facts? Is it true that Newfoundland lies northward and far out of the course? He goes and looks at a globe or atlas, and finds to his astonishment that the tip of Newfoundland lies almost on a straight line from New York to the Irish coast. That particular activity of thought now comes to an end, because the boy has got what he wants; the point is cleared up; he understands. And what does the understanding consist in? It consists in finding order or system among facts that seemed ununified and even conflicting. 'Straight across' and 'around by Newfoundland' did not fit together; but when he has arranged the various points according to the plan on the map, they do fit together, and his desire to understand is satisfied.

Understanding in this case is easy because the whole that is required is simple and homogeneous, and all that is needed is to order a few points in space. But a system that is homogeneous is not always so simple. The task of understanding geography or astronomy consists, in no small part, in relating spatially a prodigious number of bodies of land and bodies of water, of planets and suns; and the full pattern of this spatial universe runs far beyond the present grasp of the mind. So does that of events in time. Any understanding of history must begin by the placing of many occurrences in the order of before and after, but all that we can do at present is to drive a few stakes, so to speak, in a stream without beginning or end. Another such homogeneous system is that of number, within which lie all the problems of arithmetic; another is that of pure quantity, dealt with by algebra; still another is that of degree. These systems or orders are all homogeneous, yet inexhaustible.

5. When we begin to include in our whole several systems at once, the possibilities of complexity are much increased. But understanding retains the same meaning. A physical event or law is explained by putting it in a framework in which the orders of time, space and causality are combined into one whole. What understanding here consists in cannot be better illustrated than by the few lucid sentences in which W. K. Clifford brings the meaning of Boyle's law within the grasp of the layman:

'There is a law of gases which asserts that when you compress a perfect gas the pressure of the gas increases exactly in the proportion in which the volume diminishes.' And 'it so happens that this law has been explained; we know precisely what it is that happens when a gas is compressed. We know that a gas consists of a vast number of separate molecules, rushing about in all directions with all manner of velocities . . . but so that the mean velocity of the molecules of air in this room, for example, is about twenty miles a minute. The pressure of the gas on any surface with which it is in contact is nothing more than the impact of these small particles upon it. On any surface large enough to be seen there are millions of these impacts in a second. . . .' 'Suppose the vessel to have parallel sides, and that there is only one particle rushing backwards and forwards between them: then it is clear that if we bring the sides together to half the distance, the particle will hit each of them twice as often, or the pressure will be doubled. Now it turns out that this would be just as true for millions of particles as for one, and when they are flying in all directions instead of in only one direction and its opposite.'[1]

[1] *Lectures and Essays*, I. 157, 167; passages from the two pages have been pieced together. The whole essay is instructive in this connection.

Here is a good example of giving thought what it wants. 'That pressure should be strictly proportional to density is', as Clifford says, 'a comparatively strange, unfamiliar phenomenon'; and when confronted with it the reflective student is inclined to ask why it should hold. He is dissatisfied because the two changes, though they do occur together, seem to have no inner connection. To satisfy the demand of thought, to understand, would clearly mean in this case to lay hold of such a connection. In Clifford's explanation this is done; and how is it done? By reconceiving both density and pressure so that they belong to a single scheme, density as the number of particles rushing about in a given space, pressure as their impact upon the sides of the container. So conceived, elements that appear to have no relation are seen to belong together inevitably as two aspects of one whole.

Take a final example, of somewhat greater complexity again. We are reading a newspaper and come upon the remark, 'Now that the tariff on wool has gone up, we shall be paying more for our winter suits'. If we have thought at all about economics, we shall take the statement in our stride, but if we have not, it may give us pause. 'Why should the government's making Englishmen pay more to ship their wool to America make me pay more for a suit? I don't understand in the least.' Here is a typical intellectual difficulty, which consists in the annoying awareness that terms supposed to be connected with each other lie about in a disorderly litter, without pattern or evident relation. The question Why? is a demand that this litter be cleared up. Let us look at the sort of insight that would achieve this.

Such insight must be reached by a mental experiment which will somehow thread the scattered items upon one string. Start from the thought of foreigners shipping wool into this country. Add ideally a tax on this wool. It follows, if the tax is high enough, that the foreigners stop sending wool. Why? Because if they must pay shipping charges and also a tariff charge upon its entry into this country, they cannot sell it here at current prices and still make any profit. Very well;

suppose they do stop sending it; what follows? It follows that the American producers of wool will have the field all to themselves. And what follows from that? Normally a rise in price. Why? Partly because the rivals who might undersell them have now withdrawn. Partly because their withdrawal has made wool scarcer, and the scarcer it is the more expensive it is. Why? Because its producers will get all they can for it, and they can obviously get more if they sell it all to those who want it most and are ready to pay the highest prices. Thus the price of wool goes up. Hence the price of suits made in whole or in part of wool also goes up. The sequence is thus complete; impose the high tariff and I shall pay more for my winter suit.

That modifying factors commonly affect this sequence is no doubt true. Still, the thread of causal tendency is clear, and at the end the question Why? that started the course of reflection has met with an answer. Most people who followed this thread would feel that they now understood; and hence we can raise our former question, Why does such an answer satisfy? We can only reply as before. The imposition of a tariff and the higher cost of the suit are no longer isolated items, but incidents in one plot. We have constructed a little system in which we pass from one part to another, and see how a change in one part sets up responsive changes in the rest. Imports, tariffs, the scarcity or abundance of a commodity, prices, the desire for profit, are seen to be so involved with each other that a change in one of them produces effects throughout the system. And the better we have grasped this system, the better we understand the linkage between any two of its parts.

If there is a doubt whether this result is typical, it would be well for the reader to take cases at random and subject them to analysis. Why does ordinary light, in passing through a crystal, break up into a spectrum? Why did the French Revolution occur? Why do makers of machines put safety valves on boilers, or fly-wheels on engine crankshafts? Why is treason commonly punished with so heavy a penalty? Why should we accept the

equality of the angles in a triangle to exactly two right angles?
Why should winding a clock at the back make the hands in
front go round and move at an even speed? If the reader has
any doubt that what thinking endeavours to reach is a system,
more or less large, in which to connect events or facts previously
unrelated, let him take what he would regard as a satisfactory
answer to any of these questions, or to any other of his own
choice, and look at it analytically. This will give him a check
on our result.

6. Some may find apparent exceptions readily. They may
say that we have virtually settled the matter in advance by
taking, as the characteristic query of reflection, Why? If we
had looked at the sort of answers given to When? or Where?
or Who? or What? or above all, How? we should have seen
that reflection is not always seeking system. But such 'exceptions', on inquiry, strengthen our position. Answers to When?
and Where? always place something in an order of time or
space, and we have seen that these are systems, though of
comparatively simple construction. Who? and What? express
the desire to identify, and we have likewise seen that to identify
is to assign something to its place in a system of classification;
the fact that this is not fully explicit is irrelevant. How? may
excite more doubt. It may be said that the commonest use of
reflection is in helping toward some practical end, in suggesting
how to do something—to catch a train, or get a position, or
build a bridge—and that in such cases it is pedantry to describe
the purpose of thought as the construction of a system. But
the answer lies in pointing out a confusion, the time-worn
confusion, indeed, on which pragmatism thrives, the confusion
between knowing and doing. However strong may be the
interest of a bridge-builder in getting his bridge completed,
it is clear that within this interest, or alongside it, another is
at work. For unless he conforms his building to the laws of
mathematics and to the theory of strength of materials, his
bridge will never get built; and to conform his work to these

laws he must apprehend them. Now to apprehend a law is one thing, and to apply it in practice is another; it would be idle to say that a mathematician, *qua* mathematician, is also an engineer, and an engineer, precisely to the extent that he is an engineer, is also a mathematician. Granting that some understanding of the laws of nature or the construction of a machine is indispensable if one is to manipulate them successfully, it is surely clear that the understanding and the manipulation are not the same thing. And once this distinction is made, it is evident that thought, even when in the service of action, has an interest or aim of its own. That aim is at understanding the nature of things. And by understanding is meant apprehension in a system.

7. What kind of system? It would be hard to ask a philosopher a more critical question than this, for upon his answer to it hang his conceptions of intelligibility, of proof, of the task of philosophy, of the very nature and prospects of reason in the world. The answers to it have been various. Some philosophers have conceived of thought as an effort to get things into a hierarchical order of genus and species, the problem being one of right classification. Others have been so convinced of the superiority of mathematical and particularly of geometrical understanding to every other kind that they have attempted to force all philosophy into its mould. There have been eminent scientists, like Lord Kelvin, who declared that an explanation in science first became intelligible to them when it was translated into the terms of a mechanical model. There have been eclectics who held that understanding could be achieved by relating things in any one of a wide variety of categories—causality, means and end, genus and species, and others. Now it is of the first importance to decide among these conflicting claims; no precise notion of the end or office of thought is possible without it; and we shall take up the problem in earnest in due time. What must here be said, however, is that a review of reflection at ordinary levels supports the eclectic position.

Though it is always system that is aimed at, the systems accepted as satisfactory are of the most various types. The plain man would count it ridiculous to confine genuine understanding to mathematics, and, for example to deny Stanley's understanding in history, or Bradley's in philosophy, or Faraday's in physics, because these men conspicuously lacked mathematical grasp. He would even concede the name without question to a mechanic's mastery of the functions of a carburettor, a speaker's 'intuitive' perception of how to persuade a certain audience, or the judgement of an art critic as to why an artist drew a certain line. The wholes used in common thought as providing understanding are thus of the widest variety. The one feature they own in common appears to be that they are systems with interdependent parts.

8. This somewhat curious situation closes a few doors in the study of reasoning and opens up certain others. It raises an initial presumption against logical purism and fundamentalism. To confine reasoning to the movement from premises to conclusion in syllogism, or from antecedent to consequent in a mathematical system, is at least *prima facie* absurd, just as is the attempt to confine proof to such a framework, for we do in fact find intellectual satisfaction in systems of different kinds. Various possibilities in the treatment of reasoning would seem to remain open. One might review the types of linkage that are accepted in actual thought as making things intelligible: the cause-and-effect connection, for example, which is the great principle of explanation in the natural sciences; the relation of means and end, which covers so much of human behaviour; the types of implication used in mathematics; the syllogism as interpreted by the *dictum de omni*, by Mill, and by Kant. But to do this, and this only, would be both needless and a mistake; it has been very competently done already; and to leave these miscellaneous norms merely standing side by side would suggest a logical pluralism which we shall see to be untenable. So far as a treatment of the chief of these is necessary to show their relativity to the end of understanding, we shall deal with them in our final book. Another possibility would be to review these forms as part of a 'morphology of knowledge', indicating the extent to which each embodied the ideal, much as a biologist would study the evolution of a species. But this also has been done, and far too well to admit of improvement by the present writer. Part of the work has been brilliantly executed by Lotze and Bradley; it was essentially the task set himself by Hegel in the two powerful but dark barbarities he perpetrated under the name of Logic; it was done with more fidelity to fact, and explicitly as a morphology of knowledge,[1] by Bosanquet, though with a certain want of literary skill that for many has drawn a veil over its soundness of conception and workmanship.

In the account of reasoning offered by these and other writers, there seem, however, to be two comparative lacunae. On the one hand, there has been a lack of interest in showing how the logical ideal actually operates in the movement of reflection, and hence the insights achieved by the logicians and philosophers of 'the great tradition' have been imperfectly utilized in the psychology of reasoning. Thinkers of this school have been disposed to regard the treatment of the reasoning process put forward by the psychology that prides itself on being a natural science as inept, clumsy and naïve.[2] But they have not succeeded in awaking the psychologists to any conviction of sin, and not caring themselves to venture into psychology so far as to offer alternative accounts, they have too often been dismissed as obscurantists. Our own study is a modest eirenicon. It seeks to supply in outline an account of the reflective process in which the presence and operation of the logical ideal are recognized as clearly as the logicians have a right to demand, while the process is still regarded as a psycho-

[1] This is the subtitle of his *Logic*.
[2] Though they would no doubt make exceptions, Professor Pillsbury, in his little book on the *Psychology of Reasoning*, has obviously made good use of philosophical logic; Sir William Mitchell's *Structure and Growth of the Mind* is masterly; Ward and Stout have done much admirable work.

logical one, consisting of a series of steps, each one of which requires to be accounted for.

The other lacuna, which perhaps is less conspicuous, lies in the absence of straightforward accounts of the ideal itself. There are fairly good brief defences of the coherence theory, acute and detailed criticisms of it, more or less brilliant adumbrations of the Absolute in Bradley, comprehensive statements of the programme of 'speculative philosophy' by several of the Gifford lecturers. But with the possible exception of Bosanquet's *Implication and Linear Inference*, one misses in this extraordinarily able work any simple account of the ideal of systematic necessity and of the reasons why it seems so compelling, as compared with empiricism on the one hand and formalism on the other. This is the second need which this work would seek in its measure to supply. It will be dealt with in Book IV. We turn now to the steps in the movement of reflection.

CHAPTER XIX

HOW REFLECTION STARTS

1. It is sometimes said that we never think unless we have to. This in a sense is true, though the sense is not quite obvious. Some have held that we are driven to think by mere physical necessity; the pragmatists would add to this a co-operating practical necessity; we should ourselves be inclined to admit the presence of both, at least on most occasions; but we should insist upon a further element of another kind. Let us look for a moment at the three views.

Imagine someone engaged in a course of reflection. The philosopher Kant, let us say, has just come into his study, looked off through the window to the tower upon which he liked to fix his eye as an aid to fixing attention, and set out in search of the truth about causality. What has started the process? Perhaps someone will say, an unpredictable act of free will. If this means that it had no conditions or antecedents that contributed to its occurrence or to making it what it was, our question is of course inept. But then no one holds this view. No one would soberly say that the state of Kant's body, for example its being relatively fresh rather than absolutely exhausted, had nothing whatever to do with his beginning to reflect. There are those, however, who would hold that not only did this bodily state have something to do with the matter, but that nothing else did. The truth, they would say, is that Kant's organism had been conditioned to react in a certain manner to a particular type of stimulus; and the stimuli now acting upon that organism—rays of light from the familiar tower, the action upon his sense of the surroundings in his study, 'memories' of his thought of yesterday, i.e. certain physical processes partially repeated—these and others of their like combined to induce the response called reflection about causality. And the good behaviourist would have it that if we could put Kant's not uninteresting little organism into the laboratory under ideal conditions and with an adequate supply on hand of microscopes, smoked drums, galvanometers, and the rest, we should find that in its production of the *Critique* there was no mystery whatever which could not be thus dispelled.

Now we have considered elsewhere in some detail the physiological explanation of thought, and do not feel called upon to go into it again. Regarding any account of the beginning of reflection along the lines just indicated, we may say that it will almost inevitably be in part obviously true and in part obviously false. Everyone knows that the brain is closely connected with consciousness in the sense that profound changes in the one are commonly accompanied by profound changes in the other; and to a useful extent the areas and the cerebral changes that are more directly associated with certain mental processes have been made out. But it is as easy to overrate the enlightenment that this gives us as it would be foolish to underrate its importance for practice. *How* body affects consciousness we seem to be as far from knowing as ever. Nor do we know with any exactness what the differences are in cerebral change that correspond to differences in idea, nor even whether such changes always exist; it would be naïve to confuse a useful methodological hypothesis with an established fact. There is observable a tendency in some psychologists, when they fail to discover the nervous conditions of conscious processes, to fall back on conjectures which if offered as facts are premature, and if as arguments are *petitiones principii.* But we shall not press this because it is not our point, nor have we the slightest intention of casting what could only be incompetent aspersions on those who work in physiological psychology. Our point is that such an account could not in the nature of the case serve our purpose. If it keeps to physical changes exclusively, after the manner of behaviourism, it cannot even recognize a problem in the initiation of thought, since it does not believe that thought exists; we have sufficiently shown this already. But even if it concedes to the full the difference between consciousness and material change, its value as explanation is limited. It would then explain by correlation; but to correlate the members of one series with the members of another is a very different thing from showing *how* any member of the one exerts an influence on any member of the other; as a philosopher has said, to know that if you knock a man on the head he loses consciousness is not to explain the relation of body and mind. Further, and more important, it is assumed that the result of such explanation would be that the mode of causation in mental process would be found the same as that of physical process, and hence non-purposive. And I think we can see directly that no such result is possible. We can see some mental processes to be purposive with even more directness and certainty than we can see any physical process whatever to be mechanical. It is, in part, for these reasons that, while admitting the importance of nervous changes as conditions of mental, we should be unwilling to accept the physiological explanation as adequate for any step in the thought process.

For the pragmatist what occasions thinking is not, or not exclusively, this physical necessity; it is rather practical necessity, the need to think in order to act in an appropriate way. We think when we need food or clothing, when we are in fear or danger, when the road to anything we want is temporarily blocked and we must devise some means of surmounting the obstacle. Necessity of this kind was the original mother of invention, and though many of her progeny to-day are trying to disown her, a little study of their features will readily reveal their origin. All reflection arises as an instrument of action. This view too we have discussed, and have accepted as broadly true its account both of the origin of reflection and of the occasion of reflection to-day. It must be admitted that the early interest of the mind is dominantly practical, that any considerable interest in theory for its own sake is a late development, and somewhat rare even now, and that it has burnt with so feeble a flame that if it had not been fed by other and more violent interests, it might have gone out altogether. We may even say roundly that thinking always springs from a collision between present fact and some want or desire, and is called into existence to satisfy that desire. Does it follow that we must be pragmatists as to the occasion of reflection? No, it does not. Their account is plausible, as we have seen, of the dawn of reflection in the race, when practical interests were all-absorbing and theoretical interest scarcely born. Yet probably in no case, not even there, is thought *simply* an instrument to an alien end.

2. For within the grosser and more obvious conflict that calls thought forth there is always a subtler tension, a tension not between destitution and desire, but between one's present confusion and ignorance and some fulness of understanding not yet attained, if only that understanding needed to satisfy the dominant practical want. It is a tension between the crudity and chaos to be found within the present idea, and the immanent end of the knowing impulse which is at work in that idea and urging its expansion. At the higher levels of experience it is perfectly clear that this conflict is not only often present, but that it may furnish the mainspring of reflection; and the mere feebleness of the theoretic impulse is no reason for denying its presence far lower in the scale. Where consciousness is too primitive to have gained any control, the physiological account is plausible; where it is more advanced, but still dominated by practical interest, the pragmatic account is plausible; it is probable that neither account is in any case wholly adequate; but in cases like that with which we started, of a philosopher reflecting upon a problem which he finds fascinating in its own right, the unsatisfactoriness of both accounts is plain. And the factor that must be added is the restless demand of the theoretic impulse for a satisfaction of its own, the tension within the impulse itself between what we know and what we might know.

'There is this paradox about knowing', writes Mr. Joseph, 'that we seem to some extent to know what knowledge ought to be, before we know anything as we ought. We have an ideal of which we are sufficiently conscious to realize the imperfections of the actual, though not sufficiently conscious to be able to put it clearly and fully into words. This paradox is not confined to knowledge; it occurs in art and in morality also. We may recognize defect in an aesthetic whole without being able to rectify it, and yet we may be able to say in what direction its perfection must lie; we may know that "we have all sinned", without having seen "the glory of God", and still be able to prescribe some of the conditions which that must realize.'[1]

Now it is the presence of this implicit ideal, working like a yeast in the imperfect thought of the moment and setting up there a ferment of unrest, that provides the motive force in all reflection. Mr. Joseph calls it a paradox; indeed, as such, it had already attracted and puzzled the Greeks. It lay behind the ingenious dilemma with which they puzzled themselves about the possibility of seeking knowledge: if you know what it is you are seeking, the search is needless, since you have what you want already; if you do not know what you want, you would not recognize it if you found it, and the search is therefore vain. The usual solution lies in taking into account the paradox just mentioned; you may know in general what you want without knowing it in detail. But what does this mean? Does it mean that side by side in one's mind are a state of muddle and a schematic idea of that muddle reduced to order? Certainly no such account can be verified in ordinary thought. With all its restlessness, the present state of mind is single and not divided; the supposed abstract idea of the end is found on inspection not to be there. And if this abstract idea were what common logic describes as such, it would be useless even if it were there, for that idea presents rather a caricature of thought than an ideal for its pursuit. Thus the paradox remains. It was supposed to be cleared up by pointing to an abstract thought of the ideal, hovering like an angel above troubled waters. But the angel proves to be as elusive as angels generally are.

[1] *Introduction to Logic*, second ed., 368.

3. The fact is that the paradox pointed out more or less playfully in the old Greek dilemma is nothing less than the central paradox of mind. Our whole discussion of idea and reflection is an attempt to insist on it and in some measure to deal with it. In essence it presents the same problem as the relation of thought to its object. And we saw that it was idle to take something conceived as external to mind and, setting this up as reality, try to puzzle out how mind could build a bridge to it. For the only possible test of what is real is satisfactoriness to mind, and that is not to be determined from without. One can arrive at the real only through the growth of thought itself, only by allowing the expanding organism of thought to develop itself to the limit. There is no short cut; abstract or general notions of the end are themselves, as we have seen, only purposes, partially realized, whose meaning must remain indeterminate till the process is completed. Yet, in spite of the control from within, thought does succeed in getting a better and better notion of its object. Indeed we hold that the two attempts—to define its object and to embody its ideal—are really the same. Thus if it can get forward toward its goal in the one case without any explicit knowledge of where it is going, so it should in the other. And this seems to be precisely what it does.

It is notorious that men may be good who know nothing of moral philosophy. It is almost equally notorious that artists may reach a high order of performance who, when they begin to discuss aesthetics, are all at sea. The like holds of the practice of thought. God, as Locke remarked, did not make man barely two-legged and leave it to Aristotle to make him rational. The power to embody the ideal, whether of beauty or goodness or reason, happily does not depend upon our power to formulate this expressly. Not only so; even when the poet or composer or philosopher has achieved a relatively specific idea of what he wants, still he is often astonished at what comes out. Plato spoke of poets as mad because, without knowing what they did, they nevertheless did it successfully;[1] in humbler

[1] *Phaedrus*, 245.

degree we are all familiar with what this means; 'when in talking we pledge ourselves to a simile, we are a little surprised that the right one is good enough to come and redeem us'.[1] The control exercised by the ideal over the conscious and subconscious mind we shall study later in detail. Meanwhile, to suppose that these results are accidental is absurd, and the absurdity grows as one looks at the working of a mind of the first order. No explicit purpose may be there; yet it is somehow purpose that started the process and keeps it at every moment under rigorous control.

We hold that in the end there is no way to account for all the phenomena of this type, except by the theory of mind and thought here presented. Thought moves toward an end and is controlled by it; that is certain. Often no thought of the end can be discovered; that seems equally certain. And the two things are hard to reconcile. But what if, instead of thought's *having* a purpose, it *is* one? What if, in its very essence, it is a movement toward an end, the self-development of an idea, the self-determined coming to be of that which was potential only? We cannot say what an idea *is*, as has been seen, without saying what it is *of*, since its very nature lies in a seeking to compass and be what falls beyond it. And when thought reaches an immediate end in the solution of a particular problem, it does not stop there; if it is allowed to follow its own impulsion, it goes on spreading outward like a rising sea, stretching out arms of inference, engulfing what is insular, transforming from a single centre and into a single whole all that is detached and fragmentary. Or to employ a better metaphor, it is a process of organic growth. It behaves as it does because there is at work in it at every stage that which it is to become. Just as a sapling *is* a tree partly grown and strictly not conceivable except in terms of what it is becoming, so thought *is* an impulse to system; it is system imperfectly realized. It can get on without formulating its end for the reason that it *is* the end in process of self-affirmation. We can call all this a mystery, if we wish; but it seems to be the fact; and the

[1] Mitchell, *Structure and Growth of the Mind*, 354.

more we reflect upon it the more clearly we shall see that it is the central fact both of thought and of mind.

4. There are some points in our theory for which we could hardly expect support from authority. But lest the general view of thought as the coming to be in finite minds of a whole that is potentially there already should be taken by anyone as merely odd, we may point out that it is almost an orthodox western tradition. There are witnesses for it in plenty. Three of them speak at once in Bradley's comment on Hegel, repeated by McTaggart: 'The opposition between the real, in the fragmentary character in which the mind possesses it, and the true reality felt within the mind, is the moving cause of that unrest which sets up the dialectical process.'[1] Two more of them speak in this from Bosanquet: 'The evolution of knowledge is, as Plato long ago portrayed it, the emancipation of individual minds from their accidental limitations, and their education into the knowledge of the one real and intelligible world.'[2] Spinoza's view was not essentially different. It was the doctrine of a *conatus* whose fulfilment, judged by an immanent standard, was found in ideas progressively more 'adequate'. A like theory appears in Leibniz; the construction of the world which appeared in the windowless monad at maturity was only the development of what had belonged to it from the beginning. The theory appears again as the central doctrine of ethics and metaphysics for a thinker whose fidelity to the facts of mind is insufficiently recognized, T. H. Green. The evidence, Green insists, that there is an end at work in thought 'does not depend on any account of it which the learner may be able to give', for 'it is at work before it is reflected on'; 'and every step forward in real intelligence, whether in the way of addition to what we call the stock of human knowledge, or of appropriation by the individual of some part of that stock, is only

[1] Bradley, *Principles of Logic*, second ed., II. 409; McTaggart, *Studies in the Hegelian Dialectic*, 33.
[2] *Logic*, second ed., I. 233.

explicable on supposition that successive reports of the senses, successive efforts of attention, successive processes of observation and experiment, are determined by the consciousness that all things form a related whole—a consciousness which is operative throughout their succession and which at the same time realizes itself through them'.[1] To call but one more witness, a contemporary, the same general view of thought is held by Croce, though in accepting it one need not, of course, commit oneself to its whole Crocean setting: 'Truth is ... free development of one's inner powers. The light is in us; those sequences of sounds, which are the so-called demonstration, serve only as aids in discarding the veils and directing the gaze'.[2]

5. From all this it will be clear that the question, What starts the movement of reflection? is no simple one, and is not to be answered merely in terms of stimuli and practical need. One cannot explain by jogs from without what is really an impulsion from within. Ultimately thought moves because the system of ideas which at any moment *is* the mind on its intellectual side is incomplete and fragmentary, and because that completed system which is immanent and operative within it impels to explicit fulfilment.[3] But it may occur to someone to ask, Why did such a process start in the first place? Granting that thought is a perpetual struggle toward integration of experience, how is one to account for such an impulse, either in oneself or in the race? This is very different from the question what *now* occasions reflection, but before going on, it will be well to dwell on it for a moment. It may mean any one of three things: First, why should anyone take such an end as an end at all? Secondly, why should the whole implicit in thought have so far denatured itself as to appear in forms that are struggling and imperfect? Thirdly, what are the

[1] *Prolegomena to Ethics*, Sec. 73, 70.
[2] *Logic*, Eng. Trans., 51-2.
[3] The meaning of this statement will become clearer in later chapters.

conditions that started the process of its realization? Unfortunately, though for instructive and different reasons, no one of these questions at present is answerable.

The question, Why try to understand? is unanswerable because it is not a genuine question. A question expresses the desire to understand, and if I so desire, I feel the value of understanding already. The question, Why understand? can therefore not be asked unless I already possess, in a measure, the answer, and if I do, the question is hardly a genuine demand for light that is absent. On the other hand if I do not, if for me understanding possesses no sort of value, my question is not a demand for anything; it is a form of words merely, and therefore not a question at all. As for the second problem above, Why should the whole implicit in thought have so far denatured itself as to appear in forms that are struggling and imperfect? that again is unanswerable, for very much the same reason that the older theologians found *Cur Deus homo?* unanswerable. They held that it was intelligible enough why man should want to be God, but that to explain why God should want to be man, we should have to *be* God. Thought, if we are right, is a movement toward that whole where lies complete understanding. To answer the question before us, we should need already to have arrived at that whole, whereas we are immeasurably far removed from it. Hence the question is now beyond us. The third question, as to the conditions under which thought historically began, is perhaps more manageable. It seems certain that in time we shall know much more minutely the physical conditions of changes in thought. But if these conditions are the same in kind as we now know, if they are still movements of physical particles, only known in more detail, and correlated more precisely with elements in thought, they will not give the understanding we want. The reasons for this have already been stated.[1] And thus, in the kind of terms expected, the third question too is unanswerable.

These comments are a needed preface to any explanation of why thinking takes place on a particular occasion. One of

[1] Sec. 1.

the chief contentions of this work, as noted at the beginning, is that a course of thinking cannot be explained in the sense in which psychologists commonly say it can. Since it is a teleological process, no account of it is sufficient without reference to the end that guides and in a measure controls it. When, and only when, this is seen can one go on to 'explain' special cases with knowledge of what one is about. If, in what follows, we mention factors external to the process, such as sense stimuli or moods or non-theoretical interests, it will not be because these are supposed to explain why the process takes the course it does, any more than soil or rain explain why an acorn becomes an oak rather than a sunflower, though in both cases these are important co-operating factors.

Granting now that in a course of thinking an impulse toward understanding is working itself out, by what steps does it move toward its end?

6. The course begins in every case with a shock to the system of thought already present. Something is offered so alien to the present circle of ideas, so unassimilable by it, so tantalizingly isolated from it, that the impulse toward integration is stung into action. Let us take three simple cases offered by Professor Dewey as typical of the situations in which thinking arises.[1] A student is in down-town New York when the face of a clock suddenly brings to mind that he has an engagement far up-town in forty minutes. He immediately begins reflecting. 'How am I to get there? By tram? No, that is too slow. By the elevated? But I don't know where there is a station. By subway? Well—'. Here is a familiar type of thought-provoking situation. Or again, a man was crossing a river on a ferry-boat when his eye fell on the vessel's pointer. This was a long white pole, with a gilded ball on the end, stretching out from the prow of the steamer and looking a little like a flag-pole. But why should a flag-pole stick out above the water? It would be awkward to fly a flag in that position. Then what can the

[1] *How We Think*, 68–71.

pole be for? Here is another typical situation in which reflection is aroused, less directly concerned with action than the first. And here is a final one, still further removed from practice: someone is washing tumblers in hot soapsuds and placing them on a plate, mouth downwards, when he notices that bubbles are coming out and clustering round the rims. After the tumblers have stood there awhile, the bubbles reverse their movement and begin to appear inside. This is an odd performance; why do they do it? And the dishwasher is off on a train of reflection.

These situations are very different, but in all of them thinking starts in the same way. There comes, as in Macbeth, a knocking at the door by something that the mind is not prepared to receive, but must find a place for. The unity of thought is shattered; outside the continent that forms its mainland—to use a very useful figure—there appears an island that ought to be attached to it and yet is not; and this disunion on the surface sets in motion a force below, which by upheavals and rearrangements seeks to unite the fragment to the mainland. In the case of the man down-town, the island is the thought of his being up-town a short forty minutes later; the mainland is his present position, with its mass of familiar facts about New York's transportation system; he sees no way of expanding the latter to include the former; yet expanded it must somehow be. In the pointer case, the island is the thought of that conspicuous pole without any apparent function; the mainland is the knowledge that in boats, or anything else that is carefully constructed, outstanding parts have their uses. In the case of the bubbles, the analysis is similar. If in this case the mainland is harder to see than the island, it is on the principle that what is hardest to see is the obvious. A fixed part of our mental furniture, but one very seldom reflected on, is the conviction that things do not happen by chance, that everything has a cause; and for most of the events of common life this has been verified so often that they are placed in their causal context automatically. But when some event obtrudes itself of whose cause we have no inkling, we are arrested and challenged by it.

'It stands out like a sore thumb', it refuses to fit into our familiar picture of things. Hence the impulse to integrate is called suddenly into play.

In all these cases reflection starts from a divided mind and the resultant challenge to the intellectual impulse, which is always an impulse to integrate. The first step in the movement of reflection is thus the appearance of a disunion or disharmony that intelligence cannot abide. But further points must be noted about this stage. (1) Though the moving impulse is the same, the secondary or trigger impulses that set off this essential impulse differ widely. (2) In some minds these conflicts are continual, while in others they occur very seldom; hence reflectiveness varies enormously from mind to mind. These facts imply significant differences in intellectual character.

7. (1) First as to the trigger impulses, that is, the interests which set the theorizing impulse in motion. In our instances these played very different parts. In the third, their part is relatively slight; for the intellectual impulse is there self-sustaining, while in the first it is not. For all we can see on the surface, reflection about the cause of the bubbles arises solely from the tension within intelligence itself, without help from secondary compulsions. The integrative impulse, made restless by the disharmony, works itself clear by its own insistence. But in the first case it needs a goad. The man down-town did not think out his course from sheer love of intellectual order; he was forced to think by an urgent demand of a non-intellectual kind without which he would not have pursued such reflection at all. Hence it is tempting to say that the conflict from which thinking directly springs is a practical conflict, and indeed Professor Dewey holds this. He says that 'the difficulty resides in the conflict between conditions at hand and a desired and intended result, between an end and the means for reaching it. The purpose of keeping an engagement at a certain time, and the existing hour taken in connection with the location, are not congruous. The object of thinking is to introduce a

congruity between the two.'[1] In one significant detail, our own
account would differ from this. The incongruity is not strictly
between end and means, or purpose and fact. Such conflict
is hardly possible. If I form the purpose of leaping over the
moon a half hour hence, there is no conflict, strictly speaking,
between that purpose and present facts. The conflict is not
between the purpose and the fact, but between the *judgement
implied in the purpose* and the fact. My purpose to leap over
the moon implies the judgement that this is physically possible;
my purpose to be up-town in forty minutes implies that I can be
there at that time. And the conflict lies between the implied
judgement as to what is possible and the system of present fact
with its unbending rules of time and space; it looks as if both
cannot hold at once. The truly reflective conflict is thus intellectual, not practical. What is practical is the trigger impulse.
The interest in solving the theoretical difficulty is here neither
self-generating nor self-sustaining. It works because it has to
if a non-theoretical but dominant interest is to be appeased.

Never in any case is thought directly concerned with practice.
Its business is theory, and the conflicts that it can settle are
theoretical conflicts only. But since we can reach no end
whatever without taking account of the nature of things, and
thought alone can tell us what the nature of things is like, we
must call it into service continually, regardless of what we are
seeking. For example, the kindliest will for another's welfare
is so helpless in reaching its end without some degree of understanding that a contemporary writer has insisted persuasively
on 'the moral obligation to be intelligent'. Consider again the
following remark: 'the intellectual character of the musical
faculty—its connection with the capacity for the most abstract
kind of thinking—is attested by the tendency of musical and
mathematical talent to go together'.[2] If this is true, the musician
finds mathematical grasp and interest to his advantage. But it
would be plainly mistaken to say that the driving impulses
of scientist and artist are therefore the same. 'The one imagines
in order to think better, but if the artist has to think, it is in

---

[1] *How we Think*, 72.   [2] The remark is Dean Rashdall's.

order to imagine better.'[1] Thinking is a distinct activity with an end of its own, though there is no end that human nature can pursue whose attainment may not be furthered by that activity.

8. (2) Granting the variety, however, of the interests that may be furthered by thinking, it remains true that the conflict from which thought springs is always one of theory. And the next question is, Why does this conflict which is the birth of reflection occur so commonly in some minds and so seldom in others? That such variation exists is unquestionable. To some minds incessant food for reflection is supplied by things and events that ordinarily go unnoticed; other minds, in what seem to be the same surroundings, merely go to sleep, like cats. There is the greatest difference in the coarseness of the stimulus needed to set off these types of mind. On the street-corners of towns may be observed certain persons who prefer such posts of vantage because something is more likely to turn up there to provide the cue for a remark or an idea, persons whose minds, like flint, must receive a blow to produce a spark. Such minds are comfortably at home only on the perceptual level. At best they are Peter Bells, for whom the primrose is that and nothing more. But it is notorious that there are those to whom it is very much more. Indeed there are those to whom almost anything will serve as a peg on which to hang a chain of reflection. One thinks of Huxley and his piece of chalk, of Louis Agassiz's fascination with the scientific problems of his dooryard, of Spencer's difficulty in reading, which arose from the fact that any book suggested so many problems that he soon felt compelled to put it down and take them up. Any good sketch of Galton, Darwin, or Faraday will present the picture of a mind bubbling over with theories about things to which most men never give a thought. Nor is it that their environment was more generous than others' in the abundance spread

[1] Mitchell, *Structure and Growth*, 353. For a fuller discussion see Chap. X, Sec. 9–10.

before the mind, for there is no environment which to the discerning does not offer problems in profusion. But when most men see an apple fall or a kettle boil, it obviously does not arouse in them the reflective response that it did in Newton or Watt. There is an abysmal difference here which it would be simplest to dismiss without further analysis as a difference in 'mind' or 'intelligence'. 'I could write like Shakespeare if I'd a mind to', Wordsworth is reported to have said in an unguarded moment. 'Quite so', was Charles Lamb's comment; 'all that is lacking *is* the mind.'

Of course for mind in the high sense of the power to see what is right in art or thought, it would be absurd to offer prescriptions. But one can pick up clues as to what it lives by; and so far as reflectiveness is concerned, the main condition seems clear. It is a state of suitable tension between 'mainland' and 'island', as we have called them. This state is very similar to what was described in these pages long ago as the condition of fruitful perceiving. If what is before us fits in effortlessly to the apperception mass of the moment, it is not particularly noticed; the mainland swallows it automatically; we adjust ourselves, for example, to the objects in our room without closely attending to them. On the other hand, what is presented may be so utterly foreign that nothing in our minds responds to it, and then there is no tension for the opposite reason; there is no mainland to appropriate it. A case in point is that of the aborigines staring blankly at trams and motors only to break into alert delight when they saw a repair man climbing a telephone pole. The arousing of reflection has similar conditions. If some minds notably fail in reflective response, it is usually for one or other of three reasons. (*a*) They may have no mainland to start with; (*b*) challenging islands may not be forthcoming; (*c*) both may be present and integration still fail through interference from without.

9. (*a*) Thought, as we have seen, is the mind's movement toward understanding, and to understand means to relate within a whole, the more systematic and complete the better. Thinking always starts from a whole and, if it is successful, ends in a better one. As an example of a whole that has been slowly achieved, but which, once it has been achieved, gives an exceptionally firm spring-board for further adventure, one may take the world of common sense. For the 'plain man' this provides an intellectual native land, the home of truth and reality; and any theory that cannot prove citizenship in it, or at least show naturalization papers on demand, he is inclined to set down as a suspicious alien. On this rock of routine perceptions and beliefs he lives as on an island in an unexplored sea, seldom undertaking the labour of reflecting except when something threatens—a ghost, a loss of income, a loss of some prospective pleasure. When reflection does occur, it consists in extending the bounds of this world in such wise as, if possible, to domesticate the thing that threatens, or to circumvent it. Now this world is in degree a system. Intelligibility is not evenly diffused through it, but it is by no means a chaos; it is shot through with the lines of order; it is organized on principles; it recognizes one space, one time, one system of number and degree, one inclusive web of causation. And the principles of structure of the plain man's world are also the rules that govern his thinking. If he is to extend his world to include the novel it must be by bringing the novel within their domain (we omit for the moment the case of his revising the rules to include it); if it stands out and defies assimilation, intelligence has collapsed. The problem of the man down-town is to stretch the bounds of his present world, in accordance with its fixed rules of space, time, and motion, to include himself some minutes later and some miles away. The problem of the man on the boat is to include within his conception of boats as man-made things, economical of means to ends, the strange pole that for the moment resists inclusion. The problem of the bubbles is merely to catch them in the net of causation and bring them ashore. The problem of any thinking is to include challenger and challenged in one whole without internal disharmony.

Now suppose that there is no whole to start with. At once reflection becomes impossible. πῶς and ποῦ στῶ disappear together. The business of thinking is to extend or revise a system so as to include what challenges it, and with no system to extend or be challenged, there would be no problem; we could never set out. And if, *per impossibile*, we could somehow begin, we could not proceed. For the principles of our accepted basis give the rules for our procedure; they are the chains we must use to grapple and annex the new; and with no spatio-temporal, causal, or other lines to throw out, how are we to enmesh it? One cannot play a game that has no rules.

It is obvious that every sane mind has some sort of world to start with, however small and ill-organized. Why then the remark of a moment or two ago that some minds failed in reflectiveness through lack of a mainland to set out from? The answer is that one never takes one's start from the continent of knowledge in general, but always from a special part of it, and if this part is lacking, the effect is much the same as if the continent itself were lacking. To Darwin the fact of an orchid with a nectary twelve inches deep set him reflecting excitedly whether, to fertilize it, there could possibly be a moth with a proboscis twelve inches long; he concluded, rightly as it turned out, that there must be. Why would this fact, which so readily aroused reflection in Darwin's mind, awake no response in ours? It is because, whereas in his mind there was a body of biological knowledge which the new fact sharply challenged, in our mind this is absent. Darwin knew how orchids are fertilized and moths constructed, and hence the fertilization of this special orchid came to him as a puzzle and a challenge. Unless one possesses already a mass of knowledge about orchids, a fact like this would not strike one as out of the ordinary. Not that it is impossible for the layman, on the strength of general impressions, to ask questions about botany, but it is likely that his interest will be sporadic, his questions blundering, and his suggested answers merely guesses.

10. This requirement of special knowledge for reflectiveness in any field has some interesting implications. (i) It points to the importance, for a reflective life, of a various fund of information. There are those who, in enthusiasm for either discipline or creativeness of thought, disparage learning. And it is true that very remarkable feats have been performed by minds whose range of knowledge was limited, as for example by Hume and Gauss in the works of genius that were the product of their middle twenties. But it will be noted that the fields they were working in, metaphysics and mathematics, however difficult they may be, are fields for whose exploration the plain man's world gives a surprisingly adequate starting point. The traditional task of these sciences is to explore in abstraction the systems involved in the commonest of all categories, such as space, time, causation, number. But that it is impossible, even for transcendent intellect, to invade the special departments of nature and to make bricks there without straw is illustrated by such conclusions as Aristotle's that mind is seated in the heart, and Descartes's that nervous impulses are conveyed by a gas through hollow tubes. In the absence of special knowledge the conclusions of these great thinkers were hardly more valuable than those of the plain man. Undoubtedly, other things equal, there is a presumption in favour of intellect, since the caution and exactness it has displayed in one field are not likely to be simply forgotten in another. But the mere habit of caution and exactness will not even show what the problems are in a special field, let alone solve them. There is something absurd in publishing, as a popular magazine did, the opinions of Edison and Burbank on immortality, as pronouncements of great significance, to say nothing of appealing, as a great newspaper did, at the time of the Massie trial in Hawaii, to a prize fighter, an expert at cards, and a theatrical producer, for judgements as to the soundness of the verdict. A glamorous name or even a thousand casual answers to a questionnaire are worth next to nothing as compared with the special experience and responsible reflection of one true expert. But the same principle that enjoins scepticism enjoins also charity. Reflective poverty in one field need not mean poverty in all. It is said that when Canning was Prime Minister he was on a walk one day with a friend when, passing a pond, the friend remarked on the oddity of tadpoles becoming frogs. Canning was astonished. He had never heard of such a thing before. But who that is astonished at Canning's astonishment would question his policy in Portugal because of his innocence of zoology? 'I, who for the time have staked my all on being a psychologist', said William James, 'am mortified if others know more psychology than I. But I am contented to wallow in the grossest ignorance of Greek.'[1] To sum the matter up: if one is to carry on explorations in a new territory, one must have an adjoining base of operations, but in the nature of the case, the range afforded by this base will be limited.

(ii) There is another interesting implication of the doctrine that reflectiveness calls for knowledge. The larger the base one starts from, the better aware one is of its smallness. For the expansion of knowledge is less like the extension of a line than like the enlargement of the circles caused by a pebble thrown into a pool; the greater the knowledge, the wider the circuit on which it touches the unknown. It is expressly 'a little knowledge' that is 'a dangerous thing' and 'puffeth up'. The mind that has been confronted on all sides with questions it cannot answer is more likely to talk, like Newton, about 'picking up a few pebbles on the shore of knowledge'. This is natural enough when one realizes how large a part frustration plays in producing thought at every point in the orbit of knowledge. 'There is no sin . . . which philosophy can justify so little as spiritual pride.'[2]

11. It may be objected that what we have said shows only that knowledge is a necessary, not that it is a sufficient, condition of thinking. Granting that Darwin could not have raised his question about the orchid without special knowledge, it

[1] *Principles*, I. 310.   [2] Bradley, *Appearance*, 7.

does not follow that those who have this knowledge are thereby made reflective. Indeed we have admitted that one may start from a basis hardly broader than the ordinary man's and still perform feats in mathematics and metaphysics. If such knowledge were all that is necessary, it may be asked, why should we not all be philosophers? The point is well taken. Knowledge in the field is necessary, but whether it will be actively used in reflection, whether such knowledge of human nature, for example, as can be picked up in a country parsonage will be used as it most commonly is, or as Jane Austen and the Brontës used it, obviously depends on something further. This something further has been much discussed under the heads of 'genius', 'mental energy', 'creative power', 'intelligence', and so on. But these only name the problem; they do not begin to solve it, nor is it likely to be solved in any terms now known. For it is essentially the old problem over again, how comes intelligence to exist in the world? And I do not think that is a question which science can answer or philosophy can with much profit speculate on. Intelligence as the capacity for understanding, and its variations from mind to mind, are at present most usefully dealt with as initial facts. We cannot explain them; we cannot explain them away. All we can do is to explain the manner in which an intelligence that already exists goes about it to win new territory.

12. (b) We have seen that a body of special knowledge is the necessary, if not the sufficient, condition of thinking in a special field. There is also a counterpart condition. Even if the required body of knowledge is present, reflection does not normally occur unless this body is goaded from without into readjustment.

The late Professor Rignano developed an interesting theory of thought based on the tendency of all life to inertia. Every organism from paramoecium to man, he held, has a normal state that it seeks to maintain; and so long as this state is not threatened, its activity keeps an even tenor, since between its situation on the one hand and its 'mnemonic accumulation' on the other, i.e. the set of tendencies that the past has con-confirmed in it, there is peace and harmonious adjustment. But let the situation change, and it goes through a convulsive period of readjustment till a new set of habits has been established, whereupon it devotes itself to the maintenance of these. For instance, the diatom *Navicula brevis*, kept in the dark, will flee the light; keep it for a while in the light, and it will flee the dark. If actinians, clinging some to the bottoms and some to the sides of rocks, are put in an aquarium, each will seek to attach itself in the same position as before.[1] Through this tendency to maintain an established state, Rignano seeks to explain the higher activities of the mind. Now it may be doubted whether any theory resting so largely on the mnemonic, or the maintenance of the acquired, can cover the facts of mental origination. But as Rignano unrolls his cases, the impression grows on the reader that inertia does play a large part in normal mental life. Even mastery in a field is unproductive except under the stimulus of fresh problems. And where, further, the knowledge is small to begin with, reflection can scarcely occur at all. How often do we find someone reflecting critically on the rightness of a custom unless stimulated to do so by contrary customs observed in travel, by some interference with his own happiness, or by some realized inconsistency with something else that he believes or does? How often do we find someone taking up for consideration a religious belief and revising or abandoning it when nothing in his experience has suggested any defect in it? Such cases are not impossible, but they are very nearly unknown.

13. The powerlessness of the rational impulse to break by itself the fetters of established belief is a familiar fact of social history. The tendency of early society, as Walter Bagehot has shown, was to form rigid 'cakes of custom', congealing both conduct and belief. If the cakes fixed themselves so rigidly

[1] *Psychology of Reasoning*, 9.

that they could not be broken, progress ceased; society was like a colony of ants, performing the functions with a machine-like fixity, but not advancing. The hope of progress lay in a combination of fixity on the whole with accessibility to invasion and change at special points. The break in the wall was often made by commerce; 'commerce brings this mingling of ideas, this breaking down of old creeds, and brings it inevitably'.[1] Some goad of the sort seems necessary. For 'experience shows how incredibly difficult it is to get men really to encourage the principle of originality. They will admit in theory, but in practice the old error—the error which arrested a hundred civilizations—returns again. Men are too fond of their own life, too credulous of the completeness of their own ideas, too angry at the pain of new thoughts, to be able to bear easily with a changing existence. . . .'[2] Even a civilization as complex and advanced as that of the older China may become sterile if guarded against impregnation from without.

The same holds of individual minds. It was a point insisted on by Hegel that thought advances only by the continual overcoming of obstacles through combining them into a whole with what was there already, this whole then serving as the basis for further advance, made in similar manner. Hegel seems to have been convinced that with the help of the implicit system operative in the mind thought could generate the challenging factor from itself. Whether it could perform this feat ideally we shall not argue; at any rate it does not do so in fact. The external and challenging element comes normally through a rebuff from without. It may not be useless to recall that some of the turning-points in the history of culture have come when challenges of this kind happened to be addressed to first-class minds. Descartes became a philosopher when a mathematically whetted intelligence ran its edge against the scholastic theology. On the other side, Hobbes became a mathematician when his complacency about philosophic demonstration was piqued by an accidental reading of Euclid. Hume woke Kant from his dogmatic slumbers. Goethe returned

[1] *Physics and Politics*, 40.   [2] *Ibid.*, 57.

from the 'italiänische Reise' 'to all appearances, a changed man'.[1] So did Darwin from his voyage on the *Beagle*. He had seen fossils in South America and species on the Galapagos Islands that sharply challenged accepted biology, and he later entered succinctly in his note-book, 'these facts (especially latter) origin of all my views'. It is needless to multiply examples. Thought will not work in a vacuum. And even where material is abundant it will not reach the level of reflection if it can appropriate this material automatically. It must be presented with what is foreign enough to be challenging, yet not so foreign as to make assimilation hopeless. The man with any practice in thinking soon discovers for himself what Plato discovered before him and embodied in the form of his writings, that reflection is a debate or dialogue of the mind with itself. If the mind cannot make its own hurdles, it can at least increase its skill in finding and making use of them. Darwin's habit of keeping a note-book of the objections to his theory is, in degree and more or less consciously, the practice of every thinker. Thinking *is* the process of seeing and surmounting theoretical obstacles.

14. (c) We have been examining the reasons why some minds find difficulty in taking the first step of reflection. In terms of our figure (a) such minds may have no mainland to start from, or (b) no challenging islands may be forthcoming. Let us now look at a final difficulty. In some minds where there is adequate knowledge to start with, and the difficulty is clearly perceived and defined, reflection may still be blocked. If so, it is either because outside factors are entering in to obstruct the movement, or because of native stupidity. Of the first sort there are too many varieties to exhaust easily, but a few of the commonest obstacles may be mentioned. Fatigue is a familiar and universal one; for some persons the use of certain drugs offers an equally effective veto. Helmholtz, in describing how the solutions of problems came to him, wrote: 'As far as my

[1] Lewes, *Life*, 308.

experience goes, they never come at the desk or to a tired brain . . . The smallest quantity of alcoholic drink seemed to frighten them away.'[1] In the same class are physical illness and the decline of faculty in old age. Likewise external to the course of thought, though related to it more intimately, and capable of blocking or distorting it in the subtlest ways, are mood and emotion. One of the most insidious difficulties for those who measure intelligence by tests has been that examinees approach the tests with emotions so different as to affect their performance and the consequent validity of the ratings. A high performance in such tests undoubtedly means something, however hard it may be to say what; but even in so vital a point as the power to reflect, and to reflect on familiar matter, a poor performance may mean little. Such faculty as exists may be paralysed by excitement and apprehension.[2] More must be said later about how mood and emotion may determine the course of suggestion, but it is enough for the moment to see that they may block its course completely even when other conditions are favourable.

It is also perhaps enough merely to point this out regarding the other and more intrinsic obstacle, namely, stupidity. Stupidity is a blanket term that means as many different things as there are varieties of human faculty. It is sometimes

[1] Quoted by Mitchell, *Structure and Growth*, 355.

[2] This is prettily illustrated by an event of some historical importance. Till 1696, persons placed on trial in England for treason had to handle their own cases in court. In that year a proposal to abolish this inhumanity was introduced in the House of Commons. One of the supporters was the philosopher Shaftesbury, then a young man of twenty-five. 'In the course of his speech', Macaulay writes, 'he faltered, stammered, and seemed to lose the thread of his reasoning.' The House indulgently waited till he had regained some measure of composure, whereupon in dramatic fashion he used his own lapse as the most effective argument possible for the Bill he was supporting. If his own capacity to reflect in normal manner had been destroyed even by the presence of a friendly audience, what must be the position of the man 'whose faculties are paralysed by the thought that, if he fails to convince his hearers, he will in a few hours die on the gallows . . .?' The Bill passed.—Macaulay, *History* (Firth), V. 2582. Unfortunately the suspicion must be added that it was all a deliberately staged performance.

defined as the inability to use experience effectively in the solving of new problems. But that implies that intelligence *is* such ability, and it is not merely that; it may exhibit itself in the ready grasp of relations and wholes which have never before been apprehended, and which no application of past experience would enable one to apprehend, such as new branches of mathematics. And there will be as many forms of intellectual stupidity as there are types of system or whole through which understanding is achieved. How minds may differ in their ability to construct the simpler wholes has been illustrated with unusual clearness by studies in the minds of apes, particularly those of Professor Köhler; and we may perhaps let one of his cases serve as the type of all those stupidities which lie in the inability to construct an appropriate whole.

Near the cage of a chimpanzee, but out of reach, Professor Köhler would put a banana. Close to this, but within reach, he would place a stick, which, however, was too short to be of use in getting the banana. In these circumstances all his apes would seize the stick and poke at the banana frantically. He would then complicate the problem. Leaving the banana and the short stick as before, he would place outside the cage another and longer stick, this time just out of reach. And now the difference in native faculty came pitilessly to light. Sultan, one of the more intelligent of the apes, after gazing about him, 'suddenly picks up the little stick, once more goes up to the bars directly opposite the long stick, scratches it toward him with the "auxiliary", seizes it, and goes with it to the point opposite the objective, which he secures'.[1] Not so with his companion, Rana, who strove as valiantly as he, but less wisely. She would angle for the banana with the short stick, then, giving up, would strain after the long stick with her hand; and failing in both, she could only repeat them excitedly and vainly. 'The detour "short stick—long stick—fruit" simply did not arise with this animal.'[2] This looks like, and may have been, a pure defect in intelligence. So far as one could see,

---

[1] *The Mentality of Apes*, 180.   [2] *Ibid.*, 183.

the 'mainland' from which she started and the 'island' which she had to reach were the same as in the case of Sultan, but she could not get them together; the bridge that had to be built was too complicated for her powers. Like differences, and of course far greater ones, are to be found in human endowments. When every allowance has been made for fatigue and indisposition, lack of interest, lack of experience and all the rest, there remains in some minds—and indeed in all, since there are here no absolutes—a residue beyond elimination of good round native stupidity. If this is sufficiently distinguished, it will halt the reflective movement, whatever its direction, at the first step.

15. The chief conclusions of this chapter are as follows: (1) the mainspring of the process of reflection lies in a tension within thought itself between an immanent but unrealized end, in the form of intelligible system, and the relatively incomplete and disorderly state of present knowledge. Physical and practical necessities, important as these are, do not tell the whole story. (2) The immediate stimulus to reflection is always the appearance off the 'mainland' of thought—the present accepted system—of an 'island'—something which declines to be incorporated—; and the problem is always one of integration, how to bring these into an intelligible whole. (3) The theoretic process is usually goaded into action and prematurely halted by dominating interests of a non-theoretic kind. (4) The process may be blocked at the start by (a) the lack of any 'mainland' from which a problem may be approached, or (b) the lack of an adequate challenge, or by (c) a great variety of mental and physical inhibitions imposed from outside the process itself.

CHAPTER XX

SPECIFYING THE PROBLEM

1. Reflection, we have seen, is a purposive movement, whose end is understanding. And to understand anything means to place it in the context of a system that is seen to necessitate it. The movement of reflection starts when we are presented with something, a suggestion or an apparent fact, which we need for any reason to fit into the system we carry about in our minds, and which yet resists inclusion. An island appears demanding union with the mainland; we must bridge the gap, but are at a loss how to do it; tension arises, and from that tension, reflection. How does the mind go about it to bridge the interval?

The first step is to fix the point to which it must throw its span, i.e., to specify its problem. For it is as hard to build a mental bridge to a point that remains undefined as it is to construct a causeway to an island lost in the fog. Schoolboys at times have essays set them on 'George Washington', or 'the *Mayflower*'; grown-up persons who attempt to discipline their power to reflect, sometimes prescribe for themselves ten minutes of concentration on 'Progress', 'Conscience', or 'Efficiency'. Now the mere play of ideas round a topic is not what is meant here by reflection. To reflect means to solve, or attempt to solve, a problem, and where is the problem in such cases as these? George Washington is not a problem. To be sure, there are a thousand and one problems *about* him any one of which would point a direction in which thought might proceed. 'Is the story of the cherry tree true?' 'What part did Washington take in Braddock's campaign?' 'Was he a military strategist of the first rank?' As soon as objectives like these take shape through the initial mist, reflection proper can begin, but not before.

Of course, something does occur in the schoolboy's mind when the general topic is presented to him ; he puts the result down on paper and gets credit, no doubt, for having reflected. The thought of Washington burgeons fruitfully; first comes, perhaps, the image of the face with the white wig and the wide firm mouth; then a helter-skelter succession of odds and ends—the date of his birth, the look of Mt. Vernon, the crossing of the Delaware, the phrase, 'first in war, first in peace', a figure kneeling in the snow at Valley Forge. The boy rounds these items up into paragraphs, probably loose internally and looser still in their larger linkage, and hands in an essay. Has he thought? No; not unless the clustering of random associates round a centre is thought; and to call it so would be flattery. His 'thought' bears the same relation to thinking proper that a sputtering pinwheel fire-cracker, which he sets off on the Fourth of July, and watches go off in all directions, bears to a gun that fires at a mark. Thinking is not musing, or wool-gathering, or dreaming, or day-dreaming, or 'inviting one's soul'. It is the attempt to get a line from the coast to something helpless at sea, when one must find the line for oneself and make out through a shifting and uncertain light where the object is. Hence, no doubt, Emerson's remark, that thinking is the hardest work man does.

We have seen that the mind never simply entertains an idea, that to have a thought is always to judge, i.e. to assert something about a subject. Now George Washington is not a subject that can remain motionless in the mind; it either vanishes altogether or develops predicates, and it may develop these in any direction whatever. If it is allowed to develop aimlessly, first a little in one direction, and then a little in another, we have a process of musing rather than of thinking. Thinking will occur when it develops in a single direction under the control of a specific interest. A challenge is thrown down to it on one side, and because thought feels its imperfection on that side, it begins to expand in that direction. If our problem is, Was Washington a first-rate strategist? the thought will advance under the control of that idea; he will be seen as a general deploying troops against the enemy, not as the wooer of Martha Custis, or as the orator of the first inaugural. Thought is like the unstable mass of protoplasm in an amoeba, which is ready to pour out its own substance into a pseudopodium and seize any ingestible particle that attracts it. And the more precisely thought can locate its objective, the less groping, the more quick and neat and effortless, will be the manner of reaching for it.

2. Now the problems thought must deal with show, at their first appearance, every degree of specification. Some of them come in so definite a form that we can deal with them instantly. If the question occurs, What time is it?, there is no need to whittle this down; the point at once is apparent; and one proceeds to settle it by pulling out one's watch. At other times, when whittling is necessary, the process is so swift and effortless that we do not realize it has occurred. This was the case, for example, of the man down-town, who suddenly woke up to the fact that forty minutes later he must be at a place several miles away. His problem, put abstractly, was how to translate his body in a certain direction and a certain time for as many miles. This is an extremely general requirement, and theoretically any suggestion that would fulfil it would be pertinent, even that of an airplane or a magic carpet. But in an ordinarily regulated mind, these suggestions would not occur. Why? Because the problem has instantly specified itself under control of the system from which it sprang. If one started from a basis of fairyland, one's problem would 'admit of a wide solution'; if one starts from the sidewalks of New York, the problem so promptly defines itself as 'What public conveyance will take me there?' that this seems to be the problem we began with. Really it is not. That problem was a far more general one which, under the control of the system it sprang from, a system familiar, definite, and dominant, has narrowed itself down to within an inch of the solution.

But not all the problems that puzzle us specify themselves so easily. Anyone who has had to prepare a speech or paper on some topic that is not quite familiar, will probably recall an initial period that was a helpless and dreary blank. This experience has produced in many a conviction that they are stupid, and in many, too, an almost invincible repugnance to thinking, as a voluntary immersion in the misery of indecision. That thinking does involve indecision, and indecision discomfort, and that the life of the thinker is hence not the pleasantest life imaginable is, no doubt, true. But much of the distaste and humiliation that attempts to think bring with them could be avoided by a better understanding of how reflection normally moves. That numb sterility of mind with which one first faces a great problem is not abnormal, but natural and all but inevitable. While the bait held out above the deep is so ill-defined as to be barely recognizable, one cannot expect definite suggestions to come leaping up to meet it. Or in terms of our recurring simile, we must fix the point off the mainland of thought to which our bridge is to be thrown before we can tell what piers and girders we are going to need.

If one is confronted with a general topic, then, the first thing to do is to resolve it into a question, or perhaps into a series of questions. The reason is that answering questions is what thought *is* in its very essence; it springs from them; it is guided by them; unless they light the way, it is lost in the dark. One cannot think profitably on the bare 'problem of evil'; but convert it into a question—Could a God who was all-powerful and all-good allow as much pain and sin as we actually find?— and you give reflection a compass. 'Free will' is a matter one would expect ideas to cluster about like barnacles round a keel. But let anyone try thinking about it without implicitly or explicitly recasting it as a question, and his thought will be what men's thought on this subject has so often been before, a mere wallowing in the sea, with sails helplessly flapping. Once the thought is brought under the control of a definite question, however—Does a decision or choice ever occur without a cause?—it finds itself able to move; it is as if a new hand had appeared at its helm and a trade wind had got into its sails.

But even with the difficulty recast into a question, it may still be too large to manage. Is suicide ever right? If one is perfectly clear what one means by this, there is no need to specify it further. But suppose that what one means by 'right' has never been made clear; then one's thinking may resolve itself into an elaborate missing of the point. It may take the course of showing that suicide shocks men's feelings or is contrary to Scripture; or again that it may be committed with a clear conscience or a good intention. But then, one may not mean by right or wrong any of these things at all, so that to establish them will leave one's question still unanswered. To think pointedly on a question, one must know what one means by it; and to know what one means by it, in this case, calls for some more or less definite notion of what one means by 'right'. Once this has been achieved, the question has so specified itself that the answer may come as a matter of course. If, for example, to take a common definition, one means by 'right' productive of more happiness than any act that might be done instead, the original question becomes, could suicide ever produce this surplus in general happiness? And to that the answer presumably is, in certain cases, Yes.

To see what must be done if the problem is to be specified is in this case fairly easy. Sometimes it is far more difficult. Is progress an illusion? Is pantheism consistent with worship? Is the French form of representative government better than the American? Such questions cannot be dealt with directly, because the answer must be arrived at through a series of subordinate questions. These questions and the answers to them may be so familiar that the Yes or No which would settle the major question is given instantly. Indeed the man who gives the answer may be so unaware of intermediate processes that he may suppose he has given a simple answer to a simple question. But there he would be mistaken, as mistaken as the sailor who, because he merely 'feels in his bones' that a storm is coming, denies that he is making an inference. A mental process, as we have seen, may be telescoped, implicit, and quick as a flash, and nevertheless be a process. And it is by just such a process as this that specification takes place, once we have thought a problem through, particularly if we have done so repeatedly. But if we have never thought it through, and wish to do so, the way of explicit specification is hardly to be escaped.

3. Before going on to more complex problems, let us stop for a moment, and make sure that we see why this is true. The process of specification is more than a hint to the woolly-minded; it is a process necessitated by the very nature of thought. We have seen that the end of thinking is to build up a whole or system such that every part is implicated in' the rest; that our present common-sense world is an attempt at such a system, however feeble; and that whenever thought meets with an obstacle, it seeks to extend its system so as to include this. We have seen, too, that the wholes thought accepts as explanatory are many and various, and of different degrees of concreteness. And since its tendency, as we have further seen, is away from the general toward the specific, from abstract to concrete, it will seek not merely to include the obstacle in its world, but to assign it to one or other of the sub-systems of this world. When confronted with a ghost or an electron, it never merely ascribes existence to the object; it ascribes existence *as* this or that; if it is anything more than perfunctory, it wants to know whether the thing is physical or mental, and if physical, what sort of physical thing it is. Now, we never approach an obstacle without some framework into which to fit it. If we could bring no framework at all, we could not even perceive that an obstacle existed. Two things with nothing in common, as Spinoza said, cannot even collide. 'Anschauungen ohne Begriffe sind blind.' And if the 'Begriffe' brought to bear are meagre, thought is correspondingly helpless; one's thought about an object will not be very fruitful, for example, if all one can say about it is that is something physical. On the other hand, the more complete and articulated its system, the more readily does it extend itself to encircle and absorb the new. Since the problem of thought is so to enlarge the present system as to include the foreign object, the more nearly that system is already built up to and around it, the more easily is the encircling movement completed. Every problem, indeed, is solved on the same principle as a picture puzzle. Given a single piece, one is all but helpless; it seems as if anything may go next. But as the picture approaches completion, the process accelerates, and

with only one lone blank or two left, one fairly races to
fill it in.

4. What seems to hold in theory is confirmed by glancing at
practice anywhere. The method of clearing up a difficulty by
making explicit the body of knowledge that it challenges, and
so bringing into clear light both the point at which that body
is defective and the addition that would make it whole is, as
Bosanquet says, 'the natural procedure in argument'.[1] It is the
procedure always adopted in meeting a difficulty in another's
thought by the teacher, lawyer, or expositor, who is truly expert.
It was the method of Clifford, for example, in meeting the
question why pressure and volume in a gas varied inversely
with each other.[2] His readers may well have had in their possession all the facts required to answer that question. What he
did was to specify it for them, to show that pressure and
volume belonged to a familiar group of facts about particles in
motion, and that these facts would have a glaring gap in their
circle if pressure and volume did not behave in precisely the
way they did. Once this was clear, the circle snapped shut and
the question was answered.

Now no question has quite the same meaning in any two
mouths, since it is always a demand for the completion of what
is present already; and it is safe to say that what is present is
always different in different minds. The questions a student
asks measure his mastery of the subject. Some questions would
be recognized at once by any expert as questions which only
another expert would naturally ask, since the answer would be
sought only as the coping-stone of an elaborate underlying
structure.[3] And the expert teacher or expositor is the person

---

[1] *Implication and Linear Inference*, Chap. V.

[2] Above, Chap. XVIII, Sec. 5.

[3] I say 'would naturally ask,' not 'could ask,' for of course such
questions may be asked by accident. When I had to write an early
undergraduate essay for one of the distinguished teachers to whom
this book is dedicated, and cast about for a subject, I asked if I might
take 'the development of the ontological argument'. Professor Joachim

who can tell, as it were instinctively, from the questions asked what the extent of this structure is, and where it must be patched and built up if the coping-stone is to be reached. Understanding can advance only as fast as the fragmentary system in the mind permits. If that is deficient, it must be pieced out, and its piecing out, like its final completion, must be achieved from within. For strictly, knowledge cannot be communicated; it can only be appropriated; and even then, only by a mind that is ready for it. This is why a young reader when first exposed to the great reflective writers so often finds them meaningless. The answers given are to questions he has never asked, questions that, with his present knowledge, were perhaps wholly beyond his asking. It is only as the pressure of his own thought, spontaneous or forced on him by the exigencies of life, leads him to seek answers for himself, that he comes to see that these answers are awaiting him in the very writings he took as meaningless. It needs a philosopher to understand a philosopher. Intelligibility is always relative. And it is sometimes well to remember that if one finds a thinker unintelligible, that does not immediately prove him meaningless or even obscure. It was one who suffered more than most, though not quite undeservedly, from the demand that he be at once intelligible, Hegel, who made the famous comment: If a hero is not a hero to his valet, that may be rather because the valet is a valet, than because the hero is not a hero.

5. Unfortunately to be a successful pioneer of thought and to be a successful expositor are not the same thing, and, indeed, require qualities markedly different. A mind with the greatest agility in leaping about among the pinnacles of its own thought may cut an awkward figure when it tries to direct someone else how to go on with a rickety foundation. It is habituated to the

saw, of course, that if that were asked with any notion of what the question really involved, the inquirer was well past his novitiate in the business of metaphysics. Somewhat startled, he pressed me hopefully, and in a way that puzzled me at the time, as to how I had come to ask it. I am sorry to have to add that his worst suspicions were confirmed.

heights and may have forgotten how things look to people on the ground. And one who has so lost touch with the common mind can neither argue with it nor instruct it successfully, however great may be his grasp.[1] For to convince another mind you must start where that mind is, and supply it with the complement it needs to make your conclusion necessary. 'The impulse of the natural man in opening an argument is not to lay down a first premise but to explain the situation at large.' 'When, again, a barrister opens his case, undertaking to exhibit a situation from which, if he proves his facts, only one conclusion can emerge, the root of his argument is the same. . . . The systematic character of our mind unites itself with the systematic material laid before it, and, aspiring to complete and harmonize the system, necessarily proceeds—such is the reasoner's hope and expectation—in a certain way to a certain result.'[2] It may be said that the reasoner in such a case is doing far more than merely specify a problem present in his hearer's mind; he is supplying him new data which give rise to a new problem. This may be true. But again it may not; the expositor, as in the example from Clifford, may be merely ordering what is already known so as to give it 'an increased vitality springing from the juxtaposition of the original data. A fresh datum—a premise which partakes of the nature of a conclusion—may arise out of the necessities which impose themselves when the original facts are synthetically grouped.'[3] In such a case, whether it is better to say that one has specified

---

[1] I once heard a savant who had sat under both say, not wholly facetiously, that there was only one worse lecturer on physics in Europe than Kelvin, and that was Helmholtz. Cf. James: 'In every university there are admirable investigators who are notoriously bad lecturers. The reason is that they never spontaneously see the subject in the minute articulate way in which the student needs to have it offered to his slow reception. They grope for the links, but the links do not come. Bowditch, who translated and edited Laplace's *Mécanique Céleste*, said that whenever his author prefaced a proposition by the words "it is evident", he knew that many hours of hard study lay before him.'—*Psychology*, II. 370.

[2] Bosanquet, *Implication and Linear Inference*, 123–4.

[3] *Ibid.*, 116.

a prior problem or that one has added to prior knowledge is a nice question. One has in a sense done both. We are to consider in later chapters how knowledge extends itself. Meanwhile it is best, if the fragments used are already there and only need to be put in order, to view the process as one of specification.

That there always is some structure underlying a genuine question and seeking completion in it we may be sure. 'A question always includes some notion of the general nature of its answer. In wanting to know something, we must know, however indefinitely, what it is that we want to know.'[1] And the problem of specification is to bring this indefinite knowledge to explicit definition. That special sub-system of our thought that seeks completion through the answer must be brought into the light of day. Let us see in an example how this is done.

6. Jones suffers from hay fever, which lays him low every year from August to October. If we can suppose him an intelligent man who nevertheless does not know the cause, and sets out to find it through reflection, how would he go about it to specify his problem? We have said that he would bring to light the sub-system from which the question springs and which is in need of the answer to round it out. What is the sub-system in this case? It is a mass of data comprising (a) what he knows of the facts of hay fever, i.e. the phenomena that it seems to consist of, and (b) all the circumstances he can think of that might be causally connected with it. Why call such a mass a system? Because its parts are tied together, however loosely, by a presumption of causal linkage. In the back of the thinker's mind is a set of conditions which, whether explicit or not, act as a board of admission, including some circumstances and excluding others. These presiding conditions are the rules of causality. Jones is hunting for a cause; the bridge he is trying to construct is a causal bridge, and no materials can be used that will not contribute to it. What enables materials

[1] G. F. Stout, *Mind*, 1922, 393; and cf. above, Chap. XIX, Sec. 2.

to qualify Jones more or less dimly knows; for he knows that what causes anything must be present just before or along with it, will probably be absent where it is absent, and will probably also vary with it. Not that he recites these rules to himself; indeed they had been used for many centuries by almost everyone before they were codified as 'Mill's methods'. But it is they that give such unity as it has to the little sub-system that emerges. It is as if the thinker were playing a game for which these conditions prescribe the way in which he shall dispose the black and white pieces on the board, and also the rules of play. His setting of the board may be clumsy, but it is not capricious. On the one side he disposes the blacks—the sneezes and snuffles, the irritable membranes and temper, the red nose and watery eyes, the lassitude, the gradual onset in late summer and waning in the fall. Over against these is the great mixed mass of circumstances that seem to accompany and may cause—weather, dust, tiredness, dryness or rain, the variations of night and day, of presence in city and country, visits to the seaside or to the mountains or abroad, a memorable walk through the fields which was interrupted by an attack, a summer in a northern camp, where the sufferer went strangely unscathed. So far as possible for a layman, the problem is specified and the board set (a) when he is clear what it is that he wishes to include in his system, (b) when he has assembled before him the set of data from which the solution must spring, and (c) when he knows the rules of the game, i.e. the sort of connection that, in accordance with the structure of the system, would complete it satisfactorily. If the reflection achieves its end, a new picture will appear before him, in which the phases of the malady, the attack in the fields, the relative freedom in the city and at the seaside, the complete freedom abroad and in the camp, will be seen in definite connection with certain factors on the other side, which no doubt would be, in this case, the presence and absence in varying degree of the pollens of certain plants. Whether the imperfect order in his mind shall fall into the more perfect order that he wants is beyond his control. One cannot dictate to one's own genius; one can only coax it and use wiles. And the likeliest stratagem is clear enough. The mind must call its reserves together, order them as best it can, and then, making a mute imploring plea to their loyalty, turn on one's heel and leave it to their regimental spirit to form themselves in true order. If one has been a good drill-master before, it is astonishing what they may do on their own initiative.

But surely, says the student who has been reading about induction, such an approach is the very picture of impotence and confusion. This may be the way in which an ignoramus would go about it to answer such a question, but it is certainly not the method of a scientific or intelligent mind. Such a mind would never dream of assembling this rabble and trusting that luck would somehow regiment it. The command of such a mind would be authoritative; every move would be orderly; like a good general it would attack the enemy piecemeal. It would first make clear the effect it wanted to explain, and then it would try the possible causes singly until it hit upon the right one by orderly elimination. Now the answer to all this is simply that the mind does not work that way, that such a description puts the cart before the horse. It is true that *after* the problem has been specified and various solutions have presented themselves, *then* this neat method of elimination may be adopted. But you cannot eliminate before there is anything to be eliminated. This formal process is important of course; it is the way hypotheses are verified once they have been arrived at. But we are still in the stage of reflection at which hypotheses are yet to be formed, when the mind is not even ready to hazard a suggestion and is groping in the dark for some solid ledge from which the leap of suggestion may be made.

The procedure of the hay-fever sufferer gives the scheme for this stage of the reflective process. It consists in setting plainly opposite each other the island that must be included and that part of the mainland which must be extended to embrace it. Within the limits of this scheme, the matter and structure of the sub-system may vary indefinitely. The system shown in the example was a causal one because this type is both so common and so important. If further illustration of it is cared for, the reader may consider how a detective, in or out of a book, goes about it to get his quarry; how, guided by a wide experience of what causes what, as well as by the canons of causation, he assembles a mass of evidence which converges with increasing certainty upon one head. His problem is, given these assembled facts, to find an X that will fit them all. But the wholes that are operative in questions, like those that are the basis of understanding, may be of extremely different kinds. The system at work may be arithmetical, as in the schoolboy's traditional problem of papering or carpeting a room; and then the way of approach will be so to combine the component totals that, by the rules of the arithmetical game, one result and one alone is seen to be possible. Or the whole may be political. What would happen in the United States if Congress passed a measure that it deemed essential to public safety, and the Supreme Court ruled it unconstitutional? This question springs from a knowledge, clearly present but incomplete, of the American system of government. A quick answer or a guess might be hazarded from a basis barely large enough to support the question. But it would be without title to respect. A competent answer could be given only by marshalling, and very probably extending, an already considerable knowledge of the way in which, within a system of government like the American, the Supreme Court, constitution, and Congress interact.

7. From all this it follows that no discovery in the upper ranges of philosophy or science is ever made by accident. Jevons has said, it is true, that 'a great science has, in many cases, risen from an accidental observation'. And he goes on in his erudite way: 'Erasmus Bartholinus thus first discovered double refraction in Iceland spar; Galvani noticed the twitching of a frog's leg; Oken was struck by the form of a vertebra; Malus accidentally examined light reflected from distant

windows with a double refracting substance. . . . Chance, then, must giveus the starting point. . . .'[1] But if it really was chance that made Galvani notice the twitching of the frog's leg, or Oken the form of a vertebra, why would it not be just as likely that you or I should notice it? In a way, of course, and indeed in more ways than one, chance may be said to have a part. Relatively speaking, it is matter of chance that one stimulus falls upon our organs rather than another, or that the observer should be in a region where certain stimuli may be received, or that the person exposed should be Galvani, not you or I. But that the exposure should awaken a fruitful response in Galvani's mind and not in ours, is no more a matter of chance than the springing up of seed when thrown on good soil rather than bad. Even though Galvani came to the twitching leg with no definite question in mind to which this gave the answer, still he brought, so to speak, a general question, an apperceiving system for this sort of event, that put a world of difference between him and us. And if such a system, restlessly incomplete, is necessary even for using effectively one's eyes and ears, still more is it necessary in the upper ranges of theory. There is something grotesque in the thought of Planck striking by a lucky accident upon the formula that gives the value of 'h', or of Bradley stumbling absent-mindedly on a suprarelational Absolute. That such conceptions often break upon the mind suddenly and without warning has nothing to do with the matter, as we shall see. Logic may be operative through the most patched and chequered psychological history. The point of importance is that it *is* logic, an implicit but imperative logic, that gets results in all these cases—not luck, nor some isolated faculty of intuition, nor some mysterious inscrutable genius, wayward but divine.

[1] *Principles of Science*, 399–400.

CHAPTER XXI

OBSERVATION

1. We have seen that reflection is always an attempt to solve a problem. We have seen further that if one is to think to the point, one must usually specify the problem into something far more definite than its first form. And the key to this process of specification we found in the nature of questioning. A question is an attempt by a system of ideas to mend a hole in its own fabric. To specify the question means to bring the frayed edges of the rent to light so that it is clear how much space must be filled and what threads must be united. What, for instance, if Booth had missed Lincoln? We know that ensuing events would have been different, but we cannot hazard so much as a reasonable guess about them unless we know the seeds from which they must have sprung. *Ex nihilo nihil fit* holds as truly of thought about effects as of the effects themselves. In this case, we must bring clearly to mind what we know of Lincoln's character and purposes, of the issues he was concerned with, of the forces that furthered and thwarted his will. It is only when this system of ideas is as complete as we can make it that we are ready for the leap of theory. And, of course, the completer the system, the better and easier will be the solution. 'A question well put is half answered.'

But suppose we have brought to light all we possess of such a system and our minds remain obstinately barren, without a shoot or sprout of suggestion. This, of course, is all too common. 'There are few people who can truly think. Take an ordinary, intelligent ploughman who reads his Bible and his *People's Journal*, and set him down to think on a given subject out of his usual run of ideas, say on Conscription; and one of two things happens. His mind either wanders from the subject in hopeless reverie, or he falls asleep. He cannot think on Conscription.'[1]

---

[1] Sir John Adams, *Herbartian Psychology*, 100–1. 'When I am not walking, I am reading', Charles Lamb wrote; 'I cannot sit and think.' —*Detached Thoughts on Books and Reading*.

There are many reasons for such helplessness. The would-be thinker may be tired or distracted or uninterested; or on this particular subject he may be over-emotional; or he may be downright insane. But we name such causes as these only to pass them by, for they are all external to the course of thought. They are agencies that disrupt or distort it by breaking in from the outside. Not that they lack importance; there are psycho-analysts of the day who tell us that all thinking is at the mercy of just such factors as these, that it can never surrender itself to the control of the subject-matter and follow the path of an objective logic, but is pulled about like a puppet by instincts, desires and feelings. Such a position is, of course, self-destructive. If all thinking is governed by these non-logical pulls and pushes, this conclusion is itself so governed, and has no more claim on our acceptance than other products of spleen or bias. What we are here concerned with, however, is not these external factors, whatever their influence, but the deficiencies of thought itself. If, with the problem specified before us and external conditions not impeding, our minds refuse to yield a suggestion, this is due to one or both of two things, lack of knowledge and lack of inventiveness. The first will be dealt with in this chapter; the second, which lies at the heart of the reflective process, in the three chapters that follow.

2. In specifying a problem, one mobilizes one's resources in order of attack. But when they are all drawn up they may present so pitiable an array that an attack is obviously hopeless; if faced with the question, What causes hay fever? we may find specification impossible, because we know nothing about it, except barely that it is a disease. If asked what we thought would have happened if Booth had missed Lincoln, we may again find reflection checkmated by mere ignorance. To infer, in its very essence, is to extend a system already partly present in the mind, in such manner as the system requires. If the system is absent, or if it is there in such disordered pieces that its nature and structure are concealed, inference is impossible.

Not only would it be out of the question for a man who knew nothing of Lincoln's aims or of the issues he was concerned with to predict what he might have done; it would be impossible for him even to make a beginning of such prediction, for he could not properly think on the point at all.

No intellectual power will take the place of such knowledge.

> 'It is related of Coleridge and two friends that, being anxious to leave a busy inn in a hurry, they tried to harness their horse for themselves. Everything went well with the three philosophers till they came to the horse's collar. This fairly brought them to a standstill. It seemed to be made on the most unphilosophical principles, and in spite of all their efforts could not be forced over the animal's head. It was not till the press of business had so far slackened as to allow the maid-servant to make her appearance that they came to some understanding of the teleology of horse collars. She simply reversed the collar, slipped it over the horse's head, and then re-reversed it.'[1]

There is no need for surprise that one of the first minds of Europe should be instructed by the maid-servant. She had had the sort of experience that made her adept at handling a horse-collar; Coleridge, peering doubtfully at it from his 'world of dim-melting lights and shadows', had not. And if it is said that he should have been able without special experience to deal with so simple a problem, it is easy to name others which any modern school-boy with a mechanical turn of mind could solve easily, but which would have defied Aristotle himself. A suggestion as to how to repair a radio must spring from some knowledge of how a radio works, and without such knowledge, no genius will avail. This holds of artistic creation as truly as of theoretic and practical. 'Let us suppose that in the Samoan Islands there were born a child having the singular and extraordinary genius of Mozart. What could he accomplish? At the most, extend the gamut of three or four tones to seven, and create a few more complex melodies; but he would be as unable to compose symphonies as Archimedes would have been to invent an electric dynamo.'[2]

[1] Adams, *ibid.*, 158.
[2] Ribot, *Essay on the Creative Imagination*, 154, after Weismann.

3. It follows that if one's resources in the way of knowledge give too small a base for the leap of theory, the next step is to get that knowledge. In the Lincoln problem, one would go to the historical authorities and try to acquire the needed information through reading. If the problem is a new one in the natural sciences, one will turn to observation or experiment. The place of these two processes, observation and experiment, in the movement of reflection is often misunderstood. To speak of their *place* at all is a little deceptive, for the fact is, that they have, not one place or function in the thought process, but three. First, observation may start the movement off by presenting a problem, as in the case of the bowsprit and the bubbles. Secondly, observation is often needed to broaden the base for theory, as when a physician hunts for symptoms in diagnosing a disease. Thirdly, observation is commonly needed in the final check of the theory, in verifying one's suggestions. The functions of experiment are the same. Indeed from the logical point of view, experiment *is* observation. 'Herschel justly remarked that we might properly call these two modes of experience *passive and active observation.*' 'When we merely note and record the phenomena which occur around us in the ordinary course of nature, we are said *to observe.* When we change the course of nature . . . we are said to *experiment.*' 'Experiment is thus observation *plus* alteration of conditions.'[1] The two may be treated together.

4. The first function of observing we have dealt with already, and we shall comment on the third later. It is the second we are now concerned with, the use of observation in preparing a base for the leap of suggestion. No better example of this use can be found than one we have just named, medical diagnosis.[2] When a doctor first approaches a case he does not carry in his mind the data for specifying his problem; he must get them

---

[1] Jevons, *Principles of Science*, 400.
[2] A typical diagnosis is detailed in the Columbia Associates' *Introduction to Reflective Thinking*, Chap II.

by using eyes, ears and instruments. He follows the case history, takes the pulse and temperature, notes suspicious sounds through his stethoscope, perhaps examines blood and secretions with his microscope, makes a chart of the rise and fall of fever, and in some cases only after a long period of such observation commits himself on the cause. Wherever the present capital of knowledge is too slight to float a theory, other scientists must do likewise. Classical examples of such patient laying of foundations are to be found in Darwin's inquiry into the formation of vegetable mould,[1] and Wells's investigation into the causes of dew.[2] It is the same process that is followed by the 'higher critic' when he prefaces his theory as to the genuineness of a document by a minute examination of its contents, its style, its likenesses to other writings believed contemporary and its differences from them, its apparent purpose, its references to known events, its own claims and the claims of tradition regarding its authorship. To give but one more instance, it is the same process that is followed by the detective in taking up a case. His theory is a better theory than that of someone who leaps to a conclusion because it is the product, not of one obvious clue or group of clues, which might be offset by others not yet noticed, but jointly of all the clues available.

5. Now this process of observing to gather data for a theory has difficulties of its own. In the sciences they often arise from the sheer impotence of our organs of sense to deal with the magnitudes of nature. At the highest estimate, the proportion of things we can perceive to the things we might perceive if our senses were more discriminating is a miserable fraction; and the problems of the natural sciences are resolving themselves ever more generally into problems of the imperceptible. The whole science of chemistry, for instance, is now known to

[1] Reported in *The Formation of Vegetable Mould through the Action of Worms.*

[2] For a brief account of this, given as an example of scientific demonstration, see Joseph, *Introduction to Logic,* 462–3.

be based upon the behaviour of electronic particles which even the most powerful microscopes have not brought within the field of vision;[1] what we know of them must be gained entirely through inferences from their visible effects. Every sensation of sight or touch, every sound and taste and odour arises from causes that are beyond the range of our senses, and for the most part even of our instruments. And just as we are limited on one side by the smallness of things, so we are limited on the other side by their largeness. If there were a 'music of the spheres', as the ancients supposed, we could not hear it, any more than we could make out by merely looking the place of the Milky Way in the Stellar universe. Similarly again of movement. What is to be observed must move within narrow limits of speed. All about us things are in the incessant movement of growth, but we cannot see it because it is too slow. At the same time the ultimate particles in these things are moving at a speed which, even if they were magnified a million times, would still be invisible because it is too fast. A jet of water we take as continuous, though it is composed of discrete drops. An ocean we take as a permanency, though in the history of the earth or the solar system, it would appear as a swift transition from the age of steam to the age of ice.

6. It is plain from this that many of the problems that are set to reflection, and particularly the central problems of science, cannot be dealt with by observation directly. Recourse must be had to instruments and experiments; the results must be interpreted by inference; and the inferences must be woven together into an elaborate fabric of theory. The technique of such inquiry falls beyond the scope of this work. But fortunately most of the problems we think about do not demand it; the observing they call for is a simpler affair. And the ways in which observation, either of the simpler or more difficult form, may in principle go wrong, and by going wrong put reflection out of its course, do fall within our scope. These dangers

[1] Professor C. T. R. Wilson's photographs show the paths made by electrons through water-vapour, not the moving particles themselves.

are reducible to two. We may (1) observe the wrong things, or (2) fail to observe the right ones.

The first of these again has three forms: When we observe the wrong things it is (*a*) through fastening on the irrelevant, (*b*) through selecting some relevant matters for too exclusive notice, or (*c*) through manufacturing the data for ourselves. It should be noted that all these mistakes are rooted in the same fact, which we have studied in detail in our first book, namely, that perception is charged with thought. To perceive is itself to theorize; to observe as a means to forming a hypothesis is to theorize twice over. In barely recognizing a footprint, one is already performing an act of inference, as we have previously argued; and when a detective singles out a footprint for special observation from among the thousand things that he might notice instead, there is clearly a further element of theory in his mind; his selection is governed by the view that this is significant for his end, while other details are not. It follows that if one brings to the facts the wrong preconceptions, one will observe the wrong things. And we are often told, in consequence, that the way to avoid error is to avoid preconceptions altogether, to bring to the facts a free mind. This sounds well, but it would be as fatal as it is actually impossible. One cannot bring a 'free' mind to the facts, try as one will, for strictly speaking such a mind would be a blank in both interest and knowledge. Nor would it help if one could. Sherlock Holmes's superiority to Dr. Watson did not lie in the greater vacancy of his stare, but on the contrary in its fuller intelligence; it was precisely because his mind was running over with theories that details were to him significant which for Watson had no existence.

7. That observation is thus selective, and that selection must be guided by theory is now recognized by science. Its recognition in principle is one of the main differences between the mediaeval and modern views of scientific method, and its adoption in research one of the main conditions of the conquest

of nature. When the alchemists set out to discover how to convert the baser metals into gold, their method was to avoid prejudgements and patiently to try all combinations. Even Bacon, in his not very enlightened hostility to the ὕβρις, as he thought it, of the older logic toward nature, recommended this sort of approach. Stranger still was the '*hypotheses non fingo*' of one of the most fertile in speculation of all scientific theorists, Isaac Newton. But it took no very keen eye to detect that his practice was at variance with his theory. And from the time of the brilliant group of mid-Victorian scientists in England, more especially Faraday, Tyndall, Huxley, and Darwin, the battle of the free imagination for a recognized place in scientific thought was won. Tyndall hung his address of 1870 to the British Association upon a remark of Bain's that touches the point in the reflective process which we are now concerned with: 'The uncertainty where to look for the next opening of discovery brings the pain of conflict and the debility of indecision'; and he went on to argue that the debility must be removed by 'the scientific use of the imagination'. 'Let the imagination go', said Faraday, 'guarding it by judgement and principles, but directing it by experiment'; he might equally well have said 'directing experiment by *it*'. 'Elsewhere he has remarked that in youth, he was, and he might have added that he still remained, "a very lively imaginative person, and could believe in the *Arabian Nights* as easily as in the Encyclopaedia".'[1] Of the inexhaustible spring of theory that made Darwin's observation so fertile we need hardly speak since it is so well known.[2]

[1] Havelock Ellis, *Dance of Life*, 120. Cf. the account in the same essay, 'The Art of Thought', of the prodigal imaginativeness of Kepler, who was not above believing that the earth was an animal.

[2] 'I have been speculating last night', wrote Darwin, 'what makes a man a discoverer of undiscovered things; and a most perplexing problem it is. Many men who are very clever—much cleverer than the discoverers—never originate anything. As far as I can conjecture, the art consists in habitually searching the causes and meaning of everything that occurs' (writing to Horace Darwin; quoted by Knowlson, *Originality*, 82). This is disappointingly vague, though it becomes a little less so if one interprets it in the light of Darwin's own practice. His mind was in a perpetual ferment of scientific theorizing.

Whenever we collect data, then, with a view to framing a theory about anything, we must fasten on some circumstances and leave others out; we must select. And if we select, there must be some principle of selection. This principle, if beyond mere likes and dislikes, must be one of relevance to a theory already in mind. But this looks like moving in a circle. We observe as a means to theory, but unless the theory is there already we do not know what to observe. This is no sought out puzzle. It is one of those genuine difficulties in the process of thought that make rules for discovery impossible, and set the great discoverers upon seats of intellectual honour. We shall shortly have more to say about this difficulty, but for the moment let us come back to the dangers to which the fact behind it gives rise. That fact is that observation is dominated by theory. How does this domination divert the course of reflection?[1]

8. (1) It may make us observe the wrong things. This means, as we have seen, that it may make us either (*a*) fix upon what is irrelevant, (*b*) fix too exclusively upon some things that are relevant, or (*c*) create what we observe out of whole cloth. As to (*a*) fixing upon the irrelevant: suppose a novice is playing a master at chess. The master moves a pawn, and it is the problem of the novice to see the design behind the move and block it. He must proceed by observing the new lay-out of enemy pieces in order to find where the danger lies. And here the novice usually demonstrates that he is a novice. He concentrates on the obscure pawn or the pieces immediately around it, not noticing that its movement has cleared the path for a bishop at the opposite corner of the board, or made possible the deadly advance of some knight that seemed to be loitering far from the scene of action. He has fastened on the conspicuous and neglected the important. This is often repeated when the problem is more significant. The investigators of malaria, pre-

[1] For a further discussion of the influence on perception of acquired meanings, see Chap. V above.

possessed by a theory, concentrated on the night air and over-
looked the mosquitoes that were abroad in it. Max Müller had
a theory that primitive religious belief arose from confusions
about names, that the Greek belief, for example, that man had
sprung from stones came from the resemblance of λαός,
people, and λᾶες, stones;[1] and being a learned linguist and
philosopher of language, he found an amount of evidence for
this dubious theory that was amazing. If the reflection of
eminent scholars can be led astray by such selective observation,
still more may this be expected of the thought of uneducated
men. Many of the superstitions that have lasted from generation
to generation have their root in such observing—the superstitions, for example, about thirteen at table, about looking at
the moon over the left shoulder, breaking a mirror, walking
under a ladder, finding horseshoes or four-leaved clovers,
starting a new project on a Friday. Something has happened
in the far past which, idly or earnestly, someone wanted to
explain. He cast about among its antecedents for the cause.
Some fancy or prepossession, perhaps not now recoverable,
fixed his eye upon the wrong thing; and once the observation
had given birth to the theory, the two went on hand in hand.
In future the theory limited the scope of the observation, and
the observation, aided by a neglect of negative instances, perpetually confirmed the theory anew.

9. (*b*) In minds of better quality, the error as a rule is less
gross. Instead of basing its theory on sheer irrelevancies, it
selects certain of the relevant data for a notice that is too
exclusive; and the ingenuity it displays in citing scripture for
its purpose is often as diabolic as it is unconscious. It is notorious how statistics can be used in this fashion, and because an
array of figures gives an impressive effect of exactness, the
unskilled and the unscrupulous are strongly tempted to go
quarrying for themselves in treacherous statistical mines.
Thus it was easy for a patriotic newspaper during the Spanish-

---

[1] *Introduction to the Science of Religion*, 48.

American war to show that life in the navy was as safe as life in the city; it offered statistics of unimpeachable accuracy to show that the two places had about the same death rate. And these data were, of course, relevant to its end. Equally relevant, however, were the data which would have shown that the group in the city comprised all ages and conditions of health, while the group in the navy comprised only picked young men; and these data were omitted. In a celebrated recent debate between a clergyman and a theatrical producer as to the morality of the stage, the producer startled his audience by stating that there were as many ministers in jail as actors. It was only after the debate was over, that the clergyman could produce the missing part of the statistics, to the effect that the number of ministers was many times that of actors, a point which if originally mentioned would have placed precisely the opposite construction upon the facts adduced. But perhaps nowhere are the combined necessity and danger of collecting data in the interests of theory more apparent than in the writing of history. Professor Bury has gone so far as to say that no first-rate history has ever been written without a bias, and it seems likely that he could make good his case. But what this implies is that even the greatest of reflective historians cannot be read with full reliance. Gibbon's convictions about Christianity, Hume's about Toryism, Macaulay's about Whiggism, Buckle's about material well-being, Froude's about Henry, all led to a selection of data which by general agreement of scholars coloured their conclusions unduly. It has even been possible to write a plausible history of philosophy with the object of showing that philosophy in its traditional sense is futile.[1] The partiality, in both senses, with which evidence is used may be more avoidable or less, depending on the degree to which in different subject-matters abstraction is justifiable. For the historian to give all the relevant evidence is usually impossible. In the natural sciences this is commonly much less difficult. But in neither case can a theory that springs from a part only of the relevant data be right, unless of course by accident.

[1] Lewes's *Biographical History*.

10 (*c*) At times preconception goes still farther in its influence on the collection of data. It may lead to the creation
of evidence virtually out of whole cloth. Lecky has pointed out
that the judges, who in mediaeval times sentenced witches to
imprisonment and death, were among the ablest and most
upright in Europe, and that to those who did not start with
the conviction that witchcraft was a myth, the evidence before
them was overwhelming. Many honest witnesses were to be
found who testified that they had actually seen some unhappy
old woman of the neighbourhood riding a broomstick, or con-
versing with the Evil One across the back fence. Nor was
there anything in this to be surprised at in an age in which
Luther himself could ink-bottle the devil. Men tend to see
what they expect or hope or fear to see. There have been almost
endless inquiries into the occurrence of miracles and into the
phenomena of spiritualism, but the fact that precisely opposite
reports on the same kind of event have been over and over
rendered by men of apparently equal ability and integrity
makes it clear how dangerous preconception can be to straight
seeing, as well as straight thinking. And the difficulty is greatly
increased when the object observed is oneself. Are we, at the
present moment, happy or not? If we are ill, how serious is the
illness? Has the recognition we have received been greater or
less than our deserts? Is our attempt at applying a faith cure or
Christian Science a failure or a success? If we bring a pre-
formed conviction to such questions as these, we shall be as
ready to find in the facts the sort of basis we want as Silas
Marner was to see in Effie's head by the firelight his missing
pot of gold.

11. (2) We turn from the error that consists in fixing upon
the wrong things to the error that consists in failure to see the
right ones. These are really two sides of the same mistake. A
failure to observe is never a case of mere blankness of mind;
one fails to note the right things *through* fixing upon the wrong
ones. Thus all the instances we have given exemplify both

errors. Nevertheless the two sides are worth distinguishing, just as affirmation and negation are, though neither can occur without the other. And since failing to see the essential, like fixing on the unessential, is a head that includes all cases of malobservation, we can make under the new head another and not uninstructive classification of such cases.

When we fail to observe anything, it is through failing to note either (*a*) part of a whole, or (*b*) instances of a rule. (*a*) By a whole is meant here any limited system of observable fact. When watching a prestidigitator perform a trick and trying to find how he does it, one is very likely, and the more likely by reason of his misleading 'patter', to overlook the essential movements. When we are attempting to play the part of physician to ourselves or to another, it is easy to pass over through mere ignorance a frequent shortness of breath, though this may be a symptom of grave weakness of heart. Sometimes, again, the parts of the system we are attempting to put together are so remote from each other that even the experts are blind to them. None but a scientist of exceptional alertness would note that northern lights varied with magnetic storms, and both with the appearance of spots on the sun, and yet the three are causally tied together. It is clear that failure to observe in such a case implies no intellectual defect unless measured by a superhuman standard, and no moral defect at all.

12. (*b*) This is not quite so easy to say of the failure to observe instances that run counter to a rule. Here preoccupation with a theory commonly divides with emotional bias the dishonours of the day. Both distort reflection disastrously.

> 'It is difficult to find persons who can with perfect fairness register facts for and against their own peculiar views. . . . The whole race of prophets and quacks live on the overwhelming effect of one success, compared with hundreds of failures which are unmentioned and forgotten. As Bacon says, "Men mark when they hit, and never mark when they miss". And we should do well to bear in mind the ancient story, quoted by Bacon, of

one who in Pagan times was shown a temple with a picture of all the persons who had been saved from shipwreck after paying their vows. When asked whether he did not acknowledge the power of the gods, "Ay", he answered; "but where are they painted that were drowned after their vows?" [1]

There are those who believe that socialists generally are tub-thumping psychopaths; others who believe that Englishmen generally omit their h's and lack humour; others who think that all Jews are of dark hair and complexion; others who are convinced that honesty is the best policy, in the sense that it is always the most likely way to advance one's material interests; others who believe that the good are invariably happy and the wicked unhappy, that haste always makes waste, and that everything worth doing is worth doing well. Those who accept such generalizations need the warning of another and sounder saying: all that glitters is not gold. There is no logical path from 'some' to 'all'. A little observation would overthrow any of these sayings, and if, in some minds, they have become established, it is pretty certainly not because the negative instances have offered no corrective, but because the corrective has been ignored or forgotten.

13. It should be noted that there is no fallacy in non-observation by itself. Fallacies occur only in inference. What distorts reflection is the all but irresistible tendency to put a premature inference unwittingly in the place of data of observation, to argue that, because I have failed to observe something, it is not there to observe. The man who has met some state socialists who were obviously hare-brained has had an experience that, so far as it goes, is worth while; and the fact that he fails to note or to think of Plato and others who belong to their tribe but were very far from hare-brained, need not, if he is duly cautious, destroy the value of that experience. The trouble is that in his eagerness for a sweeping view, he hastens to put a construction on his failure to observe, and infers that

---

[1] Jevons, *Principles of Science*, 402.

if the few socialists he has met have been less than sane, the reason can only be that sane socialists do not exist. He then includes this proposition among the data of observation, though he has manufactured it for himself, and proceeds to build upon the 'fact' a baroque edifice of conclusions.

14. The inference from non-observation to non-existence, however, is not always illegitimate. There are two cases. When one knows that negative instances, if they existed at all, would certainly have come to notice, then their failure to appear is fair proof that they do not exist. Thus if a competent anthropologist is asked whether, in addition to the races that are white, black, yellow, red, or brown, there is a further race that is green, he is justified in saying No. His denial, however, is not based merely on the absence of such people in his own or in reported experience, but on this *plus* the legitimate further premise that if they did exist, they would somewhere have been seen. Secondly, when one's proposed generalization is necessary in itself, one may again deny exceptions without making a hunt for them. If the question is, Are men with a strong sense of justice more or less inclined to be selfish than those without? it is wasted labour to take an appeal to instances at all. One can see without them that, other things equal, such men *must* be less selfish; justice is the sort of thing that curbs selfishness inevitably; negative instances are excluded in the nature of the case. Of course, there are persons who do not believe in rational necessities of any kind, and in due time, we shall look at their contention. It is enough here to remark that such persons have no right to believe in logic either.

15. We have distinguished two types of non-observation. In the one, we fail to note some point essential to a system of explanation; in the other, we fail to note exceptions to a rule. It must be admitted that this distinction, like our main division of failures in observation, is rather expository than logical. All failures in reflective observing fall ultimately in the first class. For just as all thinking is system-building, so the observing that is done in the interest of thought aims at system also. It is never particulars that thought is really concerned with; we have argued this out in the previous book. Even when it seems to be dealing with them, it is really employed upon universals, and its desire everywhere is to find intelligible bonds that bind universals together. For it, the importance of noting instances is that this is a means to the law behind them. Similarly the evil of missing instances is that one misses the law behind them. What the man who observes socialists and generalizes about them is looking for, whether he is aware of it or not, is not instances, but a permanent connection revealed by the instances, a connection between socialistic opinions and a certain type of character. Observation is of value for thought precisely so far as by its agency such connections can be laid bare and defined.

16. There is another point that will be clear by now about our treatment of observation. What it has revealed as essential in good observing, is not so much keen senses as sound theory. We have implied that observation is dominated by thought, and since thought is partial system seeking completion, it follows that observation itself is controlled by the fragmentary systems of ideas that we bring to the business of observing. We see more with our intelligence than we do with our eyes. Theory is both the strength and the weakness of observation. Expert theory leads to expert perceiving, while all the chief faults in perceiving, apart from mere deficiencies of sense, are due, we have suggested, either to the lack of theory or to the dominance of wrong theory.

This may be questioned. We may be told that it lodges the blame for bad observing too exclusively on the intellect, whereas everyone knows that such observing is due commonly, perhaps usually, to feeling and desire. Is it not notorious that love is blind? Have we not said ourselves that 'men tend to see what they hope or fear to see'? And what can be meant by calling hate and jealousy 'green-eyed' unless they, and not theory alone, have a power of concealing the good points in their objects and exposing the bad? That there is truth here is evident, and yet the ordinary statements about the effect of feeling on perception are too loose for acceptance. Is it true, for example, that love is blind? On the contrary, love fastens on its object hungrily; there is no detail about the loved one too minute for the lover's interest. How comes it, then, that love, and feeling generally, have gained such a reputation for blinding the eyes? We hazard two suggestions. In the first place, the lover, who knows as well as anyone the irregularities of profile and the awkwardnesses of manner of his beloved, does not feel about these things as others do; his happy state is such that the feelings they arouse in others are, in him, neutralized or checked. Since he does not feel about them as others feel, he is supposed not to see them at all; and this, we suggest, is an error. It is not observation itself that is blocked by his feeling, but those other feelings that observation would normally arouse. Secondly, so far as feeling does affect observation, it seems to do so indirectly through theory. Moods may be associated with ideas just as ideas may be associated with each other. Disapproval or dislike tends to breed a judgement of its object that is consonant with its own tone. And once this judgement is accepted, it acts upon observation in the way theory generally acts. This way we have described. The man who dislikes socialists will find the theory congenial that they are not quite sane, and while under the dominance of this theory, his observation will register unequally the favourable and unfavourable cases. Thus again it seems to be theory rather than feeling that is the directly distorting agent in observation.

17. And so we come round again to the paradox that we noted some time ago. The observation that is to count in reflection must be directed, for good or ill, by theory; and yet the observation is performed in order that the theory may be

arrived at. This seems to imply that the end must be reached
before we can select the means to it, and is not that absurd?
The general answer here is the same as the answer to the paradox of the search for knowledge:[1] our grasp is general before
it becomes specific, and this general knowledge is enough to
keep our search, for the most part, within the field of the relevant. Granting that a detective at work upon a crime does not
know at the start who the criminal is, his observation is certainly
not undirected; his general purpose of identifying the agent is
enough to fasten his notice upon open windows, footprints and
fingerprints as things that are relevant, and divert him from the
colour of the victim's eyes and the state of the weather as things
that probably are not. On the basis of his experience, he quickly
forms an initial theory to the effect that whoever committed
this crime would have acted from certain motives and would
have left certain traces behind him; under the guidance of this
theory, he goes on to detailed observation; the observation,
again, suggests a theory that is more specific; and this in turn
leads to the further narrowing of his attention and a still more
specific theory, until his thought overtakes the fact.

18. For most cases this answer to the paradox will serve.
But the difficulty with it is that it assumes a previous experience
which shows where to look; it assumes that men have dealt
successfully with this kind of problem before, whereas it is the
glory of the great discoverers to have blazed a trail into unexplored territory. What knowledge was on hand that would
tell Archimedes where to look for the suggestion of specific
gravity, or Newton where to look for the clue to the nature of
gravitation, or that would take Freud's eye away from physical
conditions and fix it upon unconscious mind as the explanation
of the neuroses? That even here the necessary data had for
the most part been accumulated is true; genius itself will not
work in a vacuum. But the greatness of these men consists
almost as much in knowing where to look as in seeing when

[1] Above, Chap. XIX, Sec. 3.

they do look. Indeed the two things go together; that is the point of the paradox. Neither goes before the other. If originality were a matter of finding something within a small and clearly marked field, or of taking data known to give the answer and distilling the right result from them, we could all be inventors and discoverers. The trouble is that we must not only find the answer, but, if we are to be original in the sense that these men were, must also find the data that will yield the answer. The perception of what data are relevant and the perception of what construction these will bear are aspects of the same insight. When a true poet writes a lyric, he does not first set up an end apart from the expression, and then leaf through the rhyming dictionaries for materials to work with; nor does he start with the dictionary and hope that the words will rouse an idea. The words and what they express are so fused in his mind that they cannot be divorced; the same instinct selects both; the motif invests itself with the words and yet the words make possible the motif. So it is in the mind of the thinker. It is the same insight that reveals new truth and that discovers in the most unlikely quarters material relevant to that truth. Darwin and Wallace found in Malthus's *Essay on Population* data that bore upon the origin of man. In such a book, most of us would have found nothing of the sort. That is why we are not Darwin and Wallace. Their hitting upon natural selection and their finding of the data that would suggest it in so unpromising a quarter, were indivisible parts of one genius.

Unfortunately, for such genius, there is no prescription. There can be no rules for the seeing eye. And thus James is right when he says about the thinker who turns to observation for ideas:

'Even when his interest is distinctly defined in his own mind, the discrimination of the quality in the object which has the closest connection with it is a thing which no rules can teach. The only *a priori* advice that can be given to a man embarking on life with a certain purpose is the somewhat barren counsel: be sure that in the circumstances that meet you, you attend to the *right* ones for your purpose. To pick out the right ones is the measure of the man. "Millions", says Hartmann, "stare at the phenomenon before a *genialer Kopf* pounces on the concept." The genius is simply he to whom, when he opens his eyes upon the world, the "right" characters are the prominent ones. The fool is he who, with the same purposes as the genius, infallibly gets his attention tangled amid the accidents.'[1]

[1] *Psychology*, II. 336, note.

CHAPTER XXII

INVENTION AND ASSOCIATION

1. Reflection, we have seen, is a movement toward self-completion on the part of an imperfect system of ideas. What starts the movement is a challenge to the system by something demanding inclusion. Faced by such a challenge, and driven on by some need, theoretical, practical or other, the system seeks to incorporate the foreign element within itself. The first step is to specify the problem. This is achieved when one has made the point to be settled as definite as the case admits, and has made explicit the resources already owned which bear upon that point. The second step, necessary only if these resources do not suffice, is to broaden the base from which suggestion may emerge, to read, consult or observe until one is equipped for the venture of theory. The third step, which we are to study in this and the two succeeding chapters, is perhaps more correctly called a leap, the leap of suggestion. It is no more essential than some other steps, but of all the parts of the movement it is the most interesting and the most dramatic.

2. This step may be called with equal justice invention and discovery, and is thus essentially the same in art as in science. The scientist who discovers a new law has thought creatively just as truly as the novelist has; and the novelist who traces the development of a character has discovered something just as truly as has the original scientist. There is much misapprehension on both points. It is not uncommon, but to one who reflects on the sort of power original work in science calls for it is distressing, to find such work disparaged when compared to the 'creative writing' of some second-rate story teller, as if Faraday was all very well in his pedestrian way but lacked the divine unaccountable inspiration that produced 'Abie's Irish Rose'. This of course is rubbish, but it is easier to see that it is than to say precisely why it is. The reason is not that scientific and artistic originality are wholly different things, and that the statement therefore attempts to compare the incomparable. The absurdity is rather that of two things which *are* felt to be somehow comparable the true order is reversed. A mind like Faraday's is felt to be creative, and profoundly so, because in a certain department of nature its imagination and insight carried it far beyond where men had gone before. The mind of the ordinary novelist is felt to be relatively uncreative because it does nothing of the sort. This implies that creation in artistic work, like originality in science, is a matter of relative depth of insight, or in terms of our second point above, that it is a matter of discovery. To call it discovery may seem wilful paradox to those for whom the essential point is that the artist's figures did not exist before he made them. Why use the name discovery, these persons will ask, when the only things 'discovered' depend wholly on the will of the maker? The answer is that the relations and behaviour of the artist's figures by no means depend wholly on his will, that their world is as truly a world of law, though, to be sure, law of a special kind, as that of the scientist himself. Every Shakespearean play, for example, is an aesthetic whole whose immanent imperatives cut off all manner of developments as aesthetically impossible; and its fabric is further shot through with those lines of psychological law which, visible or not, fix the pattern for every character. These laws the artist no more makes than the scientist makes the laws of nature. He finds them, and if his work is to be more than trivial he must conform to them. His insight that a fragmentary picture or character must be developed in this way rather than that is therefore literally discovery. The more profoundly he conforms to the laws of his spiritual realm the greater at once are his discovery and his creation. Thus invention is not in essence different in science and in art. The artist discovers when he creates; the scientist creates when he discovers.

3. Another point calls for remark. We are to attempt an account of the process of creation, an account meant to hold, with due modifications, of creators as far apart as Edison, Einstein, and Galsworthy. And it is not unlikely that the first impression of such an attempt will be of the grotesque presumptuousness of it. 'So you are going to be good enough, are you, to dispense, in passing, the secret of originality, and put in our hands the key to genius? That is very gracious indeed. Would it be indelicate to remark, however, that your credentials would be clearer if you could show that you had ever used this key to unlock anything yourself? You who have this secret of creation—where are the things you have created with it?' Now this is utter misunderstanding. To follow the track of an exploring mind after its discoveries have been made does not imply the claim that one could oneself have made these discoveries; if it did, it would be presumption to study great minds at all. Nor does it imply that we shall be able fully to understand the working of such minds; 'it is not possible', as Lotze points out, 'to account for any new idea or reaction of the mind without taking into account the whole state of the soul at the preceding moment',[1] and such knowledge is beyond us. What it does imply is that the movement of mind is not lawless, that even in the coming of new insights there is nothing magical or capricious which would put the mode of their coming quite beyond our discernment. And to say that a process is governed by law is not to claim the power of controlling it. No one now doubts that the weather has laws, but no one supposes that in using these laws to explain or even predict the weather, one is claiming power to produce states of weather at will. Similarly, the believer in 'natural law in the spiritual world' makes no claim to control the 'weather of the soul'. His knowledge at best is meagre and abstract, while the forces that govern the play of mind are beyond anyone's exhausting. All that he claims, in the present context, is that when he compares cases in which the mind has dealt with problems successfully, he finds it using the

[1] *Microcosmus*, I. 219.

same devices over and over. But he admits that the abstract knowledge of these devices will no more tell us what to think in fresh circumstances than a knowledge of the syllogism will supply us with argument in an unfamiliar field.

4. It will be well now to take a case or two of a simple kind of construction and look at the commonly received account of it. The shortcomings of this account will perhaps suggest a truer one.

Let us return to the man down-town who recalls his distant engagement forty minutes later, casts about for some way to meet it, and finally decides to take the subway. This man has reasoned; he has faced a problem and solved it. And there are many to-day who think the course of this thought would be explained if we could trace the nervous connections involved. The man is an organism elaborately conditioned, and if we knew all the stimulus-response connections that had been established in it, we could see that the process of 'reasoning', like the behaviour that issued from it, was the rattling off of a concatenation of reflexes. This 'rigorously scientific' theory we have discussed at length in dealing with behaviourism, and shall here pass it by with the remark that if this is science we hope to remain in superstition.

A less uncritical view, which has many adherents among psychologists, would make the process of reasoning one of association. According to this view what goes on in the man's mind is about as follows: The thought of the engagement suggests its time; the thought of its time suggests the thought of the present time; the latter, or the two together, suggest the shortness of the time intervening; this shortness suggests that I cannot keep my appointment by walking; the thought of this means of locomotion turns my thought to others, and there come up in turn the ideas of a taxicab, a tram, the subway. This movement through similars continues until I hit upon an expedient that appears to satisfy my need. I then accept this and put it into practice. Such a process is not the same thing as a chain of conditioned reflexes, yet in this respect it strongly resembles it, that the connection between each idea and its successor has been set up through past 'experience'. For example, I have had many experiences of covering certain distances in certain lengths of time, and the law of contiguity has fixed in my mind what can and cannot be covered in the time at my disposal. Again, one kind of locomotion more or less resembles another, and thus the law of similarity acts to make me move along the series—taxicab, tram, subway. The line of reflection is thus to be accounted for by the laws of association.

5. The details and forms of the theory by which association-ists account for reasoning we shall not go into, since no multiplication of details and no novelty of form could save it from one criticism that is for us decisive, namely that at times the mind works logically or intelligently, and that for this the theory has no explanation. It escapes the ontological folly of behaviourism only to fall into its structural folly, for it still believes that the mind is a sort of machine governed by mechanical or quasi-mechanical law, whose way of running can be explained without any mention of relevance, or any resort to the working of ends, logical, moral, or aesthetic. And we have argued long ago that to hold this view is to cut oneself off at the outset from every prospect of understanding how thought works.

6. Take any step in a course of reasoning and try to show by the laws of association why this rather than a dozen other steps should have followed from the one preceding, and the theory will prove bankrupt. Suppose that in the case considered the thought of walking is followed by the thought of taking a tram. This would be explained, one gathers, as association by similarity; one mode of locomotion suggests another. But note in the first place that the law by itself is absurdly inadequate.

There are many things that are more like walking than riding in a tram-car is; if it is similarity that mainly counts, why do not these flock to mind? That there is some similarity between the two things actually thought of may, of course, be admitted; there are no two things in the universe that do not resemble each other somehow. But the point is that in this case, and indeed in most cases, thought declines to take the path of greatest resemblance; it may ignore the grossest and most obvious likenesses to fix its eye upon some object which, except for its special purpose, is wildly dissimilar. Far from controlling the course of suggestion by itself, the perception of similarity cannot work without a prior grasp of what is relevant to a purpose. In this instance the controlling force is the insight, explicit or not, that if I am to keep the appointment, some means of rapid transit is necessary. This once seen, I can review the objects that, in respect to providing such means, are alike. But the insight into the relevant controls the perception of resemblance; the resemblance does not produce the insight. To say that the latter acts either chiefly or alone is to miss the heart of the matter.

7. Indeed, in those cases where similarity holds sway unrestricted, we fall below the level of what anyone would call reasoning. It is not reasoning, 'it is mere association, for instance, which would lead a man in a conversation about peace and war to begin to talk about Peace the murderer'.[1] When we pun we follow lines of resemblance, but puns are often exasperating precisely through breaking the thread of thought. And when we give ourselves over to the rule of random resemblance, as in a day-dream, or in the 'free association' of the psychoanalysts, all semblance of reasoning has gone. Indeed, 'any familiar illustration, either of contiguity or of similarity', writes W. E. Johnson, 'will prove that association in itself does not entail inference. If a cloudy sky raises memory-images of a storm, or leads to the mental rehearsal of

[1] Stout, *Analytic Psychology*, II. 3.

a poem, or suggests the appearance of a slate roof, in none of these revivals by association is there involved anything in the remotest degree resembling inference.'[1] No train of reasoning, no step in a train of reasoning can be explained merely by association. Similarity does work, to be sure, and in a way that we shall presently examine, but it is useless except in the service of teleological insight.

8. This is the main flaw of the view that inventiveness is merely a roving eye for resemblance. Unfortunately it is not the only flaw, as may be seen in our old example. In this example the earlier associationists would have said something like this: faced with the need of a rapid conveyance, one marshals before the mind's eye a parade of past experiences in which, under like conditions, one had made use of a conveyance. The parade continues until some member appears that fits the present requirements. Thus, other things equal, the better thinker will be the man whose mind is most lavish of similar remembered particulars. But this account wears its falsity on its face. The procession of particular memories required, with its swarm of recollected buses, trams, and motor-cars of various makes is simply not there. It is so plainly not there that Bain, having committed himself to a belief that required this host of similars, had to conjure up a 'law of oblivescence' to explain why no one could find them. Nor do we find in fact the implied connections between the ability to think effectively and the power to retain past particulars. Further, even if these particulars were retained and paraded as the theory claims, they would still not account for invention. To invent is not merely to repeat. It may be questioned whether even in the region of habit we ever do quite the same thing twice, and it is clear that in the region of thought no old wares are ever used whole in the solving of a new problem. The very best of our stored-up suggestions must be trimmed and refashioned and adjusted if they are to meet precisely the

[1] *Logic*, Vol. II. 3.

new need. The past can never be transferred to the present quite intact.

It may be replied that all this is flogging a dead horse, that no one who accepts the law of similarity would now read it in this sense, that the similars I run through my mind are not particular past expedients or the thoughts of them, but only similar *kinds* of expedient. Thus when I want to keep the engagement and have reached the point where I see that some conveyance is necessary, the thoughts that file through my mind are not of this, that, and the other, tram and taxicab; they are much more general and contain far less of irrelevancy; they are ideas of the different sorts of conveyance that might be used. Certainly this account is nearer the facts than the other. It states approximately what does happen when we are puzzled and compelled to cast round before deciding. But here too it is clear that similar association comes in only so far as thought is tentative and halting. Does the expert chess-player proceed by running through the gamut of moves by which he has met like situations in the past and so eliminating the unfit? Does the poet complete a line by thumbing a rhyming dictionary, in his ear or on his table, until he hits upon the least intolerable ending? That such means are sometimes used may be admitted. But they are certainly not the procedure of thought when in command of its matter. In the degree to which such thought is present, it can dispense with this litter and go to its end directly. Not that past experience itself can be dispensed with, but rather that when the mind is thoroughly dominated by the whole that is emerging through it, it can cast aside the casings and trappings in which the complement that it needs has been presented in the past, and use the kernel pure.

9. To explain invention, then, as association by similarity will not do. It would commit all thought to bad logic, since the similars recollected would never precisely apply. It is bad psychology, since it implies facts that cannot be found. We may now add that it is bad metaphysics, since it calls for a machinery that could not exist. There seems nothing at first suspicious in saying that when we deal with a new situation we call up similar past situations and deal with it in terms of these. This looks so innocent that there is some shock in hearing it called absurd and self-contradictory. Yet in fact it is no less. Consider what it reports as occurring: the situation now before me arouses by similarity an experience I have had in the past. And this similarity must be felt or perceived, for how could the mind make use of a similarity it did not perceive to exist? Further, before it can feel things as similar, both things must be before it; to find a thing similar, yet similar to nothing, does not make sense. These points seem obvious enough, yet if they are accepted, the law will not work. The present situation is to call up through similarity a past situation like it. Now this similarity is either perceived or not. If it is not perceived, how could it be used by the mind as a tool? If it is perceived, then the experience that was to be called up by means of it must be there already, to serve as one term in the comparison, and the felt resemblance that was supposed to condition the calling up comes as a consequence of a calling up that occurred without it. What is supposed by the law to happen is thus full of incoherence. The procedure is to start through my seeing a similarity between something now existing and what, being past, does not exist. This impossible perception then calls into being that past which nevertheless must have been in being already if the similarity is to be seen.

Besides making perceived resemblance thus both condition and result of revival, it assumes a kind of revival that is itself impossible. If you take a past experience in the way psychology takes it, i.e. as an event in time, to call it up at all would be an absurdity, since this would make a past event present. If you say that it is not the past event itself that is called up but only the present thought of it, then you are saying something that association will not explain, since the present thought, occurring now for the first time, has never been associated with anything. If, troubled by these inconsequences, you say that what association connects is not events at all, but elements of content, i.e., universals which may present themselves in various times and places, then you are saying something that is true and immensely important, but you have set your face toward another view of the world. For thought now consists no longer of ideas as psychical events that are done for at the moment of their happening; it consists rather of ideas in the Platonic sense, neither generated by our own minds nor destroyed with them, nor tied to any points at all in the temporal series, though they may appear and act a part there. If we were to find in this pressure of universals through our minds any *conatus* toward a yet unrealized order, we should have something really worth saying about the nature of invention. But that for the moment must be an intimation merely.

10. It is clear that the mind's tendency to move along lines of resemblance will not by itself explain the appearance of the ideas we use in thinking. But what of the other laws of association? May not the appearance of one suggestion rather than another be explained, for example, by the frequency or the recency with which such suggestions have been used in the past? Hardly. To revert to our example, the taking of a conveyance may have been associated far less frequently, either in fact or in thought, with meeting a prospective engagement than many other things have been, but here it takes priority for all that. Again, the most *recent* association with meeting an engagement may have been the breaking off of a love-affair, an experience which may have been of the most poignant intensity; and yet neither recency, nor intensity, nor both of these together may be able to elect their candidate if there is a rival backed by relevance to an end. What about contiguity? This is a law that has commonly shared with similarity the chief burden in explaining the rise of reflective suggestions. The present state of things arouses through similarity the ideas of like states in the past; these states in the past have involved, or been contiguous with, certain processes of mind or body; the recurrence of the states brings the recurrence of the processes. Or to express the law by itself, and in the words of an able expositor of these laws: 'The fact that two psychological processes occur together in time or in immediate succession increases the probability that an associative connection between them will develop—that one process will become the associative instigator of the other.'[1]

11. There can be no doubt that this describes an actual tendency of the mind, and we shall not call it in question. Rather we shall use it as a peg on which to hang two observations. The first of these any critical associationist would accept, while the other and more important one gives our ground of disagreement with associationism generally.

First, the law will not by itself explain any mental event. It describes a tendency—the tendency of one process to call up another that has been 'contiguous' with it; but this tendency may always be set aside in the presence of a stronger tendency. The law thus states what occurs, 'other things equal', and Professor Robinson agrees that to explain anything in the concrete it must be largely supplemented. But this, he would add and with justice, is no indictment of contiguity; it is only to say of this law what holds of all laws without exception. Every law that science discloses is a nexus between abstractions; that is implied in the idea of scientific analysis; and it would be absurd to carp at a law merely because its working in the concrete is affected by further factors. Who would say that the first law of motion is not a law at all merely because it is not, and never can be, exemplified in its purity? Such a requirement would be fatal to all laws. We must take a like view· in psychology. 'Indeed', says Professor Robinson, 'careful writers have not, as a rule, ignored the fact that the precise nature and strength of any given association depends upon its context.'[2]

[1] E. S. Robinson, *The Association Theory Today*, 72.
[2] *Ibid.*, 25.

12. This suggests the second observation, which is in effect our main objection to any thorough associationism. It turns upon the meaning assigned to the word 'context'. The true believer in associationism means by 'context' other tendencies of the type described in any law of association taken singly; that is, he thinks that if all the tendencies described in these laws could be put together, reasoning would be explained. Expressions of this view are common, though in some cases they certainly do not give the better judgement of their authors. 'Conclusions all come through suggestion, and the laws of suggestion here are the laws of association as they are found in memory or imagination or in action.'[1] '. . . . if all the alleged accidental discoveries could be analysed, we should find the familiar laws of association would explain every one of them.'[2] Round statements of this kind, which suggest or explicitly state that the laws of association will explain reflective invention, are to be found in both technical and popular books. This view we are forced to reject; and for clearness' sake, let us put at once the view we intend to oppose to it. That view is that what governs invention in reasoning is the requirements of a whole already present implicitly and seeking explicit completion. The laws that govern this whole are not in the ordinary sense psychological laws, nor are they, in that sense, empirical or natural laws; they are laws of what ought to be rather than what is—rules prescribed by the nature of those wholes, moral, aesthetic, or logical, which thought is seeking to achieve. And we hold that no psychology can deal faithfully with the facts of the process of thought that fails to see it as a pursuit of ends, or fails to see what these ends are.

But let us try to be just to associationism. Suppose that, realizing contiguity alone to be insufficient, we supplement it by the 'context' Professor Robinson mentions. Why is it that

[1] Pillsbury, *Psychology of Reasoning*, 188. Cf. the same author's *Fundamentals of Psychology*, 405: 'Finding the solution, inference in our sense, consists in a process, or series of processes, of association.'

[2] Knowlson, *Originality*, 117. Cf. *ibid.*, 82: 'In what way do ideas come to us? The only proper answer is: By the action of the laws of association.'

of the countless things with which engagements and the thoughts of them have been contiguous, the particular idea arises of taking a conveyance? It must be owing to further conditions, not covered by contiguity. Very well, we proceed to bring these in. We find, let us say, that the idea actually aroused was not merely contiguous with the other; it has been most recently contiguous, most frequently contiguous, contiguous under circumstances of the most intense feeling. And these conditions each represent a further law of association. We thus go on supplementing one law by another until we have the whole lot of them, perhaps, co-operating to push the ball in one direction. And thus the direction is explained. Divided the laws fall, but united they stand. Let an idea be necessitated by the whole assortment of them acting jointly and it will follow as the night the day.

Now the trouble with this theory, guarded as it is, is that the idea may do nothing of the kind. It may have all these laws at its back, conspiring to push it upon the stage, and still it may fail to appear, while some surprising stranger turns up in its stead. Let us take an instance or two.

13. We may take first a confession of difficulty by a great doctor of the school, a confession which, in spite of its celebrity, might well be more considered by his modern disciples:

'Suppose . . . a person to have enjoyed his sight for thirty years, and to have become perfectly well acquainted with colours of all kinds, excepting one particular shade of blue, for instance, which it has never been his fortune to meet with. Let all the different shades of that colour, except that single one, be placed before him, descending gradually from the deepest to the lightest; 'tis plain that he will perceive a blank where that shade is wanting, and will be sensible that there is a greater distance in that place betwixt the contiguous colours than in any other. Now I ask whether 'tis possible for him, from his own imagination to supply this deficiency, and raise up to himself the idea of that particular shade, tho' it had never been conveyed to him by his senses? I believe that there are few but will be of opinion that he can. . . .'[1]

Hume's point in this illustration is not the same as ours; he cited it as an exception to the rule that ideas copy sensations. But it provides an exception also to the rule that ideas follow the path of association. Assuming he is right that we can form the image of the new colour, what law of association brings it up? Similarity? Clearly not. Given ideas of the shades on each side of the gap, similarity might account for the appearance of further images like them, but the point here is that the mind conjures up an image dissimilar to both. 'Ah, but it is also similar to both', may come the reply, 'and it is this requirement of double similarity that controls the issue.' True; but what is not seen is that this requirement goes far beyond the law of similarity itself or any law of its type. If mere similarity were operative, the mind would draw on its past, and in this instance draw in vain; for the novel element that in fact it produces is not to be found there. It is obvious that over and above the workings of similarity there is the prescription 'darker than one and lighter than the other', and that what this expresses is not a law of association but *the requirement of a system or series demanding completion according to a plan.* If this is what is meant by 'context', well and good. But it is something so very different from association that it can hardly be what the associationist means. And if we introduce what he apparently does mean, are we helped? Will contiguity help? No. The new shade that comes up, precisely because it is new, has never been contiguous to anything, and hence the pressure of contiguity would lie in another direction. The same holds of intensity and frequency. Both would make for the emergence in thought of something else than what appears. So likewise of the other associative forces. And if they are contemplated as acting all together, their position is still more awkward. For the idea behind which they would throw their joint strength would be, like a Tammany candidate, some old familiar with which all were in bosom relations; and, again with the political

[1] Hume, *Treatise of Human Nature*, Bk. I, Pt. 1, Sec. 1.

parallel, the one candidate they would all fight against shoulder to shoulder would be some stranger, the choice of intelligence. Happily man is not wholly a political animal, for that is often the idea that appears.

14. Let us take another example. Socrates in the *Meno* is at his favourite business of helping ideas to the birth in other minds. Here the other mind is in all but total darkness, so that it must feel its way at every step; and there is laid before us with rare art the way a groping intelligence, with or without assistance, stumbles through to insight. Socrates is at the moment defending a view of thinking that is in this respect like our own, that it conceives it as a bringing to explicitness of what is in some sense there already; and by way of showing that the mind has an inner compass, which will give guidance in fields that are totally unexplored, he calls an illiterate slave boy and proceeds to question him on geometry. He draws on the sand a square with two-foot sides, and shows by drawing inner lines that such a space would have four square feet. He then propounds a problem: in a square that was twice as large, that is, one that had eight square feet, how long would the side be? The boy is prompt with an answer: in a square twice as big the side would be twice as long. He has here produced a fresh suggestion, and let us stop to ask how he did it. Was it by similar association? Yes, it seems pretty clear that that was the chief agency, and we may add that this shows how the answer came to be wrong. The boy drifted along the line of least resistance, 'twice as big, twice as long'; strictly speaking, he has not inferred at all, since his answer has not sprung with necessity from the data from which he started. Socrates shows him his error by drawing on the sand the figure he would really get if he made the sides twice as long; in that case he would have, not eight square feet, but sixteen. This the boy readily sees, and Socrates plies him again. If a side of two feet gives four square feet, and a side of four feet gives sixteen, then to get eight you would need, wouldn't you, a side *between* two and four in length? Yes, agrees the boy, that is clear. Well, how long would it be? Three, comes the reply. Here is another suggestion, and again we may ask what produced it? Is it association? Partly, yes; the boy knows that three gives a middle ground between the numbers and he carries it over by similarity to the lengths. But it is not association only that is here at work; in the insight that the length *must* fall between two feet and three, the pressure of necessity is beginning to make itself felt. Socrates now proceeds to fill

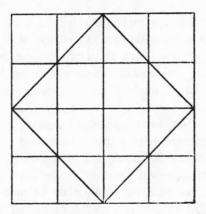

in the picture, confident that if he can get a little more of it within the boy's field of vision, the natural logic of an untutored mind will complete it of its own motion. He draws on the sand first the figure of four square feet, then, extending and including it, the larger figure of sixteen square feet, and he invites the boy to attend to these in the light of the problem before him, namely, to find an eight-foot square. From one corner to another of the smaller figure he draws a diagonal, cutting it into two triangles. How much space will there be in each of these? Just half of the square that it cuts, replies the boy. And how much is that? Two square feet, comes the answer. To many minds, perhaps most, no further help would . be called for; from this fragmentary base the figure required would complete itself in a leap of intuition. But Socrates is dealing with an intelligence for which the gap to be filled must be quite encircled before the missing piece is supplied. He goes on to draw three other like diagonals, making the four sides of an internal square. And then at last the solution darts into the boy's mind. This square contains four triangles, each of two square feet, and is thus itself of eight square feet, exactly the size wanted. And so all is clear. He has laid hold of a general principle: if you have a square, and want to get another square double the size, draw a square on the diagonal.

15. This example is particularly helpful because we see in it the struggle between association and necessity, with association slowly retreating and an implicit logic little by little gaining the day. In the final stages where insight comes, association has fallen completely into the background. The perception that the diagonal of a square *must* cut it in half, the perception that four such triangular halves *must* make another square, the perception that this square *must* be half of the square in which it is inscribed, and double the square of which it gives the diagonal—with these insights association has nothing to do. And it was Socrates' point, when he chose an illiterate slave, to exhibit this. Given the conditions of the problem, these conditions proceeded to complete themselves not along the lines of association, which in this instance were clearly irrelevant or non-existent, but along the lines of a true necessity fixed by the nature of the whole in course of construction.

Here is our chief divergence from associationism. When I am really thinking, ideas come to me, not because at some time in my past I have formed associations with them, but because they serve my present point. Such teleological control *no* associationist that is thoroughgoing can afford to admit. The idea that comes up may, with good luck, be to the point, but the fact that it is to the point has, for him, nothing to do with its appearing. We hold, on the contrary, that when a mind is really thinking this fact is the decisive fact. We hold that a psychology of reasoning that leaves logic out of account as a determinant of the course of ideas can not deal with thinking proper at all. Its insistence that psychology is a descriptive science purely, and in no degree a normative, an insistence designed to free it from half-baked theories and keep it close to the facts, is in both respects self-defeating. For it rests on a theory about the science of mind which is itself little more than a prejudice, and which distorts the central facts under observation. That there are such things as mental habits and associations we of course admit. But that mind is a bundle of habits, an enormous telephone switchboard of associations through which any incoming call takes the line of least resistance— that we deny. We deny, further, that this denial rests on ignorance, that if we could trace out all the tiny associative pushes and pulls that are now beyond us, we should then finally understand. Even if we multiplied these to infinity, we should still not understand. For thought is not a machine of any sort whatever. It is a pursuit of ends.

16. Of course associationists have their ways of defence. One is the appeal to a 'law of individual differences'. It is obvious that some minds think with far greater fertility and pertinence than others, even when they have had no advantage in the way of forming associations. How account for this consistently with associationism? By introducing, we are told, a special associative law covering a 'factor of idiosyncrasy'. This factor is very important; indeed 'the fact that individuals differ in their innate capacity to form associations of a given type is taken by Thorndike to underlie intellect, which is, of course, one of the most important conceptions in modern experimental psychology'.[1] It is reassuring to learn that modern experimental psychology has thus lent its recognition to intellect, at least until we learn what intellect is taken to mean. 'The important point' about Mr. Thorndike's theory, we read, 'is the explanation of intellect in terms of capacity for forming associations of a certain type',[2] and it is the variation in this capacity that is expressed in the 'law of individual differences'. Thus

[1] Robinson, *op. cit.*, 121.   [2] *Ibid.*, 122.

when some genius appears whose 'intellect' does not work in the familiar associative ways, we may rest assured that even his idiosyncrasy does not fall beyond the mesh of our law. Now this 'law' seems to us a limbo of inexplicables. It is less a law than an assertion that there are laws, not now known. And since they are not now known, by what right are they called associative? In the presence of other possibilities, such as better logical grasp or aesthetic insight, there is only one thing that could supply such a right, and that is the exclusive sway of associative law in the field explored already. Before that sway has been made out, as we are clear it has not, to describe the law as associative is to beg the question.

17. Another resort is to a 'law of context', which permits relevance to play a part by construing it as associative. Among experimentalists the 'opinion would seem to be that associative connections are most readily formed in a "congruous" context'. It was found, for example, 'that in associating pairs of words the process was facilitated by the presence, during learning, of words logically related to the word to be instigated or by words related both to it and to the instigator'.[1] The context here is presumed to exert its influence through being 'congruous' or 'logically related'. When such influence is described by a 'law of association', it seems also implied that there is nothing in logical congruity to set it off from association. But is this true? We must not stop to argue out here one of the classic problems of philosophy, but we may at least offer certain comments. First, there *is* a problem, a problem of immense importance, and even an experimental psychologist cannot assume with safety that it is not there. Secondly, it is not the sort of problem that experiment can deal with; whether two and two are conjoined with four by necessity or by custom will not be settled in a laboratory. The question is philosophical, and the man who is most likely to be right about it is not necessarily the man with the better instruments,

[1] Robinson, *op. cit.*, 111.

but the man who is most acute and practised in reflective analysis. And we may perhaps remind the experimentalist that there have been many men of this type, from Plato forward, who, after taking immense pains with the point, concluded that the working in the mind of logic and of association were totally different things. Thirdly, anyone who makes these the same should be willing to accept the burden of proof. Certainly to the thinker himself they do not seem the same; day-dreaming does not seem like inference. Indeed, the one often gets in the other's way, as when the eyes of the schoolboy wander away from Euclid through the open window and his mind goes wandering after them. And fourthly, the identification of the two processes offers dialectical difficulties of which the associationist should at least be apprised. To say that there is nothing in a course of reasoning except a series of associated ideas, that thought never moves under the compulsion of seen necessity, is to say that every associated series is as logical or as non-logical as every other. It is everywhere the product of conjunctions which in the last resort must be laid to chance. But such a theory cannot, except verbally, be made consistent with its own defence. Is it not put forward as a theory whose formulation has been guided by the logical necessities of the case? If such necessities have played no part in its construction, why is its claim to acceptance greater than that of any other theory which may wander into our minds? If they have played a part, then the way the theory is arrived at is itself the witness to its untruth.

18. The associationist, like Ovid, sees the better and acclaims it, then goes and does the worse. In his law of context, and implicitly in all his arguing, he admits teleological influence; he cannot but feel in thought the impulse toward an end, the pull of an implicit ideal, the stress of an obligation to think truly, or as he ought to think. But then he takes fright and hastens to explain it away. Eager to make his subject a natural science, he feels that it would not do to admit this 'ought';

he must repel its seduction and remain within the 'is'. The result is an unstable balance, with one foot in each realm. When his awkward position is pointed out to him, he tries to stabilize himself in two ways at once, neither of which is sound and which are inconsistent with each other. For one thing he hastily withdraws his forward foot, protesting that he had never meant to move it, that his science is concerned with the 'is' alone and has no dealings with the 'ought'. But then his science, as we have insisted, becomes inadequate to its own subject-matter, since ends are too plainly at work in the process of reflection. His other course is to insist that the forward foot is not really advanced at all, that the boundary separating the two fields is only an illusion, and that the seeming compulsion of the end could be explained away if only he knew more about the associative factors at work. But this goes ill with his other apology. If the two realms are really distinct, as he first asserted, their difference cannot in this fashion be explained away; if it can be explained away, as he now maintains, why the earlier insistence on keeping the line sharp between explanations in terms of value and explanations in terms of fact?

We have suggested that his second expedient, namely the denial of two realms, is not only inconsistent with the first, but in itself unsound; and the reason for this, already developed, is that a logical process cannot be reduced to association. This the associationist denies, and if we can trace the motives of his denial, we shall gain much light on his position. Why is the suggestion that thought may be controlled by an implicit ideal so invincibly repugnant to him?

19. There are various reasons. One is the suspicion, potent even when unformulated, that necessity has no place in the converse of scientists, that however useful it may be in certain types of logic, it answers to nothing that can be found in fact. This suspicion is natural enough. Historically, associationist psychology springs from the empiricist theory of knowledge, and with the empiricists the conviction that logical 'necessity' is at base psychological habit was a cardinal point. On an issue so fundamental to the nature of thought we shall have to say more later. For the present it must suffice to refer to that later discussion, or better, to those classic criticisms, such as T. H. Green's[1] and Cook Wilson's,[2] which are still awaiting an answer.

But perhaps the most important reason is the feeling on the part of psychologists that if they let in the thin edge of the teleological wedge, psychology must cease to be a factual science and hence must cease to be properly a science at all. And it is true that if you admit among the determiners of a course of thought the *nisus* of an implicit system to complete itself coherently, you are explaining the rise of certain ideas by their values as apprehended, and values, it is constantly repeated, are not facts. The question, then, is as to the sense of 'fact' to which psychology should seek to confine itself. Now there are some current conceptions of fact from which the science might well ask to be emancipated. The writer recalls, for example, an article by Dr. Watson with the title, 'Feed Me on Facts'. But a psychologist who lived on a diet of what Dr. Watson regards as fact would shortly starve.[3] To make psychology a physical science is to render homeless a great army of facts which, if not taken in by this science, must go begging. My experience of red, for example, would generally and naturally be described as a psychological fact, but it is not a fact for any physical science. Thus the charge that admitting values would take psychology out of the field of the physical sciences is no ground for alarm; its subject-matter has taken it out already.

20. To define 'fact' for any science is a dangerous venture and we shall not attempt it. But one would suppose that for psychology the term must include at least all that is presented

---

[1] *Introduction* to Hume's *Treatise*.
[2] *Statement and Inference*, II. 616–30.   [3] See Chap. IX above.

to a mind, *as* so presented. And on such a supposition it is hard to see how values can be left out. Are not the perceived relevance of an argument and the felt appropriateness of the closing lines of a sonnet as truly facts, and do they not as truly make a difference in mental behaviour as presentations of colour or sound? And if so, how can psychology ignore them?

One proposal is to exclude from psychology every sort of presented object, sense data, as well as beauties and necessities, and to confine the science to mental *acts*. But we have examined this theory already in some detail,[1] and have seen that a psychology which ignores the *whats* that engage our various acts of attention is rendered helpless in dealing with the acts themselves. To confine psychological fact to acts of this kind would mean suicide for the science.

21. But are there not other means of saving the factual character of the science? Granting that *what* is thought of must have a part in any account of mental process, may we not still distinguish within this 'what' the factual content from the content in the way of value? For example, a rose is before me; it is of such and such a variety; it has a characteristic odour; its colour is red; these elements of content are neutral, and the sensations or perceptions in which they figure may thus be taken as scientific facts. But the rose is also beautiful, and beauty is an element of a different kind; it is a value, and as such is to be excluded from the report of fact. Or take an example where the value concerned is logical. The thoughts occur in my mind of Socrates as a man, and of man as mortal; these thoughts have objects that in point of value are neutral, and they may hence be reported simply as facts. But there is present in my mind another thought as well, namely the thought of these former objects as necessitating something further, the death of Socrates. And this third thought is of a different type from the other two. Just as in the thought of the rose's beauty

[1] Chap. XI; see also the remarks in Chap. VII, Sec. 13, and in Chap. XII, Sec. 13.

there enters an element with no part in fact, so here in the form of 'necessity' there enters an element that may indeed be of concern to logicians, who discuss ideals of thinking, but whose presence is a matter of dispute, even among them, and which is clearly no component of the facts. Thus at least we have the distinction needed. We are no longer driven to the desperate expedient of excluding *what* we think from mention by psychology; we are free to describe thoughts by their objects. Only we draw a line between objects in the way of fact and objects in the way of value. The latter we hand over to the 'value sciences', logic, ethics, aesthetics, the philosophy of religion. Psychology will concern itself exclusively with the former.

Is this the substance of what was hoped for? Unfortunately no. Neither in theory nor in practice is the doctrine better off than its predecessor. Value has already infected the very facts that it sought to keep pure. For to lay hold of fact is to lay hold of truth, and truth is itself a value. There is no use in protesting that a fact may not be a truth—an unknown fact for example. Even so, our only way to get at fact is through knowing truth, and the criteria of truth and fact must be the same. The immediate aim of science is always truth. And truth, we repeat, is a value. It is what we ought to believe, just as the good is what we ought to realize and the beautiful what we ought to appreciate. Perhaps it will be replied that truth is so unlike other values that it should not be counted among them, that it is independent of being experienced while other values are not, that it is identical from mind to mind while other values vary, that it is grasped by intelligence while other values are somehow apprehended by feeling. But all these views seem to us so arbitrary that we will take a risk and pass them by. Suppose, however, that they were sound. Suppose that the proposed distinction could be made out, and that in respect to value, truth could be held apart as neutral and colourless; it would still be quite impracticable to build a psychology upon the distinction. One would have to begin by excluding two thirds of the facts one would naturally want to consider. All volitions, affections and emotions would go at once. Indeed if the line were insisted on, and only facts that were simon pure were to be admitted, there would probably be no facts left, for even the 'coldest' and abstractest thought remains subtly pervaded by value. It would seem, then, that this third attempt to exclude values from psychology can only go the way of the others.

22. Does this mean the breaking of the dykes and the flooding of the science by considerations alien to fact? There is one barrier left to its defenders, far inland to be sure, but a last hope. This line of defence is as follows: we may allow that values exist and are components of fact, but we need not thereby commit ourselves to treating them *as* values, that is, to appraising, comparing and rating them. We may admit that an artist's choice of a colour may be suggested, not merely by association, but also by his view of what is aesthetically necessary; that in the development of an argument the requirements of logic, as these are understood by the thinker, may serve as leading-strings to his thought. It may be admitted that we are here using a mind's sense of value, its sense that something ought to be, as part of our explanation of fact. Without this, we may agree, the picture of fact would be a puzzle, since it would contain elements that were inexplicable. But merely with this we are not abandoning psychology as a factual science. Between saying that an element appeared in someone's mind because *his notion* of logic suggested it and saying that it appeared because *logic really did* require it there is an immense and saving difference. There are no disastrous commitments in granting the first of these; it makes use, to be sure, of the thinker's sense of value, but it uses this merely as fact; it does not distinguish invidiously between one man's sense and another's; it does not talk of better and worse; it does not force the reluctant psychologist into the position of a judge. But that is just what the second proposal would do; it would force him to set up standards in logic, art, and morals, and appeal to these as terms in his explanation. He would find himself using such language as that a suggestion occurred to a thinker because it was logical, that is, really required by the logic of the case, and not merely prompted by what his sense of that logic happened to be. From the comparatively innocent statement that something *is* because something else *is*, namely, such sense of ought as one happens to have, he is forced on to the totally different statement that what really and objectively ought to be plays a part in determining what is. And that is fatal. It means the death of factual psychology. It means that the psychologist, as a psychologist, is to have convictions on truth and falsity, right and wrong, and even on the aesthetically good and bad, and is to inject these convictions of his into the business of his science.

This sounds decisive. And if the conventions of psychology are to be acquiesced in, it undoubtedly settles the matter. But after all that has gone before, we shall hardly be expected to hold these conventions sacrosanct. We have not dismissed them as generally inapplicable, but we have contended that they were adequate to lower processes only, which are not in strictness thinking at all, and that to impose them on thinking proper distorts it and misconstrues it. And if there is some temerity in flying in the face of psychological practice, we can only plead that it is worse to fly in the face of nature.

We must insist that anyone who looks freshly at thinking must see that it is not the sort of process which current psychology takes it to be. When we think, we mean something and are trying to do something that this psychology does not see, because it takes its stand outside us and peers at our activity distantly through the glasses of physical analogy. And in doing so, it is not only negligent; it is inconsistent. It admits that in studying thought and will we must take into account the content or meaning or *what*, that which is before the mind in the form of either object or end. But having admitted this, it will not sit down with that meaning and look at it as it is. It assumes that the meaning can be dealt with in terms of descriptive psychology; why? Because otherwise it could not be dealt with in the terms of descriptive psychology. But this is to adjust the facts to the science rather than the science to the facts. We are convinced that if the psychologist spent enough hours in that arm-chair, which now stands confessedly, even ostentatiously, empty, to get clear as to the plain man's meaning when he thinks, he would be not a little disturbed. For he would find there things that, frankly faced, would either inspire him to reconceive his science or else extort a confession of failure.

23. By 'the plain man's meaning when he thinks' we intend here for the moment both what he means and what he means to do, his reference and his intention, what he is thinking of and what he is about. With these in mind, let us look at his thought again. He is trying to solve a puzzle in geometry, for example; what is his meaning here, in the sense, first, of the object he is concerned with? Plainly it is an *order*, an order, furthermore, that he never supposes himself to have made but considers himself to be uncovering in his thought of it; 'we all feel certain, in the moment we think any truth, that we have not created it for the first time, but merely recognized it'.[1] And he thinks of this order that is before him as not only independent, but necessary. The parts could not be coupled with any other, for their places are fixed for them by the larger pattern. When the plain man thinks in geometry, it is clearly to such an order that he is referring, whether he is justified in doing so or not. And what is his meaning in the other sense, the sense of what he is trying to do? Is he presenting his mind as a public park for ideal waifs, where they may chase each other up and down the paths of habit? Nothing of the sort. What he is trying to do is get the order that he is engaged with more completely before his mind. The merely habitual and associated is precisely what he is trying to keep out. Indeed he is trying to keep himself out, in the sense of that whole vast mass of passing interests and casual memories and vagrant desires that make up so much of his life. Just as his meaning in the first sense is an

[1] Lotze, *Logic*, Sec. 318.

impersonal logical order, so his meaning in the sense of intention is to place his mind at the disposal of this order. He wants it to have its way with him, that he may follow the argument where it leads. That he really does take the argument in successful thinking as leading him rather than himself as leading the argument seems clear from this, that so far as his personal interests intrude he condemns this as prejudice, and that he counts the admission of casual associates as a surrender to wool-gathering. His business is to give the subject his attention and to let it develop itself before him. When he follows the flight of a meteor across the sky, his endeavour is merely to keep his eyes open and to let the movements impress themselves upon his mind according to their own law of succession. When he is thinking geometrically, he is doing essentially the same thing. His attention keeps to the track less easily, for his objects are now conceptual and the succession is a logical sequence. But that in both cases there is a track, that it is laid down for him not by him, that it is his business in thinking to let the plan of it possess him and direct him, that so far as attention is given to it, it will impress everyone in the same way—all these things he takes for granted. In spite of a waywardness and truancy that are perhaps incurable, thought shows everywhere that it feels the pull of an ideal order, sometimes weak, sometimes engrossing and possessive, but never absent where genuine thought is under way. And to leave out the control of this order when we are explaining the course of ideas would seem as capricious to most of us as it would to an astronomer to explain a planet's keeping to its orbit without mention of the sun.

24. When the plain man thinks, then, it is to such an order that he refers, and to such an order that he would resign the control of his thinking. And the psychologist who hears this contention would seem to have three courses open to him. He may simply deny that there is to be found in our mind any such reference or intention. This is the choice of the behaviour-

ists, that dashing band, compounded so unequally of valour
and discretion. There is secondly the course taken by Titchener
and apparently, though less explicitly, by the associationists, namely to admit thought to be self-transcending in its
reference and aim, but to ignore this when speaking pro-
fessionally. The psychologist recognizes this aspect, bows to it,
and at once passes it on to the logicians or epistemologists or
whoever else may take an interest in the transcendent. For
himself he will remain among ideas; let objects take care of
themselves. But we have seen that the relation between thought
and its object is too delicate and too momentous to be treated
so cavalierly, without careful study at any rate. This study
we have tried to make. And we have found that to exclude the
reference of thought was to decapitate it, leaving it formless
and useless, even for the purposes of psychology. In the
course of a protracted struggle with the matter, we discovered
that the only tenable relation between thought and its object
was that of the partial and complete fulfilment of a purpose.
From this it was an obvious inference that the way to understand thought was to read it in the light of its end. With this
there appears the third course open to the psychologist. It is
to interpret thought frankly and fully in the light of what it is
seeking to achieve.

And now we are in sight of the answer to the final proposal
above for keeping psychology a factual science. That proposal,
it will be recalled, was to admit the working of ends or values,
but to take account of such working only as a particular fact
or event, an occurrence in an individual mind, not as anything
so pretentious as the operation in consciousness of truth,
goodness and beauty themselves. And the answer to this is
that once you have gone so far, you are bound willy-nilly to
go farther, even if it takes you into metaphysics. Thought refers
to, and aims at realizing, a system beyond itself, an impersonal
and logical system. Its relation to that system is one of partial
realization, and you can no more see what it is and why it
behaves as it does without reference to the system than you
can explain the behaviour of a lover without reference to the

beloved. Does this mean that psychology, to be adequate to mind, must introduce into its account the necessities of logic, morals and aesthetics, must say that human behaviour is, in part, what it is because truth, goodness and beauty are what they are? We answer with another question. Is it these things that the mind is seeking to realize, or is it something less and other? This question answers itself. To say that the aim of thought, for example, is not at truth but at some mask or appearance of it, or at anything else whatever, is, on reflection, absurd. Truth is its sole and sufficient end; and the course of thought is unintelligible unless it is taken as the embodiment through the mind, brokenly always and fitfully and in continually varying degree, but nevertheless essentially, of truth itself.[1]

25. It follows that if psychology is taken in the ordinary sense, there are no psychological laws governing the course of thought. To be sure there are laws of association, but to the extent to which inference proper appears, these laws are superseded. On the other hand, if psychology is so reconstituted as to be adequate to thinking, there will be as many laws of the process as there are levels of realization of that system which forms its implicit end. The actual course of thought is a resultant of two influences, on one side the psychological or mechanical, which would drive it along the trail of association, and on the other the logical, whose attraction, if sufficiently powerful, keeps it in the groove of necessity. And a particular process of thinking can be understood only as one appreciates how, in this particular case, the two forces interplay. Such appreciation means, in practice, a power both to share another's end and to perceive the degree of system which, in the pursuit of that end, he has so far managed to achieve. The more he has achieved, the greater will be the power of that system to complete itself in his mind

[1] For the meaning of 'truth', as here conceived, see Chaps. XXVI and XXVII.

along the lines of necessity; the less he has achieved, the more broken, halting and tentative the movement will be.

26. It follows again that while the better mind will be able to understand pretty fully the movements of the inferior mind, the inferior will be at a loss before the movements of the better. To an intelligence like Burke's, for example, a mind like Shallow's, with all its difference from his own, would be fairly transparent; indeed we all know what it means to drift, with the tension of thought relaxed, along a stream that is fed by random similarities, accidental associations, and varying moods and impulses. But to Shallow a speech by Burke would remain a mystery, even if every fact in it became familiar. The spring of Burke's mind would be missing; Shallow would never really see why, having said one thing he went on to the next rather than to any of a hundred alternatives. The true reason of course was that a large and articulated view of, say, the relation of England to America lay before his mind, not explicitly perhaps, but none the less truly and effectively, and that in setting forth this view the movement of his mind was determined by the requirements of that whole; the heads and sub-heads, the contrasts, the transitions, the massing of arguments, all reflected the inner conceptual arrangement. 'But surely', it may be replied, 'he could have put things in a different order and still have communicated his view?' Yes and No. So far as the whole he was communicating was a whole of thought, he could no doubt have started elsewhere and, under the governance of this whole, set out the parts in various orders. There are many rhetorical sequences in which an identical logical order may be expressed. But in Burke's case, perhaps in degree in every case, the implicit whole that is seeking utterance is an aesthetic as well as logical whole, and a rhetorical order that is logically indifferent may be aesthetically necessary. To understand a speech by Burke, Shallow would have to add more than intellectual cubits to his stature. He must not only share the integration of Burke's mind on its logical side, but he must also feel how the norm of beauty, in a mind at Burke's aesthetic level, articulates its facts into a distinct, and at times a rival, whole.

27. From all this it is fairly clear what the problem of invention is. It is the problem how an 'end, already partially realized in the mind, gets the material to extend or complete itself. It is the problem how a purpose, instead of being encroached on and submerged by the waves of irrelevant impulse and association, plays Canute to them successfully and reclaims a further domain from the sea. Invention is purpose assuming authority over the course of ideas. If the suggestion that it calls for puts in an appearance, this never comes by accident merely; there is something absurd in the notion that in the mind of a competent thinker the laws of association, knowing nothing of propriety or relevance, yet arrive on the scene regularly and punctually to offer on a platter the idea required. We cannot believe this because we cannot believe in miracles. There is thought in the purpose itself. The whole that is under construction takes from the material offered it what it needs, and rejects the rest. Nor is its work confined to selecting from matter passively received. It takes an active part in summoning up this matter. Our contention, in short, is nothing less than this; that in the mind of the successful thinker the spirit of logic itself is at work leavening the un-formed mass, and that in the mind of the creative artist the spirit of beauty is at work, supplying both ends and means. A 'nisus toward wholeness', as Bosanquet would call it, is every-where the spring of thought.

But this is far too general. What are the devices by which the fragments already in the mind extend and complete themselves? This is the question we must turn to next.

CHAPTER XXIII

THE NATURE OF INVENTION

1. We are now to look more narrowly at the leap of suggestion or invention. Perhaps if we run over again the steps that are taken by reflection before it comes to the leap, we shall be able to follow its movement more clearly.

The movement begins, we saw, with a collision, a collision between a system or order already present in the mind and some fragment that ought to be included in this and yet remains outside it. Lord X is found mysteriously dead in his library, and the wheels of reflection start revolving in the mind of a detective. What is it that sets them off? Not simply the fact about Lord X, but a conflict between that fact and something in the detective's mind. He orders his experience on the principle that events have definite causes; here is an event that challenges inclusion in that order, but so far will not fit. How does he bring it in? His first move, we saw, is to specify the problem. He cannot do this here, as he sometimes can, by reflection alone; he must have recourse to observation. This observation will be guided by what experience has taught him about the details most likely to be relevant; and hence he will pay particular attention to the 'bruises apparently made by some blunt instrument'. But his specifying of the problem does not consist in narrowing his notice to a single point. The platform he prepares for the leap of suggestion will probably be a broad one. If the question he set himself were simply, Who might have wielded such an instrument? he would accomplish nothing, since the answers would be indefinitely many. His problem, when he is ready for the leap is, Who must have done this *in view of* Lord X's unemptied pockets, the signs of a struggle, his butler's loyalty, and perhaps a hundred other particulars? If the leap is made from any one of these alone, its success would be an accident. It must somehow be made from the mass of them taken together. Put otherwise, the problem is to fit a detached fragment of fact into a picture that very nearly surrounds it, and what the choice issues from is the entire surrounding system.

2. Since our account here diverges from that of the well-known chapter by James, it will perhaps be well to have his view before us. According to James there are two chief factors in reasoning, namely, sagacity and inference, whose part in the process may be described as follows. We are confronted, let us say, with some problem demanding solution, perhaps a very simple practical problem—how shall I get this door open? perhaps some sweeping one of theory such as, Why do the planets remain in their orbits? For the solution of such problems not all the circumstances before us are of equal value, some being of no account and some essential. It is in the selection of the essential ones that the first factor, sagacity, comes in. When the door refuses to open, for example, the reflective man, instead of beating it or tearing at it, as an animal might do, looks for the place where it catches, and having discovered this, holds the solution in his hands, for he knows that by lifting the door so as to remove the friction he can get it open. Once his sagacity takes control of his eye, he is on the way to his conclusion.

> 'The difficulty is, in each case, to extract from the immediate data that particular ingredient which shall have this very evident relation to the conclusion. Every phenomenon or so-called "fact" has an infinity of aspects or properties, as we have seen, amongst which the fool, or man with little sagacity, will inevitably go astray.' 'To reason, then, we must be able to extract characters—not *any* characters, but the right characters for our conclusion.'[1]

Why is this singling out of characters so helpful in the work of thinking? For two reasons, James answers.

> 'First, the extracted characters are more general than the concretes, and the connections they may have are, therefore,

---

[1] *Principles of Psychology*, II. 341, 343.

more familiar to us, having been more often met in our experience. Think of heat as motion, and whatever is true of motion will be true of heat; but we have had a hundred experiences of motion for every one of heat.' 'The other reason why the relations of the extracted characters are so evident is that their properties are so *few*, compared with the properties of the whole from which we derived them. . . . Thus the character of scraping the sill has very few suggestions, prominent among which is the suggestion that the scraping will cease if we raise the door; whilst the entire refractory door suggests an enormous number of notions to the mind.'[1]

In these sentences there is indicated also the second factor in reasoning, namely inference, or reasoning in the narrower sense. It consists in taking the essential character, which has been brought to light by sagacity, and following it out into what it entails. The suggestion that the door must be catching at some particular point is the work of sagacity; the work of reasoning in the narrower sense is to suggest that this catching will be relieved by lifting the door, and that I can then open it and get out. And so of other and more impressive acts of reflection.

3. It is plain that in the work of invention sagacity is by far the more significant factor. The second factor no doubt is necessary, and its work at times is extraordinarily difficult, as is seen in Newton's development of a new branch of mathematics in order to calculate what would follow from his hypothesis of gravitation. But more commonly the elaboration of a new insight, once it has been arrived at, is relatively easy; what is hard is to hit upon the essential circumstance that carries the solution with it. Here it is that the ordinary man is most helpless. When the idea of a force pulling the planets toward the sun, and apples toward the earth, has once been pointed out to him, he has not the slightest difficulty in seeing its pertinence; indeed it seems so obvious that he wonders why the discovery should have been so difficult. But the power

[1] *Principles of Psychology*, II. 342.

to hit upon it by himself is precisely what he lacks, and what marks the true discoverer. Can we follow the path of such discoverers in the finding of the essential? The more nearly we can do so, the nearer we shall come to the secret of invention.

Let us first hear what James has to say on the point.

> '*How are characters extracted,*' he asks, '*and why does it require the advent of a genius in many cases before the fitting character is brought to light?*' Why cannot anybody reason as well as anybody else? Why does it need a Newton to notice the law of the squares, a Darwin to notice the survival of the fittest?' His answer is that such discoveries require a remarkable eye for resemblances. 'This answers the question why Darwin and Newton had to be waited for so long. The flash of similarity between an apple and the moon, between the rivalry for food in nature and the rivalry for man's selection, was too recondite to have occurred to any but exceptional minds. *Genius, then,* as has been already said, *is identical with the possession of similar association to an extreme degree.*' And he quotes Bain in support: 'This I count the leading fact of genius. I consider it quite impossible to afford any explanation of intellectual originality except on the supposition of unusual energy on this point.'[1]

4. Admirable so far as it goes; but surely inventive genius is more than this. What is here described as genius might be madness. A madman contemplating a door, or standing on the deck of a boat where he can wonder about the pointer, may be a bubbling fountain of analogies. Doors resemble all manner of things, from walls to geometrical figures; a ferry-boat's pointer is equally like a lead pencil, a crayon, and a telegraph pole. If 'genius is identical with similar association in an extreme degree', such a man should qualify. Yet something more is obviously necessary. And this something more is the *control of analogy by the conditions of the problem.* Take the

---

[1] *Principles of Psychology*, II. 343, 360; italics in original. James himself, as is common with him, has supplied the material for a better theory; see *Ibid.*, I. 588. The quotation from Bain is from the chapter on 'Genius' in his *Study of Character*, p. 327.

case of the pointer; a man is wondering what this projecting pole is for. An unchecked fertility in similars would be far more likely than not to derail his thinking. A pointer with a ball on the end is very like a flag-pole, an old-fashioned porcelain-headed pin, or a walking-stick with a knob at the head. Should we call that mind the best which, regardless of their ineptness, turned up such likenesses as this in the largest numbers? On the contrary we feel that such wandering betokens a feeble grip. As the grasp of a problem strengthens, such similes are dispensed with, first in favour of analogies that are really close, and finally altogether. Their value corresponds to the value of instances in induction, where it is well known that if many and various instances are needed, thought is in the groping stage.[1]

5. That analogy is of great aid in reflection is beyond question, and we shall soon examine its service more closely. What we must insist on, however, is that it is perfectly useless, because wanton and random, except as the agent of an implicit system seeking completion by means of it. If this is mysterious, it is at least far less mysterious than the right suggestion's popping out at us from a heterogeneous crowd of similes; indeed to anyone not obsessed by the notion that thought is a mechanical process, the idea of such control is as natural as it is

---

[1] In his excellent chapter on mathematical invention, Poincaré puts the point clearly:

'To invent, as I have said, is to choose, but the word is perhaps not quite the right one; it suggests a buyer to whom many samples are presented, and who inspects them one after the other by way of making his choice. But here (in mathematics) the samples would be so numerous that a lifetime would not suffice for their examination. It is not this sort of thing that actually happens. The sterile combinations will not so much as occur to the inventor's mind. There will appear in his field of consciousness only those combinations which are really useful, together with certain others that share the character of these, but which he will reject. It is all as if the inventor were an examiner of the second degree, whose business it was to examine only those candidates warranted admissible by a prior test.'—*Science et Méthode*, 49–50.

necessary. The man who is thinking about the pointer does not find his mind thronged with irrelevant similars, because the sort of interpretation he must attach to this puzzling pole is marked out for him already; he must find, not any use whatever, but that kind of use which a pole would have if placed by design at that point on a ship. A ship is a system of means to the end of navigation; every major part of it is one of those means; and the way to understand any of them is to see its function in such a whole. It is this function that forms the *quaesitum* of the thinker; and his thought will be a competent thought just as far as the whole that he is trying to complete takes possession of his mind and governs the course even of his errant love of analogy.

The essential point is thus not so much range of analogy as mastery of the system requiring completion. The fuller this is, the more quickly and easily, the more directly and confidently will thought move to its goal. If one can imagine a man thoroughly familiar with the sailing of boats without knowing the function of a pointer, one can at any rate hardly conceive his remaining puzzled long; his knowledge of the needs of a navigator would supply the cue. The writer has described earlier how helpless he once was when his motor-car began without warning to make a hideous noise, and how readily a garage mechanic recognized the trouble as a detached muffler and set it right. Here the problems of diagnosis and cure were solved almost instantly. But there probably entered my own head a larger number of explanations, drawn from analogy, than occurred to the mechanic. They occurred to me because in this field I was incompetent; they did not occur to him because they were needless; his knowledge of the structure and running of an engine carried him to the solution without them. This is typical of all expert thinking. In such thinking the sagacity that James speaks of consists quite obviously not in the power to summon up similars, but in what, as a matter of fact, it consists in everywhere, however disguised it may be in cases of unusual difficulty, *the power to extend a partially given whole.*

6. How little such sagacity depends upon the appeal to analogy is shown by 'calculating prodigies'. There is no doubt that the process they go through is a process of thinking, or that this thinking is inventive. To refuse them the name of inventors because they did not, like Newton and Darwin, extend the knowledge of the race would be to misconceive what invention means. This means the attainment of what is new to the inventor, not what is new to others. To confine it to the discovery of what is new to everyone would be to say that in discovering the calculus either Newton or Leibniz must have been unoriginal, since they arrived at it independently, and presumably one of them did it first. Every solution of a problem is invention. And a glance at the sort of invention we find in 'calculating boys' will be enlightening as showing that there are certain things with which invention generally cannot be identified. It cannot, as we have said, be identified with the reproduction of similars; for neither the reports of these prodigies themselves, nor the abstractness of their problems, nor the amazing speed of their processes, gives any countenance to the view that they have taken a meandering circuit through analogies. Nor can their invention be identified with the dexterous use of past experience; for, to say nothing of the difficulty of accumulating at their ages the experience required, such experience must itself have consisted of the very reasoning to be explained. Furthermore, there is evidence in more than one case that as experience did accumulate and their faculty gained more exercise, it declined instead of increasing. Thus Archbishop Whately writes:

'There was certainly something peculiar in my calculating faculty. It began to show itself at between five and six, and lasted about three years. . . . I soon got to do the most difficult sums, always in my head, for I knew nothing of figures beyond numeration. I did these sums much quicker than anyone could upon paper, and I never remember committing the smallest error. When I went to school, at which time the passion wore off, I was a perfect dunce at ciphering, and have continued so ever since.'[1]

[1] Quoted by F. W. H. Myers, *Human Personality*, I. 82.

As to the appearance of such prodigies we are able to say little or nothing except that the wind of genius blows where it lists. But there is no need to make an equal mystery of their processes. They have grasped certain rules of formation for numerical wholes and certain rules for breaking these up, rules that are presumably the same as those applied by the rest of us. What chiefly makes them remarkable is the ability to carry out in their heads with ease and speed operations that others could carry through only with mechanical aids. Where the rest of us would forget some of the conditions on which the solution turned before we reached the end, they are able to retain them steadily in mind and thus to deal with more complex wholes. But their difference from us is one of degree, not of kind. Given the arc of a circle, drawn on a piece of letter-paper, we should complete it easily enough; given an arc a half-mile long, we could complete it only with tremendous effort; but the process would not be different, only the magnitude of the figure. So these calculating prodigies differ from ordinary mortals chiefly in the complexity and size of the wholes which guided by the same arithmetical law, they compose and decompose. Since they illustrate processes of thought to which the term 'genius' has been as justly applied as those to which James would confine the name, and which are yet markedly different from these, we may take an instance or two. We shall look at the faculty first as it appears in moderate development, then in very high development.

'When almost exactly six years of age', writes the brother of Benjamin Blyth, one of these phenomenal children, 'Benjamin was walking with his father before breakfast, when he said, "Papa, at what hour was I born?" He was told four a.m.
Ben. "What o'clock is it at present?"
Ans. "Seven fifty a.m. . . ."
The child walked on a few hundred yards, then turned to his father and stated the number of seconds he had lived. My father noted down the figures, made the calculation when he got home, and told Ben he was 172,800 seconds wrong, to which he got a ready reply: "Oh, papa, you have left out two days for the leap-years—1820 and 1824", which was the case.'

This is impressive enough, but the case that follows is more so.

'In the year 1837 Vito Mangiamele, who gave his age as ten years and four months, presented himself before Arago in Paris. He was the son of a shepherd of Sicily, who was not able to give his son any instruction. By chance it was discovered that by methods peculiar to himself he resolved problems that seemed at first view to require extended mathematical knowledge. In the presence of the Academy Arago proposed the following questions: "What is the cubic root of 3,796,416?" In the space of about half a minute the child responded 156, which is correct. "What satisfies the condition that its cube plus five times its square is equal to 42 times itself increased by 40?" Everybody understands that this is a demand for the root of the equation $x^3 + 5x^2 - 42x - 40 = 0$. In less than a minute Vito responded that 5 satisfied the condition; which is correct. The third question related to the solution of the equation $x^5 - 4x - 16779 = 0$. This time the child remained four to five minutes without answering: finally he demanded with some hesitation if 3 would not be the solution desired. The secretary having informed him that he was wrong, Vito, a few moments afterwards, gave the number 7 as the true solution. Having finally been requested to extract the 10th root of 282,475,249, Vito found in a short time that the root is 7.'[1]

7. This boy was certainly a genius on any reasonable definition of that term. And if so, James's definition will not do, for there is here neither evidence nor need of 'similar association in an extreme degree'. To be sure the boy was applying to new situations certain rules that he had applied to more or less like situations before. But to call this similar association would be mere confusion. What brought the suggested answer to his mind was not its likeness to something else he had known in the past; it was rather, both in this instance and in all past instances of similar calculation, the working in his thought of the laws of numbers themselves which, given the data before him, and the sort of manipulation

[1] The extracts given are from Myers, who collected a number of such accounts for the chapter on 'Genius' in his *Human Personality*; see Vol. I. 81, 84.

wanted, carried him to his result inevitably. It was nothing else than what carries our own minds to some simple result like 'three and four make seven', namely the logic of the number system.

8. In cases like this it is particularly plain that invention turns on a surrender to the working of necessity in one's mind. It is particularly plain here because the abstractness of mathematics lays bare the groove of necessity so that everyone would agree as to its existence and its path. But besides these numerical wholes there are many in which the mind clearly proceeds in the same way. If one knows that B is north of A and C is west of B, one arranges the points in a pattern and by means of it sees at once that C must be north-west of A. What carries one to the result is the same as before, namely the structure of the system—this time a spatial system rather than a numerical one. If anyone reaches a wrong result it always turns out, on review, that he had entered into the system imperfectly, either through omission of relevant, or admission of irrelevant, matter. And so of other systems or orders. If Miltiades, who fought at Marathon in B.C. 490, was a better general than Charles Martel, who fought at Tours in 732, though inferior to Napoleon who fought at Waterloo in 1815, and if Tours would not have been fought without Marathon, nor without Tours Waterloo, we have at least four different arguments in three different orders—two in time, one in causation, one in degree—all of them possessing a necessity as great as that of the mathematical examples. If one were asked which was the earliest or most capable general, or which the first battle, or the most important causally, one would dispose each set of factors in its own order and then read off the result in a manner with which neither association nor past experience had anything essential to do.

9. It may be objected that all these orders are a priori orders, and that to base on them a theory of inference is to forget that nine-tenths of our reasonings are empirical and concrete. Perhaps it will be granted that when thought is moving in the abstract frameworks of number, space, and time, it finds its channels already dug for it by agencies beyond its ken. But in the reasonings of everyday life, such as reflection about to-morrow's weather or what to do for a cold, how to open a sticking door or to make a sale in business, there is no such abstract system, nor is there any such compelling necessity. In view of the fact that inferences like these make up the larger part of our thinking, can the movement from point to point in an abstract and a priori order be offered as typical of reasoning generally?

10. Yes, it can. It is typical in both the respects that we would here insist on, in showing true necessity and in revealing this necessity as the demand of implicit system. But while offering it as truly typical, we must add certain qualifications. In the first place, there is no need that the system should be so highly abstract. Indeed one might have inferred as much from some of the illustrations already used. We have pointed out, for example, that the parts of a ship make a system, supporting each other and contributing to a common end, and that our attempt to understand some part is an attempt to grasp its function within this system; yet as compared with the numerical order the system is concrete and empirical. Bosanquet opens his *Implication and Linear Inference* with a list of conclusions all of which emerge from this sort of whole. They are arrived at neither from a set of explicit premises nor along lines that would be called a priori, but within systems that would be unhesitatingly called empirical. Here are a few examples:

'In a good electrical installation, a fuse will be blown before any conducting wire can be overheated.'

'In a country with large foreign trade, if you want to fix prices, you must control imports.'

'In a body like that of any higher animal the separation of the head from the trunk must be fatal to life.'

'According to the British Constitution, the King can act only through his ministers; and therefore in and subject to that special complex, "the King can do no wrong".'[1]

In all of these we arrive at something new along lines determined by special types of system, but the reasoning is at the opposite extreme from what is commonly called a priori.

11. 'But if not a priori, then empirical', comes the reply, 'and if empirical then not really necessary, and if not really necessary, how are you a whit better off than the associationists you claim to have left behind?' Now, plausible as it is, this objection rests on an illusion, and its exposure will supply our second qualification to the statement that mathematical reasoning is typical. The first qualification was that everyday reasoning is less abstract than the mathematical. The second is that it is less a priori. To some ears such a suggestion may sound absurd, as if one had described a number as less odd or less prime than another. An insight, it is supposed, is either a priori or not; there is no more or less about it. But this is a mistake. At all events, apriority is a matter of degree in any use we can make of it, for our only measure of its presence is itself a matter of degree. Its traditional tests have been universality and necessity, but as the first of these must be tested by the second, the double criterion becomes a single one and necessity stands alone. Is there, now, any test of necessity? The only test is internal and lies in its own self-evidencing force, its objective certainty as opposed to the mere emotion of conviction. And such certainty plainly varies. If I run over in mind the following beliefs, for example: Three and four make seven, Bigamy is immoral, There once was a man named Belisarius, Homer was not a woman, I find no two of them that I could place on the same level of certainty, even if I were sure I believed them all. It may be said that this is confusion, that the first is completely certain because the meaning of the terms is clear and all the relevant evidence lies before me,

[1] Pp. 4, 5.

while the others are all uncertain because one or other of these conditions is not fulfilled. If they were fulfilled, it will be added, I should see at once that the proposition was either necessarily true or necessarily false. In short, there are no degrees in necessity; there are degrees only in our knowledge of the conditions that play a part in it. In a sense we may admit this. The assumption that to completed knowledge the world would show no contingency is, though it must probably remain an assumption, a natural and reasonable one. What must be doubted is whether the absolute necessity that is thus assumed in the nature of things can ever get into our experience. To say that it sometimes does is to say that in some cases we apprehend a proposition in the light of everything whatever on which it depends and nothing whatever on which it does not depend. And there is no good reason for believing that we ever do. The only view that could make it plausible to think so is one which would break the world up into atoms or pieces, each with its necessity wholly within itself. This view indeed has its advocates, and we shall later have to examine it. Meanwhile we can only say that since everywhere our grasp of conditions falls short of purity and completeness, any necessity or apriority that our reasonings may possess must remain a matter of degree.[1]

If a priori insight means insight that is made possible by the nature of the mind, then all thought is a priori. If it means that in which the knower imposes a structure upon the known, a structure that cannot be taken as shedding light upon the real, then it amounts to self-destructive scepticism; there is nothing it could offer us as true of the real, not even this insight about itself. What a priori rightly means is *revealing the character of thought through revealing what satisfies thought*. This conception of it corrects the common tendency to identify the a priori with the mathematical. It still leaves to mathematics its a priori character, for in this field we shall still find our most striking instances of demonstration within a system.

[1] For further consideration of this point, see Chap. XXV, Secs. 32–33, XXVII, XXXI 9 ff.

But it also draws attention, in a way that nowadays is needed, to the fact that demonstrative reasoning can be done in other fields as well. Is not Bosanquet clearly right when he says that 'a judgement of our instructed perception upon a colour harmony is in principle as good an a priori judgement as that three angles of a triangle are equal to two right angles'?[1] If apriority is denied to such thought on the ground of the wider disagreement on such matters, Bosanquet's own simple reply is sufficient: 'in many persons the perception is inadequately trained. Right perception is not every man's affair'. The truth is that no judgement or inference is ever made that is not in some degree a priori as revealing the pressure, however slight it may be, and however difficult to define, of that necessity which thought in its essence is an effort to realize.

12. There are many ways in which ordinary thinking falls short of the complete necessity it seeks. The terms of its conclusion may not be clearly defined; when it affirms, for example, that bigamy is immoral, neither 'bigamy' nor 'immoral' may carry any definite meaning, and necessitation can hardly be satisfactory when it is not known what is necessitated. Again, when puzzled we may select the right data and be drawn aside to the wrong conclusion, or select the wrong data and hit upon the right conclusion; or we may admit too much into our data and get too much in our conclusion, or admit too little in our data and hence in our conclusion also; or more commonly, we may pass from data in which there is both excess and defect to a conclusion marred with the same double vice. We may misconceive the degree of relevance of any datum to our result in as many different ways as there are degrees of relevance themselves. It is just such ventures as these, confused and groping and tentative, that form the staple of our thinking. But to say that because thought is condemned to this uncertain and twilight path it is following no track at all is to deny in the end that there is any such thing

[1] *Implication and Linear Inference*, 15; cf. also 95.

as sanity. It must be admitted, of course, that in the rigorous demonstrations of geometry and algebra there is something deeply satisfying to both the aesthetic and the logical senses. But for the enthusiast over these sciences to set up in their name an exclusive claim to necessity and to deny it to the thought of statesman, artist, and moralist, is a kind of dogmatism which betrays, one suspects, an ignorance of the rightful basis of all such claims.

13. The achievement of new insight through the completion of the fragmentary, a completion carried out under the control of an inner necessity and within a system that in neatness and abstractness is poles apart from the mathematical, might be illustrated in countless cases. I shall take one that happens to be at hand. In a book I was reading recently I found an exclamation of admiring wonder at the way in which Shakespeare, after the harrowing series of mischances, deceptions, and murders that threatens to carry *Othello* to an insupportable close, contrives to set all right again with the Moor's magnificent speech at the end:

> 'Speak of me as I am; nothing extenuate,
> Nor set down aught in malice: then must you speak
> Of one that loved not wisely, but too well;
> Of one not easily jealous, but, being wrought,
> Perplex'd in the extreme; of one whose hand,
> Like the base Indian, threw a pearl away
> Richer than all his tribe.'

and so on to the gorgeous and tragic close. If the dramatist had kept to the abstract, there were many possibilities open to him when he composed this speech. And it would seem to follow from the theory adopted by James and many other psychologists,[1] that the author's genius, consisting in a prodigal

---

[1] 'Just as a new voluntary movement is "discovered" by means of selection in an over-production of movements, so in an exactly similar way, new reasoning always proceeds by the method of *selection in an over-production of acts thought of*.'—Rignano, *Psychology of Reasoning*, 91-2. Italics in text.

power of analogy, did actually array before him a range of
alternative endings from which he went on to make his choice.
One may be fairly confident that nothing of the sort occurred.
It is far more likely that as the drama moved to its close in
Shakespeare's mind, only one possibility presented itself, with
no alternatives at all. He wrote what he did for the same reason
that we, in reading or hearing it, find it satisfying, namely
that with the given dramatic situation in mind he 'could no
other'. He had carried his hero from a height where nobility,
courage and strength made him an object of love and honour,
to a depth where nothing seemed left of him but a murderer
mad with jealousy. But the descent has been gradual, and at
the end the initial picture is obscured. How could the extent
of the appalling tragedy be brought home, and the reader
reconciled to it? To such a question in the abstract, there
may be many alternative answers, but is there not something
a little inept in supposing that such a writer would either
propound himself this question or make a list of the abstract
solutions of it? Even if he did both, any answer would be
worthless until specified in terms of the concrete situation.
He might conclude, for example, that a satisfying whole
would be achieved if the hero could appear again to us in all
his old strength and honour and blot out with his own hand
the thing he had become, and Shakespeare does give us this.
But so far we have nothing but the bare skeleton that would
be revealed by reflective analysis. And for all Poe's famous
and curious views on the philosophy of composition, it is clear
that this is not the way in which the mind of the artist works.
What Shakespeare actually gives us is something completely
organic with what has gone before, a speech in which we feel
in every syllable what Stuart Sherman would have called 'the
formative pressure of the tone and structure of the entire
work'. Given the character of Othello, his prevailing mood,
his habits of speech, the situation in which he was placed, and
given the need to round out the whole in accordance with the
implicit demands of the aesthetic ideal, there was only one
course for the Moor to take; and that he did. It is precisely

because the deeper we go into Shakespeare's better work, the less fortuitous do such things seem, that we give him superlative praise. He was so true an artist and so great an inventor because he succeeded, as perhaps no one else has succeeded, first in entering with full measure and variety of feeling into the situation before him, and secondly in giving it a development that is free and satisfying because it remains, in every detail, under the control of aesthetic necessity.[1]

14. Since we have taken instances of invention both from wholes that are extremely abstract, like those of number, and from others that are extremely concrete like those of art, it is perhaps needless to offer examples from the intermediate levels that are occupied by most of the sciences. But if it is true, as has been remarked, that 'poetic inspirations come, in anything like finished form, only to persons who have read poetry, studied it, and attempted to produce it; mathematical inspirations come to mathematicians only; musical inspirations come to musicians only',[2] then we should expect to find that in chemistry and biology new suggestions of any value would come only to those who were at home among the facts and the special patterns of these fields. And this is what we do find. It is perhaps not quite impossible that discoveries should be made by free-lances who venture on happy guesses; but normally, unless one's guesses grow from a mass of relevant

[1] Cf. Alexander: 'Great artists know or believe that they are inspired from something outside themselves. Why should we suppose them to be deceived? It is true that to make the discovery (of Hamlet) the gifts of Shakespeare were needed; that is why great artists are rare. But equally the gifts and skill of Newton were needed to discover the law of gravitation. . . . "Ripeness is all." . . . The artist's creativeness conceals from us his real passivity.'—*Beauty and Other Forms of Value*, 74.

Considering the amount of analysis in Shakespeare's plays, it is striking how little interest he seems to have taken in the more abstract types of analysis. 'Shakespeare never once made a simile from Euclid, or from Thomas Aquinas, notwithstanding that his range seemed to know no bounds.'—Bain, *Study of Character*, 333.

[2] G. A. Coe.

facts and a sense for the special order that holds these facts together, they are almost certain to be wild. Mere cleverness will not serve. 'Many men', writes Darwin, 'who are very clever—much cleverer than the discoverers—never originate anything.' Nor will profound knowledge and even creative genius in one field carry with them inventiveness in another. 'Think of Laplace, the man who made the theory, dismissed by Napoleon for *incapacity*, and say whether the greatest mind may truly be called great, when tested apart from the apperception masses with which it is familiar.'[1] Nor are there any rules that greatly help; the laws of deductive logic and even the canons of induction are tests for theories already achieved rather than devices for achieving them; the famous *regulae* of Descartes are too general to be of much use outside mathematics.[2] As Professor Pillsbury says, 'No rules can be given for making the unfertile brain fertile'.[3] If we accept the view of an experienced student of biology, Professor Lloyd Morgan,

> 'it is idle to expect through the application of rules of scientific procedure to attain scientific insight; for the man of science, so far as he is creative, is an artist. One can only say to him, as to other artists: Saturate yourself through and through with your subject and with all that bears, or may bear upon it, and *wait*. If the flash of insight comes, treasure it, and then patiently work it out in all its bearings, remembering that no art product is made convincing without labour. *Then* you may apply your rules of scientific method with profit and advantage. And if it does not come, still *wait*. . . .'[4]

15. From all this it will be clear that the process of invention is anything but the hit-or-miss business of trial and error that it is often taken to be. 'The mathematician might as well expect to integrate his functions by a ballot-box', writes Jevons, 'as the experimentalist to draw deep truths from haphazard

---

[1] Adams, *Herbartian Psychology*, 127.
[2] Cf. Serrus, *La Méthode de Descartes et son Application à la Métaphysique*, 77 ff. [3] *Fundamentals of Psychology*, 407.
[4] *Comparative Psychology*, 307.

trials.'[1] So far as the system within which the problem arose
is really mastered, its development is under control. The control
is negative as well as positive. It not only holds the mind to
the road but also closes the blind alleys along the way. As
Professor Stout puts it, 'mental elements which share in the
activity of one mental system are for the time disabled from
acting either in any other systematic combination or independently. When we are engrossed in writing or speaking about
some serious topic, it does not occur to us, unless we are
inveterate punsters, to play upon the words we use. When we
are interested in a game of billiards, the idea of the billiard
balls does not set us thinking about the trade in ivory and
African slavery.'[2] A mind which thus darted from system to
system would be either insane or a super-mind; the former
if the systems were unrelated except through these associative
links, the latter if the systems themselves were intelligibly
ordered within a wider system.

16. At its best, then, creative thought is not a tentative
groping, but a straightforward march. But where the problems
are at all difficult, it must be admitted that the conditions are
seldom present which make this march possible. As Whewell
said, 'to try wrong guesses is, with most persons, the only way
to hit upon right ones'. And here it is that analogy comes in.
It is the chief and constant resource for thought that is imperfectly in command of its matter. If the mind cannot solve
its problem in terms dictated by the situation itself, it will
try to solve it in terms of some other but similar situation.
'The aborigines of Australia called a book "mussel" merely
because it opens and shuts like the valves of a shell-fish.'[3]
'Men, taken historically', says James, 'reason by analogy long
before they have learned to reason by abstract characters. . . In
all primitive literature, in all savage oratory, we find persuasion
carried on exclusively by parables and similes, and travellers

---

[1] *Principles of Science*, 579.   [2] *Analytic Psychology*, II. 117.
[3] Ribot, *Creative Imagination*, 26.

in savage countries readily adopt the native custom.'[1] No wonder they adopt it readily, for it is essentially the one they follow themselves whenever they are in difficulty.

There are writers of weight, as we have observed in another connection, who have regarded the eye for analogy as virtually one with intellect itself. For example, Bain: 'In every subject implying *thought*, as distinct from mere memory, the power of identifying like things, through distance and disguise, is the main element of intellectual force'.[2] Jevons writes: 'There is a rare property of mind which consists in penetrating the disguise of variety and seizing the common elements of sameness; and it is this property which furnishes the true measure of intellect.'[3] 'The difficulties of suggestion are all in reducing the strangeness of our task by specifying it as a case', says Sir William Mitchell.[4] And Havelock Ellis reminds us of the 'fine and deep saying of Aristotle's that "the greatest thing by far is to be a master of metaphor". That is the mark of genius; for, said he, it implies an intuitive perception of the similarity in dissimilars.'[5] We have insisted that this goes too far if it means that intelligence and originality *consist* in the command of analogy. What these really consist in is the power to grasp and develop a system, and if the system is highly abstract, as in the case of number or space, analogy may scarcely appear in the course of reasoning. Where it does play a part, it is not in the guise of intellect itself, but in that of an assistant. We have now to see, however, that its aid is of the first importance, for it is the great magazine of suggestions for puzzled minds. How is it used?

17. It is used to show how a system which in a given context is incomplete may be completed. It does so by showing that this system, when it appears in another context, is completed

[1] *Psychology*, II. 363.   [2] *Study of Character*, 341.
[3] *Principles of Science*, 5.
[4] *Structure and Growth of the Mind*, 357.
[5] *The Fountain of Life*, 52.

in a particular way, and by suggesting that in the present case it may be completed in the same way. Let us see this in an example; and since familiarity helps, let us take as our example an incident which, though apocryphal perhaps,[1] is the most widely known use of analogy in the history of science. Newton is said to have hit on the law of gravitation through analogy with the fall of an apple. What was the probable track of his thought? In his mind, to begin with, was a mass of ordered data about the planets; he knew that they were material bodies moving in elliptical orbits round the sun at certain approximate velocities and at certain approximate distances. These and other connected data were ordered in his mind in accordance with such laws as he knew of logic and physics. Conspicuous among these laws was the first law of motion, which had been stated by Galileo, and which laid it down that a body moving straight forward will continue to do so unless some other body interferes. It was with this 'apperception mass' in his mind that Newton contemplated the moving planets, and in the course of this contemplation one fact stood out arrestingly and refused to fit into the picture, namely that, instead of shooting off at a tangent, each planet so bent its line of advance as to go round and round the sun. This was not at all what Galileo's principle would lead one to expect; yet the fact was unquestionable. How account for it? This was Newton's problem. He must find some cause which would link this errant fact with the body of his physical knowledge and make it thus intelligible.

Now the mind that would build a bridge to an isolated fact must start its construction, as we have seen, from some particular point on the mainland. The problem in this case was to find that point. Of course it might not exist at all; the sort of causal factor that could deflect a planet from its path might never have found its way into the thinker's experience,

---

[1] 'The story that Newton first saw the gravitation of the earth in the fall of an apple in the orchard, which Voltaire has transmitted to us from a fairly good source, has no first-hand authority. But the crowd has always accepted it as a gospel truth, and by a sound instinct.'— Ellis, *ibid.*, 53.

and then, though he would not know it, the problem would be for him insoluble. If it is soluble, that is because some fact is already known to him which, if brought to light, would provide the pier for a construction, that is, in this case, reveal the cause of the given effect. Nor will he be quite in the dark as to where to look. Newton would never have dreamt of looking for the cause among his own emotions or among the political events of the day; his experience would have impressed upon him that the cause of a planet's motion was to be found among its physical relations or attributes. But where? Hundreds of these were known to him, any one of which might be relevant. It is in a situation like this that appeal is made to analogy. Is there any other set of facts which parallels this in essentials and in which the missing factor may stand out? Can we think of another instance where a body, instead of going straight on, as the first law of motion would by itself require, leaves its path and appears to cling to some other body? Yes, said Newton, we can. An apple blown off by the wind, or a missile thrown at it from the ground, presents in essentials the same picture; neither will continue on a straight course; each will describe an arc and fall to the earth. The earth and the moon, the apple and the missile, may all be conceived as *falling* objects, the apple, the missile and the moon as falling toward the earth, the earth as falling toward the sun. Once this likeness had been seen, the path to the goal was straight. For the motion of falling was firmly linked to that of a force that exerted a pull and caused the fall, and if this pull was present in one case it was presumably present in others. Thus thought passed on, in a way that now seems so natural as to be inevitable, to one of the most fruitful of all discoveries, the identity of celestial attraction with terrestrial gravitation.

18. But however natural this analogy seems, it is a matter of no little difficulty to explain the movement of thought that proceeds through it. For example, if the account just given is taken as an explanation, but little reflection is needed to see that it is circular. The thinker goes to his result, we said, by using another case which in essentials is the same. An apple and a planet were both essentially falling bodies. But what do we mean by 'essential'? Something, presumably, on which the missing element depends, and which, once seen, would carry that element with it in our thought. It is clear, further, that the analogy will succeed only if it *is* an analogy in essentials. An analogy in unessentials, that is, in respects that had no connection with the element sought for, would conduct the movement up a side track. Now how are we to select this essential analogy? Is it not clear that if the mind is in a position to select, out of hundreds of possible analogies, the one that is based upon essentials, it must know what is essential already? But if it does, it owns, to begin with, all that is necessary for its end, and the resort to analogy is needless. Hence the circle: new insight is made possible by the use of analogy, but the analogy is made possible only by the prior insight. For clearness let us put it otherwise: You want to explain an element X, and you know that the factor it depends on is one of a group. Any member of this group would serve as a base for analogy, but since only one is relevant, this alone can give a relevant analogy. How are you to select it? Your only ground for selection would be the perception of a link with what you are seeking. But if you perceive this, you know already what you are seeking; if you do not, you have no ground for selection at all.

19. One answer to this puzzle lies in escaping between the horns. Analogy is partly directed by insight and partly not. No one ever puts a question who is wholly in the dark about the answer, if only for the reason that a question, in its very nature, implies that the new fact, at least in part, can be assimilated to a system that is familiar. We always presume that this fact conforms to the general laws of the system we bring to it, and as a rule we also presume that it will conform to the laws of some special province. Newton was confident that the factor he was seeking was at least physical; no doubt he was confident of much more. When Adams and Leverrier, to account for the perturbations of Uranus, inferred the existence of Neptune by analogy, they had before them such a mass of data, governed by laws so firmly established, as to confine the analogy to the narrowest range, and almost to prescribe the result.[1] Even Jevons's famous hypothesis, which is a classical case of apparent wildness and disconnection, that commercial crises are connected with the appearance of spots on the sun, would never have been thought of except under pressure of a familiar causal presumption. As Bosanquet has pointed out, 'it was the suggestion of a rationale through the connection of a deficiency in solar heat with a deficiency of harvests that made the hypothesis worth embodying in a proposition'.[2]

20. That is one side of the answer; before we resort to analogy we know roughly or in general what is essential to our result, and this knowledge bounds our choice. Now for the other side. Within these boundaries we are free, and we frame analogies at random. Since the inventor is in the dark, he can only proceed by trial and error, striking out the unfruitful guesses until he stumbles upon a fruitful one. That within the limits of their controlling theory discoverers commonly do this is too plain for doubt. The process is one of groping, and in their success is a large element of luck. 'We are apt to imagine that all the suggestions, analogies, and hypotheses of the great scientists were right; it is mainly of the correct ones that we hear. But this is far from being the case. Months and even years are often spent in formulating and testing a hypothesis which has in the end to be discarded, and the one that is suggested in its place may have to pass through the

[1] Even before the planet was seen, Sir William Herschel said: 'We see it as Columbus saw America from the shores of Spain. Its movements have been felt trembling along the far-reaching line of our analysis with a certainty hardly inferior to that of an ocular demonstration.'   [2] *Implication*, etc., 90.

same process. We are told that Kepler tested and rejected nineteen wrong hypotheses before the right law of the orbit of the planets occurred to him; and they were mostly the result of false analogies.'[1] Of Einstein a contemporary writes: 'He told me once in Berlin: "I think and think, for months, for years. Ninety-nine times the conclusion is false. The hundredth time I am right".'[2] Nor is the matter different in the fine arts. To 'analysis and reflection' Bach added 'much writing and ceaseless correction' as giving 'all my secret'. Of Beethoven's *Fidelio* 'it is said that he made as many as eighteen different versions of one famous passage, and ten of another, and similar changes and experimental improvements throughout'.[3] The more developed is the whole demanding completion, the less is the range of blind experiment and the need for it; the less developed is that whole, the greater the need. When pioneer work is called for, the most tropical imagination and the wildest shots in the dark are the order of the day; and to suppose that these are incompatible with scientific exactness is false to historic fact. As has been said of Kepler: 'he possessed the most absurdly extravagant imagination'; 'he was willing to believe that the earth was a kind of animal, and would not have been surprised to find that it possessed lungs or gills', yet 'he developed a greater regard for accuracy in calculation than the world had ever known'.[4] Faraday, of whom it has been written that 'his method was the method of the *Arabian Nights* transferred to the region of facts', wrote of scientific investigators: 'in the most successful instances not a tenth of the suggestions, the hopes, the wishes, the preliminary conclusions, have been realized'. His own suspicion of a special bond between magnetism and light was turned over in his mind for twenty-three years at least before he gained the first experimental suggestion that

---

[1] Latta and Macbeath, *Elements of Logic*, 314.
[2] Alfons Goldschmidt in *New York Times*, April 1, 1934.
[3] Parry, *Studies of Great Composers*, 176.
[4] Ellis, *The Dance of Life*, 122: 'Some of his most elaborate calculations were repeated, and without the help of logarithms, even seventy times.'

led to a positive result; and though the notion of an underlying identity between gravitation, electricity and magnetism was one of his obsessions, he never, to the end of his life, could hit upon a way of proving it.[1]

21. Here then is an answer to our puzzle. To the criticism that analogy is the key to invention and yet that we could not select the analogy unless we had the key already, we reply with a distinction. We do have the key to the outer door; analogy does not supply this; it is only when prior insight has produced it and turned it in the lock that analogy can begin to work. On the other hand we do *not* have the key to the inner door where the specific solution is hiding, and here it is that analogy, through mere unguided simian play, may find for us the further key. But does this answer wholly satisfy? In the main it is both true and instructive, but we must admit that it is unsatisfactory in the same way that the dilemma it answers was unsatisfactory. The inventor would find it hard to discover in his somewhat nebulous musing anything corresponding to these explicit and hard distinctions. He may bow to the logician's insistence that he must either know a certain connection or not know it. But he could reply that he is curiously uncertain as to what he does know and what he doesn't, that he sometimes succeeds in solving problems without ever reaching clearness on this point, and that when success does come, he would often find it hard to tell whether analogy had played a part in it or not. We are all familiar with this state of mind. When, in virtue of something we have seen, we conclude 'X is timid' or 'X is a southern European', are we clear whether our result has come from analogy, and if it has, what its basis is? Yet we reach the conclusion somehow. And so, sometimes, of more original thinkers on matters of greater weight. How can any definite conclusion issue from what is so vague?

The answer is that we may lay hold of a connection and that it may work within our minds without ever becoming

[1] Cf. Jevons on Faraday, *Principles of Science*, 587–91.

explicit. Long ago, in our study of perceptual thought, we found instances of this. A physician, for example, walked along a hospital ward, his eye fell on a child in one of the beds who had presented a difficult case, and he remarked, 'That child has pus in the abdomen'. When asked how he knew, he was unable to answer convincingly; but that he had made more than a lucky guess was attested by the fact that his 'lucky guesses' were continual.[1] What more was involved? It was the implicit grasp of a general connection between certain appearances now before him and their hidden cause. No earlier case that is similar may have come explicitly to mind, and even if it did, the point of identity might have been veiled. Yet below the level of explicitness identity was at work. Somewhere, probably, the doctor had observed a case of pus in the abdomen, and in the case now before him certain features of the earlier case were repeated. At that time an ill-defined connection impressed itself on his mind between the diseased condition and these other accompanying features, and when these turned up again, the connected character itself was reinstated. What effected the reinstatement was an identity that from first to last may have lain buried out of sight.

> 'We all know very well that in our daily life we reason habitually from the results of past experience, although we may be wholly unable to give one single particular fact in support of our conclusion. We know again that there are persons whose memory is so good that they recall past details in a way which to us is quite impossible, and who yet cannot draw the conclusions which we draw, since they have never gone beyond the reproduction of these details. It is not the collection of particular facts, it is the general impression one gets from these facts which is really the *sine qua non* of reasoning; and it is that from which we really go to our result.'[2]

22. 'And so', it will be said, 'associationism once more. Granting, as Bradley would have us grant, that association

---

[1] Above, Chap. VI, Sec. 10.
[2] Bradley, *Principles of Logic*, I. 352.

marries only universals, still this connection is conjunction merely; when a universal reinstates another it does so because this has in fact been given along with it.' We answer, Sometimes so, and sometimes not. That the link between universals is at times conjunctive only is, ultimate refinements aside, to be conceded. What we must insist on, however, is that sometimes it is very much more. Universals are less like little blocks that will fit together in any order than like the tangled branches of vines. They are implicated with each other in every degree of intimacy. And sometimes, even when the terms and their links never appear in the focus of consciousness, thought divines this intimacy. It has a sense which, falling short of demonstration and definition, is yet far from merely capricious, that if certain terms are together, this is not because they have fallen together, but because they belong together; and it keeps these terms distinct from those whose connection is mere coincidence. For example, along with the malady at its first appearance there may have been various accompanying factors occurring only there, and thus it would seem connected uniquely with the malady in question; so that if diagnosis is made to turn on conjunction only, it should declare the disease to be present wherever any of these occurred. The earlier sufferer may have had hair of a brighter red than the physician had seen before or ears of an unparalleled shape. But he would never, on the appearance of such features in others, go on to ascribe the disease also. Why? Because he has seen that some of the associates are relevant and some are not, and he declines to base diagnosis on irrelevancies. It may be replied that all this amounts to is that features of the type called 'relevant' have been conjoined with such maladies frequently, while those of the type rejected have been found independent of them. This implies that in causal inquiry we have ultimately no guide but the bare rules of presence and absence. And this is incredible.[1] It would still be incredible even if it were shown that only through the noting of presence and absence

---

[1] For the position that causality involves necessity, see Chap. XXXII, Sec. 10 ff.

do we ever come to note causality. Thought never takes constant conjunction as brute fact only; its attempt is to thread the conjoined on a string of necessity, and whether it finds this or not, it always assumes it to be there as the real ground of the union. Sometimes this thread of necessity comes quickly to definition, as when the child arranging trinkets in pairs sees that regardless of the trinkets he uses, two and two make four. Sometimes it remains unisolated because the interest is smaller in isolating it than in ordering terms in accordance with it, as when an artist puts in his foreground just the right figure to give perspective or a musician keeps in key. Sometimes the interest in analysis does appear but only to be frustrated, while yet the conviction remains that one has divined a true necessity. This is very commonly so of our knowledge of causation. The plain man is convinced, and rightly, that between the blow of the hammer and the sinking of the nail there is more than sequence in time, even though to strip off from the two events their unessentials and lay bare a differential equation is very probably beyond him. We do not mean to deny that the rules of presence and absence are useful, or even in practice indispensable. But they are means of directing attention, and not themselves sources of insight; they can only provide the theatre for a perception supplied by reason; accompaniment is not the *causa essendi* of necessity but the *causa cognoscendi* only. As for the insight itself, there is no explanation for it short of one in terms of the essence and end of mind. For such insight is simply mind coming into its own, mind realizing in the material given it its own distinctive ideal. It is one stage of that *nisus* for necessity which forms the very nature of thought.

23. Now diagnosis, however humble, is invention or discovery, and the simple instance we have used illustrates the process generally. What evidently gets the result is not analogy, but that which lies at the basis of all analogy and all similar association, the presence of a universal which develops itself in differences. Both the 'universal' and the 'differences' need emphasis. On the one hand, what works in the mind is no present particular event; any such event, as now appearing for the first time, could never have been linked with anything. What works now is what also *has been* connected, and this is an identity or universal which is not tied to one time or place, but may appear in many. And a universal, as we saw long ago, has an identical logical context wherever it may appear, that is, a set of further relations without which it would not be what it is. This context, of course, it carries with it always. Hence if we have ever discerned its connection with any part of this context, we may, on its reappearance, go on to infer that this part also is there. That is one side of the matter; invention works through identity, which reinstates what we have seen to be bound up with it.

But the other side is of equal importance. The identity that is at work is not a bare identity, nor need the term inferred be barely identical with the term inferred before. 'An existing connection of thought, when confronted with new matter, is able to reproduce itself in a new form which is at once appropriate to the new matter, and continuous with the connection as previously thought.'[1] Indeed unless such development and accommodation are allowed, the achievements of creative thought are unaccountable. Even in so humble an instance of discovery as a doctor's diagnosis, it is to be doubted whether the path of thought is ever merely through 'the same linked to the same'. The doctor who, in diagnosing a case, was helpless to proceed unless exactly the same symptoms appeared, exactly the same shade of sallowness, for example, and exactly the same pulse or temperature, and who assumed, further, that the disease could not be present unless in precisely the same form that he had found in an earlier case, would probably never arrive at a diagnosis of anything. The truly inventive mind must be able to reason both *from* and *to* new forms of the identities it uses. To invent is to develop an old connection into an altered version of itself. Whether the

[1] Bosanquet, *Science and Philosophy*, 70.

development is what is called creation, in which the universal evolves variety out of itself, or recognition, in which we identify in what is presented to us a new form of an old object, is a point of minor importance. What is important is that, with or without help from the given, the universal and its consequence should develop themselves into something new. It is not enough when we have to deal with a problem to single out A and so get carried along to B. For in cases of any difficulty, A is sure to appear as *a*, which will no longer give us B, but *b* instead. And unless we can carry both identities into their differences, we shall be lost. To invent is to pass from a modification of one identity to a corresponding modification of another and implied identity.

24. With this in mind, we see why, as feats of thought, some discoveries rank so high and some so low. The man who first made a fire, perhaps by striking rocks together, changed the face of civilization, but he required no special intellectual endowment; his achievement was less an invention, or in the scientific sense a discovery, than a happy accident. In point of understanding, he may have been well behind the child who has arrived at the insight that three times three are nine. And yet if the child understood this when he learned his multiplication table, we should not say he was inventing or discovering when he later saw for the first time that it held for apples and matches. Why? Because he would be seeing nothing new; threeness in the new context is the same threeness as before, and in doing the multiplication he is merely repeating an old process. When we come to the doctor's diagnosis, we seem to be again on a higher level. This is not because the connection grasped has more of necessity in it, for it plainly has less, but because the identity one must start from is masked, and only an intelligence of a fair order can recognize or make use of it. From this level thought again leaps upward in making such a discovery as Lavoisier's of the nature of oxidation. Having found burning to be a process in which the body burnt takes oxygen from the air and unites it with itself, Lavoisier went on to study the further processes of rusting and breathing. He divined that in spite of their differing appearances and the differing substances involved, these processes were identical in essence with the process of burning. This is considered one of the triumphs of the scientific mind. It is so considered partly, no doubt, because so keen an eye was required to see identity in things so different; but partly also because of the enormous range of the implied revision of concepts. Every form of burning, breathing or rusting was now linked with some underlying form of oxidation.

And when we reach the supreme scientific discoveries, such as Newton's of gravitation and Darwin's of the origin of species, it is this range of implied revision that stands out as the chief element. Newton's perception of identity between falling apple and moving planet was of course a signal achievement, but it was no stroke of unprecedented genius; indeed the suggestion had been made before. What made his achievement so great was less the discovery of an identity A from which he could pass to a correlated identity B, than the grasp of the law of variation in this correlated identity itself. From that identity in difference, falling, he passed to the thought of another identity, a natural force which, though everywhere the same, yet varied directly as the mass and inversely as the square of the distance. And by means of this conception he threw a new light on every motion in the universe. In the same way, it was not merely or chiefly Darwin's guess that the Malthusian law, faster race horses, and an improving humanity, might all illustrate selective mating, that made his discovery what it was. Indeed this is implied in the general consent by which the credit has gone to Darwin rather than to Wallace, who made the same point simultaneously. Darwin, having grasped the identity, a mating of the best, and having grasped the implied universal, alteration in type, went on to develop their corresponding changes up and down the evolutionary scale with such exhaustive and convincing detail as to leave no form of life, or its relation to any other, unaffected by the discovery. Invention in his case, as in all the supreme cases, was no mere gimlet-eyed discernment of some out-of-the-way point of identity; it was the grasp of a connection between universals which, through all their protean forms, were still linked firmly together by a nexus that was itself an identity in difference. If it is said that this wipes out the line between discovering an idea and verifying it, the answer is that this is a defence of our theory, not an objection to it. In actual thinking no clear line of this sort exists. 'What is not proved', as Bosanquet says, 'is not really discovered.'[1]

25. Thus invention is the emergence in the mind of novelty under the control of system. A connection between A and B such that the changes A^1, A^2 . . ., on the one side are responded to by changes B^1, B^2 . . ., on the other is already a system; and in a discovery like Darwin's, where, in the fully developed thought, each side had thousands of members, it may itself have a high complexity. But probably the system at work in invention is never merely a connection of simples, a form of A operating alone to redintegrate a form of B. The leap of suggestion is actually made from a far broader base; the datum from which the physician passes to his diagnosis is a complex state which includes flushes, temperatures, pulse-rates, and perhaps much else, which all converge upon his theory. Nor must it be forgotten that this complex base, already a partial system, is itself a sub-system in an enormously wider system, namely, the nature and laws of the organism as represented, for the most part implicitly, in the physician's knowledge. We have seen long ago how comprehensive such an apperceptive mass may be, and how powerful is the control it may exert from behind the scenes on the processes of explicit thought. What primarily acts to produce suggestion is a sub-system that is relatively small, but this acts with the co-operation of innumerable moulding pressures from this larger background.

[1] *Logic*, II. 119.

26. 'But granting all this', the patient reader may complain, 'we are still waiting to learn how the *right* sub-system, the *right* suggestion, arises. You rejected James's key of fertility in similars. You went on to argue that sometimes problems are solved without resort to analogies, and that even when they are used it is not they that are really effective, but a universal working through them. But all this leaves one in the dark on the really vital point, namely how the mind hits on the *right* universal. You have pointed out that when Newton, on seeing an apple, thought of the planets, what was working in his mind was the essential point of identity, their both being falling objects; that what worked in the mind of Darwin was not a mere random resemblance between race-horses and men but what, for his end, was the essential resemblance, the presence in both of natural selection. In each case the identity at work was the important one, and how did they arrive at it? What was it in their minds that brought up the right suggestion, while others, no less learned, perhaps, or diligent, missed the mark?'

It will not do to evade this question, for it is the essential and central puzzle of invention. But we can now see that the sort of answer that the questioner probably wants cannot, in the nature of the case, be given. Why could our calculating shepherd boy pass to the solution so surely and swiftly while we cannot? The question is ambiguous. It may mean, What are the conditions, physiological and psychological, that gave him his advantage in this field over others? To this question the answer is that we do not fully know, but that they are apparently such conditions as special structures among the neurones in certain regions of the cortex, and special ways of functioning on the part of certain glands. Some progress has been made in defining these conditions, but much more remains to be done, and our darkness on the whole is abysmal. But the discussions of the last book have made it clear that even if we knew them we should not know what we most want to know; there are important further conditions. And our question may perhaps refer to these. It may mean, Granting the first conditions to be present, what bent the boy's line of suggestion along the logical path it took, rather than along some different road? And to this question no answer is possible except that the government of his thought is now in the charge of an ideal order. Given the requirements and data before him, he thinks as he does because he has to if he is to go on thinking at all. His mind is under compulsion from the system he is engaged with. And this system is compulsory because it is the fulfilment of thought as such. It is the embodiment, so far, of that ideal of intelligibility which is the implicit end of all thinking. And he thinks as he does because if, under these conditions, he is to realize that ideal, he *must* think so and not otherwise. To ask why the ideal should demand one course rather than another is meaningless, since if the reason for the course were not evident in the structure of the ideal itself, it would not be the ideal.

27. Now it is the same with invention that proceeds through analogy. Of two minds engaged with the same problem and possessing, so far as may be seen, the same data, one catches the essential cue and the other does not; why? Because, it is said, one is more intelligent than the other. Now what we really mean by this is not some perverse cleverness or fertility that goes off in dazzling disregard of fact; we mean the sort of thinking that is under control by the necessities of the case. So far as the analogies are random and heterogeneous, thought is adrift on the tide of association. So far as they become less random and heterogeneous we can see necessity taking the helm. And when it does take the helm, why does it steer the course it does? We can only answer as before. That the universal connection hit upon should be the right one; that Newton, contemplating planets and apples, should light on the concept of 'falling' as leading to the force he was in search of; that Darwin should select from men and race-horses the feature essential to improvement of type; that the suggestion should come to Leverrier of an undiscovered star; that Shakespeare

should be carried, with or without analogies, to the last speech of Othello—all these are explicable in one way only, namely that the ideal order which their thought is attempting to realize has so far come to the birth in them. The matter, as they brood over it, begins to take shape in their minds, part throws out lines to part, and hidden affinities come to light, not because they so order it, but because they have succeeded beyond the measure of most men in surrendering to a necessity that is at once within them and beyond them. What De Quincey calls their 'electrical aptitude for seizing analogies, and by means of these aerial pontoons passing over like lightning from one topic to another' is not at all what it seems to be; far from being a grasshopper fickleness, it is an expression of logic itself. The eye that can trace the lines of necessity and single out the relevant from the crowd of irrelevant associates is under guidance which to the descriptive psychologist is and must remain invisible. It is the guidance of the immanent end of thought, of the ideal of rational order, whose pressure, felt at its strongest in such minds, organizes the chaos of experiences into relatively orderly ranks. And if in the minds of the great discoverers these ranks form themselves more readily and in closer alignment, what reason in the end can be given but that this immanent logic has so far gained control?

CHAPTER XXIV

THE SUBCONSCIOUS IN INVENTION

1. We turn now to another aspect of invention which, though less important and equally difficult, is to many minds more interesting. It has already been remarked that inventive thinking, instead of being a tense assertion of the will, seems rather to be a surrender of the will to an order whose structure is quite independent of it and whose affirmation through the mind is very largely so. That in the realm of art, at least, creative thinking appears in this light to those engaged in it is almost a commonplace. 'Poets seem to agree that "real" literary work is done without conscious effort. They feel compelled to write, they do not know what is coming. . . They may dream it like Stevenson or believe it is dictated to them like Blake.'[1] 'Poetry is not, like reasoning', said Shelley, 'a power to be exerted according to the determination of the will. A man cannot say "I will compose poetry". The greatest poet even cannot say it; for the mind in creation is as a fading coal, which some invisible influence, like an inconstant wind, awakens to transitory brightness.'[2] In Wordsworth there is much to the same effect.

> 'Think you, mid this mighty sum
> Of things forever speaking
> That nothing of itself will come
> And we must still be seeking?'

Mozart wrote, 'When I am, as it were, completely myself, entirely alone, and of good cheer—say, travelling in a carriage, or walking after a good meal, or during the night when I cannot sleep; it is on such occasions that my ideas flow best and most abundantly. *Whence* and *how* they come I know not nor can I force them.' 'I had for long', wrote Schumann, 'to

---

[1] Saxby, *The Psychology of the Thinker*, 69.
[2] *Defence of Poetry*.

rack my brains, but now I hardly need to rub my brow. Everything comes from within, and often I seem able to play right on without coming to the end.' 'Gluck said thoughts flowed to him, and he knew not whence they came.' 'In the arts of genius', said Voltaire, 'instinct is everything'; and with reference to his tragedy *Catalina*, which he wrote in a week, he says that if men could know 'how a poet in spite of himself, idolizing his subject, devoured by his genius, can accomplish in a few days a task for which without that genius a year would not suffice—in a word, *si scirent donum Dei*—if they knew the gift of God—their astonishment might be less than it must be now'.[1] 'Beethoven, when asked to improvise, would strike some notes or chords at random, and forthwith entwine them in a rich succession of images; three notes of a bird would inspire him with a leading motive.'[2] Goethe said of *Werther* that he had written it 'somewhat unconsciously, like a sleepwalker'. Milton, after long drought, would sometimes call for his daughter in the middle of the night and ask her to seize a pen to help him catch the verse that was descending in unexpected floods. Thackeray wrote of his novels: 'The characters once created lead me, and I follow where they direct. I have no idea where it all comes from. I have never seen the persons I describe, nor heard the conversations I put down. I am often astonished myself to read it after I have got it on paper.' 'Ce n'est pas moi qui pense', wrote Lamartine; 'ce sont mes idées qui pensent pour moi.'

2. Can conscious effort be as largely dispensed with as this in science and philosophy? Apparently not. James writes that 'minds of genius may be divided into two main sorts, those who notice the bond (of identity) and those who merely obey it. The first are the abstract reasoners, properly so called, the

[1] Quoted by Myers, *Human Personality*, I. 75.
[2] Mitchell, *Structure and Growth of the Mind*, 353, quoting L. Arréat. The citations from Gluck, Goethe, and Schumann are also from Mitchell.

men of science and philosophers—the analysts, in a word; the latter are the poets, the critics, the artists, in a word, the men of intuitions.'[1] For the purpose of the poet it is enough if the identity so far works as to call up some telling parallel; and when we read

> 'Then felt I like some watcher of the skies
> When a new planet swims into his ken;
> Or like stout Cortez',

we never dream of demanding that the resemblance be set out formally. Not only would this be pointless; the poet would often find it impossible; the identity has worked below the level of explicit thought, and neither by interest nor by discipline is he adept at recovering it. With the scientist it is otherwise. One can imagine how much value would have attached to Darwin's announcement if he had merely reported a felt resemblance between race-horses and men. It is the business of the scientist not only to feel identities but to define them and make them explicit; for in general he is searching for law, and a law is a nexus between abstractions that require precise definition. Such conceptual precision is notoriously a matter for conscious effort. Hence philosophy and science can hardly hope for that independence of voluntary attention and focal consciousness which has marked much genuine achievement in the sphere of art.

3. But that a large measure of such independence can be attained, even in the sphere of speculative thought, is suggested by a recent passage from the pen of Archbishop Temple, a passage so interesting that I quote it in full:

> 'Men seem to differ very profoundly in the fashion of their thinking. If two men are presented with a novel suggestion and both exclaim "I must think about that", one will begin by putting together what he knows with reference to the subject, his former opinions based upon that knowledge, his general

[1] *Psychology*, II. 361.

theories concerning that department of enquiry, and so forth; piece by piece he will work out his conclusion with regard to the suggestion made to him. The other will find that his mind goes blank; he will stare into the fire or walk about the room, or otherwise keep conscious attention diverted from the problem. Then abruptly he will find that he has a question to ask, or a counter-suggestion to make, after which the mental blank returns. At last he is aware, once more abruptly, what is his judgement on the suggestion, and subsequently, though sometimes very rapidly, he also becomes aware of the reasons which support or necessitate it.

'My own mind is of the latter sort. All my decisive thinking goes on behind the scenes; I seldom know when it takes place —much of it certainly on walks or during sleep—and I never know the processes which it has followed. Often when teaching I have found myself expressing rooted convictions which until that moment I had no notion that I held.'[1]

Mysterious as this subconscious reasoning is, there can be no doubt that it occurs, or that it can carry through operations of great length and complexity.[2] The biographies of discoverers abound with examples of it, and by way of showing what it can do in regions of high abstractness, we may take a few illustrations from the work of mathematicians. A well-known case is the discovery of the method of 'quaternions' by Sir W. Rowan Hamilton, a discovery of which he has left a graphic description. For fifteen years, he says, he had been haunted by the problem which this method finally solved. When at last the solution came, it came abruptly and unannounced; it 'started into life, or light, full-grown, on the 16th of October, 1843, as I was walking with Lady Hamilton to Dublin, and came up to Brougham Bridge. That is to say, I then and there felt the galvanic circuit of thought close'; all that was necessary was to seize a note-book and jot down the new equations. It was as if they had been worked out for him by some co-operating intelligence and had now presented them-

---

[1] *Nature, Man, and God*, the preface.
[2] The term 'subconscious' is applied in this chapter broadly to any processes which produce results like those of fully conscious processes without being fully conscious themselves. We are deliberately excluding for the time the problem of their metaphysical status.

selves without summons.[1] We hear it said sometimes that such results are not achieved by subconscious processes at all, but rather by a conscious faculty that has been restored or freshened by rest. But this will not suffice. There are many cases in which a solution is correctly given, while the steps by which it was reached remain unknown. Thus Gauss had been trying to prove a theorem in arithmetic for four years. 'At last, two days ago, I succeeded, not by dint of painful effort, but so to speak by the grace of God. As a sudden flash of light the enigma was solved. *For my part I am not in a position to point to the thread which joins what I knew previously and what I have succeeded in doing.*'[2] Most of the original work of Henri Poincaré seems to have been done in the same way, and he has left a valuable account of it. On one occasion, after two weeks of fruitless effort on a problem of great technicality, he went sleeplessly to bed, when suddenly

> 'the ideas came surging up in a crowd; I could feel them jostling each other until two of them would lock together, so to speak, and form a stable combination. By morning I had established the existence of a class of Fuchsian functions.' 'I now wished to represent these functions by the quotient of two series; this idea was fully conscious and reflective. . . . I asked myself what should be the properties of these series if they existed.' He goes on, 'at this point I left Caen, where I was then living, to take part in a geological expedition undertaken by the School of Mines. The events of the journey drove my mathematical work from my mind; but, arriving at Coutances, we were getting into an omnibus for some excursion or other when, at the moment of putting my foot on the step, and without anything, so far as I could see, in my previous thoughts to prepare me, it struck me that the transformations I had used to define the Fuchsian functions were identical with those of non-Euclidian geometry. I did not verify this; I had no time. Once seated in the omnibus, I resumed the conversation, but with a confidence sudden and complete.' His further progress in this field was of the same sort, an alternation of intense but apparently fruitless

---

[1] Cited in Carpenter, *Mental Physiology*, 537. This old book contains many interesting cases of the kind.

[2] Cited in Montmasson, *Invention and the Unconscious*, 77; italics mine.

application and sudden bursts of insight. 'It is needless to multiply instances; the reports I should have to make about my other researches would be entirely similar . . . the role of this unconscious work in mathematical invention seems to me incontestable.'[1]

Is there anything in such invention that is different in principle from the invention already discussed? I think not. In both cases intelligence moves in the same way; the only difference is in the division of labour between conscious and subconscious processes. And even here the difference is smaller than appears. Even in the most fully conscious reasoning much goes on behind the scenes. The identities that link the old with the new and carry us on to fresh perceptions usually operate underground and need an effort to bring them to light.

> All discovery', writes Mr. Joseph, 'is made unconsciously; we are conscious of it only when we have made it. Solutions come to us; but yet we find them. They are not given, like buns to a bear; it is the working of intelligence in us that reaches them. Not wrongly did Socrates compare the mind that thinks to a mother bringing children to the birth; and "as thou knowest not how the bones do grow in the womb of her that is with child", so the mind works in darkness until it is delivered.'[2]

4. The darkness that Mr. Joseph speaks of is a matter of degree; and not, as our examples may have suggested, a matter of mere blackness and mystery. It will be useful to distinguish

[1] *Science et Méthode*, 51–3.
[2] H. W. B. Joseph, *The Concept of Evolution*, 30. Cf. the following from Shelley: 'A great statue or picture grows under the power of the artist as a child in the mother's womb; and the very mind which directs the hands in formation is incapable of accounting to itself for the origin, the gradations, or the media of the process.'—*Defence of Poetry*. And cf. the following in lower key: 'If the reader will note down his line of thought after he has solved a problem which did not yield to customary forms of attack, he will find that his new ideas seemed to appear full fledged from the unconscious, and that the conscious self confined itself to the work of testing each idea as it became conscious.'—Saxby, *Psychology of the Thinker*, 68.

some of these degrees. Sometimes the mechanism works so near the surface that if we are not at the moment conscious of it we can become so by shifting attention; thus the man on the ferry-boat who identifies the pole on the prow as a pointer can see that what has been working is an identity between this and other pointers, whose use and relation to the eye are roughly similar. In a second class of cases, while the final steps seem fully conscious, they are reached by hidden stepping-stones which introspection would not reveal and which can be brought to light only by special methods. Thus one of Dr. Prince's patients, a lady who has been trying to translate a difficult passage in Virgil, suddenly finds her problem solved. She does not know how she has solved it, but when placed under hypnosis and asked to recall the preceding events she is able to bring them back. She reports that though the problem was put aside, it 'still remains in the secondary consciousness' and there gathers a set of associates in the way of 'fragmentary memories', 'different meanings of words in the passage, in fact, anything I had read, or thought, or experienced in connection with the problem'. These are not themselves the solution, and they contain much that is irrelevant, but they provide the raw material from which a solution may be framed. 'Later when my waking consciousness thinks of the problem again, these fragmentary thoughts of my secondary consciousness arise in my mind, and with this information I complete the translation. The actual translation is put together by my waking consciousness.'[1] It is natural to ask how such memories can be tested; how are we to prove that these latent processes actually did go on? In many cases this is impossible; in others effective checks can be devised; and suffice it to say that often their results leave little doubt about the accuracy of the reports.[2]

In a third type of case, still more of the process is buried. It is not only the materials used that remain hidden, but also the process of inference, so that the conclusion emerges as from the darkness of a cave. Fortunately the cave is not beyond

[1] Morton Prince, *The Unconscious*, 172–3.
[2] See, e.g., *ibid.*, Chap. III and pp. 164 ff.

exploration. Thanks chiefly to Freud and his followers, a good deal is now known about it. Indeed the literature is so large and familiar which describes how irrational beliefs and fears may spring from memories repressed but active, how these memories may be brought to light, and how, once they are brought to light, the beliefs and fears may disintegrate, that illustrations, for all their interest, are hardly needed. What does need to be said is that the work of the subconscious is by no means confined to the irrational, though the preoccupation of the psycho-analysts with diseased conditions might lead one to suppose that it is. The secondary consciousness is as truly capable of straightforward inference as it is of wild associations. It is possible, for example, to assign to the secondary consciousness of a subject under hypnosis the task of solving a mathematical problem after the subject has awakened, and of reporting the solution at a specified time. A solution both prompt and correct may be presented, though the subject is unaware that he has been engaged on a problem at all. The method he pursued in solving it may then be recovered hypnotically.

But there is apparently a fourth and deeper degree of darkness in which reasoning may go on. This is to be found when those processes that come to light in secondary consciousness are themselves but symbols of a further process, to which we can hardly refuse the name of inference, since it gets the required conclusion, but which remains beyond the reach of any methods so far devised. For example, processes of inference underlie some dreams, but the irrational play of the images that make up the 'manifest content' is not itself the reasoning process; that lies deeper, and is often if not always inaccessible. When one of Dr. Prince's patients, as a result of hypnotic suggestion, had arrived subconsciously at the product of 453×6, and was pressed to recall the method, she could only report an odd coming and going of visualized figures, which now added themselves, now subtracted, and went on with this random behaviour until suddenly the result stood before her. It is plain that this succession of images was not all there was to the thought; they can only be taken as the indications in a secondary consciousness of a process that was buried more deeply still.[1]

5. It is happily no part of our task to discuss the relations between these levels, the methods of probing them, or the differences in their nature. We shall confine ourselves to one point of not a little theoretical interest and still greater practical interest, namely, In what way and to what extent can subconscious thinking be controlled? No one is yet in a position to answer this finally, but it is safe to say that anyone who availed himself fully of the limited knowledge we have would enormously increase the effectiveness of his thinking. The chief ways in which control may be exercised are the following.

6. (1) Normally, and other things equal, practice reduces attention and effort; mere familiarity makes thinking easier. On one side there is no more than the law of habit. As practice continues, we find that any complex activity like piano-playing or typewriting can be more and more left to the subconscious without loss of speed or accuracy.

'The great thing, then, in all education', writes James, 'is to make our nervous system our ally instead of our enemy. It is to fund and capitalize our acquisitions, and live at ease upon the interest of the fund. . . . The more of the details of our daily life we can hand over to the effortless custody of automatism,

[1] *Ibid.*, 170. As to dreams, Dr. S. Herbert writes: 'The dream is, generally speaking, incapable of rendering intellectual processes and logical relations. In this respect it is like a kind of ancient picture writing in which only the main ideas are represented by pictured signs, the grammatical and logical relations being implied.'—*The Unconscious Mind*, 57. As to the range of performance possible in these subconscious or co-conscious processes, cf. the following: 'The automatic script that describes the memories of a long-forgotten childhood may at the same time reason, indulge in jests, rhyme, express cognition and understanding of questions—indeed (if put to the test), might not only pass a Binet-Simon examination for intelligence, but take a high rank in a Civil Service examination.'—Prince, *ibid.*, 153.

the more our higher powers of mind will be set free for their own proper work.' And he continues in a way that must have heartened many a student: 'Nothing we ever do is, in strict literalness, wiped out. Let no youth have any anxiety about the upshot of his education, whatever the line of it may be. If he keep faithfully busy each hour of the working day, he may safely leave the final result to itself. He can with perfect certainty count on waking up some fine morning to find himself one of the competent ones of his generation.'[1]

It is not merely that practice makes perfect; it is also that practice has secret allies who take over part of the labour of instruction, so that, as James puts it in another well-known passage, we learn to swim in winter and skate in summer. The impetus given by effort goes on when effort ceases, and on coming back to the work we find, after the first brief period of adjustment is over, that we are farther along than we knew.

So it is in the practice of thinking. Most of the problems we have to face are of a type we have dealt with again and again, and as we have done so, our handling of them has become more and more automatic. The bank-teller can add his columns, the grocer fill his orders, even the judge pass rulings on petty cases, with little of the effort or attention he had to bestow on them at first, and this without relaxing in the least his grasp of their detail. It may seem impossible that the teller should run down his column as fast as he does and still have noted all the figures; indeed at the end he may have no memory that he did note certain ones; but the correctness of his result shows that he must have taken account of them. Of course as one turns to problems of new type one cannot rely so largely on this help from the subconscious. But even there it is considerable. We have admitted, to be sure, that there are no rules whose application will solve our problems generally; and we concede to the full that proficiency in one field, say classics, will not guarantee like proficiency in some very different field, say art or mathematics. But it is as idle to say that thought in these various fields has nothing in common as to say that it is precisely the same. The thinker with a thorough discipline

[1] *Principles of Psychology*, I. 122, 127.

in one department may carry into another the same style of attack—the same care in defining the problem, the same patience in gathering evidence, the same orderliness in disposing of it, the same resistance to snap conclusions. There is such a thing as logical habit. It need not be acquired through the study of logic itself, though it may be. On these points John Stuart Mill, by reason of his extraordinary training, his much reflection on it, and his achievement in consequence of it, has a peculiar claim to be heard. Concerning the study of formal logic, he says:

'I know of nothing in my education to which I think myself more indebted for whatever capacity of thinking I have attained. The first intellectual operation in which I arrived at any proficiency was dissecting a bad argument, and finding in what part the fallacy lay: and though whatever capacity of this sort I attained was due to the fact that it was an intellectual exercise in which I was most perseveringly drilled by my father, yet it is also true that the school logic, and the mental habits acquired in studying it, were among the principal instruments of this drilling. I am persuaded that nothing in modern education tends so much, when properly used, to form exact thinkers. . . .'[1]

7. But it is not merely logical habits that may be subconsciously carried over; it is also the mass of consciously accumulated knowledge. The fact has long been known that details of early life which have gone completely from normal memory may come flooding back in delirium; Sir William Hamilton, a century ago, collected some striking instances.[2]

[1] *Autobiography*, 11. In a recent popular book one reads: 'Often, skill in one type of work overlaps with that required in another utterly different activity. A former doctor recently told me how he had applied the principle of medical diagnosis to reorganizing a receivership and bankruptcy office. He studied every job, made a list of every unfavourable symptom in organization or method, arrived at principles of reorganization, and finally prescribed the necessary changes in equipment and procedure. His skill in medical diagnosis contributed greatly to his success in the receivership job.'—Pitkin, *More Power to You*, 247. There is no reason to doubt this.
[2] *Lectures on Metaphysics*, Chap. XVIII.

But it has remained for our own day to show that even in normal minds these memories remain in abundance, though at a secondary level, and colour the main stream of consciousness. There are those who hold that we never quite forget anything. It is needless to go so far, however, in order to realize the importance for thinking of the new discoveries. They imply that experience is more truly cumulative than the narrow bounds of conscious memory would lead us to believe. They imply that we are wiser than we know; that the knowledge we gained with such effort and lost so swiftly is in an important sense still available and still used. We have seen already that in the perceptual judgement of the skilled critic far more is represented than the critic himself can put into words or give any adequate account of. His judgement is the deposit of his relevant experience as a whole; and if his experience is a scholarly one, he may write, as Mr. Eliot suggests, 'not merely with his own generation in his bones', but with 'the whole of the literature of Europe', so far as he knows it, exerting its influence on his perceptions.[1] It would be surprising if what is so valuable to the critic should be valueless to the creator, since criticism of one's own suggestions is so important a part of the process of thought. And besides serving as a court of appraisal for suggestions already risen, one's latent store of impressions serves at once as source and censor for these suggestions before they arise. Variety of retained experience means range of available analogy, and this, as we saw, while not the essence of invention, is a very valuable aid to it. As for censorship, the control exerted by retained experience, promoting candidates that have been found promising and thwarting others, is a matter of common knowledge. The farther we go in any field, the more point there is in our thinking and the less irrelevancy.

[1] *The Sacred Wood*, 49. Cf. the passage from Wordsworth's preface to *Lyrical Ballads*: 'Poems to which any value can be attached were never produced on any variety of subjects but by a man who, being possessed of more than usual organic sensibility, had also thought long and deeply', etc.

8. Once it is seen how a volume of past experience, while remaining itself behind the scenes, can invest a present judgement with its plenary authority, much that has been mysterious in mystic intuition becomes intelligible. Professor Montague seems clearly right that 'it is from the subconscious stores of memory and instinct that the intuitive judgement is derived'.[1] The fact of its being intuitive, that is, directly seen as true without awareness of grounds, shows nothing about its truth or falsity; it may show only a lack of skill in making the grounds of belief explicit. There is reason to think that between different minds there is much variation in the manner and ease of interplay between conscious and subconscious levels. In some minds the hidden self is remarkably rich and productive, remarkably able to assemble the spoils of its past campaigns, to work them over profitably, and present them as fresh and new to the upper consciousness; and yet the same mind, when called on to defend its position through dialectical thrust and parry, may be singularly helpless. Emerson is an example. The appeal of Emerson is less to the abstract intelligence than to the mind as a whole. One feels in reading him that these rhythms and these thought-connections, superficially so loose, yet felt as coherent fundamentally, are not so much the product of explicit reasoning as of forces that used the conscious self as their voice or instrument. Certainly this was Emerson's own view.

> 'When I watch that flowing river, which, out of regions I see not, pours for a season its streams into me,—I see that I am a pensioner,—not a cause but a surprised spectator of this ethereal water; that I desire and look up and put myself in the attitude of reception, but from some alien energy the visions come.'[2]

There was nothing tentative in the announcement of his doctrines; they came to him as compulsory, and he reported them with something of the air of a prophet; but he admits

[1] *Ways of Knowing*, 66. Galton (*Inquiries*, 148) and others have expressed similar views.   [2] *The Over-Soul.*

that if a school-boy were to ask him *why* he accepted them he could render at best but a stumbling account.[1] Does this reduce their weight? Not necessarily. It does reduce the cogency of Emerson for one to whom they do not appeal at once as true and who insists on having the argument; but our point here is that a mind may reach a true conclusion, and one that is based on extensive evidence, while quite unable to adduce this evidence on call. This is not to say that the capacity for formal argument is worthless or indeed anything but valuable in the extreme, but it is to insist that formal argument is not the only means by which sound conclusions can be reached. Mr. A. C. Ewing, in discussing the conspicuous chasm between the 'Cambridge school' of philosophers and the idealist tradition, ventures to remark 'that the former argues better but that the latter arrives at wiser conclusions'.[2] Whether one agrees as to the fact or not (the present writer does agree), one must admit that wisdom and argumentative adroitness are not the same thing.

9. Now what holds in high degree of the mystic, and, one may perhaps add, the poet and the artist, holds in lesser degree of the rest of us. We are called upon continually to deal with problems whose factors are far too numerous to be brought at once within the focus of consciousness; and when we try to reckon with these explicitly and attach definite weights to them, we may find ourselves constrained, as Spencer did when thinking about his prospective move to New Zealand,[3] to flout conscious decisions.

'The supreme issues of life are settled for us, all the way up and down the scale, by unreasoned adjustments, by intents rather than contents of consciousness, by value-responses which far overflow any knowledge explanation which we can give. It may, I think, be said, that all great work, all work which has

[1] This was not mere modesty. See, e.g., Stratton and Buckham, *G. H. Howison*, 54.
[2] *Idealism*, 2.　　　　　　　[3] Above, Chap. VI, Sec. 16.

the touch of genius on it, comes from persons who in special degrees draw upon this matrix consciousness. Such persons often feel as though a Power not themselves were working through them; as though, without tension and effort, the creation at which they are working was "given" to them or "brought" to them.'[1]

For both Rufus Jones and Emerson the active agent in the subconscious may be more than psychological; on occasion it is a 'Power not ourselves', an 'Over-Soul'. To some readers such a doctrine will be too 'tenderminded', too speculative and visionary to be seriously entertained. And certainly the invoking of the supernatural to explain the effortless as such would be mere indolence or superstition. But then this is not the meaning of such writers. And it is needless to go into that meaning in detail to recognize that our own view has something in common with it. Our view, so often repeated, is that thought in its very nature is the affirmation through the mind of that system which is truth, the realization, in degree and partially always, of a purpose whose fulfilment would be truth complete. And since identical laws govern our thinking and an identical end is at work in all of us, since the very existence of universals implies community in our objects, we have argued that the apparent severance between our minds does not in strictness hold, and that one identical mind is finding expression through them. 'The greater the spiritual activity within a man, the less is he able to ascribe this activity to himself.'[2] If this is mysticism, then our doctrine is mystical. But what tests the presence of the immanent intelligence is no psychological test; it is not involuntariness, or ease of production, or any rapt or ecstatic feeling; it is the test of inherent worth, the objective and logical test of intelligible order. So far as that is achieved, mind on its intellectual side has come to expression through us; so far as it is not, we are still in 'chaos and old night'.

It is thus a mistake to take subconsciousness, because there

---

[1] Rufus Jones, *Studies in Mystical Religion*, xxiv.
[2] A. C. Bradley, *A Miscellany*, 236.

is something mysterious about it, as the one source of inspiration. Inspiration is judged by its fruits, not by its roots. An insight arrived at by conscious reflection is not the less inspired because it is conscious; nor is the voluble incoherence of automatic speech or writing to be taken as inspiration because it springs from deeps that are imperfectly known. By the same token, one is not robbing the subconscious of any legitimate dignity in saying that it builds with the bricks of experience; creation always does this. To point this out is not to explain creation, still less to explain it away. In the last resort the only way in which invention can be explained is to show that it has followed the track of intelligence, that it has been governed by the implicit necessities of the whole it sought to construct; and the path of necessity is the same whether it runs through daylight or twilight or the dark. Thus the interest of our present discussion is less explanatory than practical. Recognizing that the path of creation does often dip down into the subconscious, we are asking how thought can be kept in that path, even when it winds off into the mist.

10. (2) The first suggestion was an extremely general one: we are contributing to the character of the subconscious whenever we do anything at all. Whenever we think, whenever we attend to anything, we are adding to our secondary selves some element of discipline or capital. In their sum, these increments are of great moment, but of course they give no help in solving one problem rather than another. Our next question must be whether the conscious self can so control the subconscious as to set it to work along a special line. The answer is that it can. It may, with marked success, commit its conscious concern to the subconscious to be elaborated, or its problem to be solved.

Now it may do this with very different degrees of definiteness. (i) It may pursue some special interest in the hope of generating creative activity, but with no particular problem before it. (ii) If it does bring a particular problem, it may leave this undefined, formulating it only in general terms or blocking out only roughly the whole it is intent on creating. Or finally (iii) before committing the problem to the subconscious it may specify it as far as it can. Each method has its own reward.

11. (i) First as to the furtherance in subconsciousness of a special interest. There is a sense in which all attention reflects special interest, for attention is always selective. And if we tend to retain whatever we attend to, our 'mnemic mass' must accumulate at an almost portentous rate, since it is known that some degree of attention is given even to extremely marginal impressions. Indeed this rapid increase seems to be the fact. We may attend to something so feebly as to be unaware of having heeded it, though clear proof may be forthcoming later that we both noticed and retained it. Such proof was a favourite employment of Morton Prince.

> 'For instance, to cite one out of numerous examples, on one occasion I saw her (one of his patients, a Miss B.) pass by in the street while I was standing on the door-step of a house some fifteen or twenty feet away, well outside the line of her central vision. She was in a brown study. I called to her three times saying, "Good morning, Miss B.", laying the accent each time on a different word. She did not hear me, and later had no recollection of the episode. In hypnosis she recalled the circumstances accurately, and reproduced my words with the accents properly placed.'[1]

If attention as feeble as this will print an experience in memory, it is hard to set any limit to what may become subconscious capital. But of one point there can be no doubt. What is attended to intently and explicitly is far more likely to remain in such manner as to be usable. If Dr. Prince's patient had heard the greetings with a full and explicit awareness, she could have recalled them the next day without any such desperate recourse as an appeal to hypnosis. But even these explicitly

[1] *The Unconscious*, 56.

grasped details would not long have retained their vividness; the incident was too ordinary, too lacking in special significance or special interest. The value of such interest is, first, that it fixes our attention on some particular class of facts, secondly that by means of this attention it fixes the facts in memory. And it serves a third and further purpose. A strong interest in a set of facts is never an interest in those facts merely; it carries with it an interest in the relations of those facts. The artist is interested in details, but still more perhaps in their harmonies. The botanist wants facts, but largely as an aid to his classifications. It is impossible to take an interest in such facts without dwelling on their relations. Now as consciousness is bent, so is subconsciousness inclined. When the upper self is dominated by a strong and special interest, the lower self takes it up and carries it on, as a fly-wheel takes up the motion of a suddenly stopping engine. It digests and assimilates, combines and rearranges, much as the upper self would do if it were at work on the same matter. Our first point about the subconscious was that whatever we attend to makes some difference to our latent capital. Our present point is that an intense and special interest not only determines our type of stored goods; it may greatly further its own ends by making deliberate use of this fly-wheel of the mind. Let us see how this has actually been done.

12. George Eliot once remarked to Herbert Spencer that, considering the thinking he had done, she was surprised to see no lines in his forehead. 'I suppose', answered Spencer, 'it is because I am never puzzled.' 'Oh that's the most arrogant thing I ever heard uttered', she exclaimed. To which the philosopher rejoined, 'Not at all, when you know what I mean.' He went on to say what he meant, and it is so pertinent to our point that I give it here at some length:

> 'It has never been my way to set before myself a problem and puzzle out an answer. The conclusions at which I have from time to time arrived have not been arrived at as solutions of

questions raised; but have been arrived at unawares—each as the ultimate outcome of a body of thoughts which slowly grew from a germ. Some direct observation, or some fact met with in reading, would dwell with me: apparently because I had a sense of its significance. It was not that there arose a distinct consciousness of its general meaning; but rather that there was a kind of instinctive interest in those facts which have general meanings. For example, the detailed structure of this or that species of mammal, though I might willingly read about it, would leave little impression; but when I met with the statement that, almost without exception, mammals, even as unlike as the whale and the giraffe, have seven cervical vertebrae, this would strike me and be remembered as suggestive. Apt as I thus was to lay hold of cardinal truths, it would happen occasionally that one, most likely brought to mind by an illustration, and gaining from the illustration fresh distinctness, would be contemplated by me for a while, and its bearings observed. A week afterwards, possibly, the matter would be remembered; and with further thought about it, might occur a recognition of some wider application than I had before perceived: new instances being aggregated with those already noted. . . . When accumulation of instances had given body to a generalization, reflection would reduce the vague conception at first framed to a more definite conception. . . . Eventually the growing generalization, thus far inductive, might take a deductive form: being all at once recognized as a necessary consequence of some physical principle—some established law. And thus, little by little, in unobtrusive ways, without conscious intention or appreciable effort, there would grow up a coherent and organized theory. Habitually the process was one of slow unforced development, often extending over years; and it was, I believe, because the thinking done went on in this gradual, almost spontaneous way, without strain, that there was an absence of those lines of thought which Miss Evans remarked—an absence almost as complete thirty years later, notwithstanding the amount of thinking done in the interval.'[1]

Now whatever one's view may be of the quality of the 'thinking done in the interval', one must agree that its quantity was extraordinary, and that its production in this effortless way is a striking witness of the value of incubation in reflective thinking.

[1] *Autobiography*, I. 399–401.

13. A different kind of testimony, but one that is in some ways more impressive still, has been supplied by Professor Lowes. In *The Road to Xanadu* he has shown how the impressions of Coleridge's multifarious reading lived on and combined and germinated to produce the *Ancient Mariner* and *Kubla Khan*. By running down every clue in Coleridge's notebook, by ransacking the books he read, and by pursuing fugitive references to other and still other forgotten works, Professor Lowes placed himself in possession of an enormous store of matter that Coleridge himself had been engaged upon. The result is a proof too circumstantial to be doubted that images and phrases which in these two great poems seem to be made for each other and to belong organically to just these poetic wholes, were pieced together from Coleridge's reading. It is not that he did the reading in order to write the poems. Many of the things he read were as unlikely as old ragbags to produce anything of value. The point is that his mind, at the time he reviewed these things, was pledged and abandoned to poetry; whether he knew it or not, he was alert, in all he read, for the fine image and the telling phrase. And thus 'the unique value of the Note Book lies in the insight which it affords us into the polarizing quality of a poet's reading—a reading in which the mind moved, like the passing of a magnet, over pages to all seeming as bare of poetic implications as a parallelogram, and drew and held fixed whatever was susceptible of imaginative transmutation'.[1] He had stored up such abundance of the material of poetry that when he set about writing consciously the phrases and images came crowding to his pen.

Indeed they came crowding without benefit of conscious design. The story of Kubla Khan is enough to show that in a well-stored mind, intent upon creation, the auxiliary self does not always wait for explicit orders; it may borrow the design unobserved and proceed to build for itself. Though the story is familiar, it is so clear and classic an instance of subconscious invention that we give the gist of it as Coleridge

[1] *The Road to Xanadu*, 34.

tells it. The author, he says, had been ill and had taken an anodyne;

> 'he fell asleep in his chair at the moment that he was reading the following sentence, or words of the same substance, in *Purchas's Pilgrimage*: "Here the Khan Kubla commanded a palace to be built, and a stately garden thereunto. And thus ten miles of fertile ground were inclosed with a wall." The author continued for about three hours in a profound sleep, at least of the external senses, during which time he has the most vivid confidence, that he could not have composed less than from two to three hundred lines; if that indeed can be called composition in which all the images rose up before him as *things*, with a parallel production of the corresponding expressions, without any sensation or consciousness of effort. On awaking he appeared to himself to have a distinct recollection of the whole, and taking his pen, ink, and paper, instantly and eagerly wrote down the lines that are here preserved. At this moment he was unfortunately called out by a person on business from Porlock, and detained by him above an hour, and on his return to his room, found, to his no small surprise and mortification, that though he still retained some vague and dim recollection of the general purport of the vision, yet, with the exception of some eight or ten scattered lines and images, all the rest had passed away like the images on the surface of a stream in which a stone has been cast. . . .'[1]

Here it was the last lurking images as sleep descended that gave the cue to the creative process. But they did not themselves give the order that set the lower looms at work, or supervise their weaving. What they did was to supply a bright bit of fabric which the secondary self took up and wove into a pattern of its own. Yet it would be wrong to say that the pattern was exclusively its own. No explicit orders to follow a special course seem to have come from the conscious self, but we cannot believe that what Coleridge called 'the streamy nature of association, which thinking curbs and rudders' was here completely rudderless. His upper mind in those days seems, as we have said, to have been peopled with bright imagery and haunted by floating melodies, indeed to have been in something like that continuous poetic excitement in which we are told

[1] *Complete Poetical Works*, ed. by E. H. Coleridge, I. 296.

The Shropshire Lad was written.[1] And this in itself in some instances gives 'curb and rudder' enough. To be sure it guides with a looser hand. Because less exacting logically, it gives freer play to rhythm. In the incoherence of thought on the one side, and on the other the victorious surging stride in which logical crevasses are taken we find the special mark of the dream, whether in prose or in verse.[2] The subconscious self takes over more easily from above the patterns of rhythm than those of reason; it has often proved able, as in *Kubla Khan* and in the gorgeous dreams of De Quincey, to pick up a complex rhythm and, by selection, trimming, and furbishing, to fashion a chaos into accord with it. In such cases the pattern indeed comes from the conscious; but it is pilfered from it rather than prescribed by it.[3]

[1] Lowes, *Ibid.*, 598; A. E. Housman, *Last Poems*, Preface.

[2] Cf. Professor Saintsbury: 'It has, I have no doubt, occurred to other students of elaborate rhythmical prose that curiously large proportions of the most famous examples of it are concerned with dreams. . . . Dreams themselves are nothing if not rhythmical; their singular fashion of progression (it is matter of commonest remark) floats the dreamer over the most irrational and impossible transitions and junctures (or rather breaches) of incident and subject, without jolt or jar. They thus combine . . . the greatest possible *variety* with the least possible *disturbance*. Now this combination . . . is the very soul —the quintessence, the constituting form and idea—of harmonious prose' (*History of English Prose Rhythm*, 311). This is *à propos* of De Quincey, but as Saintsbury points out, it could be illustrated from Landor, Kingsley, Ruskin, Pater, and many another master of imaginative prose.

Whether the following observation of the Abbé Dimnet is correct I am less sure, but I add it for its interest: 'Some rhythms—taking the word in its fullest meaning—keep the writer nearer his subconsciousness than any other. You will feel it in Mr. Belloc's books, even if the author does not tell you, as he once admitted to me, that Homer is the only novelist he reads. You will feel it in Barrès' best Book, *La Colline Inspirée*, about which I also had the author's own testimony. The habit of working on such a rhythm results in an almost physical sensation informing us that we are drawing on our innermost.'—*The Art of Thinking*, 201.

[3] Cases in some ways similar, though less cut off from ordinary consciousness, are those of William Sharp, who, in his secondary personality, as 'Fiona Macleod,' at times 'would sweep aside all conscious control' and 'write at good speed, hardly aware of what, or

14. (ii) But such creation is rare, and the more so as one passes from constructions in which the artificer is imagination to those in which it is intellect. Even in art, however, the normal type is not *Kubla Khan* but *The Ancient Mariner*, that is, a construction in which the secondary self is guided by a conscious and explicit design. It is true that beneath this poem also lie

> 'innumerable blendings and fusings of impressions, brought about below the level of conscious mental processes'. 'But the poem is not the confluence of unconsciously merging images, as a pool of water forms from the coalescence of scattered drops; nor is the poet a somnambulist in a subliminal world. . . . On the contrary, every impression, every new creature rising from the potent waters of the Well, is what it now is through its participation in a *whole*, foreseen as a whole in each integral part—a whole which is the working out of a controlling imaginative design. . . . And that form is the handiwork of choice, and a directing intelligence, and the sweat of a forging brain.' 'And over the throng of luminous impressions and their subliminal confluences "broods like the Day, a Master o'er a Slave", the compelling power of the design.' 'Whatever their origin, the component images have been wrought into conformity with a setting determined by the conception which constructs the poem.' 'For through that wavering inconstant flow has moved a controlling, conscious energy, accepting, rejecting, moulding them into keeping with each other and with a lucidly conceived design.'[1]

how, he wrote'; and of William Blake, who said of his poem *Milton and Jerusalem*, 'I have written the poem from immediate dictation . . . without premeditation, and even against my will'.

[1] Lowes, *ibid.*, 304–7. Professor Lowes's contrast between the modes of production of the two poems seems a little too sharp. He says of the *Kubla Khan*, 'the sole factor that determined the form and sequence which the dissolving phantasmagoria assumed, was the subtle potency of the associative links' (401). We have held, on the contrary, that what operates in true invention is necessity, that this, whether logical or aesthetic, is quite different from association, and that it may control subconscious processes. *Kubla Khan* gives perhaps as clear a case of aesthetic necessity as the Poincaré example gives of logical necessity. In view of Professor Lowes's remarks on 'the finished, even cunning, craftsmanship' of the poem (597–8; cf. also Stevenson on the same poem, *Some Technical Elements of Style in Literature*), we can only believe that if the meanings of certain words were cleared up we should have his support.

15. This process, in which conscious design is a guide and control for subconscious process, is far commoner than that in which the product is thrown up by the subterranean waters on their own motion alone. 'For the true poet—as Goethe has somewhere said—the melody of his coming poem floats as a self-created and impalpable entity within him, before words have shaped themselves. . . .'[1] The composition of one of Goethe's own works, as he describes it, illustrates well the comparative effectiveness of the two methods for most minds. For some years in his youth he was given to a sentimental melancholy; he surrendered himself to the 'graveyard schools' of poetry; he fancied himself as a young Hamlet, awake to the vanity and hollowness of life; he reflected much on suicide, and laid nightly by his bed a polished dagger against the time when the burden of existence should become insupportable. But with his essentially healthy mind he knew that this was a morbid state and decided to pull himself out of it. In a passage with a Freudian ring he writes:

> 'In order to gain this end serenely I felt it necessary to carry through some literary work in which everything I had felt, thought, and dreamed on this important topic (suicide) should come to expression. To this end I gathered the ideas together that had been vegetating in my mind for some years; I presented to myself with all vividness the circumstances that had most oppressed and distressed me. But nothing would take shape; an event was needed, a plot, in which they might be embodied.'

Out of such mere brooding Coleridge might have produced something, but hardly Goethe. The needed guidance was soon and tragically supplied by a young friend named Jerusalem who did actually take his own life.

> 'Suddenly I heard the news of Jerusalem's death; and dogging the steps of gossip there came the most exact and circumstantial account of what led up to it. At this instant the plan of *Werther* stood revealed; the whole shot together from all sides and became a solid mass, just as water in a vessel, which has stood at the point of freezing will be converted in an instant and with

[1] Myers, *op. cit.*, I. 101–2.

the slightest shaking into solid ice.' The composition, after this, offered little difficulty. 'I wrote *Werther* in four weeks without the design of the whole or the arrangement of any part having been previously put on paper', and 'somewhat unconsciously like a sleep-walker'.[1]

16. This way of dividing the labour, the conscious self supplying the scheme, the subconscious its development, can be exemplified almost endlessly from the practice and precepts of creators in the arts. Henry James, for example, describes how in writing *The American* he took his main idea, and 'dropped it for the time into the deep well of unconscious cerebration: not without the hope, doubtless, that it might eventually emerge from that reservoir, as one had already known the buried treasure to come to light, with a firm iridescent surface and a notable increase of weight'.[2] Such help from below was a topic to which Oliver Wendell Holmes recurred again and again in his writings.

> 'I question whether persons who think most—that is, have most conscious thought pass through their minds—necessarily do most mental work. The tree you are sticking in "will be growing when you are sleeping". So with every new idea that is planted in a real thinker's mind: it will be growing when he is least conscious of it. An idea in the brain is not a legend carved on a marble slab: it is an impression made on a living tissue, which is the seat of active nutritive processes. Shall the initials I carved in bark increase from year to year with the tree? and shall not my recorded thought develop into new forms and relations with my growing brain?'[3]

A graphic brief description of the process is given by Dryden, who in presenting his play, *The Rival Ladies*, to a patron, wrote that it 'was designed you, long before it was a play; when it was only a confused mass of thoughts, tumbling over one another in the dark: when the fancy was yet in its first

[1] *Dichtung und Wahrheit*, Buch XIII, *Werke* (Kurz), IX. 502.
[2] Quoted by Lowes, *ibid.*, 480.
[3] From his *Mechanism in Thought and Morals*, quoted by Carpenter, *op. cit.*, 534; see also the *Autocrat*, Chap. V. 6.

work, moving the sleeping images of things towards the light,
there to be distinguished, and then either chosen or rejected
by the judgment'.[1] Stevenson has left an account of how,
when a story was brewing in his mind, he could commit the
theme of it to his 'Brownies', who would elaborate it for him in
sleep. The distinguished classical scholar Wilamowitz-
Moellendorff used the same method in some of his researches.
'That the spirit goes on working in sleep, many will have
experienced; I have often put it to the proof, learning by heart
a passage I did not understand, or a strophe of a chorus which
would not scan, that I might accomplish the task when fully
or half asleep.'[2] Henry Ward Beecher, whose variety and
effectiveness as a popular preacher were exceeded only by his
almost incredible output—we are told that he once preached
daily 'through eighteen consecutive months, without the
exception of a single day'[3]—used to keep a number of themes
ripening at once in the cellars of his mind; early in the week
he would select one that seemed particularly well advanced,
attend to it a while expressly, and commit it again to the
cellar. On Sunday morning there was a mass of material ready
to his hand and he would sketch out the whole with great
speed.[4]

[1] Quoted by Lowes, *ibid.*, 63.   [2] *My Recollections*, 289.
[3] Brastow, *Representative Modern Preachers*, 121.
[4] One gathers that Walter Scott was something of a strategist in his
use of the subconscious. 'I lie *simmering* over things', he once remarked,
and if he failed to get hold of an idea he would sometimes say, 'Never
mind, I shall have it at seven o'clock tomorrow morning'. In Lock-
hart's *Scott*, VII. 143, there is a letter from a young man who had
served as an amanuensis to Sir Walter in the days when he was writing
from six to six daily. Of Scott's composing he says, 'it seemed to be
only the manual part of the operation that occasioned him any inconve-
nience'. When he dictated, 'his thoughts flowed easily and felicitously,
without any difficulty to lay hold of them or to find appropriate
language; which was evident by the absence of all solicitude (*miseria
cogitandi*) from his countenance. He sat in his chair, from which he
rose now and then, took a volume from the bookcase, consulted it,
and restored it to the shelf—all without intermission in the current of
ideas, which continued to be delivered with no less readiness than if
his mind had been wholly occupied with the words he was uttering.
It soon became apparent to me, however, that he was carrying on two

In many cases this process can hardly be distinguished from another. In this other process, instead of consciousness supplying the framework, and subconsciousness filling it in, consciousness supplies a litter of fragments and leaves it to the lower self to introduce order among them. Since we have used a pulpit example for the first type, we will follow it with a similar example from the other side of the line. A 'distinguished prelate' wrote:

> 'I am frequently asked, as you may suppose, to preach *occasional* sermons; and when I have undertaken any such duty, I am in the habit of sitting down and thinking over the topics I wish to introduce, without in the first instance endeavouring to frame them into any consistent scheme. I then put aside my sketch for a time, and give my mind to some *altogether different subject*; and when I come to write my sermon, perhaps a week or two afterwards, I very commonly find that the topics I have set down have *arranged themselves*, so that I can at once apply myself to develope them on a plan in which they then present themselves before me.'[1]

Every teacher who has repeated a 'course' knows how mastery grows with repetition. It is not merely that the matter has grown more familiar to him, but that it has sent out tendrils of connection and woven itself into the context of his ideas, so that it admits of readier illustration, and altogether seems more real to him; as James says, 'the power of judging in all that class of matter will have built itself up within him'. 'Put an idea into your intelligence and leave it there an hour, a day, a year, without ever having occasion to refer to it. When at last you return to it, you do not find it as it was when acquired. It has domiciliated itself, so to speak—become at home—

distinct trains of thought, one of which was already arranged and in the act of being spoken, while at the same time he was in advance considering what was afterwards to be said. This I discovered by his sometimes introducing a word which was wholly out of place—*entertained* instead of *denied*, for example—but which I presently found to belong to the next sentence, perhaps four or five lines farther on, which he had been preparing at the very moment that he gave me the words of the one that preceded it.'

[1] Carpenter, *op. cit.*, 533; italics in original.

entered into relations with your other thoughts, and integrated itself with the whole fabric of the mind.'[1]

17. (iii) Most of our instances so far have been drawn from minds of genius, the 'quarto and folio editions of mankind'. It is part of the endowment of such minds to be able to attend with absorption, to retain firmly, and to redeem their mental pledges with easy and lavish drafts on the subconscious. But is anything like this possible to the uninspired majority? Certainly not on the same scale; the capital of most of us is too meagre and too inaccessible. It is courting disillusion to suppose that because in the head of Goethe or Stevenson or Beecher the plot of a novel or the sketch of an address completed itself in this effortless fashion, it will do likewise in our own.

Yet many make this mistake. They have not discovered the right ratio of effort and automatism for their own thinking. 'There are thousands of idle "geniuses" who require to learn that, without some degree of industry in Preparation and Verification, of which many of them have no conception, no great intellectual work can be done, and that the habit of procrastination may be even more disastrous to a professional thinker than it is to a man of business.'[2] It is no doubt to this third type of thinker, who requires much conscious effort to get the best from his subconscious, that the larger number of us belong. What form should this effort take?

We may reach the answer by inference. The outstanding minds, as we have seen, obey the same laws as our own; they

[1] Holmes, *The Autocrat*, 128–9. Professor Lowes, who also quotes this passage, illustrates it by showing how his own subconsciousness played tricks with it in the thirty years between his first seeing it and his referring to it again.—*Xanadu*, 57.

[2] Graham Wallas, *The Art of Thought*, 88. Cf. Galton: 'Although the brain is able to do very fair work fluently in an automatic way, and though it will of its own accord strike out sudden and happy ideas, it is questionable if it is capable of working thoroughly and profoundly without past or present effort.'—*Inquiries into Human Faculty*, section on *Antechamber of Consciousness*.

differ in degree, not in kind. And in their thinking we have just distinguished two forms of conscious preparation, first the presenting of a conscious design which the subconscious is to follow; second, the gathering of conscious detail which the subconscious is to order. It is natural to infer that these same devices will serve the rest of us, but that as we go down the scale of spontaneous power, more will depend on conscious effort. What is suggested by inference is also impressed on us if we try to piece together suggestions from the pertinent literature. Of the writers last quoted, for example, each emphasizes one side of the matter. Graham Wallas insists on a question definitely formulated. 'Our mind is not likely to give us a clear answer to any particular problem unless we set it a clear question, and we are more likely to notice the significance of any new piece of evidence, or new association of ideas, if we have formed a definite conception of a case to be proved or disproved.'[1] Francis Galton emphasizes the other side, the setting out explicitly of such capital as we have already. 'The character of this effort seems to lie chiefly in bringing the contents of the antechamber more nearly within the ken of consciousness. . . .'[2] These two sides, express definition of the problem and express summoning of present resources, have both been dealt with already in the chapter on 'Specifying the Problem', but in this fresh context they are worth a little further notice.

18. (a) Properly speaking one cannot reflect simply about Napoleon or the Great Pyramid. One can form associations with them and spin day-dreams; but reflecting is an attempt to answer a question, and these are not questions. Taken thus in the large, any suggestion they may produce is as much or as little relevant as any other; relevance does not enter in. But

[1] *The Art of Thought*, 84.
[2] *Inquiries, ibid.* In the context, Galton seems to be describing the final stage of reasoning, but a little later he gives a similar account of the preparatory stage.

thinking is a struggle for relevance; it is an effort to surmount some difficulty; and if our suggestion is to avail, it must meet this difficulty specifically. Hence if our problem itself is unspecified we are leaving subconsciousness without guidance and consciousness with no measure of success. Let us convert the topic 'Great Pyramid' into the question, 'How was the Great Pyramid built?' and thinking can begin. Since even this question, however, covers more than we are really interested in, we shall have to specify it further, perhaps into 'How did the Egyptians, with no machinery driven by power, lift those great stone blocks some hundreds of feet?' Drop a query as definite as this into the question-box of the subconscious and there is some chance of getting an answer. But there will be no reply to a slip left blank.[1]

19. In one of Bertrand Russell's later books there is a bit of autobiography that shows the value of intense application in setting the lower processes at work.

> 'I have found', he says, 'that if I have to write upon some rather difficult topic the best plan is to think about it with very great intensity—the greatest intensity of which I am capable —for a few hours or days, and at the end of that time give orders, so to speak, that the work is to proceed underground. After some months I return consciously to the topic and find that the work has been done. Before I had discovered this technique, I used to spend the intervening months worrying because I was making no progress; I arrived at the solution none the sooner for this worry, and the intervening months were wasted, whereas now I can devote them to other pursuits.'[2]

The importance of thus thinking on one's problem with 'the greatest intensity of which one is capable' is stressed also by Poincaré. Unconscious work is 'impossible', he says, 'or at least unfruitful, unless it is both preceded and followed by a period of conscious labour'. He reports that in his own case

[1] On specifying the problem, see Chap. XX above.
[2] *The Conquest of Happiness*, 75–6.

'sudden inspirations never occur except after days of voluntary effort which seemed quite fruitless', and points out that if such effort after all made a difference, it was because the ideas in the subconscious were selectively set in motion toward '*un but parfaitement déterminé*'.[1] Brahms makes the same report of his creative work in music. 'There is no real creating without hard work. That which you would call invention, that is to say, a thought, an idea, is simply an inspiration from above, for which I am not responsible, which is no merit of mine. Yet it is a present, a gift, which I ought even to despise until I have made it my own by right of hard work.'[2] Wallas even thinks that in the difference between Mill and Spencer on this point 'lies the chief cause which made Mill's thought, though done by a tired man after or before office hours, more valuable to mankind than Spencer's thought, though he gave his whole time to it'.[3] This difference lay in

> 'a mental habit,' to use Mill's words, 'to which I attribute all that I have ever done, or ever shall do, in speculation: that of never accepting half-solutions of difficulties as complete; never abandoning a puzzle, but again and again returning to it until it was cleared up; never allowing obscure corners of a subject to remain unexplored because they did not appear important; never thinking that I perfectly understood any part of a subject until I understood the whole'.[4]

20. Some will be disposed to say, 'That is just what you would expect of thinking like Mill's, so obviously ground out and uninspired, so "wintry", "sawdustish" and "logic-chopping".[5] To think abstractly in this fashion means to hold the mind to a narrow track, and that is hard because really unnatural; it keeps the impulses and other faculties in abeyance

---

[1] *Science et Méthode*, 54, 61. Cf. Baudouin: 'Suggestion acts by subconscious teleology. When the end has been suggested, the subconscious finds means for its realization.'—*Suggestion and Auto-suggestion*, 117.

[2] Quoted by P. A. Scholes, *The Listener's Guide to Music*, 18.

[3] *The Art of Thought*, 155.   [4] *Autobiography*, 70.

[5] The adjectives are Carlyle's.

that this one faculty may have play; it is rather the feat of a highly drilled gymnast than the free flow of creation. In thought that is truly creative, these struggles and crabbed inhibitions are left behind.' We answer: First, the notion that thinking which is highly abstract is therefore not creative is nonsense. Secondly, it seems to be true that in the realm of high abstraction success requires a preparation more concentrated, intense, and analytic than it does in the arts. But thirdly, such preparation is by no means peculiar to high abstraction; in a sense all thinking is alike unnatural and hence alike difficult. In most of us the impulses to act are far more powerful than the impulse to know. That comes of our animal heritage; we are still biological organisms; we remain, as James suggests, hair-trigger mechanisms made to act. And for beings so organized, thinking of all kinds is hard because of the tensions it requires. It demands that we maintain at once two sets of inhibitions, first of the 'bias of impatient impulse' that would have us be up and doing, then of the runaway fractiousness among our thoughts themselves that would carry us off down every alley of association. Creation, even in the arts, must generally be preceded by intense and painful thinking.

This has been denied. A host of facts and sayings could no doubt be adduced to support the denial. Those miraculous Shakespeare manuscripts, reputedly without erasures or corrections; the patroness of Milton who

> Deigns
> Her nightly visitation unimplored,
> And dictates to me slumbering, or inspires
> Easy my unpremeditated verse';

indeed all we have been saying about Coleridge and Goethe, Emerson and Scott, may be taken as showing that the born artist, or anyone at all in truly creative moments, has left the dust and heat behind him. 'What writer does not realize', asks Abbé Dimnet, 'that his most successful pages are the ones which gave him the least trouble?' 'Genius never plods.'[1] 'Remember Plato', says A. E. Housman: ' "he who without the Muses' madness

[1] *The Art of Thinking*, 199, 197.

in his soul comes knocking at the door of poesy and thinks that art will make him anything fit to be called a poet, finds that the poetry he indites in his sober senses is beaten hollow by the poetry of madmen" '.[1] 'I appeal to the greatest poets of the present day', Shelley writes, 'whether it is not an error to assert that the finest passages of poetry are produced by labour and study. . . . . Compositions so produced are to poetry what mosaic is to painting.'[2] But that there is a fly in this ointment somewhere is clear from Shelley's own reference, not to a piece of prose argument, but to one of his greatest poems, whose writing was fresh in his memory, as springing from 'the agony and bloody sweat of intellectual travail'.[3] This contrary view of the matter could be supported by an equal array of authorities, from Bach's 'Analysis, reflection, much writing, ceaseless correction—there is all my secret', to Carlyle's 'Genius is an infinite capacity for taking pains.' 'There is hardly a bar in his music', writes Sir George Grove of Beethoven, 'of which it may not be said with confidence that it has been re-written a dozen times.' 'Mendelssohn used to show a correction of a passage by Beethoven in which the latter had pasted alteration after alteration up to 13 in number. Mendelssohn had separated them, and in the 13th Beethoven had returned to the original version.'[4] Even Coleridge, who has provided us the *ne plus ultra* of automatic invention, wrote of his *Christabel*: 'Every line has been produced by me with labour-pangs.' 'I turn sick and faint when I reflect on the labour I have expended on the mere endeavour to avoid or remedy imperfections, which not one in ten thousand would have noticed.'[5] Here are two sets of views that appear to be in flat conflict. Are they really so? I do not think they are. Both are true and both important; the point is that they refer to different parts of the creative process. The 'agony and bloody sweat' comes first; it belongs to the stage of conscious analysis,

---

[1] *The Name and Nature of Poetry*, 37.   [2] *Defence of Poetry*.
[3] From a letter to Godwin given in Dowden's *Life*, II. 172.
[4] *Dictionary of Music*, I. 272.
[5] Quoted in Lowes, *op. cit.*, 304, note.

of elaboration of the problem or design. The full and effortless flow comes later when the preliminary work is over and the tide is setting in from below. Both are present in almost every creative work of any worth. 'Almost', we must say, not 'every', for it must be admitted that there are cases of invention where plan and performance alike are apparently effortless. But certainly this is not the rule. And if we knew all the facts, we could probably bring most or all of the exceptions under the rule. As we proceed either down the scale of genius or up the scale of abstractness the exceptions become increasingly rare.

21. (*b*) In general, then, an effort, and an intense one, to define and specify the problem is needed to get the full co-operation of subconsciousness. The other thing needful, it will be recalled, is to mobilize present resources. Why is this required? It is required, first, because one cannot effectively specify one's problem without it; and secondly, because the greater one's conscious knowledge, the more subconsciousness has to work with. To deal with the first point by example: how would one extract from 'the great pyramid' any problem that could be thought about except by making clear what one knows about it already and where the gaps are in one's knowledge? As one runs over this knowledge, partly fact but chiefly inference, much in the pyramid's history comes clearly enough to light—armies of workmen, the careful measurement, the hewing or sawing of stones—but in the attempt at reconstruction, one is sooner or later brought up short. How did these primitive builders manipulate and hoist their great stone blocks? Here we get a specific problem, and it has been reached by reviewing present resources and exposing a gap in them. The builders' achievement, to use our old metaphor, is an island, standing off from the mainland tantalizingly and inviting a passage to it. How are we to make the passage? By constructing an approach from the mainland of present knowledge. We bring together whatever we know that may be relevant— the size of the pyramid and its blocks, the facilities the Egyptians had in the way of man-power, oxen, tools and sledges; if this is still too narrow a base, we supplement the resources of memory with data from books. As our facts increase, they restrict the range of credible theory and it is likely enough that their joint pressure will soon produce the idea sought for. If it does not, we can only turn the matter over to the workshop of the subconscious. But in doing so, we may take hope from the fact that we have supplied the artisans there with the two things they most desiderate, a definite problem and a litter of likely evidence.

This discussion shows amply, I think, that we do succeed, in various degrees, in controlling and guiding subconsciousness by means of conscious suggestion. Sometimes, as we have seen, such control means no more than the maintenance of a conscious interest, by which the stores of the secondary self are gradually enlarged. Sometimes it goes farther and sets before the lower agencies a rough but explicit design. Sometimes—the typical case—it must go farther still; in order to secure a full co-operation, it must define its problem and mobilize all its reserves.[1]

---

[1] We might have let Emerson summarize. There is a paragraph of admirable description in his essay on *Intellect* which serves as companion-piece and corrective to the passage we have cited from the *Over-Soul* (Sec. 8). To some it may be an encouragement to learn how coy was even Emerson's muse, and how uncapturable except by stratagem.

'What is the hardest task in the world? To think. I would put myself in the attitude to look in the eye an abstract truth, and I cannot. I blench and withdraw on this side and on that. I seem to know what he meant who said, No man can see God face to face and live. For example, a man explores the basis of civil government. Let him intend his mind without respite, without rest, in one direction. His best heed long time avails him nothing. Yet thoughts are dimly flitting before him. We all but apprehend, we dimly forebode the truth. We say, I will walk abroad, and the truth will take form and clearness to me. We go forth, but cannot find it. It seems as if we needed only the stillness and the composed attitude of the library to seize the thought. But we come in and are as far from it as at first. Then, in a moment, and unannounced, the truth appears. A certain wandering light appears, and is the distinction, the principle, we wanted. But the oracle comes because we had previously laid siege to the shrine.'

22. (3) We come now to a third means, or set of means, for gaining subconscious help in thinking. The behaviour of these hidden processes is profoundly affected by *feeling*, and hence so far as this feeling may be brought under command we achieve control of the subconscious itself. To find what is possible here, we must first see how feeling acts upon suggestion.

23. Everyone will agree that to certain ideas there are emotions which are closely akin. The thought of an impending illness has an aura of depression about it; with the thought of a wilful insult there is usually a feeling of anger; the thought of one's new house in the country brings a stirring of elation. Just as a thought may call up another associated thought, so it may arouse one of these associated feelings. It is less commonly seen, however, that the course of causation may be the other way about, that what is present to start with may be the emotion, which then calls up cognate ideas. 'The same objects do not recall the same associates when we are cheerful as when we are melancholy. Nothing in fact is more striking than our utter inability to keep up trains of joyous imagery when we are depressed in spirits. Storm, darkness, war, images of disease, poverty, and perishing afflict unremittingly the imaginations of melancholiacs.'[1] 'The fact that one is in a state of depression when he scratches his finger has a great deal to do with the prompt thought of blood poisoning. Another mood might have brought the thought that the coagulation of blood is a blessing.'[2] Happily, there is a corresponding pressure from the sunnier emotions in the direction of their own type of ideas. If everything has a way of suggesting to the St. Francises and Emersons, the Walt Whitmans and the Brownings, that 'God's in His heaven, all's right with the world', that is not necessarily because their road has been a smooth one nor because they have made an effort, persistent, unjudicial, and desperate, to think no evil; it is a matter of

[1] James, *Principles*, I. 576.
[2] Robinson, *The Association Theory Today*, 44.

congeniality rather; it is very largely because their native temperament, their habitual and dominant mood, puts a premium on such thoughts. This dominant mood may never produce an idea by itself, but it does supply an atmosphere in which some types of thinking flourish while others rapidly wither.

24. Care is needed in interpreting this. It does not follow, for example, that the recipe for writing a tragedy is to achieve a fit of depression. Nor is the reason for this merely that the ideas aroused by emotion may be in no degree creative— nothing but gloomy memories or fatuous pieces of self-adulation—though that is true enough. The real reason we find, I think, in a valuable distinction of Alexander's between material and formal emotion, feeling appropriate to the matter before us and feeling appropriate to the form we seek to give it. Feeling of the first sort may or may not be present; it is feeling of the second sort that is important; it *must* be present if we are to create at all. Wordsworth once said that there are many poets in the world who have 'the vision and the faculty divine, yet wanting the accomplishment of verse'. Alexander takes him to task for this. It is just the verse-producing impulse that makes men poets, he thinks, an imperative and special emotion which, confronted with much the same impressions as are supplied to other men, seeks restlessly to recast them into forms of its own. Anyone may go afield at noon, for instance, and note the drooping flowers with the bees busy around them, and experience the natural languorous feelings; these last would be the 'material emotions'. But if he is a poet, he may mould his impressions and feelings into

> 'The purple flowers droop, the golden bee
> Is lily-cradled,'

and the fancy and music of that did not come from the poet's languor merely. ' It was wrung from him by his delight in his

picture, and completes the feeling from which he worked.'[1]
It expresses and fulfils a feeling peculiarly aesthetic and is
quite different from the material emotions it uses as means.
Not that this creative emotion is always the same, nor even
the same in any two cases. One gathers from Alexander that
it is as various as the forms that express it. By itself it is wholly
amorphous and indefinable; it can be described through its
products only; and yet it is a potent shaping impulse prescribing
the form of the creation and defining itself more exactly in
every subsequent revision.

25. This is a fruitful notion, and there is no reason why it
should not be applied, as indeed Alexander suggests, outside
the field of art. Does it not hold, for example, of philosophers
and mathematicians? Strangers to the abstracter studies
sometimes wonder how travellers can keep alive in these arid
wastes, so barren, it seems to them, of any sustenance for the
heart; and to stay there deliberately appears an asceticism
that is perhaps heroic, but is really only possible to an already
lean and somewhat fanatical mind. But of course to the worker
in this field it does not seem at all like a desert, and if it did,
he would hardly succeed in making it blossom. One can force
oneself for a time to attend to something devoid of interest,
but one cannot bully one's subconscious into brooding over
it lovingly; the secondary self is accustomed to freedom and
will play truant at the first opportunity. Hence if we find the
devotee of the abstract forms of reason living among them
contentedly and puzzling out continually new relations and
systems among them, we may be assured that his feeling about
them is not quite as other men's. What sort of feeling is it?
Pragmatists have supposed it a passion for practical advantage
which has been compelled by special circumstances to take
this roundabout route. The psycho-analysts would say that
it is a sublimation of sexual feeling, which has discharged
into 'autistic thinking' because it lacked a normal outlet. But

[1] *Beauty and Other Forms of Value*, 67.

is it not more natural to take a fascination so deep and inveterate as having some authentic root in human nature? It is hard to believe that mathematician and philosopher are mere twisted and self-deceived inverts, and it is perfectly clear to all who know such persons that they have not forgone passion for an existence wholly cerebral. 'All philosophy', Hazlitt remarked, 'depends no less on deep and real feeling than on power of thought'; 'there is no light', says Joubert, 'in souls in which there is no warmth'. To be sure this warmth or passion is of a special kind. It is the kind that finds its fulfilment not in the rough and tumble of existence, though it may seek such experience for purposes of its own, or in the various kinds of practical success, or even in the forms and harmonies of art, but in the 'form of intelligibility'. It would impose on things a rational order much as the artist would impose an order prescribed by aesthetic feeling. Indeed, though different from aesthetic feeling, it is so like this that some masters of abstract reasoning have identified the two outright.

26. Poincaré is an example.

> 'One may be surprised to hear feeling mentioned in connection with the demonstrations of mathematics, which can appeal, it would seem, to intelligence only. But this is to forget the sense of mathematical beauty, of the harmony of numbers and forms, or geometrical elegance. This is a truly aesthetic sense, which all real mathematicians know. It is indeed a form of feeling (*sensibilité*).'[1]

Poincaré says it is this feeling, co-operating with his subconsciousness, that enabled him to make his discoveries. The subconscious, he says, when given a mathematical problem, produces all manner of strange combinations in answer to it. For the most part these never come to light. Why? Because of the presence of this special feeling, which acts as a censor and allows the appearance for explicit attention only of those that

---

[1] *Science et Méthode*, 57. Cf. the remark of Weierstrass: 'a man who is not somewhat of a poet will never be a perfect mathematician.'

satisfy its demand. And what is the nature of this demand? It is for a self-luminous logical whole, in which the mutual relations of parts are all made clear. It will be obvious from what has gone before that we cannot accept this account altogether; there is no good reason to suppose that the subconscious does indulge in this orgy of irrational answers; and the responsibility for selection that Poincaré assigns to mere feeling is more than it can bear. We have seen that the emergence of the right answer cannot be accounted for unless there is acting in the subconscious a genuinely logical compulsion which itself selects and eliminates. Nevertheless we may follow Poincaré in believing not only that this feeling is present, but that it is indispensable if the logical impulsion is to be sustained in carrying through its difficult work.[1]

What holds of mathematics holds also of other forms of systematic speculation. To do creative work in philosophy, even to enter into the spirit of the great philosophers, calls for a peculiar intellectual passion. In some minds this is deep and habitual, as it appears to have been in Spinoza, who went so far as to identify pleasure generally with increase in understanding.[2] It is probably the powerful undercurrent of this sober but exalted emotion, quite impossible of concealment beneath the apparatus of propositions and proofs, and running up at the close to the almost lyric strain about 'the intellectual

[1] Mr. Russell also thinks that the mathematical researcher is supported by a quasi-aesthetic feeling. 'Mathematics, rightly viewed, possesses not only truth, but supreme beauty—a beauty cold and austere, like that of sculpture . . . and capable of a stern perfection such as only the greatest art can show. The true spirit of delight, the exaltation, the sense of being more than man, which is the touchstone of the highest excellence, is to be found in mathematics as surely as in poetry . . . the world of pure reason knows no compromise, no practical limitations, no barrier to the creative activity embodying in splendid edifices the passionate aspiration after the perfect from which all great work springs.' And again: 'In the greatest (mathematical) works unity and inevitability are felt as in the unfolding of a drama. . . . The love of system, of interconnection, which is perhaps the inmost essence of the intellectual impulse, can find free play in mathematics as nowhere else.'—*Mysticism and Logic*, 60–1, 66.

[2] *Ethics*, Pt. III, Prop. 11, note.

love of God', which, more even that the close-knit logic, has made the *Ethics* so persuasive a manual to many generations of students. But not in many minds is it so persistent and consuming a passion. In most men, as in Goethe, periods of Spinozism alternate with others in which 'grau ist alle Theorie, und grün des Lebens goldner Baum'. Nor can the case be wholly different even with the great metaphysicians. 'The shades nowhere speak without blood', says one of them, 'and the ghosts of Metaphysic accept no substitute. They reveal themselves only to that victim whose life they have drained, and, to converse with shadows, he himself must become a shade.'[1] But this can hardly have been the typical Bradley, and it was certainly not the one who wrote *Appearance and Reality*. Of that Bradley we get a glimpse in this:

'Some in one way and some in others, we seem to touch and have communion with what is beyond the visible world. In various manners we find something higher, which both supports and humbles, both chastens and transports us. And, with certain persons, the intellectual effort to understand the universe is a principal way of thus experiencing the Deity. No one, probably, who has not felt this, however differently he might describe it, has ever cared much for metaphysics. And, wherever it has been felt strongly, it has been its own justification. The man whose nature is such that by one path alone his chief desire will reach consummation, will try to find it on that path, whatever it may be, and whatever the world thinks of it; and if he does not, he is contemptible.'[2]

Here the strain is unmistakable that we find also in Spinoza. Speculation is too arduous a business to be supported without passion.[3]

---

[1] F. H. Bradley, *Aphorisms*, No. 98.

[2] *Appearance and Reality*, 5–6.

[3] It is clear that in both Spinoza and Bradley the speculative passion was blended with feeling that one can only call religious. These are not the same, though they are very often found together. There is perhaps no metaphysician of the first rank who could not have said with Sir Thomas Browne, 'I love to lose myself in a mystery, to pursue my reason to an *O altitudo*!'

27. Such 'formal passion' seems necessary, then, for either artistic or speculative creation. It supplies the 'intellectual climate' in which cognate suggestion flourishes. But, remembering that our interest for the moment is chiefly practical, we must go on to ask, Can such feeling be controlled? Is it something that may be achieved with effort or is it a gift of the gods? The right answer seems to be, as so often in issues of nature *versus* nurture, *both*. That it is in part the result of discipline is suggested by the immense improvement in product that commonly follows persistent effort, and by the facts of deterioration through disuse. That there is something native about it is shown by the early age at which it may appear and the ease with which instruction at times elicits it; witness such prodigies as Mozart and Gauss. Indeed, the opinion may be risked that 'formal passion' is so largely a matter of native temperament that efforts at control are more profitably directed to the 'material passions'. But so directed, the efforts would have to be differently applied. For the material passions—not love, perhaps, but certainly fear and anger, grief, lust and jealousy—are more commonly important as inhibitors of creation than as aids to it.

Note, for example, that physicians, when a life that is dear to them is at stake, give the case into other hands. The excitement of playing football before thousands may make a player's instincts alert and give him dash and abandon in using his acquired resources, but it is precisely what makes it impossible for him to elaborate any new and intricate strategy. 'Ask young people returning from a party or a spectacle, and all excited about it, what it was. "Oh, it was *fine*! it was *fine*! it was *fine*!" is all the information you are likely to receive until the excitement has calmed down.'[1] 'When the war broke out in 1914', writes Graham Wallas, 'I expected that the emotions stimulated by it would at once create memorable poetry or prose, and prepared to collect a small anthology of war-philosophy and war-poetry. I soon found, however, that the terrific emotions of a modern war are apt to benumb rather

[1] James, *Talks to Teachers*, etc., 220.

than stimulate all the higher processes of the mind which are not applied to the work of fighting.'[1] His search netted practically nothing. If we are to deal effectively with intellectual problems, we had best take Bishop Butler's suggestion and 'sit down in a cool hour'. If we are attempting expression in art, we should pretty certainly do better if we followed Wordsworth's suggestion and let the expression come, not straight from the heats of feeling, but from 'emotion recollected in tranquillity'. The intimations from beneath are likely to reach us in whispers so low and tentative as to be drowned out utterly if brass bands are blaring in the room above.

Reflection is inhibited by any material passion that rises to violence. Unhappily some emotions are inhibitive even when they fall far short of violence. Of these the chief is fear. Creation is all but impossible when subconsciousness is given over to apprehensive preoccupation with the necessities of life; 'the poor poet has not in these days, nor has had for two hundred years, a dog's chance', writes Quiller-Couch, since he is denied 'that intellectual freedom from which great writings are born'.[2] The fear of failure may benumb the mind of the examinee; the fear of a loss of faith may inhibit the critical faculty of the religious man; just as the need for self-respect may make us find bogus reasons for what we are doing, so the fear of the loss of it may blind us to good reasons why we should cease what we are doing.

Such emotional inhibitions can be removed. The two best ways of removing them are, first to understand them, to unbare their causal root and see them as the irrational influences they probably are, and, secondly, to follow up the exposure in practice, to starve the feelings out by refusing to act on them. The first method has been so fully canvassed by the various schools of psycho-analysis, and the second so effectively urged by James,[3] that enlargement upon them is needless.

We have now discussed some of the more important ways in which the workings of the subconscious can be made to

---

[1] *The Art of Thought*, 160.   [2] *On the Art of Writing*, 46–7.
[3] See, e.g., his *Principles*, II. 463.

co-operate with conscious design. We have seen that every act of attention makes a difference to the secondary self, that a definite committing of one's problem to this self makes a still greater difference, and that subconsciousness may be influenced by control of feeling. There is still another aid to the management of subconscious thinking that should here be briefly mentioned.

28. (4) We may help ourselves at times by a judicious alternation of effort with passivity. It has already been pointed out how necessary effort is in specifying the problem. But even when the problem is specified fully, one may go on trying, and the question is whether this is worth while. To take a convenient old example, we are trying to recall a name. There is no doubt whose name we want, and yet it refuses to come. Everyone knows what it means to strain after such a name, and to feel oneself getting nearer and nearer until one can almost seize it. Everyone has found, too, that a mere intensifying of the strain, an indignant head-on assault, may only drive it farther away and leave one bogged more deeply than ever in helpless exasperation. Two courses are then open. In the first place we may give up the struggle and turn our attention elsewhere. If we do this, the name will often pop up in the course of the next few minutes without any apparent cause and without the slightest relevance to what we may then be thinking about. Or we may exchange our frontal attack for a leisurely enveloping movement, calling to mind the person's looks, his voice and dress, his house and his friends, and so far as possible the entire setting in which he has figured in our experience. This method also is effective. Indeed the methods are essentially the same, the second being the conscious version of what is subconscious in the first. Both are superior in the same way to the method of direct assault. 'It is easy for the focus to become tyrannical, to refuse due representation to the counsels of the subconscious',[1] and this is what is happening when we strain

[1] Hocking, *The Meaning of God in Human Experience*, 530.

at the name directly. The method of subconscious recall is based on the assumption that 'as soon as our attention is relaxed, it becomes possible for all our inner life to flow together, to collect itself within us';[1] to relax the conscious strain allows the associates of the name to proceed with their silent encirclement until the quarry falls into their hands now unresistingly. In both methods it is this encirclement that yields the result, but because in the one case it is subconscious and in the other fully willed and explicit, the two are superficially very different. Of course the success of the subconscious method is not achieved by passivity merely. What counts is passivity preceded by conscious effort. Indeed it is not unlikely that this first alternation will have to be followed by several further waves of effort and quiescence before the goal is reached. It is as if the subconscious momentum spent itself and had to be renewed occasionally by charges from above.[2]

29. If there were space, we could add many details about the special conditions of work which men of genius have found of aid in wooing their particular muses. It would be a diverting story. And it would help to convince the sceptical that enough is known about the subconscious to supply the beginnings of a technique for its control. But after all, *only* the beginnings. The difficulty is not merely that it cannot make a dull mind inventive; no technique can do that. The difficulty

[1] Baudouin, *Suggestion and Autosuggestion*, 137.
[2] We are really applying to a special process that 'principle of alternation' which Professor Hocking has applied illuminatingly to religious experience. Explicit thought and explicit will are both alike abstract, he points out; the very strenuousness of their concentration cuts them off from that 'whole-idea' by which in the end they must be interpreted and appraised. And since the subconscious, as the deposit of experience generally, may be more representative of this whole-idea than conscious thought itself, it is natural that the mystic should have frequent recourse to it. But he, too, defeats himself if he relies on it continually. Advance must be through the swing of the pendulum between 'work and worship,' effort and passivity.—*The Meaning of God*, etc., Chap. XXVIII and appendix, note 1.

is that subconscious processes are affected by factors so manifold and subtle, by so many repressed fears and wishes, so many forms of fatigue in mind and body, such obscure and unpredictable changes in resolution, in interest, in mood, in cortical nutrition, that no knowledge we can hope to get will make our control over suggestion complete, even when the problem to be dealt with falls within our intellectual range. Even for the best meteorologists of the spirit, the winds will go on blowing pretty much where they list. The day will never come when the best work in art and science can be done to order. But then it is also true that such work never has been done and never will be done by mere caprice. Like everything else, the uprush from below of creative thought is governed in detail by laws. We said at the beginning that, however much we have still to learn about these, most men could improve very greatly their methods of reflection if they were merely to use what is known already. We trust that this chapter will have made that statement good.

CHAPTER XXV

THE TESTS OF TRUTH

1. The steps we have thus far considered in the movement of reflection are three: first, the defining or specifying of the problem; second, the amassing of data through observation and memory; third, the leap of suggestion. To this third step, as the central one of the whole movement, where genius appears if at all, and where the behaviour of thought is at once most baffling and most fascinating, we have naturally devoted the largest space. But suppose now that this third step has been accomplished and that a suggestion, pointed or pointless, toward solving our problem has actually been produced. What next?

Two further steps are commonly recognized. The suggestion that has arisen must first be elaborated into its implications, and then these implications must be compared with fact. Newton, for example, once the suggestion had come to him that planets fall toward the sun in obedience to the same law as bodies falling to earth, had two further steps to take. He must first deduce what the motions of the planets would be *if* his theory were the true one; and secondly, he must compare the motions that on his theory ought to follow with the motions observable in fact.

2. Now there is no doubt either that these steps can often be distinguished, or that the distinction serves a useful purpose. But it is easy to show that this succession of steps is neither universally present in a completed course of thought nor, therefore, fundamental to it. Sometimes the one step, sometimes the other is absent; sometimes both are missing together; and when both do appear, the two processes, except for a single point, to be dealt with shortly, are in principle the same.

Sometimes the missing step is the process of reasoning by which a suggestion is elaborated. If the data we begin with are so complete as virtually to surround the gap in our knowledge, the right suggestion when it occurs may be seen at once to be the wanting element, without any help from elaboration. Thus our insertion, at a venture, of a piece in a picture puzzle may be followed so immediately that it seems to be accompanied by the perception that it squares with the facts. The if-then process has vanished into the process of verification. Sometimes, on the other hand, it is not the elaboration but the process of squaring with fact that has disappeared. A child who concludes that seven times eight are fifty-six may wish to make sure about this, and reasons that if it is correct he should also be able to arrive at it by adding eights to each other. He tries this and succeeds. Here the process of verifying is swallowed up in the elaboration. The elaboration consists of conceiving fifty-six as a sum of eights; but that is also the verification. Sometimes, again, *neither* the working out of implications *nor* the squaring of these with fact can be distinguished as a separate step. We may take as an example the attempt to recall a name, which is as truly an effort of thought as many other processes that we should accept as such unhesitatingly. When the right name darts into mind, bringing with it the awareness of its being the right one, where are we to find either the elaboration of consequences or the checking against fact that the ordinary account demands?

3. Even when both processes are present and distinguishable, they do not show the sharp difference that is commonly alleged. In elaboration we start from a hypothesis and work forward to its consequences; in verification we take certain judgements of fact as pointing backward to our hypothesis. The two processes are the same process looked at from different ends. Both are aspects of one insight, the insight that theory coheres with relevant fact.

We should not deny that when looked at each from its own end, the processes appear very different. Elaboration consists essentially of inference; verification consists usually of observation; these two processes appear as different as two processes could well be; and since they do often appear successively in a course of thinking, it would seem as if full and separate treatments of them were called for. No such treatments are offered here, and for the two reasons following.

First, neither inference nor observation is confined to a single stage in the movement of thought, and we have preferred to deal with them in other places. Inference has been dealt with at the point where its workings are most interesting, namely, in creation or invention; and implication, which supplies the track that inference follows, will form the subject of Book IV. As for observation, we have discussed it already as fully as space will permit.[1]

Secondly, the more steadily we regard the two processes of elaboration and verification as used in actual thinking, the more clearly do they resolve themselves into the phases of one insight, the insight into coherence. What makes them appear so different is the unanalysed belief that in verification we have left behind us the region of internal web-spinning and system-building and got at last into contact with naked fact. It will readily enough be admitted that verification does appeal to coherence, but it will be contended that the only value of this coherence lies in its resting, at one end, on what is independently given. In the last resort, it will be said, we take tables and chairs to be facts, not because our judgements about them cohere with something else, but because they are given in perception. Thus coherence is not the whole story, and to make it the whole story would be like building a bridge without any piers to support the span. Now in a sense we admit all this, in the sense, namely, that there is such a thing as givenness. How then can we continue to treat verification as if it involved nothing beyond coherence? For this reason, that as soon as we attempt to say *what* is given, we find ourselves thrown back upon coherence anyhow. The solid piers of fact, supposed to be standing there in broad daylight as the bases of our

[1] Chap. XXI; see especially Sec. 3 for the various points at which observation may be required in the process of thought.

structure of theory, are illusion. There are no such things. The 'facts' that were to support our system are themselves relative to the system. In short, the coherence of judgements within a system is our test, and our only test, of any truth or fact whatever.

4. This 'only' commits us to much. It requires us to show, not simply that there is no alternative to coherence that is in use as a general test, but none that supplies a test in any instance. And these points are hard to prove; the first because it is hard to be sure one has exhausted the possible alternatives, the second because it is barely conceivable that there should be several tests of truth, of which one might be used in one case and another in another. For example, while truth might *be* the same thing everywhere, our test of it in geometry might be self-evidence, in morals a satisfied conscience, and in botany accordance with perceived fact. But neither of these difficulties turns out, on nearer inspection, to be as formidable as it looks. The last point would be sufficiently met if it were shown that, whatever test may be used for a first approximation to truth, there is a particular one that is always resorted to when a final test is needed. The same proof would meet the first point also. That point was that there is perhaps some alternative to coherence which is used implicitly but universally as the court of appeal. But of course if it can be shown that coherence is the court to which ultimate appeal is always taken, we shall have destroyed this contention in the most effective possible manner, by establishing not only its contradictory but also its contrary.

Now I think it can be shown that coherence *is* our test, the final and invariable test, when our beliefs are under pressure. Not that nobody could be found to maintain that his belief had a different basis, even to maintain this to the end through all manner of logical bombardment. But of course pertinacity is hardly evidence, and the contention here put forward is that, this apart, the person who rejects coherence can be shown, in such fashion as to convince him if he is unbiased, that he is doing one or other of two things: either resorting to coherence without knowing it, or else applying a standard that he himself would reject as soon as its nature was made explicit.

5. Now there are six distinct tests of truth that are today accepted in various quarters as providing a court of last appeal. Indeed there are no doubt more; but at any rate these are the most widely accepted. They are: (1) correspondence with fact, (2) self-evidence, (3) coherence, (4) 'working' as defined by the pragmatist, (5) the peculiar warrant that attaches to mystical intuition, and (6) the voice of authority. The pragmatic test has been dealt with. Correspondence, self-evidence and coherence are all so important that the reader will be invited shortly to listen to a debate between them. As for the other two, authority and mysticism, a brief discussion will perhaps suffice.

6. First, then, as to authority. Suppose that a man is confronted with some problem of faith or morals, that he arrives at a tentative solution of it, and that he looks round for some means of verifying the solution. It occurs to him that this may be one of the matters on which the Pope has spoken *ex cathedra*; on investigation it turns out that he has, and moreover has put the seal of his approval on the very suggestion the inquirer himself had arrived at. Many persons, of course, would regard this as a sufficient and final guarantee. Is such a position intelligible? I think not. When the person who accepts the pronouncement as authoritative is asked why he does so, there are two possibilities before him; he may give reasons for his acceptance or he may not.

7. Suppose he does give reasons. Suppose he says that the dogma of infallibility has been accepted by the Church for centuries, that it was expressly defined and adopted at the great council of 1870, that it is clearly implied in the commission to

Peter, that some seat of final authority is imperatively needed in practice. For our purpose the reasons matter little, since whatever they are, they carry with them an implication that is plain and fatal. That implication is this, that authority itself is not the ultimate ground of his belief. Authority may be the immediate ground, but if the authority itself is accepted for other and further reasons, it is these that form the real ground. Of course it is conceivable that these also should be based on authority. But that only means that with regard to them the original dilemma is repeated. Either *their* acceptance as authoritative is based on reasons, in which case once more authority is not their ultimate ground, or else it is made with no reasons at all.

8. Let us turn, then, to this second alternative, that the appeal to authority is taken *without* reasons. One accepts the authority, not on the ground of arguments, nor even on the ground that one feels it to be the right authority, since this itself is a kind of reason, but for no reason whatever and simply as an act of faith or will. Unfortunately, though this attitude is beyond criticism for its reasons, it is intolerable in its consequences. For if one person is justified in appealing to authority without reasons, then others are similarly justified. They would even be justified in accepting authorities that said precisely the opposite of what is said by one's own authority. But it is obvious that in this event one or other authority is wrong, and therefore that whatever justified appealing to it must similarly be wrong. In the light of its consequences, the unreasoning appeal to authority is thus self-destructive.

Is it replied that to draw inferences from the authoritarian's position, to say that he must *in consistency* admit some hing, is to impute to him an acceptance of the authority of reason which he is under no obligation to avow? If he holds that authority is the only ultimate ground for accepting any belief, are we not begging the question when we seek to hedge that authority with any prescriptions of reason? Why should he not reply, If my acceptance of authority leads to inconsistencies, so much the worse for logic? The answer is that such a position would be destructive even to authoritarianism. For unless the primary laws of logic are accepted as valid, no assertion of any kind can be made legitimately; deny the law of contradiction, for example, and the truth that X is an authority would no longer exclude its untruth. An authority that declines the limitations of logic renders its claim unintelligible.

Is it replied, again, that in demanding the submission of an authority to logic we are only exchanging one authority for another, and setting up reason as itself an authority? Undoubtedly in appealing to logic we do appeal to authority in *some* sense. Whoever recognizes any criterion of truth at all may be said to take that criterion as for him authoritative. But it is important to see that 'authority' is being used here in two different senses, a wider and a narrower. In the wider sense, all believers in a criterion are authoritarians. But the typical defenders of authority plainly take it in the narrower sense, as a criterion that is to be distinguished from others and preferred to them. It is regarded as conferring on propositions or systems a guarantee which they themselves could not supply. Those who reject authority do so because they disbelieve in this external warrant, the rationalist holding, for example, that the warrant for a system of belief lies in its own character. If 'authority' is so extended in sense as to cover not only the guarantee from without, but also the internal self-evidencing power of a proposition or system, it has lost its *distinctive* meaning.

9. It may be said, once more, that the acceptance, not resting on reasons, that X is an authority, does not compel me to admit the opposing beliefs of others, since that implies that authorities are equal, and this I expressly deny; if my recognition of authority is right, as I contend it is, theirs must be wrong. But how am I to know whether I am right? If I base my claim on evidence, I am returning to the course we have just seen to be excluded. If I say the insight is *self-*

evident, I am appealing to another test of truth, which we
shall consider presently. If I say the authority itself guarantees
the insight, the argument is of course circular; the insight
guarantees the authority, and the authority the insight. It may
be replied that the establishment of any ultimate test of truth
must be circular. If a man believes that the only ultimate test
is self-evidence, for example, he will naturally use it as the test
of this proposition itself, and to ask him to adopt any other
would be absurd. This is true. It must be admitted that no
valid *argument* can be offered for any exclusive criterion of
truth. For the supporter of such a criterion is always in a
dilemma: if he rests his case upon the use of his own criterion,
he begs the question; if he rests it on any other criterion, he
is either admitting the validity of that criterion, and then his
own is not the only one, or else offering an argument that he
must grant is worthless. If an opponent is to be convinced,
then, it must be by a process, not of proving one's own criterion
or of refuting his, but of showing him that what he thinks he
holds he does not really hold, since the supposition that he does
is inconsistent with the facts of his intellectual practice. The
considerations we have just been offering are of this type. We
have pointed out that if the authoritarian is strictly true to
his own test, and rests his acceptance of it on nothing whatever
but its own assertion, he cannot protest against others accepting
their authorities for the like reason, which would mean conflicting authorities and the justification of conflicting beliefs.
If he protests against this conclusion as illogical, he is only
abandoning his exclusive criterion in another way, for then
he is using the logicality of an argument as an independent
criterion. If he protests on another ground, and says that
the acceptance of *his* authority does not justify others in
accepting *their* authorities because his is unique by reason
of the soundness, or weight of experience, or penetration, or
profundity, of its pronouncements, then so far he is making
the character of the pronouncements the criterion of the
authority, not the authority the criterion of the pronouncements. Indeed it seems safe to say that no belief is ever held

simply because authority enjoins it. The believer always accepts this authority rather than that on some grounds or other, of age, prestige, alleged origin, or what-not, which, if destroyed, would carry down the authority with them; he always imposes on its pronouncements certain conditions of consistency and intelligibility, and withholds his assent unless they are conformed to. And it is meaningless to say that authority is his ultimate criterion if there remain ulterior considerations by which the authority itself must be judged.

10. How easy it is to overlook these considerations, how obvious they are when pointed out, and how dependent on them is the validity of any claim to authority, may be made clearer by illustration. Take a case where the appeal to authority would be most generally felt to be justified. Suppose some result is announced in quantum mechanics that one does not in the least understand; but one knows that the equations leading to it have been worked out by Dirac, and have been checked and verified by Planck. Probably most of us would accept their authority in these matters without hesitation. But is our acceptance of their results really based on their authority? There is one reflection that is enough in itself to destroy any such supposition. This is the fact that we could not so use their authority without an implicit rebuke from the authorities themselves. For if we did ultimately accept their results merely on their authority, we should be accepting them on grounds which they themselves would ridicule. When Planck and Dirac accept certain results, they do not do so on the ground that their authority is so great and infallible; they would regard this as an absurd ground for believing anything; and if we really regard them as authorities, we must accept this authoritative abjuration of authority. If we ask why they do accept certain results, the answer is very simple; given the conditions, they have seen these results to be necessary; and they are ready to supply the data and the reasoning to anyone who can follow. In short, they do not take these things to be true because they are authorities; they are authorities because they can see these things to be true. And clearly, if pressed about the beliefs we accept from them, we should agree that their sort of ground is the only decisive one. The court to which in the end we shall take our appeal is not authority, but those reasons through seeing which an authority becomes an authority, namely, those that condition or determine the truth itself. To be sure, our own reasons for accepting the statement of authority may not be those ultimate reasons. They may be only reasons for believing that our authority can see the real reasons. But if we accept him as an authority at all, it is because we believe he has a fullness and clearness of grasp which, if we had it, would render the appeal to his authority needless. If this higher warrant is there, authority is superseded; if it is not there, authority fails. In neither case is authority itself the final court of appeal.

11. Verification by mystical insight—if we may now turn for a moment to that—is of course far less frequently resorted to than the appeal to authority. But if we interpret it broadly enough to include such warrant for various convictions as came to Socrates through his 'demon', Joan of Arc through her 'voices', and George Fox through his 'inner light', it must be conceded at least historical importance. Is it among the legitimate methods of ratifying belief?

Mysticism is hard to deal with because it is not really a single thing, but a great many different things of extremely different values. Without attempting to go into these, we may distinguish three relations that seem to appear in mystic experience between the truth apprehended and that which verifies or assures it. In the first class of cases, this truth and the insights that guarantee it are both ineffable; the mystic comes down from his mount of vision sure that his eyes have been opened to truth without defect, but helpless to say what it is that he has seen or what are the grounds of his assurance. In a second class of cases the veil is partly lifted. *What* he has seen to be true the mystic can now tell us with some degree of definiteness; it is the personality of God, or the doctrine of the trinity, or the immortality of the soul. But what makes these beliefs so overwhelmingly certain remains ineffable, as before; though all doubt is gone, he cannot, try as he will, make clear to us what dispelled it. In a third class of cases, the veil is removed altogether and we are able to share both the truth that has been revealed to him and the grounds on which his certainty rests.

12. (i) Suppose, first, that both are ineffable. This is a frequent case, and if we follow James in taking ineffableness as one of the marks of mystic experience, it is the typical case. What are we to say of it? Or rather, what could we possibly say with any profit? Since everything laid hold of is by hypothesis inexpressible and incommunicable, anything we tried to say about it would be condemned to inadequacy beforehand. It is needless to deny that such insight is possible; indeed we shall see in due time that any knowledge of ultimate truth would break the abstract moulds of our understanding and expression. But that is no proof that the mystic has reached such knowledge; and even if he had, it is clear that we have not, however we may hang on his broken speech. And since the endeavour of a man on the plain to describe what he would see from an unscaled mountain top is not very likely to be profitable, we will spend no time in the attempt.

13. (ii) Suppose, however, that the truth the mystic brings back to us is one that on our presumably lower level we can still make sense of, and that by his own profession it is essentially what we all mean when we express certain familiar beliefs. His claim, then, is that of these propositions he has had a special assurance, not open to our more pedestrian reason. Here again we can hardly deny his claim dogmatically; it is idle to deny when we do not in the least understand what we are denying. But in the present case we have one check that we did not have in the former case. The beliefs now reported as true are more or less definite beliefs, which may be seen to agree or not agree with others. And if some of them, fully supported by this special insight, disagree with others equally supported by it, then the credit of such insight is bound to be impaired. Unfortunately, these contradictory results are common. We have already mentioned three beliefs of moment that mystics have reported as confirmed by their insight. All three of these beliefs have been denied through apparently similar insight. The first of them was the doctrine that God is a person; the great tradition of Catholic mysticism in Spain has strongly supported this, while the pantheistic mystics of Buddhism have rejected it. As to the trinity, St. Theresa reports that in one of her visions she was made to 'comprehend in what way it is that one God can be in three Persons. He made me see it so clearly that I remained as extremely surprised as I was comforted.'[1] On the other hand it was revealed to Plotinus that God was the Absolutely One, whom no plurality could rightly represent, since He is 'the source from which the differentiation of unity and plurality proceeds'[2]; while the mediaeval mystic, Richard of St. Victor, seems to have received still another assurance, namely, that though the Deity was really triune, this trinity was contrary to reason. In like manner, as regards immortality, mysticism can be cited on both sides. One vision concerning it is described as 'not a confused state, but the clearest, the surest of the surest, utterly beyond words— where death was an almost laughable impossibility. . . .' But in another such state, which seems to have carried an equal certitude, there was 'the apprehension of a coming dissolution, the grim conviction that this state was the last state of the conscious self, the sense that I had followed the last thread of being to the verge of the abyss. . . .'[3] Now our only way of

[1] Quoted by James, *Varieties of Religious Experience*, 411–12.
[2] Cf. Inge, *Philosophy of Plotinus*, II. 108.
[3] Both passages are quoted in James, *ibid.*, 384, 385; the first from Sir James Crichton-Browne, the second from J. A. Symonds.

knowing what mystics mean is by what they say. And if what they say gives any intimation of what they mean, it casts grave doubt upon the value of mysticism as a warrant for truth. For it is apparently willing to affix its great seal, with royal impartiality, to both sides of a contradiction.

14. (iii) We have pointed out that in a third class of cases, however, both the proposition of major interest and those relations that serve to verify it are presented together in clear and communicable fashion. The mental life, we have seen, shows alterations of effort and passivity, and sometimes in one's passive states the horizons of the mind are thrown back; one sees with new range and clearness, and probably too with a peculiar exultation; one becomes, as Emerson puts it, 'porous to thought and bibulous of the sea of light'. After Hamilton and Poincaré had been wrestling for long with their very difficult mathematical problems, the solution, with its right bearings upon their data, suddenly stood clear before them, almost as if revealed to them from without.[1] It may be said that such experiences are not mystical at all. Quite possibly not; it is enough for our purpose that they have often been taken as such. And regarding them our point is this: that however they may be classed, the special security they afford for truth is plainly non-mystical. If, in such cases, a truth is seen in its relations to other knowledge, and so with something of the certainty that goes with demonstration, it is no unique and mystical warrant that guarantees it, but mere coherence, the same sort of coherence precisely that is used in workaday verifications. It is of course a striking experience to find so wide and clear a prospect opening out before us, and not unnaturally there comes along with it an elevation of mood that perhaps is genuinely akin to the mystic's exaltation; but we can see on reflecting that the mood itself gives no criterion, and that the greater clearness of vision is nothing whatever

[1] See above, Chap. XXIV, Sec. 3.

but the sort of insight we are using daily, intensified somewhat in its clearness and enlarged in sweep.

We may conclude that from mysticism there is to be derived no distinctive or applicable test. Where proposition and grounds are both ineffable, we can find nothing to take away. Where the proposition itself is definite while the verifying insight is mystical, that insight lends its support to contradictions. Where both proposition and support are laid hold of distinctly and communicably, the ground of certainty is not mystical at all, but plain coherence.

15. Three important tests are now left us, coherence, correspondence, self-evidence. The plausibility of the last two varies with the field in which they are applied. When we are thinking about historical facts, or events reported in the newspapers, or things actually seen and heard, it seems to the plain man obvious that our thought could be tested only by correspondence with fact. But if we were to take this same man by the hand, lead him off to another room in the gallery of knowledge, and set him down before a law of logic or a mathematical proof, he would probably desert his former standard without misgiving. These insights do not need comparison with fact; they are self-evident as they stand. If he had met these first, instead of judgements about things and events, he would probably have laid it down with confidence that the test was a certain clearness and convincingness apparent at once to anyone who could grasp the truth at all. But then disillusionment would again have overtaken him when he began to move from one region to another. For just as correspondence deserts us when we move from facts to abstractions, so self-evidence deserts us when we move back again from abstractions to facts. Where is the self-evidence in the judgement that it rained yesterday in Guatemala?

On the face of it common sense is without any consistent standard. It keeps swinging back and forth between two different standards, correspondence for matters of fact and self-evidence for the abstract and formal. But we hold that this oscillation and inconsistency are superficial only. We hold that these two standards are not so far apart as they seem and that both resolve themselves on analysis into a single standard, coherence. The way to establish this is to show that even in matters of fact it is coherence rather than correspondence that we actually use, and that even in regions of the abstractest formality it is once more coherence rather than self-evidence that is in the end our court of appeal. We shall not argue that these types of judgement cover between them the whole of knowledge, though many philosophers would say they do. It is enough to point out that they are the kinds traditionally placed at the poles of knowledge. If types so far apart can be shown to depend on a single criterion, it is unlikely that any third type will come forward to challenge its universality. We shall open the case for coherence, then, by considering the two types of judgement that seem to demand most obviously another standard.

16. Take first the judgement of fact. 'Burr killed Hamilton in a duel.' 'That is a cardinal on the branch yonder.' To the plain man it seems obvious that the test of such judgements is whether they correspond with fact. But as regards the first of them, there is a simple distinction which, if perceived, would shake his confidence. When he reflects on the judgement, 'Burr killed Hamilton in a duel', he sees, or thinks he sees, that its truth *means* correspondence; and it is natural to say that if truth means this, then it must also be tested by this. But the two questions are distinct, and in saying that the test here is correspondence, he is pretty clearly confusing the test of truth with its meaning. For the slightest consideration will show that the use of correspondence as a test is here out of the question; one of the terms that are to correspond is irrecoverably gone. There is no person living who could have witnessed the famous duel; and even if there were, he could not, through correspondence merely, validate his memories. Our test in such cases must clearly be found else-where. And the more we reflect, the plainer it becomes that this test is the way our judgement is implicated with a host of further judgements that we are compelled to make when we investigate. If this belief about Hamilton is true, then a thousand references in newspapers, magazines, and books, and almost endless facts about the fortunes of Hamilton's family, about the later life of Burr, and about American constitutional history, fall into place in a consistent picture. If it is false, then the most credible journalists, historians and statesmen, generation after generation, may be so deluded about events that happen before the eyes of a nation that no single historical fact is any longer above suspicion. If evidence of this weight is to be rejected, then in consistency we must go on to reject almost every hint that takes us beyond immediate percep-tion. And intellectually speaking, that would pull our house about our heads. What really tests the judgement is the extent of our accepted world that is implicated with it and would be carried down with it if it fell. And that is the test of coherence.

17. 'But in any such judgement', it may be replied, 'the value of correspondence is seen in a false light. *Of course* it cannot be used in those special cases where one of the terms has vanished. But that does not disqualify it where it *is* applic-able, nor does it show that any other test can really supplant it where it is not. Indeed, in an instance like this, where correspondence cannot be applied, we see that our judgement is incapable of proof altogether, by coherence or anything else; every judgement of historical fact must retain to the end a touch of uncertainty. It must do so for the reason that it is beyond reach of the one thing that could establish it, namely, that perception of the event itself which would make appeal to correspondence possible. On the other hand, when we turn to the judgements where appeal to correspondence *is* possible, we find that it is always resorted to, and that in such cases uncertainty is banished. Take the judgement, "That bird is a cardinal". If you heard someone make that remark, how would you test it? You would look and see. If there was a correspondence between what was asserted and what you saw, you would call the judgement true; if not, false. This is the way we actually assure ourselves of the truth of all such judgements, and it is correspondence that assures us.'

18. Now, plausible as this argument is, it goes to pieces on inspection. It assumes that, corresponding to our judgement, there is some solid chunk of fact, directly presented to sense and beyond all question, to which thought must adjust itself. And this 'solid fact' is a fiction. What the theory takes as fact and actually uses as such is another judgement or set of judgements, and what provides the verification is the coherence between the initial judgement and these.

Consider the cardinal. This is supposed to be fact, unadulterated brute fact, given directly to our senses and providing a solid reality to which our thought is to correspond. But no bird is a mere sense datum, or even a collection of sense data. Suppose that standing in our place were an animal with all our senses, each developed to the highest acuteness, but unable to attach meanings to sense data as we do, or note likenesses, implications, and differences. Would such a creature perceive what we perceive? Plainly not. To recognize a cardinal is a considerable intellectual achievement, for to do it one must grasp, implicitly but none the less really, the *concept* of cardinal, and this can only be done by a leap far out of the given into ideal classification. The most ignorant person among us who achieves such recognition could unpack from it a surprising wealth of contents. The idea of living organisms, the thought of the bird kingdom and its outstanding characteristics, the notions of flight and a peculiar song and a determinate colour—these and many other notions are so bound up with the identification that our thought would lose its character with the removal of any one of them. Not that they are logical implicates which later analysis might find to be entailed by our identification; they are parts or components of it, as truly as 'plane' is part of 'plane triangle'; they are part of what we mean when we use the word 'cardinal'. And these essential elements, at least at the time and for the most part, are not given in sense at all. They are elements in a theory, and a theory of no little complexity, which is based on sense data if you will, but could not possibly consist of them.

Indeed, that the brute-fact view of perception is untrue is proved by this alone, that perception may be mistaken; I may take the cardinal for a robin. If the object were mere given fact, such a mistake would be impossible. A fact is what it is, and cannot possibly be something else. If it appears to be something else, the seeming must be in our thought, and the perception that involves such seemings has advanced beyond the given into the region of judgement. What makes the error possible is a theory of ours.

It may be said that if perception is itself theory, that only means that we must look a little further for the verifying fact. Somewhere the bow of theory must come to earth; it cannot float loose in the clouds; a theory that rests on nothing but theory is a mere intellectual caprice. Very well; let us go on in our search for fact. By way of testing our perception, we stealthily approach the bird, observe it from new angles, and note fresh characteristics. Does *this* bring us our ultimate fact unmixed with theory? Obviously not. Suppose we proceed with this method to its farthest possible limit; suppose we shoot the bird, seize it, carry it off to a biological laboratory, and subject it to minute and exhaustive dissection; would *that* give us our solid facts? No again. For every notation of a new trait, or even remarking of an old one, would as truly go beyond brute fact and as truly involve an element of theory as would the original judgement. And so long as it contains this element of theory, it must of course be checked by further perceptions; but then these further perceptions once again are judgements; in no case are they brute facts. Thus the facts with which our judgements were to tally seem forever to elude us, and we find ourselves in a region where, on every side, there are only judgements and still more judgements.

19. This, it may be said, is intolerable. It suggests that we are turning in a maze of thought and never make contact anywhere with sense data or other particulars. But there is nothing in coherence itself that need drive us to this extreme. To be sure we lost belief long ago in what are called particulars,[1] and we have expressed doubts whether the 'sense data' in the form of red patches which figure largely among contemporary writers are either so sensory or so plainly given as their name implies. But even if our scepticism on these matters were removed, our doubt about correspondence would stand. For the point is, assuming that there are sense data, can they *as such* verify anything? A mere judgement of fact is not ultimate, since it is in principle capable of error; and the question then, is whether we can get below this to something at once indubitable and sufficient to verify. Let us turn then to the sort of perception where mistake seems impossible, where the wrappings of association and inference seem so completely torn away as to leave the kernel of sensation bare. Take, for example, the fact of a toothache. Does this not give us mere primitive unclothed pain, and does it not verify 'I have a toothache' with the most complete and precise correspondence? Now with no desire to cavil, we would ask the reader to look at this judgement and tell us whether the elements that are involved in it *could* be given in brute fact. 'I', that is, a self; 'have', that is, a relation of ownership; 'a', that is, one member of a class; 'toothache', that is, a special kind of pain connected with a particular point in the body; every one of these elements is included, and asserted as real; every one of them goes beyond sense data; yet every one of them must be given in fact if the verification is to be complete. Now it is obvious that to look among sense data for things like

[1] See above, Chap. XVII.

these is hopeless. We could never in the world find them there, because they are not the sort of things that could exist there, and if at any time we seemed to find them, it would be only to realize a moment later that what we had was another judgement in the now familiar masquerade of fact.

But perhaps we can strip our judgement barer. To be sure, this is a desperate suggestion, since it means abandoning correspondence for all but the very simplest judgements. But it is unavailing even so. Suppose we lop off the 'I', the 'have', the 'a', the 'tooth', and leave nothing whatever but the ache. Our judgement would then be the impersonal 'it is aching', or 'there is an ache', or perhaps a mere anguished 'Ouch!' Of course, if this is pure exclamation, we are not concerned with it. The test whether it is or not is whether there is sense in denying it; if there is, it is a judgement; if not, it is an exclamation. Let us suppose that it can be denied; it is then a judgement; and the question is: Does it contain any element that is beyond verification by sense data? And surely it does. *What* this is, it is hard to say, but *that* it is, is unquestionable. There is always a difference in content between the general idea used in the judgement, the thought of pain or ache as such, and any wholly specific pain. This may be shown variously. It is shown, first, by the fact that a different kind and degree of pain would correspond equally with the universal used in judgement. It is shown, secondly, by the presence in the judgement of the element of time; the pain is declared to be *now*. But 'now' means membership in a series; 'the present', as Landor says, 'like a note in music, is nothing but as it appertains to what is past and what is to come'; and past and future are not data. Thirdly, we can distinguish degrees in which experience approximates pure pain, and can see that in the judgement we are short of our goal. Fourthly, there is the undoubted fact that we may be mistaken about our own suffering. This is illustrated at least in principle by the remark of George Eliot's heroine, whose malady was the ancient one of love, that she would have been unable to distinguish her state from an experience of extreme suffering except by the reflection that she would not part with it for any that might have been vouchsafed her instead.[1]

20. To all this it may be replied that we are begging some important questions. It is true enough that in the judgement there are elements not to be found among sense data. But in the first place, why assume that given facts must be confined to sense data? Surely 'two and two make four' and 'pleasure is better than pain' are as much given facts as pleasure and pain themselves. And if so, this attempt to show that given fact is too meagre to verify anything proceeds on a false assumption. In the second place, it begs the question of the structure of judgement. Granting that in the judgement there are elements not present in the answering fact, still there does remain in the judgement the reference to that fact, and it is absurd to say that because the correspondence is incomplete, there is no correspondence at all. When I think of this toothache I may also have to think of irrelevancies, but the fact remains that I do think of this toothache, and that my thought does in part correspond to it.

To the first point we answer as follows: It is true that fact may be, and often has been, identified with something other than what is given in sense. It is generally so taken by the Cambridge philosophers, for whom a fact is a *fact that*, such as that I now have a toothache, or that this table is black; nor is there anything in such usage to object to. But to adopt it here would not help us in the least. Let us suppose that such facts exist, and ask how we can know them. We plainly do not sense them; to say we sense *that* A is B is mere confusion. We apprehend the Bness of A through the judgement, A is B. But judgements, as we have seen, are in principle capable of error; this judgement, therefore, stands in need of verification. But if we attempt to verify it by correspondence,

[1] There is an effective page or two on the difficulty of ridding perception of classification and inference in Sidgwick's essay on the 'Criteria of Truth and Error', *The Philosophy of Kant, etc.*, 452–4

what is the fact that it corresponds to? The Bness of A? But we have seen that we can get at that fact only by the judgement, A is B. To take this as infallible is groundless and arbitrary; to take it as self-evident is to resort to another criterion of truth; to appeal to its coherence with the rest of our knowledge is to join us in this criticism; to say that at any rate what one means by truth is correspondence with such fact is to shift the issue. Indeed, that correspondence is the test seems more difficult to defend on this definition of fact than on the other.

21. Returning then to that other, we are told, secondly, that the correspondence between judgement and fact may be at least partial. Whatever extras judgement introduces, it does contain the assertion that a particular pain exists. Now are we to say that the content of this special assertion cannot correspond just because certain extras that come along with it do not correspond? Surely not, it is said. We can analyse this out from its context and consider its correspondence in isolation. But this itself makes two assumptions, neither of which, I think, can be justified. First, it assumes that the nature of the component it is to isolate is unaffected by the others. There is a fact b^1 and there is a judgement abc, and between the b^1 which stands outside the context and the b that stands within it there is to be precise correspondence. And the element b would still correspond with b^1, no matter how varied or complicated became its context within the judgement. It is thus assumed that the nature of b is unaffected by its context. This is not only an assumption but, we believe, a false assumption. Unfortunately since to discuss it would involve us at once in the tortured question of internal relations, we must defer its consideration.[1] But the notion of partial correspondence contains another assumption, which is perhaps the main assumption of the theory generally. It assumes that sensory fact is accessible in its purity, and usable in this form as a test.

[1] See Chaps. XXXI, XXXII.

We have looked into this matter critically in our study of thought in perception, where we were forced to conclude that it is without grounds. This is not to deny, for example, that there are approximations, greater and less, to pure sensory pain. But more particularly in an adult mind, with its innumerable and subtle influences from past experience, its fears and premonitions, its knowledge of causes and results, its flights of classification in which everything received through sense is given its place in a hierarchy of species and genera and related to extensive ranges of remote experience—to suppose that in such experience pain has the sort of purity that it may be presumed to have in the lower orders of life is certainly false to fact.

22. But even if such purity were to be had, it would still not serve. For the facts with which thought corresponds are commonly supposed to be independent facts, not sensations or fancies of our own; and if our criterion cannot discriminate these, it is failing at a crucial point. On this matter, what is proved by givenness in sense? Nothing. When the sufferer from insane delusions, or the man with delirium tremens, or the patient in hypnotic suggestion, reports his painfully vivid perceptions, he is experiencing something given in sense. (To judge givenness by the presence or absence of physical stimulus is of course futile, since one can judge of the presence of the stimulus only by something accepted as given.) No one believes that in these cases what is given is fact, as the term is used by common sense and science. But if whatever is given is fact, and whatever corresponds to this is true, then the judgements of these unhappy people that there are snakes and goblins about are as true as any other judgements, since they are verified in just the same way, according to the theory, as our own beliefs about tables and chairs. One may attempt, of course, to differentiate the two kinds of givenness, but to do that one must go beyond givenness as a test. And then one has abandoned the theory.

23. On this problem different types of mind are moved by different types of argument. For some, a brief dialectical proof that this sort of correspondence cannot be used would settle the matter: others are suspicious of such displays and demand evidence from the practice of science. It seems to me possible in this case to give both parties what they want. As a formal proof, we suggest the following: The matter asserted in judgement of the ordinary categorical type, is of the form, A is B. It asserts at the least a relation between two terms. But a purely sensory fact would lack even this complexity; it would be a mere red, or sweet, or pain. And between A is B on the one side, and a mere A *or* B on the other, correspondence is meaningless. It may be replied of course that a sense datum may be itself complex, that I may sensibly apprehend the red as bright or the spatial nearness of A and B. But, strictly speaking, this is not true. Granting that the brightness belongs to the red, one cannot *see* the relation of 'belonging to'. Nor can one *see* nearness. As Professor Kemp Smith says, 'the factor of thought is no less necessary than the factor of sense, in order that "spreadoutness" be apprehensible in intuition'.[1] But even if we concede to sense such relations as these, there are numberless others commonly asserted in our judgements that quite obviously are never given in sense. 'P implies q'; 'to give is better than to receive'; '*fugaces labuntur anni*'; where should we look among sense data for the relations here asserted?

24. To those who wish the other kind of evidence it is easy to show that in the actual work of science correspondence is not considered enough. In 1874 Sir William Crookes published an account of an extended series of observations made in his own laboratory to test the claims of a spiritualist medium that while in a state of trance she was able to produce fully-formed materializations of disembodied spirits. Crookes arranged the conditions in a way that, to his own satisfaction, completely

[1] *Prolegomena to an Idealist Theory of Knowledge*, 159.

precluded both deception and the co-operation of other persons with the medium; and under these circumstances he reported the following: There appeared a fully materialized figure of a woman some four and one half inches taller than the medium, whose features were larger and complexion lighter, whose pulse-rate by count was 75 while the medium's was 90, who was seen simultaneously with the medium, 'by myself and eight other persons, in my own house, illuminated by the full blaze of the electric light',[1] and who was photographed by a battery of assorted cameras. Now Crookes was a careful and exact observer, of unimpeachable honesty and great scientific distinction. Did science accept his observations? It did not. Though he published in technical journals precise accounts of what he had seen and heard, and described in detail his elaborate precautions, and though a quarter-century later, in his presidential address of 1898 to the British Association he took occasion to say that in all this he had nothing to retract, still in the scientific world his statements met with an incredulity that was steadfast and all but universal. They still do. Nor is this really untypical of the attitude of science toward the claims of perceived facts. If these facts may be read as cohering with the body of established science, in the way of supporting it or extending it, well and good; if they conflict with it, then 'observation and experience are not treated as guides to be meekly followed, but as witnesses to be broken down in cross-examination. Their plain message is disbelieved. . . .'[2] This does not mean, of course, that no observation at variance with received beliefs can get accepted; science would be bound hand and foot if this were true. What it does mean is that observation of this kind is never taken by *itself* as conclusive, as it ought to be if correspondence with perceived fact is to be our test. In case of conflict it is accepted only if the consequences of rejecting generally the sort of evidence here

---

[1] From a letter reproduced in Conan Doyle's *History of Spiritualism*, I. 239.

[2] From a presidential address to the same Association in 1904 by A. J. Balfour; quoted in Joseph, *Logic*, 506.

presented would be intellectually more disastrous than those of accepting it. And this is the appeal to coherence.

25. We have been considering the correspondence test in the region of its greatest strength, namely, in judgements where the natural appeal is to perception. If it fails here, it will hardly succeed where the reference to sensible fact is remote or absent. A few judgements of this kind have been given already; let us cite two or three more; they will suggest how much easier our case would have been if we had not discussed the matter on ground where correspondence is at its strongest. 'I ought to pay my just debts'; 'between any two points on a line an intermediate point may be inserted'; 'if I had served my God as diligently as I have done the king, He would not have given me over in my grey hairs'. How would one go about it to apply correspondence in such cases? Even its initial plausibility has here vanished.[1]

26. But it is time to turn to the second main rival of coherence. Just as it seems at first obvious that statements about perceivable things are to be verified by correspondence, so it seems obvious that such statements as '2 + 2 = 4' and 'a proposition cannot at once be true and false' are to be tested by their self-evidence. To search for evidence outside them implies that they fall short of being clear and certain as they are, whereas they seem to possess already the greatest clearness and certainty of which any judgement is incapable. To try to prove a proposition when the proof is no more certain than the proposition itself and probably far less so, would appear to be idle or stupid.

---

[1] Some contemporary writers seek to evade the difficulty by denying that such statements are assertions at all. Their views will be considered in Chap. XXX. For a useful study of the application of the coherence test to various types of propositions, see Hobhouse, *The Rational Good*, Chap. III.

An enormous number of such 'truths' have at various times been taken as self-evident. Among these are propositions about conduct, such as 'it is my duty to produce the greater good rather than the less'; propositions about existence, such as 'I am'; propositions about quantity, such as 'things equal to the same thing are equal to each other'; spatial propositions, such as 'two straight lines cannot enclose a space'; temporal propositions, such as, 'what is before A is before all that is contemporay with A'; laws of logic, such as 'x must be either A or not-A'. These and great numbers of others from the most diverse fields of knowledge have been put forward as absolutely certain 'within their own four corners'. But this very profusion of self-evident truths gives rise to a suspicion which many writers have thought enough in itself to annul their claims.

27. For it is admitted that a great many propositions taken as self-evident have actually turned out false; and if a test when fairly applied can lead to error anywhere, then it is in principle untrustworthy, that is to say, no test at all. The stock examples are the former judgements about the shape of the earth; if the earth were really round, water would flow out of both ends of the Strait of Gibraltar, and the people on the under side of the earth, having to walk head-downward, would fall off into space. These propositions, once 'self-evident', are to us obviously false. And there is perhaps no department of knowledge that could not furnish similar examples of outmoded 'certainties'. The judgement 'an eye for an eye and a tooth for a tooth' no doubt appeared self-evident to ancient Jewry. Before Galileo it seemed self-evident that heavier bodies would fall faster than lighter ones. The philosophy of causation has swarmed with assertions supposed to be self-evident: 'every event must have a cause and an effect'; 'the effect cannot be greater than the cause'; 'two things with nothing in common cannot interact'; 'nothing can act where it is not'. But to many philosophers all of these statements have seemed either questionable or downright false. Indeed there is not a statement we could make, however transparently true it may seem, that would not meet with the objection somewhere, 'It is by no means evident to me'. And is not this fact alone enough to discredit self-evidence? How can a proposition be self-evident when to some people it is not evident at all?

28. There is some force in this argument, but it is far from decisive. 'Self-evident truths are not truths which are evident to everybody',[1] and 'much that is certain may be very hard to discover'.[2] Because there are aborigines in Australia whose counting becomes confused when they have exhausted their fingers and toes, are we to say that the certainty which the multiplication table presents to our own minds is nothing more than muddle? Because our own grasp of the theory of functions is feeble and uncertain, are we to say that the grasp of the accomplished mathematician must be likewise? Such an argument would throw out any test whatever. It would set up the least intelligent man as the final judge, though to such a man probably all standards alike would be unintelligible. The fact is that there is no sort of inconsistency in accepting both self-evidence and divergent opinions about it, for the reason that this divergence may spring from a great many other things besides the lack of self-evidence. It may spring from a difference in native intelligence, for example, or from a differing understanding of the proposition, or, as so commonly in morals, from a differing apprehension of the values entailed. At the same time the candid defender of self-evidence must admit that this is not a complete answer. For he must admit that there are many propositions so abstract and simple that the hypotheses of varying meanings and conflicting values are scarcely plausible, whose self-evidence is really in dispute between minds of apparently equal ability. And to insist that

[1] Rashdall, *Theory of Good and Evil*, I. 85.
[2] Laird, *Knowledge, Belief, and Opinion*, 219.

a proposition is self-evident when someone else who is equally competent is unable to see this is to invite the charge of dogmatism.

29. How far has disagreement among the doctors gone? Has it broken out only in those border-line cases where the defenders of self-evidence would themselves be doubtful, or has it extended to the propositions on which the defenders would make a last stand? To answer that, we must know what the propositions are that are taken as most indubitably certain. They appear to be of two classes, axioms and logical laws, whose place in the process of thought may be shown as follows. The approved way of demonstrating anything is to cite other propositions from which the one in question follows. But how do we know these other propositions to be true? If by still other propositions, where is the series to end? It ends ultimately, on the theory before us, in certain propositions which need no proof because they are certain in themselves. These are the axioms. They are the sort of propositions that Euclid took to start with, and from which he deduced his theorems. But secondly, such deduction is itself possible only if it accords with the laws of logic. Suppose these laws are called in question; how are they to be established? Obviously not by proof, since they are themselves the laws of proof and we should have to assume them in any proof we offered. We are in the position of being unable to demonstrate them, and yet of accepting them as certain. And what can that mean if not that we take them as self-evident?

Let us consider these two prime cases of (i) axioms and (ii) logical laws. It is true that to consider them fully is here impossible, since the case against self-evidence is so linked with the case for internal relations that we could not complete the one without introducing the other, and this would take us, at the moment, too far afield. But the test of self-evidence can be shown questionable without this, even here in its twin citadels.

30. (i) As for axioms, we are met at the outset by the fact that mathematicians themselves no longer accept these as self-evident, and are even abandoning the name for more non-committal expressions like 'postulate' and 'primitive proposition'. As Professor Laird says, 'there is a growing tendency on the part of mathematical logicians to renounce every claim to the certainty or self-evidence of the "primitive propositions" from which (as they maintain) their science may be generated by a series of logical inferences. According to the latter view the choice of logically primitive propositions is principally a matter of technical convenience. What is logically primitive in one system may be derivative in another. . . .'[1] Of course 'it has not always been so; the term axiom for example was long used to denote "self-evident proposition", which is a kind of proposition that modern mathematicians have not been able to discover'.[2] The assault on tradition has been concentrated on a particular axiom, the axiom of Euclid that through a given point only one line could be drawn parallel to a given line.[3] To the orthodox geometers all the other Euclidean axioms seemed self-evident; and since it was something of a scandal that anything less than certain should lie in the foundations of their subject, they tried to deduce this axiom from the others taken jointly. But that, they found, was impossible. This discovery seems to have been made early in the eighteenth century by the Italian Saccheri, but his results 'alarmed him to such an extent that he devoted the last half of his book to disproving them'.[4] A century later the French mathematician Legendre, the Russian Lobatchewsky, and the Hungarian Bolyai, all returned to the attempt only to fail again. To Lobatchewsky this failure was significant. He began to wonder whether the Euclidean system was as finally and exclusively true as for many centuries it had been taken to be. By way of experiment he asked what would

[1] *Op. cit.*, 218–19.   [2] Keyser, *Mathematical Philosophy*, 41.
[3] 'The liquefaction of Euclidean orthodoxy is the axiom of parallels, and it was by the refusal to admit this axiom without proof that Metageometry began.'—Russell, *Foundations of Geometry*, 7.
[4] Russell, *op. cit.*, 8, note.

follow if he slipped in among the axioms a substitute for this about parallels, and instead of saying, as Euclid did, that only one parallel to a line could be drawn through a given point, said that two or more could be drawn, each of them meeting the line at infinity. He found that by making this assumption he could develop with perfect consistency a whole new system of geometry. A little later the German mathematician Riemann, working in ignorance of these predecessors, raised another but similar question: what would follow if it were assumed that *no* parallels could be drawn? Once more it was found that a complete new geometry would follow, different from both of the others but equally coherent in itself. These pioneers for the most part thought their results had only speculative interest, and did not doubt that actual space was Euclidean.

Their successors were bolder. Helmholtz declared that non-Euclidean space was not only conceivable, but imaginable, though such imagining was difficult because unfamiliar;[1] and rejecting the certainty of axioms, he held that they were all empirical, that they might have been quite different if our sense experience had been different, and that even now they might not hold in regions inaccessible to us. Henri Poincaré, whose view has been increasingly accepted, held that axioms were *neither* self-evident as tradition supposed, nor empirical, as Helmholtz supposed; they were 'conventions' whose choice and development were unrestricted except by the requirement of consistency. It is conceivable that various geometries should fit the facts of experience, though we should naturally choose the simplest because it is the most convenient. But convenience is not truth. Since a plurality of systems might all accord with the facts, questions of truth and falsity are beyond settling by geometry, and indeed by any science. 'Une géométrie ne peut pas être plus vraie qu'une autre; elle peut seulement être *plus commode*.'[2] In the very next sentence, however, Poincaré goes on to swear his allegiance to Euclidean geometry as the one that will always be most convenient. Here the scepticism of his successors has outrun his own. Einstein holds that in dealing

---

[1] Russell, *op. cit.*, 72–3.   [2] *La Science et l'Hypothèse*, 70.

with problems of astronomical physics the Euclidean geometry is actually less simple than the non-Euclidean.[1] Thus for a century past those propositions that are the 'die-hards' among self-evident truths have been beating a slow retreat. A well-known mathematical logician indicates their present plight as follows:

> 'The traditional rationalist conception that metaphysical first principles can be shown to be logically indispensable, or that what is logically prior is thereby proved to be certain or self-evident, is one to which the actual structure of logical and mathematical systems lends no support. In genuinely rigorous deductive systems, as these are understood today, "logically prior" means only "deductively more powerful" or "simpler". The supposed necessity, or logical indispensability, of pre-suppositions most frequently turns out to be nothing more significant than lack of imagination and ingenuity.'[2]

It is easy to push this development so far as to make logic and mathematics merely a complicated game without significance as to the nature of things, in which play consists in the deducing of endless conclusions from arbitrary postulates, or perhaps only in arranging marks on paper. When we come, as we must shortly, to consider the views of necessity held by formalists and logical positivists, we must inquire into the significance of such systems. Meanwhile there is importance for us in the history just recounted. Mathematicians are the students *par excellence* of the place and nature of axioms. And generally speaking, at the present time mathematicians neither consider axioms self-evident nor believe that, if they do appear self-evident, this is a guarantee of their truth. Such an opinion among experts, particularly when it is swelling toward a consensus, is not to be taken lightly.

31. Significant as these opinions are, however, it is probably needless to appeal to them to shake the belief in self-evidence

[1] For an illustration, and a brief but lucid account of some current theories of mathematics, see Cohen's *Reason and Nature*, 178; 171–205.

[2] C. I. Lewis, *Mind and the World-Order*, 204.

as this is commonly held. Considerations far less technical would ordinarily serve. Ask the plain man how he knows that a straight line is the shortest line between two points or, what seems to him equally axiomatic, that $2 + 2 = 4$, and he will probably answer that such things wear their truth on their face. But if this were challenged, would he not naturally say something like this: 'So you doubt, do you, that a straight line is the shortest line? But you can't really live up to such a doubt. If a straight line isn't shortest, why do you cut across a field? Why are roads built straight? For that matter, is there anything we have been taught to believe about space and motion that wouldn't have to be given up if we gave up belief in the axiom? As for the $2 + 2$ example, it is really the same thing again. Try making the sum anything but four, and see where it takes you. If $2 + 2$ were 5, $1 + 1$ would not be 2, and then 1 would not be 1; in fact not a single number, or relation between numbers, would remain what it is; all arithmetic would go.' This is the sort of defence, I think, that the plain man would offer; at any rate he would recognize it as reasonable if offered by someone else. And that means that his certainty does not rest on self-evidence merely. He is appealing to the coherence of his proposition with an enormous mass of others which he sees must stand or fall with it. Perhaps it will be replied that certainty may rest partly on self-evidence and partly on coherence also. But consider what this implies. If a proposition is fully self-evident, it is completely certain as it stands, and to say that such certainty can be added to is to contradict oneself. It follows that if a proposition is really self-evident to the plain man, then when he goes on to show that its untruth would destroy all our views about space and motion, this insight adds nothing whatever to the certainty he has already. Can we accept that? I do not think we can. The insight that a proposition has the support of an entire science, so that it cannot be rejected without rejecting the science with it, does surely increase its certainty. But if it were fully certain already, this would be impossible. Its certainty, therefore, does not rest on self-evidence alone.

32. Indeed it is clear on reflection not only that the certainty of these axiomatic propositions is bound up with a system which includes them, but that the same is true of their meaning. ' "A straight line is the shortest distance between two points" is true of Euclidean space, i.e., within a system defining Euclidean geometry, but may be false of certain non-Euclidean spaces. *The very meaning of "straight", "line", "short", and "point", is a function of the system*'.[1] Whatever 'real' space may be like, and whether or not there is any meaning in speaking of such space, at any rate the space of ordinary thought is of the sort that Euclid described; and when we think of lines, surfaces, and figures, we construe them in accordance with it. The axiom that a straight line is the shortest line, belongs to the geometry of the only space that most of us know, and the general nature of this space has so eaten into the meanings of our terms that being the shortest distance between two points seems less a consequent of straightness, deducible if we think, than part of what the term means. The characters of space and line have so blended and interfused that dissociation seems, and probably is, impracticable. Similarly of $2 + 2 = 4$; we think of the items as numbers, that is as members of a numerical order; and if, *per impossibile*, all reference to that order were omitted from our concept and we were no longer to think, for example, of 4 as *the number* 4, it is hard to say what would be left. To hold that such propositions are self-evident, in the sense that we can see their truth without reference to anything beyond them, is thus to leave their meaning unanalysed. Even this meaning cannot be apprehended, to say nothing of their truth, without going beyond them. And it is of no use to seek a residuum of self-certainty by stripping off all external reference, for the stripped remainder is then no longer the proposition we had, and has become so indeterminate that we are not even clear what it is for which self-evidence is to be claimed.

[1] K. Rosinger, *Journal of Philosophy*, XXX (1933), 296; my italics.

33. We add only one more point about axioms. Their 'self-evidence' varies from case to case, and it is instructive to consider whether this is really a variation in self-evidence or in something else on which the seeming self-evidence depends. Mr. Russell writes: 'Self-evidence has degrees: it is not a quality which is simply present or absent, but a quality which may be more or less present, in gradations ranging from absolute certainty down to an almost imperceptible faintness.' If we consider at random a number of propositions that have been accepted as self-evident, we do seem to find these grada-tions. 'The sun is rising'; 'the Venus de Milo is a more perfect work of art than the Laocoön'; 'ex nihilo nihil fit'; 'cruelty is wrong'; 'two parallel lines cannot enclose a space'; 'a pro-position cannot be both true and false'. These vary widely in certainty. The judgement about the sun, taken in earlier times as self-evident, is now rejected flatly; the judgement about the statues would be made, one suspects, with great uncertainty; the others would probably all be accepted. But here again I do not think their certainty would be rated equal; it may be hazarded that most people would regard this as gradually increasing and as reaching a maximum at the end in the law of contradiction.

Now as one reflects on such a series, does one find that the increasing certainty is an increase in pure self-luminousness, or is there some other variant that may serve to account for this increasing certainty? I suggest that there is such a variant. It is the half conscious recognition that what we are asserting is connected with a sub-system, more or less important, of our real world. The proposition about the sun's rising is now rejected; why? Because it conflicts with our established system of astronomy. The judgement about the Venus de Milo is uncertain; why? Is it not chiefly because, of that mass of perceptions, feelings, and stored aesthetic experience which alone would entitle a critic to pass judgement on masterpieces, we know that we have only a fragment? In the first instance, falsity accompanies conflict with a system; in the second,

[1] *Problems of Philosophy*, 183.

uncertainty accompanies absence of a system. And a little reflection will reveal the influence of system insinuating itself throughout. The judgement that nothing can come from nothing has all physical science behind it, but still in the mind of the average man it is a little less than certain because hovering on the outskirts of his science is the wraith of another system, still vaguely inviting, in which miracles were frequent, and creation from nothing was accepted fact. He is perhaps a shade more certain that cruelty is wrong, and again the judgement may seem immediate. But it is a commonplace of ethics that in what looks like an intuition may be condensed a wealth of reflection and experience; and the implications of this judgement are such that the denial of it would involve our plain man in the wreck of his ethics generally.[1] As for his judgement about parallel lines, we have seen this to be so bound up with his view of space that the two stand or fall together, though if he were a mathematical speculator the certainty would probably diminish as the power to conceive alternative systems grew. But as to the law of contradiction, even this would hardly affect his certainty. He would probably say that this law was self-evident absolutely. But is it not significant that it is just this law whose denial, more plainly than that of any other, would cut him off from truth altogether, through leaving him no truth in any region that might not also be false?[2] To summarize: in the judgement about creation from nothing, we can say, 'this or no law of causation'; in the judgement about cruelty, we can say, 'this or no world of values'; in the judgement about parallel lines, we can say,

---

[1] 'It is just as certain that deliberate cruelty is wrong, as it is that grass is green or that two and two make four. Cruelty cannot be consistently willed by men who are trying to live coherent lives in the service of a coherent society. Indeed there is no conceivable society in which it could be so willed, for if it were, each man would will that others should be cruel to himself, and in that case cruelty would not be cruelty at all but simply kindness, and the pain in which we all found our satisfaction would be not pain but pleasure.'—Paton, *The Good Will*, 371.

[2] See below, Sec. 41 ff. And for further discussion of degrees of necessity, see Chap. XXXI, Secs. 10–12.

'this or no spatial world as we know it'; in the judgement
about contradiction, we can say, 'this or nothing'.

The inference from such a review is plain. It is hardly
credible that so much correspondence between degree of
certainty in our propositions and depth of inherence in our
real world should be an accident. The suggestion is a very
strong one that for the increasing 'self-evidence' there is a
reason, which means that 'self-evidence' is really a mask for
something else. This something else may not at the time be
apprehended explicitly, but we have seen, both in the study of
perception and in our more recent study of the subconscious,
that apprehension may be none the less real for being implicit.
The identity of the missing variant will have surprised nobody.
It is coherence once again.

That self-evidence is not a matter of black and white is
further brought home to us when we consider how we come to
apprehend it. The difference between a proposition that is
not self-evident and one that is, ought, on the theory, to be
immense—all the difference between uncertainty and absolute
finality, and the process of seizing the self-evident should be
a sudden leap from twilight to noon. If we regard the way in
which the great mass of supposedly self-evident insights
have been achieved, do we find either individuals or the race
arriving at them by these discontinuous leaps? The record
reveals a very different process, a process of more or less
painful intellectual gropings and long-continued stumblings
toward clear light, rewarded only gradually by success. That
nothing comes from nothing, that cruelty is wrong, that a
musical scale must be continued by one interval rather than
another, even the mathematical demonstrations which 'every
school-boy knows' must go thus and not otherwise—these
have only been gained by protracted wrestlings of the racial
mind, which even now is none too firm in its hold upon them.
We are not contending that the belief in self-evidence is inconsistent with the belief that some self-evident propositions are
more difficult to grasp than others, and are therefore apprehensible only at a higher intellectual level. What we are saying is

that the self-evidence already achieved has attached itself only gradually to the propositions now said to own it, that their certainty, far from leaping at once to the full, has been a slow acquisition, gained as the mind, in the course of a cumulative experience, has turned to them again and again. Such a process is not what we should expect if self-evidence is an all-or-nothing affair, a character simply absent or present within the bounds of an isolated proposition. It is precisely what we should expect if self-evidence is, as we have suggested, the voice in explicit consciousness of systems that vary in magnitude and are achieved in varying degree.[1]

34. (ii) The proposition at the end of our series was the law of contradiction. This is of course one of the traditional 'laws of thought', and with it we have arrived before the second citadel of self-evidence. Thus far we have been inquiring whether there are any self-evident *axioms*; we now face the parallel question about logical laws.

We may begin as before. For it is not only the axioms of the sciences that have been called in question of late years; it is also the laws of reasoning. Naturally enough the latter development is the more recent. When the traditional axioms were questioned, and alternative sets proposed, logic at any rate seemed safe. The following argument was accounted decisive. 'When you adopt these alternative sets, you do so for the sake of drawing inferences from them. Now reasoning must have canons, and you will find when you examine your reasoning, no matter where you start, that its canons are always the same. Abandon these and you cannot advance a step. You may start if you will with alternative postulates, but there is only one logic by which to develop them; alternative logics are unthinkable.' This answer is now challenged, and to convey some notion of the nature of this challenge, we quote from an article by Professor Lewis on 'Alternative Systems of Logic':

[1] I owe the suggestion of this line of thought to Dr. J. E. Turner.

'From Aristotle down, the laws of logic have been regarded as fixed and archetypal; and as such that they admit of no conceivable alternatives. Often they have been attributed to the structure of the universe or to the nature of human reason; and in general they have been regarded as providing an Archimedean fixed point in the realm of thought . . . modern studies in exact logic reveal certain facts in the light of which any such belief becomes highly problematic. For example, in *Principia Mathematica*, the fundamental laws of mathematics are derived from a logic which is distinctly not in accord with traditional Aristotelian conceptions; yet this deduction is notably successful, and certainly could not be called fallacious. There are, moreover, an indefinitely large number of other such non-Aristotelian systems . . . it can be demonstrated beyond all reasonable doubt that the number of different implication-relations, in terms of which our inferences might be drawn (with complete validity in every case), is unlimited.' The main conclusions of the article are: (1) 'There are no "laws of logic" which can be attributed to the universe or to human reason in the traditional fashion.' (2) 'There are an unlimited number of possible systems of logic, each such that every one of its laws is true and is applicable to deduction.' (3) 'Any current or accepted canon of inference must be pragmatically determined.'[1]

Professor Lewis is far from alone in these beliefs; and they have been illustrated of late by a number of eminent contemporaries who have contrived systems in which the laws of deduction are held to differ fundamentally from those of the traditional logic. Brouwer has produced a system in which the law of excluded middle is discarded. Hilbert has produced a number-system that makes invalid the commutative law of multiplication ($a \times b = b \times a$), which, if not a part of the traditional logic, is at least a natural extension of it. One can vary the definition of implication by admitting different numbers of 'truth-values' for the propositions of one's system, and these varying definitions of implication, it is held, will give different logics. A two-valued logic such as *Principia Mathematica* takes account only of the values of truth and falsity in propositions, and defines implication as meaning,

[1] *Monist*, Vol. XLII (1932), 481–4.

'either p (the implier) is false or q (the implied) is true'. And since this gives several possibilities (p and q both true, p and q both false, or p false and q true) any proposition will imply another when any of these possibilities is realized. In the three-valued logic of the Polish logicians Lukasiewicz and Tarski, propositions have the values of true, false, and doubtful, and the ways in which propositions may imply each other are thus very much more numerous. But to work with these apparently is child's play compared with the manipulations of Dr. W. T. Parry's four-valued system, whose unprinted original lies in the Widener library. In this Professor Lewis calculates that propositions may imply others in over a million different ways.

Now the purpose of referring to these alternative logics is neither to expound them nor to criticize them.[1] The object is simpler. It is to point out that, assuming the laws of logic to be self-evident, it is the professional logicians above all who should be able to certify this. If there are many logicians of high competence (and no one will deny this character to Messrs. Russell, Whitehead, or Lewis) who consider that the laws of traditional logic are no more self-evidently true than a variety of alternative laws which they are ready to supply, that in itself is a significant argument. It is an argument that still holds whether their belief that there are alternative logics is right or wrong. For the belief that there *cannot* be alternative logics is supposed to be self-evident; and while we

---

[1] Such discussion as seems called for is offered in Chaps. XXIX and XXX. But it may perhaps be remarked here that I do not see how the criticism offered by Paul Weiss, *Philosophical Review*, XLII. 520–5 (1933), can be effectively met. And so far as the systems are really thinkable, I agree with Messrs. Cohen and Nagel that 'what have recently been claimed to be alternative systems of logic are different systems of notation or symbolization for the same logical facts.'—*Logic and Scientific Method*, v. 'If we admit the conception of "alternative logics" into logic, we are implying that we need not all employ the same principles of reasoning, and there is an end to argument. There is no basis even for disagreement, and logic in effect commits suicide.'—A. J. D. Porteous, *Arist. Soc. Proc.* Sup. Vol. XV (1936), 135.

cannot demand that what is self-evident shall be self-evident to all, still if one's assertion is denied by the most competent of experts, the insistence upon its certainty, amounting as that does to the charge that one's opponents are myopic about the simplest of logical laws, suggests something less than the open mind. If eyes like these cannot see what we say is there, whose eyes are better?

35. The suspicion aroused by such disharmony is confirmed when we come to examine the laws in question more narrowly. They possess one prominent character that is so very like self-evidence as to be commonly taken for this, but which is really different. It is in the nature of any ultimate logical law to be incapable of a self-consistent denial so long as one remains within its system. Thus to deny the law of contradiction is presumably to say that the law is false rather than true; but this is to make use of the very law one is denying, since in denying it one certainly does not mean that though false it may also be true. Thus in rejecting the law of contradiction one is implicitly contradicting oneself. And unless one is careful, the confused notion will arise that perceiving this fact is what we mean by perceiving the law as self-evident, or perhaps even that it is a demonstration of self-evidence. But it is neither the one nor the other. To perceive self-evidence is one thing; to perceive that a judgement is true because of what is implied in its denial is something else. The suggestion that self-evidence can be *demonstrated*, in this manner or in any other, is a sort of Irish bull. There is no need to question the proof in itself; it is circular to be sure; but that is the only sort of demonstration of which any proposition in pure logic is susceptible. What we should point out is, first, that it *is* a demonstration and not an appeal to self-evidence; secondly, that the demonstration lies in showing that acceptance of the law is necessary on pain of incoherence. The argument is: *if* the law of contradiction holds, then within the system governed by it even the assertion that it does not hold assumes that it does. The incoherence is between the principle of the system and the content of a proposition supposed to be made within it.[1]

When self-evidence is attacked, its defenders are likely to fall back on this dialectical defence without realizing that they have thus betrayed their cause. But it may be felt that this is still not the best defence of the laws of logic, that whatever its attractiveness to those of nimble wit, the sober citizens who feel only distaste for such exercises have a solid and more convincing proof of their own. With this we agree. When confronted by such a law, one has a sense, to use Bosanquet's phrase, that it is 'this or nothing'. When we lack evidence for a proposition, there are in general two ways of reflectively satisfying ourselves about it. The first is to assume its truth and ask what follows; if we find that it leads us on to much that is acceptable and little that is not, we take this, so far, as ground for believing it. Assume that evolution is true, and numberless reported facts become not only acceptable but mutually sustaining, while nothing comparable to this mass must be rejected. But as we ascend the scale of abstractness, we stand in increasing need of some further principle, since if we start from a proposition of very high abstractness such as a law of mathematics or logic we cannot derive concrete results. So if we are prudent we change our policy, and instead of asking what follows if our law is true, we ask what follows if it is false. To work out what is geometrically entailed by the proposition that two straight lines cannot enclose a space is a formidable undertaking, but it is easy enough to see that if the proposition is rejected, Euclidean space must go with it. So of the laws of logic. The man who is quite incapable of dialectical manipula-

---

[1] Professor Lewis would not admit that, if a proposition is reaffirmed through its denial, this has any bearing on its truth. 'Since a bad logic, whose principles are false, may still be such that the denial of any one of these principles will lead to its reaffirmation, it follows that the test of "reaffirmation through denial" does not in logic prove the truth of the principle thus reaffirmed.' (*Mind and the World Order*, 209–10). This is clearly the correct view for one who believes in alternative logics. But for anyone who believes, as the writer does (see Chap. XXX), that there is and can be one logic only, this test will have a different value.

tion can still see that unless these hold, his beliefs generally are undermined, and thus that the laws possess a charter conferred by knowledge in its entirety.

36. Whether such verification is possible for ultimate laws has been questioned, and three plausible objections have been brought against it. First it is held that the method of defending a logical law by deriving absurdities from its denial is invalid, since from such a denial nothing follows; secondly, that the absurdity supposed to be derived, namely, 'nothing is true', is not a proposition at all; thirdly, that the argument, 'this or nothing', is a disjunctive argument which must accept at least the principle of disjunction as evident in itself. These objections are technical, but they are hardly to be evaded, and I believe they can be briefly met.

(*a*) If one argues for a logical law by starting from its contradictory and then applying denial of the consequent, it is clear, as the objection points out, that one will arrive nowhere. The argument runs: 'if the law is false, then such and such consequences follow; these consequences are untenable; hence the law must be true.' The trouble here is that in making our inference to the consequent we are assuming as valid the law our antecedent declares invalid; we have denied a law of logic; and how are we to proceed when we have denied that which makes logical procedure possible? The answer is that we *cannot* proceed, and it is precisely this inability of thought to take any step whatever that disqualifies the antecedent. The sceptic naturally grows derisive over the sort of proof for a logical law that uses the law itself to draw inferences from its falsity; and if the argument here were an ordinary denial of the consequent, we could only plead guilty to his charge. But the argument is of a special type. It is not based on the inference to an impossibility, but on the impossibility of inference. As Bosanquet says: 'if thought is estopped from experimenting, i.e. from thinking, then it has no means of displaying its necessity. Here *is* actually our ultimate contradiction. If we are not allowed to think, we are not allowed to exercise the act which these pervading laws need for their establishment. They are not premises. They are principles evident throughout our thinking as the manners of its self-assertion.'[1] The contention here is obviously not that if we deny the law of contradiction thought will move on to an absurd conclusion, but that under such a condition it will not and cannot move at all. If it is forbidden to assert anything as true rather than not, it is forbidden all assertion whatever. We have thus a genuine case of 'this or nothing'. 'Yes, but a *de facto* paralysis of thought is not the same as a logical necessity; what you have here is psychological necessity only.' It is to be doubted whether those who say this have any clear idea of the relation of logical and psychological necessity, but we can only reply that from the point of view maintained throughout this book Bosanquet's answer is decisive: 'This is not a "psychological" necessity. It is a necessity of the nature of reality which it is thought's function and character to reveal. How do we know it is thought's function and character to do so? Because every act of thought says so. Thought, in asserting, does not say "I think so". It says "it is so". "I think so" is merely one case of "it is so", and is as absolute as any other assertion of a fact about reality.'[2]

37. (*b*) The second objection to establishing logical law by the this-or-nothing method, was that one horn of the disjunction, namely 'no propositions are true', was a statement without meaning. Professor Broad writes: 'It is gravely doubtful whether

[1] *Mind*, XXXI. 181 (1922). In these pages I am much indebted not only to this article of Bosanquet's, but also to Broad's review of *Implication and Linear Inference* (*Mind*, XXIX, 323–38). on which the article is a commentary.

[2] *Ibid.*, 181. 'It is really because we cannot conceive ourselves denying the complete world of our experiences that we are obliged to hold the simplest *a priori* truths to be affirmed in their negation. They have to be affirmed because they are the world at its minimum, with only "a single neck". But non-contradiction has really a stronger purchase, the more there is to lose by contradiction.'—Bosanquet, *Principle of Individuality*. 267.

the statement, *Nothing is true*, is either true or false. In actual fact this set of noises or marks does not stand for any proposition at all; for the theory of logical types condemns such expressions as meaningless. Thus it would be unfortunate if all inference really did depend on a disjunction, the second member of which is not a proposition at all, but a mere noise like Jabberwocky.'[1] So it would. But if we look at the assertion in its context, we shall see that it is needless to wait for agreement on one of the most controverted issues in symbolic logic before we know whether we mean anything by it. Indeed a meaning that will serve our purpose has just been suggested. The assertion that is forced upon us is not in strictness that all propositions are false, but that under the condition no propositions can be made. This does not mean—to repeat—that we are inhibited psychologically from doing what we might do otherwise. The point is rather that if the assertion of something did not exclude its contradictory it would have no intelligible content, and therefore would not be in the logical sense an assertion at all. Perhaps 'nothing would be true' is a bad way of expressing this; if so, we suggest the alternative, 'no proposition would have an intelligible meaning'. When we say then of the law of contradiction, 'this or nothing', the notion we attach to 'nothing' is definable clearly; it states the obvious alternative to the law of contradiction; and it is absolutely destructive.

38. (*c*) The third criticism of the this-or-nothing proof was that it proceeded on a certain principle, the principle of disjunctive reasoning, and that this, being the canon of the proof, cannot itself be established by such proof. There is nothing in essence new in this objection. It is merely the insistence through a new example that the test we have proposed as the true one will not apply. The answer is as follows: the law of excluded middle, which is applied in any argument from complete disjunction, is as much 'a necessity of the method by which

[1] *Mind*, XXIX. 327 (1920).

thought proceeds'[1] as the principle of contradiction itself. That law is that x must be either a or not-a; and the question is, can it be established by 'this-or-nothing'? The method is to try what happens when the law is suspended. What thought then has to work with is an x which is neither a nor not-a. And once more, under such a condition it plainly cannot start. What it is called upon to conceive is inconceivable. Permit it to move in accord with the law and it will validate the law through constructing under it a system that turns out satisfactory; forbid it so to move and you forbid it even to be. There is thus for the principle of disjunction, as for the principle of contradiction, a perfectly intelligible test by 'this or nothing'

39. It may be said that this support of logical laws by showing that their denial involves paralysis is a painfully roundabout way of applying coherence, and that it would be better if we could show their necessity positively, by exhibiting their part in the system of knowledge. In a manner this can be done. To be sure, we cannot establish them as we might a biological theory, by drawing inferences that experience verifies; we have seen that the abstract pattern will not fill itself in at our bidding. It would be unreasonable to demand that we show the coherence of logical laws with the rest of our knowledge in the same way as we show this of propositions about matters of fact. But these laws do cohere with empirical knowledge in the way that is natural to them, and to such coherence all experience is a witness. Before proceeding with this point, we may remark that it disposes of one of the subtlest objections to our position. The objection runs as follows: suppose we make some proposition, discover that it coheres, and accept it as so warranted; still the insight *that* it coheres possesses a truth of its own, and *this* is surely not warranted by coherence. Without accepting this view, we must admit that there is a

---

[1] Bosanquet, *ibid.*, 181. Again I am restating Bosanquet as I understand him.

somewhat different type of coherence in the two cases. In the first case it is the coherence with each other of the parts of a system; in the second it is the coherence of a principle with the instances that exemplify it. But the implied demand of this argument is one that would be fatal to all criteria, for it would object to the criterion's having instances; for example, we should have to reject self-evidence, since the insight that a particular case exemplifies self-evidence does not have the same kind of self-evidence as the proposition itself.[1] But the whole demand is illicit. To speak for coherence only, the principles of a system cannot in the nature of the case cohere with its contents as those contents cohere with each other. Still they do cohere after their kind. While the principle of syllogism does not cohere with some particular syllogism as the propositions of the latter cohere with each other, still to *deny* coherence between principle and instance would be felt at once as unreasonable. Such principles cohere with experience in the completest way that is open to them, by supplying a framework into which everything actual or conceivable fits harmoniously. If they make this system possible and they alone, then in a special but legitimate sense they too are validated by 'this or nothing'. The Kantian deduction of the categories is not the argument that would first suggest itself as an application of coherence, but there is no reason to deny that it is one.[2]

[1] While we do not consider this a sound criticism of the self-evidence theory, there is another somewhat similar criticism that we should accept. As Professor Spaulding says, 'the question must be raised whether it is self-evident that that which is self-evident is necessarily true'. He concludes that it is not, and we agree. If the theory of self-evidence is tested by itself, it will not stand. See *The New Rationalism*, 130.

[2] Cf. Dr. Ewing: 'We must suppose that there is in some cases an immediate insight to the effect that X is coherent or incoherent with the system, which insight is not itself based on a further argument from coherence, otherwise the criterion would not be applicable to anything at all. But such an admission might still leave coherence in the position of the sole criterion, for the immediate insight would consist simply in seeing whether a proposition conforms to this criterion and so is true, or contradicts it and so is false, and the essen-

40. It is time to summarize. Our defence of coherence as the test of truth took the form of examining its rivals and showing that, far from having any virtue of their own, such virtue as they had was borrowed from coherence. We first attempted to show this briefly of two less impressive rivals, authority and mystic insight. We then turned to the more formidable claimants, correspondence and self-evidence, and, taking each at its strongest, the former among judgements of fact, the latter among axioms and logical laws, we attempted to show that even here these principles in their own right can validate nothing, and are compelled like the others to fall back upon coherence. If the case against these tests has seemed less than complete, we would remind the reader again that they have been dealt with on their own grounds. We have taken them at their best; if we had taken them at their worst, their claim to provide general tests would have been immeasurably weaker. But if we have succeeded, the result is significant. It is that when really pressed, we never anywhere or at any time use any test but one. Coherence is our sole criterion of truth.

tial force of the coherence theory would not be impaired at all. To use any criterion we must be able sometimes to see whether a given object conforms to it or not.'—*Idealism*, 241.

CHAPTER XXVI

COHERENCE AS THE NATURE OF TRUTH

1. It has been contended in the last chapter that coherence is in the end our sole criterion of truth. We have now to face the question whether it also gives us the nature of truth. We should be clear at the beginning that these are different questions, and that one may reject coherence as the definition of truth while accepting it as the test. It is conceivable that one thing should be an accurate index of another and still be extremely different from it. There have been philosophers who held that pleasure was an accurate gauge of the amount of good in experience, but that to confuse good with pleasure was a gross blunder. There have been a great many philosophers who held that for every change in consciousness there was a change in the nervous system and that the two corresponded so closely that if we knew the laws connecting them we could infallibly predict one from the other; yet it takes all the hardihood of a behaviourist to say that the two are the same. Similarly it has been held that though coherence supplies an infallible measure of truth, it would be a very grave mistake to identify it with truth.

2. The view that truth *is* coherence rests on a theory of the relation of thought to reality, and since this is the central problem of the theory of knowledge, to begin one's discussion by assuming the answer to it or by trying to make one out of whole cloth would be somewhat ridiculous. But as this was our main problem in the long discussions of Book II, we may be pardoned here for brevity. First we shall state in *résumé* the relation of thought to reality that we were there driven to accept, and sketch the theory of truth implicit in it. We shall then take up one by one the objections to this theory and ask if they can pass muster.

To think is to seek understanding. And to seek understanding is an activity of mind that is marked off from all other activities by a highly distinctive aim. This aim, as we saw in our chapter on the general nature of understanding, is to achieve systematic vision, so to apprehend what is now unknown to us as to relate it, and relate it necessarily, to what we know already. We think to solve problems; and our method of solving problems is to build a bridge of intelligible relation from the continent of our knowledge to the island we wish to include in it. Sometimes this bridge is causal, as when we try to explain a disease; sometimes teleological, as when we try to fathom the move of an opponent over the chess board; sometimes geometrical, as in Euclid. But it is always systematic; thought in its very nature is the attempt to bring something unknown or imperfectly known into a sub-system of knowledge, and thus also into that larger system that forms the world of accepted beliefs. That is what explanation is. *Why* is it that thought desires this ordered vision? Why should such a vision give satisfaction when it comes? To these questions there is no answer, and if there were, it would be an answer only because it had succeeded in supplying the characteristic satisfaction to this unique desire.

But may it not be that what satisfies thought fails to conform to the real world? Where is the guarantee that when I have brought my ideas into the form my ideal requires, they should be *true*? Here we come round again to the tortured problem of Book II. In our long struggle with the relation of thought to reality we saw that if thought and things are conceived as related only externally, then knowledge is luck; there is no necessity whatever that what satisfies intelligence should coincide with what really is. It may do so, or it may not; on the principle that there are many misses to one bull's-eye, it more probably does not. But if we get rid of the misleading analogies through which this relation has been conceived, of copy and original, stimulus and organism, lantern and screen, and go to thought itself with the question what reference to an object means, we get a different and more hopeful answer. To think of a thing is to get that thing itself in some degree within the mind. To think of a colour or an emotion is to have that within us which if it *were developed and completed*, would identify itself with the object. In short, if we accept its own report, thought is related to reality as the partial to the perfect fulfilment of a purpose. The more adequate its grasp the more nearly does it approximate, the more fully does it realize in itself, the nature and relations of its objects.

3. Thought thus appears to have two ends, one immanent, one transcendent. On the one hand it seeks fulfilment in a special kind of satisfaction, the satisfaction of systematic vision. On the other hand it seeks fulfilment in its object. Now it was the chief contention of our second book that these ends are one. Indeed unless they are accepted as one, we could see no alternative to scepticism. If the pursuit of thought's own ideal were merely an elaborate self-indulgence that brought us no nearer to reality, or if the apprehension of reality did not lie in the line of thought's interest, or still more if both of these held at once, the hope of knowledge would be vain. Of course it may really be vain. If anyone cares to doubt whether the framework of human logic has any bearing on the nature of things, he may be silenced perhaps, but he cannot be conclusively answered. One may point out to him that the doubt itself is framed in accordance with that logic, but he can reply that thus we are taking advantage of his logico-centric predicament; further, that any argument we can offer accords equally well with his hypothesis and with ours, with the view that we are merely flies caught in a logical net and the view that knowledge reveals reality. And what accords equally well with both hypotheses does not support either to the exclusion of the other. But while such doubt is beyond reach by argument, neither is there anything in its favour.[1] It is a mere suspicion which is, and by its nature must remain, without any positive ground; and as such it can hardly be discussed. Such suspicions aside, we can throw into the scale for our theory the impressive

[1] See further, Chap. XXX, Sec. 15.

fact of the advance of knowledge. It has been the steadfast assumption of science whenever it came to an unsolved problem that there was a key to it to be found, that if things happened thus rather than otherwise they did so for a cause or reason, and that if this were not forthcoming it was never because it was lacking, but always because of a passing blindness in our-selves. Reflection has assumed that pursuit of its own immanent end is not only satisfying but revealing, that so far as the immanent end is achieved we are making progress toward the transcendent end as well. Indeed, that these ends coincide is the assumption of every act of thinking whatever. To think is to raise a question; to raise a question is to seek an explanation; to seek an explanation is to assume that one may be had; so to assume is to take for granted that nature in that region is intelligible. Certainly the story of advancing knowledge un-winds as if self-realization in thought meant also a coming nearer to reality.

4. That these processes are really one is the metaphysical base on which our belief in coherence is founded. If one admits that the pursuit of a coherent system has actually carried us to what everyone would agree to call knowledge, why not take this ideal as a guide that will conduct us farther? What better key can one ask to the structure of the real? Our own conviction is that we should take this immanent end of thought in all seriousness as the clue to the nature of things. We admit that it may prove deceptive, that somewhere thought may end its pilgrimage in frustration and futility before some blank wall of the unintelligible. There are even those who evince their superior insight by taking this as a foregone conclusion and regarding the faith that the real is rational as the wishful thinking of the 'tender-minded'. Their attitude appears to us a compound made up of one part timidity, in the form of a refusal to hope lest they be disillusioned; one part muddled persuasion that to be sceptical is to be sophisticated; one part honest dullness in failing to estimate rightly the weight of the combined postulate and success of knowledge; one part genuine insight into the possibility of surds in nature. But whatever its motives, it is a view that goes less well with the evidence than the opposite and brighter view. That view is that reality is a system, completely ordered and fully intelligible, with which thought in its advance is more and more identifying itself. We may look at the growth of knowledge, individual or social, either as an attempt by our own minds to return to union with things as they are in their ordered wholeness, or the affirmation through our minds of the ordered whole itself. And if we take this view, our notion of truth is marked out for us. Truth is the approximation of thought to reality. It is thought on its way home. Its measure is the distance thought has travelled, under guidance of its inner compass, toward that intelligible system which unites its ultimate object with its ultimate end. Hence at any given time the degree of truth in our experience as a whole is the degree of system it has achieved. The degree of truth of a particular proposition is to be judged in the first instance by its coherence with experience as a whole, ultimately by its coherence with that further whole, all-comprehensive and fully articulated, in which thought can come to rest.

5. But it is time we defined more explicitly what coherence means. To be sure, no fully satisfactory definition can be given; and as Dr. Ewing says, 'it is wrong to tie down the advocates of the coherence theory to a precise definition. What they are doing is to describe an ideal that has never yet been completely clarified but is none the less immanent in all our thinking.'[1] Certainly this ideal goes far beyond mere consistency. Fully coherent knowledge would be knowledge in which every judgement entailed, and was entailed by, the rest of the system. Probably we never find in fact a system where there is so much of interdependence. What it means may be clearer if we take a number of familiar systems and arrange them in a series tending to such coherence as a limit. At the

[1] *Idealism*, 231.

bottom would be a junk-heap, where we could know every item but one and still be without any clue as to what that remaining item was. Above this would come a stone-pile, for here you could at least infer that what you would find next would be a stone. A machine would be higher again, since from the remaining parts one could deduce not only the general character of a missing part, but also its special form and function. This is a high degree of coherence, but it is very far short of the highest. You could remove the engine from a motor-car while leaving the other parts intact, and replace it with any one of thousands of other engines, but the thought of such an interchange among human heads or hearts shows at once that the interdependence in a machine is far below that of the body. Do we find then in organic bodies the highest conceivable coherence? Clearly not. Though a human hand, as Aristotle said, would hardly be a hand when detached from the body, still it would be something definite enough; and we can conceive systems in which even this something would be gone. Abstract a number from the number series and it would be a mere unrecognizable x; similarly, the very thought of a straight line involves the thought of the Euclidean space in which it falls. It is perhaps in such systems as Euclidean geometry that we get the most perfect examples of coherence that have been constructed. If any proposition were lacking, it could be supplied from the rest; if any were altered, the repercussions would be felt through the length and breadth of the system. Yet even such a system as this falls short of ideal system. Its postulates are unproved; they are independent of each other, in the sense that none of them could be derived from any other or even from all the others together; its clear necessity is bought by an abstractness so extreme as to have left out nearly everything that belongs to the character of actual things. A completely satisfactory system would have none of these defects. No proposition would be arbitrary, every proposition would be entailed by the others jointly and even singly,[1]

---

[1] Coherence can be defined without this point, which, as Dr. Ewing remarks (*Idealism*, 231), makes the case harder to establish. In no mathematical system, for example, would anyone dream of trying

no proposition would stand outside the system. The integration would be so complete that no part could be seen for what it was without seeing its relation to the whole, and the whole itself could be understood only through the contribution of every part.

6. It may be granted at once that in common life we are satisfied with far less than this. We accept the demonstrations of the geometer as complete, and do not think of reproaching him because he begins with postulates and leaves us at the end with a system that is a skeleton at the best. In physics, in biology, above all in the social sciences, we are satisfied with less still. We test judgements by the amount of coherence which in that particular subject-matter it seems reasonable to expect. We apply, perhaps unconsciously, the advice of Aristotle, and refrain from asking demonstration in the physical sciences, while in mathematics we refuse to accept less. And such facts may be thought to show that we make no actual use of the ideal standard just described. But however much this standard may be relaxed within the limits of a particular science, its influence is evident in the grading of the sciences generally. It is precisely in those sciences that approach most nearly to system as here defined that we achieve the greatest certainty, and precisely in those that are most remote from such system that our doubt is greatest whether we have achieved scientific truth at all. Our immediate exactions shift with the subject-matter; our ultimate standard is unvarying.

7. Now if we accept coherence as the test of truth, does that commit us to any conclusions about the *nature* of truth or

to deduce all the other propositions from any proposition taken singly. But when we are describing an ideal, such a fact is not decisive, and I follow Joachim in holding that in a perfectly coherent system every proposition would entail all others, if only for the reason that its meaning could never be fully understood without apprehension of the system in its entirety.

reality? I think it does, though more clearly about reality than about truth. It is past belief that the fidelity of our thought to reality should be rightly measured by coherence if reality itself were not coherent. To say that the nature of things may be *in*coherent, but we shall approach the truth about it precisely so far as our thoughts become coherent, sounds very much like nonsense. And providing we retained coherence as the test, it would still be nonsense even if truth were conceived as correspondence. On this supposition we should have truth when, our thought having achieved coherence, the correspondence was complete between that thought and its object. But complete correspondence between a coherent thought and an incoherent object seems meaningless. It is hard to see, then, how anyone could consistently take coherence as the test of truth unless he took it also as a character of reality.

8. Does acceptance of coherence as a test commit us not only to a view about the structure of reality but also to a view about the nature of truth? This is a more difficult question. As we saw at the beginning of the chapter, there have been some highly reputable philosophers who have held that the answer to 'What is the test of truth'? is 'Coherence', while the answer to 'What is the nature or meaning of truth?' is 'Correspondence'. These questions are plainly distinct. Nor does there seem to be any direct path from the acceptance of coherence as the test of truth to its acceptance as the nature of truth. Nevertheless there is an indirect path. If we accept coherence as our test, we must use it everywhere. We must therefore use it to test the suggestion that truth *is* other than coherence. But if we do, we shall find that we must reject the suggestion as leading to *in*coherence. Coherence is a pertinacious concept and, like the· well-known camel, if one lets it get its nose under the edge of the tent, it will shortly walk off with the whole.

Suppose that, accepting coherence as the test, one rejects it as the nature of truth in favour of some alternative; and let us assume, for example, that this alternative is correspondence.

This, we have said, is incoherent; why? Because if one holds that truth is correspondence, one cannot intelligibly hold either that it is tested by coherence or that there is any dependable test at all. Consider the first point. Suppose that we construe experience into the most coherent picture possible, remembering that among the elements included will be such secondary qualities as colours, odours, and sounds. Would the mere fact that such elements as these are coherently arranged prove that anything precisely corresponding to them exists 'out there'? I cannot see that it would, even if we knew that the two arrangements had closely corresponding patterns. If on one side you have a series of elements a, b, c . . . , and on the other a series of elements α, β, γ . . . , arranged in patterns that correspond, you have no proof as yet that the *natures* of these elements correspond. It is therefore impossible to argue from a high degree of coherence within experience to its correspondence in the same degree with anything outside. And this difficulty is typical. If you place the nature of truth in one sort of character and its test in something quite different, you are pretty certain, sooner or later, to find the two falling apart. In the end, the only test of truth that is not misleading is the special nature or character that is itself constitutive of truth.

Feeling that this is so, the adherents of correspondence sometimes insist that correspondence shall be its own test. But then the second difficulty arises. If truth does consist in correspondence, no test can be sufficient. For in order to know that experience corresponds to fact, we must be able to get at that fact, unadulterated with idea, and compare the two sides with each other. And we have seen in the last chapter that such fact is not accessible. When we try to lay hold of it, what we find in our hands is a judgement which is obviously not itself the indubitable fact we are seeking, and which must be checked by some fact beyond it. To this process there is no end. And even if we did get at the fact directly, rather than through the veil of our ideas, that would be no less fatal to correspondence. This direct seizure of fact presumably gives us truth, but since that truth no longer consists in correspondence of idea with fact, the main theory has been abandoned. In short, if we can know fact only through the medium of our own ideas, the original forever eludes us; if we can get at the facts directly, we have knowledge whose truth is not correspondence. The theory is forced to choose between scepticism and self-contradiction.[1]

Thus the attempt to combine coherence as the test of truth with correspondence as the nature of truth will not pass muster by its own test. The result is *in*coherence. We believe that an application of the test to other theories of truth would lead to a like result. The argument is: assume coherence as the test, and you will be driven by the incoherence of your alternatives to the conclusion that it is also the nature of truth.

The theory that truth *consists* in coherence must now be developed more specifically. The theory has been widely attacked, and the average reader will not improbably come to it with numerous and dark suspicions. In presenting the theory we shall therefore follow a somewhat unusual procedure. We shall go down the line of these suspicions and objections, trying to deal with them in roughly the order in which they naturally arise, and seeking in our answers to bring the nature and implications of the theory gradually to light.

9. (1) It is objected, first, that the view entails scepticism. What is it that our judgements must cohere with in order to be true? It is a system of knowledge complete and all-inclusive. But obviously that is beyond us—very probably forever beyond us. If to know anything as true, which means simply to know it, requires that we should see its relation to the total of possible knowledge, then we neither do nor can know anything.

The answer lies partly in an admission, partly in an explanation. The admission is that the theory does involve a degree

---

[1] Cf. the criticism of the copy theory above, Chap. VII, Sec. 9. And see the appendix to the present chapter for comment on a current defence of correspondence.

of scepticism regarding our present knowledge and probably all future knowledge. In all likelihood there will never be a proposition of which we can say, 'This that I am asserting, with precisely the meaning I now attach to it, is absolutely true'. Such a conclusion may bring disappointment, but disappointment is not discredit. And in the light of the history of science, this refusal to claim absoluteness for our knowledge appears even as a merit. For the road of history is so thick with discarded certainties as to suggest that any theory which distributes absolute guarantees is touched with charlatanism. Those who would define truth as correspondence or self-evidence commonly believe that in certain judgements these characters can be found to the full and hence that the judgements are true absolutely. But it is easy to point to past judgements which, in the best opinion of the time, satisfied both definitions at once—judgements for example about the flatness of the earth or the rising of the sun—which nevertheless turned out false. In the light of such facts, theories that give patents of absoluteness to any of our present truths have antecedent probability against them. It may be answered that if judgements seeming to be true have turned out false, this does not show that truth has been wrongly defined but only that men have made a mistake as to whether its defining character was present. But the answer is obvious. The objection now before us is that, in contrast with other theories, coherence leads to scepticism. If it is now admitted that the other theories themselves are so difficult to apply that one can have no certainty, even in leading cases, whether the character they define as truth is present or not, then these theories are sceptical also.

We may reply, secondly, with an explanation, which comes essentially to this, that the coherence theory, like other theories, needs to be applied with some common sense. While the truth of a judgement does consist in the last resort in its relations to a completed system, no sensible person would claim to know these in detail, or deny the judgement *any* truth till he did know them, any more than he would deny some beauty to a picture because it failed of beauty absolute. The system we actually work with is always less than *the* whole; at the best it is the mass of scientific knowledge bearing on the point in question; on the average it is a cloudy congeries of memories, suggestions and inferences, ill-organized in the extreme, and yet capable of subconscious mobilization and use. And for all of us, except in rare moments, the interest in truth is satisfied by exercise within these limits. Even the scientist is commonly satisfied if his theory receives the *imprimatur* of the organized knowledge of his time, and he would think it fantastic to attack him on the ground that organized knowledge has been known to change, that it may do so again, and hence that his theory may have to change with it. This last he would no doubt admit, adding however that to allow one's pursuit of science, or one's confidence in it, to be practically affected by this is merely silly. We agree. For all the ordinary purposes of life, coherence does not mean coherence with some inaccessible absolute, but with the system of present knowledge; and since this is by no means beyond determining, to describe the theory as simply sceptical is misleading. In practice it is not sceptical at all; in theory it upholds the scepticism that is a mainspring of progress. It justifies our acceptance of beliefs scientifically tested, while providing a salutary warning that science itself may become a fetish. While supporting the belief in scientific advance, it refuses to believe that this advance has reached the end of the road. It is absolutistic without dogmatism, and relativistic without countenancing despair.

10. (2) This answers by implication another objection to the theory. It is said that a truth once true must be always true, whereas on the coherence theory what *was* true may now be false, and what is now true may become false with expanding knowledge. That which coheres with the knowledge of an earlier time may conflict with the knowledge of a later time. Thus propositions may put on truth or falsity, and take them off again, with changing scientific fashions; which is absurd.

But the objection is baseless. The measure of truth, which, judged by the ultimate standard, belongs to the proposition 'x is y' is quite unalterable, for the coherence theory as for its critics. But as just admitted, we cannot in practice make use of that ultimate standard, and are compelled to fall back on a second best. What the ultimate standard means *in practice* is the system of present knowledge as apprehended by a particular mind. That system changes; hence what coheres with it at one time may not cohere with it at another; thus in practice we shall be justified in accepting at one time what later we must reject. This is all true, but where is the inconsistency? We have neither said nor implied that truth itself changes. What we have said is that while truth as measured by the ultimate standard is unchanging, our knowledge of that truth does change—which is a very different thing. Our system of knowledge fluctuates; it is not now, for example, what it was in the Dark Ages, or even in the middle of the last century; and if we use as our standard this variable measuring-rod we shall naturally get varying results. But these varying results are in our knowledge, or in truth-as-revealed-in-our-knowledge, not in truth objective and complete. Between a truth that is itself invariant and varying degrees of manifestation of this truth, there is no sort of inconsistency.

11. (3) This answer suggests a third objection. We have held that while the truth of any particular proposition must be tested by its coherence with present knowledge, the truth of this knowledge as a whole could be measured only by its approximation to an absolute system. But it has been charged that 'approximation' covers a surrender to correspondence.[1] For do we not really mean by this that our present system is true so far as it *corresponds* to the further reality, and false so far as it fails of this?

We may call the relation 'correspondence' if we wish. Indeed some of the most uncompromising advocates of coherence

[1] As, for example, by Schiller, *Studies in Humanism*, 122.

have used the language of correspondence in their discussions of this point; Bradley, for example, speaks of our judgements as 'representatives' of reality which are true 'just so far as they agree with, and do not diverge from', the real.[1] Again, 'truth, to be true, must be true of something, and this something itself is not truth. This obvious view I endorse.'[2] But he adds, 'to ascertain its proper meaning is not easy'. And what he arrives at as the 'proper meaning' is certainly very far from correspondence as meant by its advocates. It is neither copying, nor a one-to-one relation, nor an indefinable 'accordance'; 'I mean', he writes of judgements, 'that less or more they actually possess the character and type of absolute truth and reality. They can take the place of the Real to varying extents, because containing in themselves less or more of its nature. They are its representatives, worse or better, in proportion as they present us with truth affected by greater or less derangement.' 'We may put it otherwise by saying that truths are true, according as it would take less or more to convert them into reality.'[3] Or, if we may put in our own terms a meaning that is certainly not far from Bradley's, the relation is one between a purpose partially fulfilled and a purpose fulfilled completely. Thought, we have insisted, *is* its object realized imperfectly, and a system of thought is true just so far as it succeeds in embodying that end which thought in its very essence is seeking to embody. If we want analogies for the relation of our thought to the system that forms its end, we should leave aside such things as mirrors and number systems and their ways of conforming to objects, and think of the relation between seed and flower, or between the sapling and the tree. Does the sapling *correspond* to the tree that emerges from it? If you say it does, we shall agree that a system of thought may correspond to reality. If, as seems far more likely, you say it does not, and that to use 'correspondence' of such a

---

[1] *Appearance*, 362–3.
[2] *Essays on Truth and Reality*, 325; and cf. 'If my idea is to work it must correspond to a determinate being it cannot be said to make'. ˉ
[3] *Appearance*, 362–3.

relation is confusing, then you are at one with us in considering 'correspondence' a misdescription of the relation we have in mind.

12. (4) Just as certain critics have attempted to reduce coherence to correspondence, certain others have attempted to reduce it to self-evidence. They say: 'When we grasp the coherence of a proposition with a system, we are seeing that it necessitates and is necessitated by the other elements in the whole; and what we mean by necessary relations is relations logically self-evident.'

Again we must answer by defining terms. When anyone says he believes in self-evidence, he is commonly taken to mean that he believes in self-evident *propositions*, that is, in propositions whose truth can be seen without considering how they are related to the systems they belong to. Thus Descartes believed in self-evidence because he believed that there were certain 'simple propositions' which, however fertile of consequences when the mind reflected on them, could be seen to be true by themselves before any such consequences were deduced. This is a useful way of conceiving self-evidence, and as it is also the commonest way, it seems wisest to conform to it. But if we do, it is plain at once that to reduce coherence to self-evidence is out of the question, since the two theories contradict each other on an essential point. The self-evidence theory says the truth of some propositions at least can be seen in isolation; the coherence theory says that the truth of *no* proposition can be seen in isolation.

However, the defender of self-evidence may reject the proposed definition; he may insist that what he means by self-evidence is something attaching equally to propositions in isolation and to the coherence of these with a system. This is a distinct view and demands a distinct answer. That answer is not difficult, and it is to our mind decisive against any form of self-evidence that may be offered as an account of truth. Self-evidence, in its essence, contains a reference to being seen; if a truth were too complicated and difficult for any human apprehension, no one would call it self-evident. And if not self-evident, then on the theory it could not be a truth at all. Now this is a violent paradox. It involves the conclusion that if the best human brains cannot *see* a proposition to be true, then it cannot *be* true. It suggests that when Newton, having hit on the law of gravitation, laid this aside for a while because his calculations failed to confirm it, the law was really not true, since it possessed self-evidence for no one. It is surely more natural to believe that there are numberless truths too recondite and elaborately conditioned for human wit. So long as self-evidence is offered merely as a criterion of truth, there is some plausibility in it, as we have seen; but when offered as the nature of truth, the plausibility vanishes.

13. (5) We come now to an objection more frequently made than any we have been considering. Granting that propositions, to be true, must be coherent with each other, may they not be coherent without being true? Are there not many systems of high unity and inclusiveness, which nevertheless are false? We have seen, for example, that there are various systems of geometry each of which seems to be as coherent internally as the others. Since they are mutually inconsistent, not more than one of them can be true, and there are many mathematicians who would say that *none* of them are true; yet if truth lies merely in coherence, are we not compelled to take all of them as true? Again, a novel, or a succession of novels such as Galsworthy's *Forsyte Saga*, may create a special world of characters and events which is at once extremely complex and internally consistent; does that make it the less fictitious? To say that it does would imply that if we could only dream constantly enough and consistently enough our dreams would literally come true.

(i) This objection, like so many other annihilating criticisms, would have more point if anyone had ever held the theory it demolishes. But if intended to represent the coherence theory as responsibly advocated, it is a gross misunderstanding. That theory does not hold that any and every system is true, no matter how abstract and limited; it holds that one system only is true, namely the system in which everything real and possible is coherently included. How one can find in this the notion that a system would still give truth if, like some arbitrary geometry, it disregarded experience completely, it is not easy to see.

14. (ii) The objection gains point, however, when it goes on to inquire whether all that is actual might not be embraced in more than one system. When a murder is committed, there may be two theories of the crime which do complete and equal justice to all the known facts and yet are inconsistent with each other. Is it not conceivable similarly that there should be two perfect but conflicting systems in which all known and knowable facts should fall into place? If so, our standard would require us to say that both were true; yet since they conflict, this would be absurd. Now we might reply that such a contingency, though possible, is highly improbable. In the case of the murder, every new bit of evidence narrows the range of available hypotheses, and it does not even occur to us that if we knew *all* the relevant facts we might find ourselves at the end with conflicting theories. If such an issue is improbable where the facts are so few, is it not far more improbable where the facts are infinitely many?

Still, this answer seems inadequate, since a theory that leaves it even possible that in the ultimate nature of truth there should be inconsistency ought to be met, we feel, with some decisive disproof. Can it be shown that such an issue is not only improbable, but impossible? I think it can. There are to be two systems, each including all facts known or knowable, but differing in internal structure. Now if the first system is constructed according to plan A, and the second according to plan B, then the possession by the first of plan A is not a fact that is included in the second, and the possession of plan B by the second is not a fact included in the first. The two systems are thus *not*, as they are supposed to be, each inclusive of all the known facts. To put it otherwise, if the systems differ neither in facts nor in structure, they are not two systems but one. If, with the same facts, they are to differ at all, they must differ in structure, but then there will be at least one fact that each of them must omit, namely, the fact that the other possesses the particular structure it does. Thus that all actual and possible facts should be embraced in conflicting systems is unthinkable.

On the other hand, if the objector lowers his claim and says only that the facts *as so far known* may be ordered in different systems, he is saying nothing against our theory. For this certainly does not show that if all the facts were known these rivals would still stand as rivals; it shows only that with the facts now available we should not on our view be justified in making a choice. And this really confirms our view, through bringing it into line with science. Such suspension of judgement is precisely what is enjoined by scientific practice, which holds that so long as two rival hypotheses equally cover the facts, neither is to be preferred to the other, but that as soon as there appears an *instantia crucis* which one hypothesis can assimilate and the other not, we are justified in adopting the first.[1]

15. (iii) Suppose, however, that no crucial instance ever did arise. Suppose (to put an extreme but conceivable case)

[1] It may be said that the truth is not established until *all* rivals have been eliminated. But this is not the view on which the natural sciences actually proceed. Of course in formal logic an argument from the affirmation of the consequent is fallacious, and when this is carried over into science it is often said to provide verification without proof; the proof is attained only when it is shown that from no other antecedent could these consequences have sprung. But it will be evident that in the ordinary work of science proof of this kind is seldom if ever practicable; one cannot be sure that *all possible* alternatives have been excluded. 'The character of relativity and non-finality, which attaches to mere verification and causes it to be called the fallacy of the consequent, is really inevitable in the pursuit of truth.'—Bosanquet, *Implication and Lin. Inf.*, 102.

that we spent from twelve midnight to twelve noon of every day in dreaming, that our dreams were as vivid and orderly as our waking life, and that when we resumed them every night we did so at exactly the point at which we left off the day before. Would there then be any difference between sleep and waking? Would there be any sense in saying that one world was real and the other unreal, that in the one our perceptions and beliefs were true and in the other delusions merely? I think not. And our inability to make any choice in such a conjuncture confirms our theory. The argument runs: if truth did lie in coherence, then, confronted with two worlds equally coherent, we should be unable to select one as truer than the other; on reflection we can see that such inability is just what we should find; hence the equation of truth with coherence is so far verified.

16. (iv) It is further verified by our way of choosing between systems which in the above sense are *not* equal. There are various cases. Consider (*a*) how we recognize dreams or delusions for what they are. When we are suddenly roused from a vivid dream, we may be momentarily dazed, not knowing the dream from the actuality. How do we establish which is which? Mere vividness does not decide the matter; the dream may be of nightmare intensity while the perception of our familiar surroundings may be comparatively dim. The deciding factor in the battle is what may be called the mass and integration of the household troops. The bureau and windows of our familiar bedroom and the sound of a familiar voice throw out innumerable lines of connection that bring our everyday world around us again in irresistible volume. Against the great bulk of this world, and without any lodgement in it, the figures of our dream appear unsubstantial and fugitive, quickly dissolving for want of support; and it is just the recognition that what we have been experiencing will not fit into our common-sense world that we mean when we say we wake from dream. The power to measure such fancies and phantasms against the ordered mass of experience is the logical meaning of sanity; its disappearance is insanity. There may be organic differences between the man who thinks himself Napoleon, the man who is sure he has committed the unpardonable sin, and the man who is persuaded that there is a universal conspiracy to keep him down; but intellectually they are alike; there are certain beliefs which resist appraisal by the mass of their general experience, and stand in the midst of it like solid capsules impervious to outer influences. In these cases that is what insanity means.[1]

17. (*b*) Again, it would be a natural consequence of the coherence theory that those minds whose vision was at once broadest and most perfectly integrated would have the best hold on truth, not only in the sense that they had compassed more of it, but also in the sense that in appraising particular suggestions they would exhibit the soundest judgement. This, once more, is what we find. Granting that for judgement on technical difficulties expert knowledge is necessary, we may recognize that there is a still more important character of mind which is called, in some of its grades, 'common sense', 'good judgement', and 'wisdom'. Everyone feels that there are some men whose voice on the conduct of life, and whose opinion on matters of belief that are of universal concern—on the difference between superstition and insight, between meretricious and genuine values, between conservatism and stupidity, progress and mere change—are of quite extraordinary weight. They are not necessarily the most learned men, though to such ripeness of judgement learning undoubtedly contributes. They are not necessarily minds of great dialectical subtlety, though again such subtlety, if they have it, adds to their power. Nor are they invariably the men who

[1] Much evidence could be adduced for the above suggestions as to the nature of sanity and of aberrations from it. See, e.g., McDougall's account of relative dissociation as explaining the lack of normal inhibition in hypnosis. *Abnormal Psychology*, 110 ff.

are most adept at giving reasons for their decisions, or who in conversation have the readiest and most interesting wares. They are the men who are best able to see the whole in the part, and the part in the light of the whole. They bring to bear on particular suggestions a larger weight of experience, because that experience has been so assimilated, so knit up, part with part, that when a suggestion is offered, its remote bearings are seized as though instinctively, and, by an intuition that is none the less rational for being largely subconscious, it is perceived as of a piece with the fabric of knowledge, or else as adventitious and incongruous. This large and close-knit fabric is itself the product of further agencies, of a sound native intelligence, a considerable experience, direct or imaginative, of men and things, and the habitual practice of reflection. And so far as the end of education is intellectual, the achievement of such a fabric is a measure not only of approximation to truth, but also of cultivation of mind. Newman's vivid description of the educated intelligence could be taken word for word as supplying the meaning of insight in terms of the coherence theory.

'That only is true enlargement of mind which is the power of viewing many things at once as one whole, of referring them severally to their true place in the universal system, of understanding their respective values, and determining their mutual dependence. . . . Possessed of this real illumination, the mind never views any part of the extended subject-matter of Knowledge without recollecting that it is but a part, or without the associations that spring from this recollection. It makes everything in some sort lead to everything else; it would communicate the image of the whole to every separate portion, till that whole becomes in imagination like a spirit, everywhere pervading and penetrating its component parts, and giving them one definite meaning. . . . To have even a portion of this illuminative reason and true philosophy is the highest state to which nature can aspire, in the way of intellect; it puts the mind above the influences of chance and necessity, above anxiety, suspense, unsettlement, and superstition, which is the lot of the many. Men, whose minds are possessed with some one object, take exaggerated views of its importance, are feverish in the pursuit of it, make it the measure of things which are utterly foreign to it, and are startled and despond if it happens to fail them. They are ever in alarm or in transport. Those on the other hand who have no object or principle whatever to hold by, lose their way, every step they take. They are thrown out, and do not know what to think or say, at every fresh juncture; they have no views of persons, or occurrences, or facts, which come suddenly upon them, and they hang upon the opinion of others, for want of internal resources. But the intellect which has been disciplined to the perfection of its powers, which knows, and thinks while it knows, which has learned to leaven the dense mass of facts and events with the elastic force of reason, such an intellect cannot be partial, cannot be exclusive, cannot be impetuous, cannot be at a loss, cannot but be patient, collected, and majestically calm, because it discerns the end in every beginning, the origin in every end, the law in every interruption, the limit in each delay; because it ever knows where it stands, and how its path lies from one point to the other.'[1]

18. (c) So sound and fine a passage had best be left without comment. But it must be added that in appraising particular beliefs, not only the individual mind, but also the social mind acts as if the coherence theory were true. If theological beliefs which in a certain age of the world are generally presumed to be truths both revealed and demonstrable are regarded by later ages as false and absurd, it is not as a rule because of specific refutation, but because of failure to accord with the 'intellectual climate' of succeeding times. For example 'the general belief in witchcraft has died a natural death, and it has not been worth anybody's while to devise arguments against it'.[2] Its abandonment, as was shown by Lecky, 'was not effected by any active propagandism. It is not identified with any great book or any famous writer. It was not the triumph of one series of arguments over another. On the contrary, no facts are more clearly established in the history of witchcraft than that the movement was mainly silent, unargumentative, and insensible; that men came gradually to

---

[1] *The Idea of a University*, Discourse VI, Sec. 6.
[2] Balfour, *Foundations of Belief*, 219.

disbelieve in witchcraft, because they came gradually to look upon it as absurd.' 'The pressure of the general intellectual influences of the time determines the predispositions which ultimately regulate the details of belief.'[1] The notion that certain old women behaved eccentrically because they were maintaining some sort of intercourse with the Devil has not to this day been refuted, and in the nature of the case can hardly be refuted; yet we reject it unhesitatingly. We do so because it is incoherent with our intellectual world. That world is one whose outlines have been fixed by science. The success of science on every side in bringing to light natural causes for supernatural seemings has made demonic guidance and possession all but unthinkable; to accept such things would threaten our universe with ruin. For if natural law is suspended at this point, we may hold it suspended also wherever we are equally ignorant, and then the world becomes a chaos in which law, Divine interposition, and perhaps chance, are mixed in unknown proportions. Not that the modern man explicitly draws these inferences before rejecting witchcraft, any more than the biologist soberly deliberates before rejecting a report about a centaur. Our logical sense far outruns our explicit thinking. Most of us feel at once that this doctrine is incongruous with the scientific outlook and consider that enough.

The argument here is that our ordinary appraisal of particular beliefs is *as if* the coherence theory were true; they are accepted if they square with what we take to be the system of established belief,[2] rejected if they do not. It may be said, however, that if such considerations are to be effective they should be carried farther; it should be shown not only that at any particular time men appeal to coherence as giving truth, but that when one system is abandoned in favour of another the system that wins the victory is uniformly more coherent, that is, more comprehensive and consistent, than the one displaced. Obviously no such law as this could be made out. Many

[1] *History of Rationalism in Europe*, Vol. I. 13, vii.
[2] The objection that this would make impossible the revision of received belief is dealt with below, Sec. 20.

factors besides rational ones play a part in determining both the dominant system of a time and the particular beliefs of an individual; and any argument purporting to show that men, alone or in groups, have always voted for reason, even when the issue was clear-cut, would be plainly sophistical. At the same time, there is a continual pressure and tendency in this direction; to deny it would seem to me merely perverse; introspection and history testify to it alike. The ordinary man, faced with a theory that he perceives to do justice to all the facts more completely than some other theory which he would very much rather accept, may continue to advocate the view he prefers, but he will do so against an inner resistance that leads at first to false shrillness and emphasis, and ultimately, if he is honest, to open surrender. As for history, the same tendency can be seen in it. Without committing ourselves to predictions, or suggesting that a Hegelian dialectic movement, or even Comte's three stages, can be verified in history, still less with any notion that in matters of belief 'die Weltgeschichte ist das Weltgericht', we must recognize that if we place in a series the Weltanschauungen of periods widely removed from each other, for example the narrow world of primitive men, the curious Greek mixture of polytheism with naturalism, the 'Christian epic' of the mediaevals, and the new world of contemporary man, so fragmentary even still, and yet so wide in its horizons and so clearly shot through, as he believes, with law, such a series shows a constant nisus toward an ordering of the world which, as coherently comprehensive, may be taken also as true. Eddies and backwaters there may have been, without number; but on the whole the movement of the social mind, like the behaviour of the individual mind, is as if coherence and truth were one.[1]

We have been dealing with the objection that truth cannot

---

[1] To the thoroughgoing authoritarian, the suggestion that essential doctrines, or one's general system of doctrine, must be revised in the light of advancing knowledge, is anathema. Cf. the papal syllabus of 1864: 'Si quis dixerit: Romanus pontifex potest ac debet cum progressu, cum liberalismo, et cum recenti civilitate sese reconciliare et componere, anathema sit.'

be coherence because different systems are possible which should include the same facts and indeed all the facts. Against this we have argued that the notion of two systems, each all-inclusive, is meaningless; and we have gone on to show that when two systems less than all-inclusive come in conflict with each other, as they do when dream conflicts with reality, or vagary with science, or one world-view with another, the issue tends always to be settled by acceptance of the view that, in the sense defined, is more coherent.

19. (6) It may be said that such a view is a 'rationalization' of conservatism. 'We are to accept whatever agrees with the body of received belief, and reject whatever disagrees. But the great advances in human knowledge have been precisely those in which the mind broke loose from the received system, set up claims that ran counter to it, and in spite of opposition and derision made them good. Scientific progress, like political, has sometimes come through revolutions. But how can revolutions occur, how can there be any but the most trivial sort of progress, if it is acknowledged in advance that nothing can be true which does not accord with what is already established?'

A little reflection will show that this begs the question. It is assumed that according to the coherence theory what is established, in the sense of merely holding the ground, is to be taken as established logically, whereas the theory expressly denies this. It says on the contrary that no system can be taken as final except that system, all-inclusive and perfectly integrated, in which the ideal of thought is realized. Indeed the two charges of dogmatism and scepticism, the charge that the theory accepts received truth as final and the opposite charge that it admits no truth at all, might well be left to cancel each other out, except that, rightly interpreted, they reveal complementary values in the theory.

An objector who concedes this may feel a genuine difficulty, however, about the way in which the dogmatism of a particular period is, on the theory, to be broken down. Granting our right to say in the abstract that the system of beliefs of any particular time is defective, how is the system in practice to be corrected if there is no measure of its correctness but itself? Judged by the system of Ptolemy, the system of Newton was false; judged by the system of Newton, the system of Einstein is false. In each of these cases the older system has in fact given way; but if the only measure of its truth was coherence with what was already received, then it ought *not* to have given way. And to say that seems ridiculous. We commonly believe that in each case the newer system won a justified victory, but how could it ever have done so if the coherence view had been followed?

But the critic is here limiting in arbitrary fashion the body of beliefs from which we start. He is assuming that the only beliefs it contains are beliefs of the first order. By 'beliefs of the first order' are meant beliefs about any objects of direct experience such as tables and chairs; by 'beliefs of the second order' are meant beliefs about these beliefs. Now, of course, scientific observation runs counter very frequently to established beliefs of the first order, and if these alone were decisive, the new result would have to go. Take, as a recent example, one of the observations by which the general theory of relativity was verified. It was implied in this theory that as light rays passed the sun on their journey from distant stars they would be bent by the sun's attraction, and hence that stars seen under such conditions would appear to be slightly displaced from their normal positions. Accordingly observers waited impatiently for a moment when an eclipse of the sun would render such stars visible. When it came, they found the stars displaced as Einstein had predicted. The positions actually seen conflicted with those required by Newtonian astronomy; and it may be said that if truth is to be measured by its accord with existing belief, the new observations would have had to be rejected. But at this point beliefs of the second order enter the scene. We not only hold beliefs about tables and chairs, the sun and the stars; we also hold *beliefs about the technique of acquiring beliefs*. We believe that perceptual judgements made under conditions exclusive of bias, ambiguity and vagueness are more to be relied upon than judgements made only casually. Now let us suppose that such careful observations as the one described are rejected because of their conflict with accepted 'fact'. Consistency would require us to hold that *all* observations made with similar care and accuracy must be set down as giving uncertainty and perhaps falsehood, and that would conflict with the very important second-order belief just mentioned. We are thus left in a position where acceptance of the observed result would conflict with our first-order beliefs, while rejection of it would conflict with an important second-order belief; and it may be thought that the first-order beliefs would win by their sheer volume. This is a mistake. For if the second-order belief goes, an enormous mass of first-order beliefs will obviously go with it. If every judgement made under conditions as stringent as those described must be called in question, is there any perceptual judgement that can be any longer relied on? A policy that would reject such judgements consistently would involve science in general ruin. To be sure, if they are accepted, certain old first-order beliefs must be revised, but this is as nothing to the chaos that would follow from a loss of faith in the observations of science. Thus stability itself demands that the new results be given admission.

The charge of conservatism is thus a mistake. It assumes that the system we must take as base is a system of first-order beliefs. But we have seen that when beliefs of the second order are included, as they have every right to be, we have a system that provides for its own correction.

20. (7) Closely related to the charge that the theory would impose conservatism on our thinking is the charge that it would impose circularity. Suppose we have a system of beliefs, *abc* . . . *n*, each accepted because it is coherent with the rest. Then the reason (in part) why *a* is accepted is that it coheres with *c*, and the reason (in part) why *c* is accepted is that it coheres with *a*. And this, it is said, is a circle. *A* leans on *c*, and hence to know whether *a* is true, we must first know whether *c* is true. But how do we know that *c* is true? Only by first knowing that *a* is true. Thus in establishing the truth of *a*, we assume its truth to begin with.

Now this is confusion again. We have said, to be sure, that part of the reason for accepting *a* as true is its coherence with *c*, but there is nothing in this to imply that we must already know *c* to be true. This is just the sort of thing the coherence theory does *not* say, even though its critics insist that it ought to say it. They write, for example: 'A "coherent" system of propositions is presumably a system such that if any one proposition in it is true, it strengthens the probability of all the rest. But some people seem to conclude from this that any one proposition in the system strengthens the probability of the rest *whether it is itself true or not*.'[1] This suggests that to give support to a system, a proposition must establish its truth *independently* of the system. If the coherence theory denies this, it is not in the least through inadvertence, but because on reflection it can see no force in this 'must'. It insists that one cannot start out with a proposition, or even a limited system of propositions, as true apart from its relations, and test others by reference to this.[2] It holds that a set of propositions any one of which, if taken in isolation, would be doubtful in the extreme, may lend each other such support through systematic coherence as to render all of them virtually certain. Let us take a simple and actual instance. Consider the two propositions (1) that certain Neanderthal skulls belong to a primitive human type, (2) that the hard point on the rim of the ear, and near the top, is the vestige of an original tip. Standing alone, either of these propositions would be disputable in the extreme. Standing, as they actually do, in an enormous webwork of 'facts' co-ordinated by the theory of

[1] Price, *Perception*, 183; italics in original.

[2] ' "Coherence" cannot be attached to propositions from the outside; it is not a property they acquire by colligation, whilst retaining unaltered the truth they possessed in isolation.'—Joachim, *Nature of Truth*, 72–3.

evolution, each (we take it) is overwhelmingly probable. This probability is not an inference from the truth of the other, nor even an inference from the system, taken as *independently* true. The system itself is made up of just such propositions, many thousand in number, none of which could be taken as true in isolation, but each of which, through coherence with the others, confirms those others and derives confirmation in return. Such a system is not circular. We are not using (1) as a touchstone for (2), and then (2) as a touchstone for (1). We are saying that truth is a function of neither when taken independently, but of the system of which both are members. So far as they cohere with each other and with the rest of the system, both are taken as true; and for either or both, extrusion from the system means falsity.[1]

21. (8) Sometimes to the charge of circularity is added the charge of contradictoriness. We have admitted that according to the coherence theory the truth that attaches to any judgement can never be precisely known till its place in the whole is known; and since we have also seen that under the influence of expanding knowledge 'certainties' have a way of shrinking into partial truths, there would appear to be no proposition that we can lay down with confidence as absolutely true. But is not this exactly what we are proposing to do with the coherence theory itself? When we affirm that truth is coherence, we can scarcely mean that *this* is only partially true. When we say of propositions generally that they are only partially true, we surely mean this

---

[1] 'The more connected and consistent is the testimony of a witness in a law court, the more likely are his separate statements to be true. . . . The law of gravitation is confirmed by its application to explain the motion of projectiles, the course of the planets, the tides, the common pump, etc.; on the other hand, the fact that these phenomena can thus be connected within a coherent system corroborates our view of each of them severally. Nor is there anything exceptional or mysterious in the conception of mutual support. We cannot make one card stand up on end; but if we take two we may prop them against each other at an angle so that each prevents the other from falling.'—Stout, *Studies in Philosophy and Psychology*, 318.

assertion about them to be wholly true. But if we do, we are contradicting ourselves, for we are saying that all propositions are partially true, only this one is not.

This argument gains apparent support from the dictum of logicians that we can never, at the moment of judging, entertain the possibility that our judgement is false. If we do entertain that possibility, then what we are really judging is that the judgement proposed is only possibly true, and *this* we affirm without reservation. The defender of coherence is thus placed in an odd position. When he says, All propositions are partial truths, he means to assert this either absolutely or not. If he does assert it absolutely, then, as we have seen, he is contradicting his theory. But even if he asserts it as only conditionally true, he is again involved in contradiction, and doubly so. In the first place, a theory that was to be adequate to the nature of truth is now offered as admittedly inadequate. And it is violated, secondly, even in the pronouncement of its inadequacy. For so to pronounce it is to say that only under certain conditions would it be adequate or wholly true. But *that* assertion is not taken as conditionally true; it is meant as true without reservation. Thus all escape for the defender of coherence seems to be cut off. His attempt to save himself by denying absoluteness to his assertion that all truths are partial, ends in absolute assertion after all.

This looks effective, but chiefly, I think, because it attaches an untenable meaning to the dictum of the logicians. That dictum says that at the moment of judging we cannot entertain the possibility of our judgement's being false, and no doubt in a sense this holds. It holds in the sense that if I see my proposed judgement to be only conditionally true, I am still judging unconditionally; for what I am really asserting is that the judgement *would* be true under conditions, and this I assert unconditionally. But that is less significant than it sounds. For however self-enclosed and absolute this judgement may be in form, it is far from being so in content. What the conditions are that would render the apodosis true I may not know, nor even whether the conditions that actually exist may not invalidate it. My assertion may be merely this, that in the light of the conditions I know, the proposition is credible, while if all the relevant conditions were taken into account, it might possibly not be. Indeed this is the commonest kind of judgement. If I say that trial by jury is to be approved, or that water consists of H_2O, I am asserting that, on the evidence we have, this proposition is sound; I am not asserting that with no possible extension of evidence could it require the least modification. So of the coherence theory of truth. When I assert that this is true, I am asserting that the theory, as I now understand it, is true according to the evidence now available; I am not holding that omniscience itself must subscribe to it exactly in this present sense. The natural scientist would not accept the imputation of such dogmatism regarding his theories, nor is there any reason why the defender of coherence should accept it.

It may be replied that this in effect is a complete emasculation of the logicians' dictum, and a denial that any unconditional statement can be made. For we are saying that when the partly blank form that stands for the conditions is filled in, our conclusion may no longer hold. Even the statement, 'S is P under the conditions I now know', may not strictly hold, since these conditions themselves may turn out conditional, while again further knowledge may reveal impurity in the connection. What is the answer? I cannot see that any answer is called for. The criticism merely states the facts. We have seen that to judge at all is to enter upon a particular kind of enterprise, which consists in trying to get reality before us in a way that will satisfy the mind. What will fully satisfy the mind is nothing short of a completely systematic insight, and when fragmentary insights are accepted, it is with the tacit reservation that they might be otherwise if the whole tale were told. The logicians' dictum is so far true that since judgement in its very nature is an affirmation within this whole, no judgement of bare exclusion from the whole is thinkable. But if the dictum means that what is explicitly before us we always predicate absolutely, just as it now appears, it is a superstition we are well rid of. Not, of course, that we go about like children grown morbid about veracity, and murmur 'perhaps' to ourselves after everything we say, or indeed that the plain man is conscious of making reservations at all. The reservations that on a moment's reflection he would agree to —that his judgements are conditional on a limited knowledge, on more or less accurate testimony, and the like—are so universally taken for granted that he need not think of them; and those remoter conditions that limit the truth even of scientific judgement lie beyond the pale of his interest. But they ought not to lie beyond ours. For we are studying the nature of thought, and we have seen that thought as such, and therefore everywhere and always, is the impulse after a complete and ordered vision. Short of that, in any special and limited judgement, there is no rest for it; and if we listen for its own voice, discriminating this from the louder voices of conceit and convention, with their love of sonorous finalities, we shall never fail to catch its persistently dissatisfied 'No, not this'.

To the charge, then, that the coherence theory contradicts itself because it is the unconditional assertion that all truths are conditional, we reply that there is no contradiction because these types are not exclusive. The attempt to divide judgements into two mutually repellent classes, the conditional and the unconditional, is a mistake. Every judgement is both. It is unconditional because it asserts that in what I am now affirming there is something that, no matter what the conditions, belongs to reality. It is conditional in the sense that the conditions implicitly recognized may disallow what is explicitly before me as in the end completely true. And the assertion of the coherence theory, like every other assertion, is absolute in the one sense and conditional in the other.[1]

[1] That the notion of coherence cannot be put forward, under the terms of the theory itself, as a quite adequate account of truth has of course been recognized by its leading defenders. Thus Joachim writes: 'Assuming that the coherence-notion of truth is sound, no theory of truth as coherence can itself be completely true, but is at most possessed of a "truth" which we may believe, but have not proved, to be "symptomatic" of perfect truth.'—*The Nature of Truth*, 175.

22. (9) Coherence means more than consistency. It means not only that the various constituents entering into the system of truth are compatible with each other, but also that they necessitate each other. The system assumed is a system ideally perfect, for nothing less than this would satisfy intelligence as stable beyond rectification. In such a system there would be no loose ends. Difference anywhere would be reflected in difference everywhere.

Now it has been held that this ideal is merely a cloud-castle, that it can never be made to embrace the facts of our actual disorderly world. There are many who would freely admit that nothing exists or occurs out of relation to *some* other things, but would regard the view that everything is related by necessity to *everything* else as demonstrably false. If the fact is that Bishop Stubbs died in his bed, this surely might be false without everything else being false that is now accepted as true.

23. Now it is obvious that we cannot show *in detail* that a difference anywhere in the system of truth must be reflected everywhere; we do not know enough, nor is it likely we ever shall. But we can do something else that is as near to this as can be reasonably asked. We can show that in the system of truth, *so far as reflected in our knowledge*, such interconnection holds, and that the denial of an apparently isolated judgement does in fact have implications for every other. The argument is as follows: When I say that Bishop Stubbs died in his bed, or indeed when I say anything, I always do so on evidence. This evidence may be hard or easy to bring to light, but it is there invariably; I never simply discharge judgements into the air with no ground or warrant at all. And by the rules of hypothetical argument, to admit the falsity of a judgement is to throw doubt upon its ground. Indeed it is to do more. It is to throw doubt, if I am consistent, upon *all* evidence of this kind and degree. Now the evidence on which it is believed that Bishop Stubbs died a natural death is of the kind and degree that would be accepted without hesitation by any historian or scientist. It is the sort of evidence on which science and history generally rest. Hence if I deny this proposition, and thus call in question the value of this sort of evidence, I must in consistency call in question most science and history also. And that would shatter my world of knowledge. Thus the truth about Bishop Stubbs is anything but isolated. However unimportant practically, it is so entangled with my system of beliefs that its denial would send repercussions throughout the whole.[1]

To some this reply may seem an *ignoratio elenchi*. It is one thing, they may say, to show that the abandonment of a *belief* would logically compel the abandonment of other beliefs; it is another thing to show that in the real world about which these beliefs are held, a change in one fact or event would necessitate that all others be different. Suppose I climb the hill behind my farm house in Vermont and look across at Mount Washington. I am wearing a felt hat at the time. Is it sensible or quite sane to argue that if I had worn a straw hat instead, that fact would have made a difference to Mount Washington?

I not only believe it would, but that the argument for this conclusion is strong almost to demonstration. In outline it is as follows: my putting on this particular hat had causes, which lay in part in the workings of my brain; these workings also had causes, which lay in part in the workings of other bodily organs; these in turn depended upon countless physical factors in the way of food, air, light, and temperature, every one of which had its own conditions. It is plain that before we took many steps in this retreat, we should find ourselves involved in millions of conditions, and that if we were able *per impossibile* to traverse all the diverging branches, there would probably be no region of the universe that would remain unpenetrated. Now if we reject, as I suppose we must, the plurality of causes, and hold that the causal relation is reciprocating, then a denial

[1] Contrast Russell, *Philosophical Essays*, on 'The Monistic Theory of Truth' with Bradley, *Essays on Truth*, etc., 212 ff.

of the causal consequent will require a denial of its antecedent. A different event, then, from that on which these various lines converge would require differences throughout the range of the countless conditions themselves. Very well; let us assume such a different event to have occurred—my wearing a straw hat instead of a felt one—and having ascended the causal lines, let us now descend them. If the antecedents of the present event were scattered throughout the universe, and we suppose them altered throughout, is there any reason whatever to suppose that the present state of the world would be as we find it? The answer is obvious. The world would not only be different, but so extensively different that we could point neither to Mount Washington nor to anything else and say that it would be exempt from change.

This is the argument in outline. It offers no proof that all events are causally related; still less does it attempt to show that behind such a causal unity there is to be found the unity of logical necessity. Evidence for these points would very much strengthen it. But it is best to leave the statement of such evidence till we consider internal relations, where the present outline will be developed in detail. Meanwhile enough has been said to turn the edge of the objection we have been examining. That objection was that on the coherence theory, a difference anywhere in the system should be reflected everywhere else, whereas a particular fact or event might have been different without entailing any extensive change. We have seen that this contention does not hold.

24. (10) Still the view that everything in the universe is relevant to everything else has been thought by many to be a millstone round the neck of coherence. They say that 'if a judgement cannot be true without reference to all the others, and this is true of all judgements, truth will be a shifting meaningless vortex with no fixed standards anywhere'.[1] The very life of knowledge, they continue, consists in holding to the relevant and excluding the irrelevant; yet we are told that

[1] L. A. Reid, *Knowledge and Truth*, 34.

everything is to be relevant and nothing whatever irrelevant. How could thought or discussion go on under such conditions? I can no longer accept what any moralist or economist or literary critic says if I discover that he has omitted from his account 'the sweet influence of the Pleiades'. If a man remarks that it is a fine day, it will be in point to reply, 'Quite so, since umbellifers have imbricated petals', or anything else that may come into my head. What, if possible, is worse is that science will now be indistinguishable from prejudice. Scientific men insist on special connections; they insist, for example, that tuberculosis is caused by a bacillus. But this must now be taken as prejudice, since they have omitted the equally essential fact that Miltiades commanded at Marathon. Now surely all this is nonsense. If everything is to be equally relevant, we shall be asked, how can you argue for your own theory? How can you think at all? Does not thought in its very essence involve the selection of grounds and consequences?

25. One way to meet this onslaught would be to admit that if coherence is true, science and traditional logic are *not* ultimately true, and to ask why they should be taken as arbiters in metaphysical questions. But such a reply would need much explaining, and less provocative replies are at hand. (i) For one thing, the objection contains a bad inference. To say that all things are relevant does not entail that they are all *equally* relevant. When I see an apple fall, I may reflect that if it had been a little larger, a widespread difference would be implied in the nature of things; but am I therefore committed to saying that no greater difference would be involved if the law of gravitation itself were radically different? I do not see that I am. Tuberculosis in a given patient would not be quite what it is if bacilli and the outer temperature did not co-operate to the result. Both factors are therefore relevant. But that does not imply that they contribute equally to causing the result or explaining it. With the outer temperature replaced by another, ten degrees lower, we have every reason to think the disease would still be there, though somewhat different in its complexion; with the bacilli absent, the disease would not be there at all. Whether our criterion of relevance is making a difference in the result, or throwing light on it, the conclusion would appear the same. Admission of relevance is not the admission of equal relevance.

26. (ii) Nor is there anything here with which scientific theory need conflict. Probably most scientists would agree with Mill that the cause of an event is not some single condition, but rather the sum of the conditions. They would probably also agree with him that to follow out these conditions would involve, in the long run, the whole state of the universe. They would therefore admit that in selecting the cause of an event, they were naming *a* cause rather than *the* cause. Countless factors are relevant, but this does not prevent their selecting certain ones, or a certain one, as more relevant than others. It must be admitted that comparative relevance is often determined for them by considerations other than logical. If *the* cause is identified, as it commonly is, with the efficient or precipitating cause, it is not seldom because this is most important in practically controlling the event, or because it is the most striking of the immediate and constant precursors, or because it is the only exclusive one. But the selection is not wholly extra-logical, often as this has been held. If the presence of bacilli is taken as *the* cause of tuberculosis, it is partly because this is more relevant in the logical as well as causal sense, because it explains the disease more fully, because it throws more light on its nature than other concomitant factors. Reflective science, like coherence, would admit a context of relevance that is indefinitely extensive. But if coherence does not consider that this prohibits degrees of relevance, neither does science. There is no necessary conflict at all.[1]

---

[1] Causal and logical relevance are of course not identical. In speaking of them at times interchangeably, we are anticipating the result of a later argument (Chap. XXXII, Sec. 10 ff.), in which it is sought to show that in causality an element of logical necessity is present

27. (iii) That relevance is thus a matter of degree is impressed on us farther by reflecting on the traditional distinctions between essence, property, and accident. According to the traditional logic everything of any complexity had an essence, and associated in its nature with this essence were two further sets of characters, which were to be sharply distinguished both from the essence and from each other. The *properties*, while not part of the essence, followed from it with an absolute necessity; their logical relevance was complete. The *accidents*, on the other hand, merely *happened* to be present; they might equally well be absent; to both essence and properties they were irrelevant absolutely.

Now under scrutiny these sharp lines turn into such broad smudges or blurs that distinctions which at first seemed absolute are perceived to be only distinctions in degree. The essence of anything is what is common and peculiar to its class; but then so are the properties. How distinguish between them? Apparently by turning to geometry and generalizing the method there employed.

> 'The essence of any species of figure includes so much as need be stated in order to set the figure as it were before us: whatever can be proved of such a figure universally is a property. Thus the definition is assumed, the properties are demonstrated; and that is the true Aristotelian distinction between essence and property.'[1]

But this distinction leaves us unsatisfied. (i) No *logical* priority is involved; if we must start at one point rather than another, that is in virtue of our limited powers. If these powers were not limited, we could demonstrate the essence from the properties as certainly as the properties from the essence. (ii) And even when the properties are demonstrated, it is not from the essence solely that they follow.

> 'It is seldom from considering merely the definition of the figure which we contemplate that the perception of its properties follows; we must set the figure into space-relations with other lines and figures, by an act of *construction*; and the truth of our

[1] Joseph, *Introduction to Logic*, 96–7

conclusion involves not solely the essence of the figure as set out in our definition, but that taken together with the nature of space.'[1]

Now if the essence of a thing is really that from which the properties follow, the nature of space will be part of this essence. If the essence is that which is given in the definition, the nature of space, since it does not appear there, will fall outside the essence. On the traditional view, essence is conceived in both ways, and hence the nature of space should fall both within the essence and without it. Thus the notion of the essential lacks definiteness of meaning. (iii) Wherever such constants as the nature of space are made to fall, demonstration cannot leave them out. And if they are included, then *everything* demonstrated with their aid must logically be ranked as properties, not some things only. But in that case property becomes as ambiguous as essence; there is scarcely anything in geometry that will not now rank as a property; every theorem in the science is a property of the axioms and postulates. (iv) But the distinction of essence from property *within* geometry is easy compared with the distinction outside it, particularly in the sphere of the organic, where the problem is notoriously insoluble. To select the essential characteristics of an organism, i.e. those which by themselves carry the properties of a kind, is quite impossible, and hence it is also impossible to demarcate the properties clearly. And thus neither in mathematics nor in the natural sciences is there any sharp distinction between what belongs to a thing essentially and what belongs merely as a property. Does it follow that the distinction is worthless? No. It does still have value if taken as a distinction in degree. There is still good sense in saying that the possession of a heart is *more* essential to man than the possession of a little finger. Again, starting from the figure of a triangle, and with the help of the axioms and postulates, we can, I suppose, demonstrate a great number of propositions. Are these all properties of the triangle? Yes and no. Logically they are. Yet the traditional logician would not say this. He

[1] Joseph, *Introduction to Logic*, 97.

would presumably take as properties those that followed more immediately, and lacking the geometer's special interest, he would disregard the remoter implications. If his practice thus differs from his theory, there is a sound enough instinct behind it. He is recognizing, consistently or not, that there is a distinction among properties themselves, that some are bound up with the triangle more intimately and specially than others. And surely in this he is right.

28. Classical logic conceived of relevance as having three levels. There were, first, the characters that constituted the essence of anything; these were essential to it in the sense that it could not even be conceived except by means of them. Then there were its properties, which were no part of its essence, but logically followed from it. Finally, there were the accidents, which were mere external concomitants of the first two classes. We have seen that between the first and the second it is impossible to draw any absolute line. The same holds of the distinction between the first two and the third, particularly when we try to apply it in the concrete. For then we are everywhere faced by a dilemma: if essence and property are given the abstractness that invest them with some plausibility in mathematics, they are too thin, even when put together, to provide the essence of anything; if so enlarged as to give a plausible essence, the so-called accidents, which should be irrelevant, cease to be so. We may illustrate again from Mr. Joseph's admirable discussion of the predicables:

'Hodge drives a plough . . . but it is not of him that driving the plough is predicated as an accident. But a man drives a plough. That is an accident; for the subject now is not Hodge wholly, but a man, and it is not in his nature as a man that the ground or reason of his driving a plough lies; else should we all be at the plough-tail. And yet no animal but man can drive a plough: so that it is partly because he is a man that Hodge drives it; and therefore, when it is said that a man may drive a plough, the relation of the predicate to the subject seems not completely accidental.'[1]

[1] *Logic*, 79-80.

This is typical of the difficulty we find everywhere. A man may be a man without driving a plough; therefore driving a plough is an accident. But one cannot drive a plough without being a man, so being a man must have something to do with driving the plough; hence the latter is not an accident. Both arguments are convincing; yet the conclusions are contradictory; there must therefore be something wrong with the way we are conceiving of essence and accident. And the difficulty is that in the first case we are conceiving humanity as a bare abstraction, and ploughing as another bare abstraction, and between these two bare bones there is no living connection; in the second case we are conceiving humanity as exemplified in a concrete man who drives a plough. And clearly it is this second kind of conception that we must work with if our reasoning is to apply to actual things. The humanity that can be lifted identically out of all men is the sort of abstract universal which, as we have seen long ago, could not even intelligibly have species.[1] But if we work with humanity as actually embodied in the man Hodge, it will be so modified and permeated by the influences of its context that every action of the man will begin to take on the aspect of necessity. Our conception of essence is at present so vague that driving a plough is neither a property nor an accident, but something between. We are convinced that if we knew enough of humanity as it is in Hodge, we should see its influence exemplified in all he did; as it is, we see this exemplified only dimly and partially. We take his acts as accidents in degree.

29. But this carries the suggestion that implication or necessity is itself a matter of degree, strange as at first this appears. We have seen in dealing with self-evidence that it is not easy to escape that suggestion, and shall find more evidence for it later.[2] But for the believer in coherence it carries with it another strange suggestion, namely that truth and falsity are likewise matters of degree. In fact the two conceptions

[1] Chap. XVI, Sec. 14.　　　　[2] Chap. XXXI, Secs. 10–12.

are for him co-extensive; a proposition is true precisely to the extent to which it is necessary, and necessary to the extent that it is true. Further, since he believes that complete necessity is never attained, no truth will be quite true, nor will any false proposition, provided it has meaning at all, be absolutely false. To those who have learned to believe that propositions are true or false simply and *in toto*, such doctrines are likely to seem nonsense. Indeed the set of implications referred to under the heading, 'the doctrine of degrees of truth', forms for many the chief stumbling-block of the theory of truth as coherence. Nevertheless they are so vital to it that we believe it must stand or fall with them. We shall accordingly devote a special chapter to the meaning of degrees of truth, the connection of the doctrine with coherence, and its significance for the work of understanding.

APPENDIX TO CHAPTER XXVI

The view put forward in Section 8 above has been recently and ably challenged. We held that if truth consisted in correspondence, it could not be adequately tested, since comparison of idea and original was impracticable. Of a similar argument, Dr. Ewing writes: 'This argument presupposes that there is no relation of correspondence in cases where we have direct awareness, which is not true. The fact that I am directly aware of a fact at the time of judging does not prevent, but is rather likely to ensure my judgement's corresponding to (being in accordance with) the fact about which I judge. We must not indeed suppose, and this is perhaps how the misunderstanding originated, that the judging and the direct awareness of the real which tells us that the judgement corresponds are separate acts and that the second would have to be performed afterwards to test the first. On the contrary, to judge is in the case of a true and justified judgement to see, and in the case of a false and unjustified judgement to think we see, that what we judge corresponds to real facts. If the correspondence theory be right, to know that something is true is just to know that it corresponds, and so its truth need assuredly not be tested again by, so to speak, looking at reality to see whether it does correspond.'[1]

I have failed to understand this. Dr. Ewing clearly thinks that we can know objects directly, for he says: 'it is the real fact about which our judgements claim to be that we are cognising, and not merely propositions or something else in our mind corresponding to it'.[2] But so long as the object we apprehend is the thing itself, where is there room for correspondence? *What* corresponds? A thing can hardly correspond with itself. Nor can the 'act of knowing' be what corresponds, for acts are not true or false. Dr. Ewing seems to be holding at once that knowledge is direct and that it corresponds, whereas so far as it really is direct, there is nothing to correspond, and so far as it takes place *through* ideas that correspond, it is manifestly not direct. But though Dr. Ewing lays it down that what we apprehend is the real fact, he reflects that this has an intolerable consequence, for 'the paradoxical conclusion would follow that in cases of knowledge the knower knows nothing which is true'. 'We must therefore suppose that there is a propositional factor in knowledge,' 'which propositional factor we can in a sense be said to know, though in a sense different from that in which we can be said to know the reality to which it corresponds'.[3] The position then seems

[1] *Idealism*, 204.   [2] *Ibid.*, 205.   [3] *Ibid.*, 205.

to be this: when we judge, 'that is a chair', (*a*) we apprehend directly by one kind of knowledge that that is a chair, (*b*) we apprehend, by another kind of knowledge the proposition 'that is a chair', and (*c*) we apprehend by what is perhaps a third kind of knowledge the correspondence between the objects of the first two. Dr. Ewing does not develop the differences between these types of knowledge; and correspondence, or, as he prefers to call it, 'accordance', while denied to be either copying or one-to-one correspondence, is taken as indefinable.

On this view we should comment as follows: (1) The presence of all this machinery is hard to verify. Granting that introspection is scarcely decisive here, one suffers a shock worth recording on being told that in an ordinary wordless perceptual judgement one is performing three such different acts of cognition, apprehending a fact, a proposition about the fact, and the correspondence between the two. (2) Propositions here seem otiose; the awareness needed we can get through 'a direct cognition of reality'; and with such direct cognition open to us, it is curious that we should fabricate a proposition merely that there may be something to correspond. Again, when we apprehend the proposition itself we apparently do so directly; we apprehend the proposition, not the proposition that there is a proposition to apprehend. It is difficult to see why, if we can grasp propositions without intermediaries, we should interpose these when dealing with facts. Dr. Ewing suggests that the direct knowledge of propositions is a different kind of knowledge from the knowledge of fact. But if knowledge at all, it is presumably true, and if true, we have a truth that does not consist in correspondence. (3) Dr. Ewing would perhaps protest against our sharp distinction between the awareness of fact and the perception of the truth of a proposition. These, he says, are not 'separate' acts. But they are apparently distinguishable acts, for he tells us that they involve different kinds of knowing. Having got this clear, however, we read, 'to know the truth of the propositional factor (in one sense of know) is the same as (in another sense of know) to know the real to which it corresponds'.[1] I have not succeeded in following this. It seems to say that direct and indirect knowledge, the immediate awareness of fact and awareness through propositions are one and the same. And I do not find this intelligible.

I cannot see, then, that in the hands of its most recent advocate the correspondence theory has been rendered satisfactory, nor do I think it likely that if Dr. Ewing cannot make it so, others will.

[1] *Idealism*, 205.

CHAPTER XXVII

COHERENCE AND DEGREES OF TRUTH

1. Thought aims at understanding, and to understand anything means, we have seen, to grasp it as necessitated within a system of knowledge. If the system is fragmentary, it will itself require understanding within a more inclusive system. The end that thought is seeking, the only end that would satisfy it wholly, because the only end that would bring complete understanding, is a system such that nothing remained outside and nothing was contingent within. We have as yet made no attempt to argue that such a system is realized in the world we know. But in the last two chapters we have maintained two theses about it. First, our test of any theory is its coherence with the system of knowledge, and ultimately its coherence with this larger whole to which the system of knowledge itself is seeking to approximate. Secondly, what supplies the test of truth supplies also the nature of truth. To say that a proposition which was completely intelligible and necessary within such an inclusive system was also false would be meaningless. Systematic coherence is not only the criterion we use for truth; it is what in the end we mean by truth.

If these contentions are sound, it follows that truth is a matter of degree. That only is perfectly true which could be transplanted into such an inclusive and completely integrated system without subtraction or alteration. That only is perfectly false which is wholly outside the system, and since nothing meaningful falls there, no assertion is false absolutely. Between these untouched limits of perfect truth and perfect falsity thought moves in a middle region where all its insights, however varying in acuteness and sweep, can be called true in degree only. A given judgement is true in the *degree* to which its content could maintain itself in the light of a completed system of knowledge, false in the *degree* to which its appearance there would require its transformation. The meaning of this doctrine of degrees has been so frequently misconceived that it will be well to begin by cutting off ambiguities.

2. Among the mistaken senses that have been ascribed to 'degrees of truth' two are particularly natural and common. The first may be described as the mosaic sense. Any ordinary judgement can be read, with a little analysis, as an omnibus affair made up of component judgements. For example, if I say, 'That is Colonel Bailey yonder', the point I wish chiefly to make is probably that the man before me is a certain person rather than another. But it is clear on a little reflection that besides this main point I am making others, not in the sense that I single them out and affirm them severally, but in the sense that they are so involved in my original meaning that if any one of them were denied I should feel that something I meant were denied. Suppose, for instance, that I were to receive one of the following replies: 'You're mistaken; that man is not a Colonel; he's a Major'; 'that man isn't a military man; he's a member of the band'; 'why that isn't an *American* officer; I can hear him and he's talking English'; 'my dear sir, look again; that isn't a man at all, but a military tailor's dummy'. I should certainly recognize any of these as denying something I meant to assert, and it is clear, therefore, that along with my assertion that the person yonder was Bailey, I was also asserting that he was a man, that he was an American, that he belonged to the military, and that he held a particular rank. Now these judgements are not closely linked; some of them may be false without obviously involving the rest; and thus the notion of degrees of truth gains a perfectly natural meaning. If my judgement is mistaken to the extent of thinking the man Colonel Bailey when he is really Colonel Carter, is it simply and totally false? In the ordinary way of speaking, yes. But in the present sense that would be inaccurate; the judgement is only partially false, since the falsity attaches to one only of the five components, while the others are all true. Similarly we can say of any other judgement that the more of its components are true, the *more true* it is, and the more of its components are false the *more false* it is.

This is a useful meaning for 'degrees of truth', but it is not the meaning implied in coherence. The trouble with it is that while it does in a sense admit degrees, it also deals in absolutes. The truth or falsity of every component is taken as absolute; if the components are all true, the truth of the judgement is absolute; if they are all false, the falsity is absolute. And hence to speak of it at all as a doctrine of degrees is a little loose; it is like saying that if there are ten men and ten women in a room the assembly as a whole is masculine to a degree.

3. The second sense is the approximative sense. A remarkable middle-western runner has recently set a record for an indoor mile of four minutes, four and four-tenths seconds.[1] Suppose three men are disputing what the record really is. One sceptic holds that a man cannot run a mile under seven minutes; another insists that the record is 4:4:0 instead of 4:4:4; the third states the 'fact' as given above. Here we should commonly say that the first two are both wrong, but that since one made a mistake of nearly three minutes and the other of less than a second, the first was *more wrong*. This no longer means that the truth is a whole of which each had seized a part, for the question, What part? asked about either, would be senseless. It means that truth is a limit which may be approached with varying degrees of nearness and in some cases attained. And from our point of view the word 'attained' gives the case away. No doubt for certain purposes this is a useful way of regarding the matter, but that it is not the meaning implied in coherence is clear from this, that it still assigns absolute truth to many of our ordinary judgements, while the coherence view, as we have seen, would say that all such judgements—even judgements of the exactest measurement —are true only in degree.

[1] Glenn Cunningham, as reported in the N.Y. *Times*, March 4, 1938.

4. Now scepticism of this sort runs so contrary to received opinion that many regard the doctrine of degrees as paradoxical in the extreme. That it does have technical difficulties may be freely admitted. But so do its alternatives. And the main grounds for it are so easily seen and so hard to deny that, once they are attended to, the paradox rapidly vanishes. I take it that these main grounds are two, one of them psychological, the other logical. Let us look at them in turn.

It will perhaps serve the ends of clearness if we take the well-worn case of the school-boy who begins with the reading of school history books and ends as a historian. As a boy he makes the judgement, 'Napoleon lost at Waterloo'. What is it exactly that he is asserting? Is what he asserts—that which he takes to be true—precisely the same as what you or I or a historian would be asserting if the same words were used? Quite clearly it is not, and if anyone says it is, we can only say that he is confused. He may say that the boy is referring to the same fact as his elders and using the same words, and hence must be asserting the same thing. But here the relations are being confounded between three different things—what is technically called the metaphysical subject, the judgement or proposition asserted, and the words in which this is expressed. The metaphysical subject is reality, or more immediately the region or point of reality of which assertion is made, in this case a point in human history; the judgement,[1] so far as true or false, is what is declared to hold in this region; the words

---

[1] I have felt free to use the old term 'judgement' rather than the popular 'proposition' partly because the latter itself has become ambiguous, partly because, in an important and common use, it stands for an entity that I am inclined to think mythical. When one speaks of a judgement as true or false, what is meant by judgement would seem to be reasonably clear, and to call the term ambiguous because some thoughtless reader might take it to mean the act of judging or the whole psychical state seems needlessly fastidious. In the present context it means simply *what* is asserted, that which is judged true or false, the 'propositional content', that in which two minds would most obviously agree if they were 'making the same judgement'. This element can quite well be discussed in abstraction from its mental accompaniments, whether it can exist apart from them or not.

are the form in which the judgement is expressed. Now the metaphysical subject may be the same, and the form of expression may be the same, while the judgement differs. Hence it is inept to argue that because two persons are talking about the same thing, in the sense of the same metaphysical subject, and are using the same expressions, they are therefore making the same judgements. The gamin who reads in the evening paper a statement by Einstein, is surely not making the judgement that Einstein did. Similarly it is clear about the school-boy that even if his ultimate subject and his form of words are the same as the historian's, his judgement is *not* the same. What he can and does take as fact is limited by what he can grasp. It partakes vitally and essentially of the character of his childish mind, so that his thought about everything is the thought of a child. When he says that Napoleon lost Waterloo, what he is really thinking is perhaps that a plucky little fighter in a cocked hat and riding a big white horse had to gallop off at top speed to get away from pursuing red-coats. That may be as much of the battle of the century as the screen of his infantile interests will allow to come through to him. To deny that his powers and interests have any effect upon his meaning is a position so extreme as not, I think, to be worth refuting; to grant them the importance they deserve is to say that this meaning has been so deeply infected by childish feelings, tastes and fancies that no one who is not a child himself, no one indeed who is not this particular child, could know exactly what it is.

5. Now let us set this child a-growing. With mental growth his powers expand so that he is able to grasp causes and effects, distinctions and implications, that once were lost on him. There comes, again, a widening of interest, so that he no longer sees the picturesque and dramatic only, but tries to go behind the scenes. This leads, once more, to expanding knowledge and the crowding into his view of extensive masses of new detail. What is the influence of these changes upon the beliefs

he held earlier? Is it simply that more beliefs are pieced on, while the earlier ones remain as they were? Nothing could be farther from the fact. To say that when a boy's interest in winning at marbles grows into a man's interest in political power, or that when a girl's interest in dolls becomes an interest in her own child, the original interest is there unchanged, but with new ones added on, is hardly more than caricature. The mind grows like a flower, not like a snowball; it is a unit in its unfolding. This holds of knowledge as well as of interests. As the boy's historical grasp advances, he may repeat verbally many times his judgement about Napoleon, but it may be that at no two repetitions of it is he asserting precisely the same thing. His accumulating knowledge penetrates his earlier conceptions through and through. He cannot think of Napoleon in the old way, now that he has explored the Napoleonic character; Waterloo has become a complicated set of military evolutions; the loss of the engagement is no longer a white horse flying, but the dominance of Europe by new political and national ideals. The earlier thought has been not so much annihilated or directly contradicted as dissolved in a new medium. From all this it is clear that meaning, in the sense of what we mean to affirm when a certain form of words is used, is undergoing incessant and insensible change. And change so organic and continuous is properly to be described only as change in degree. Now there is no need to confuse degrees of meaning with degrees of truth, though for us the mistake would not be serious. What we have to point out is that the one entails the other. If meaning is used in the sense suggested, truth is the adjective of meaning and follows it like a shadow. The school-boy's advancing thought, so far as it is an advance in knowledge, implies also an advance in truth, and it is incredible that the first of these should admit degrees and the others not. Of course the argument is abstractly possible that while thought may change continuously, advances in truth are discontinuous, just as in certain theories of the quantum the receipt of energy is continuous while the resulting leap of the electron occurs only at nodal points. But the analogy would imply that the thoughts or meanings falling between the nodal points would have neither truth nor falsity, and this is unintelligible.

It may be said that we are here returning to the second sense of degrees of truth explained above, in which 'more true' means 'nearer the truth'. The altering meanings with which a growing mind may utter the same words do not contain successively more of the truth, we may be told; strictly, none of them are true at all; they only depart from the truth less widely as they go on. It is still possible on such a theory for thought to arrive at a stage where it will correspond to the fact exactly, and then there will be no more degrees about it. But this is the old dogma that we examined in an earlier chapter, the dogma of a fixed and given fact with which thought may somehow be equated. We could find no such thing. Indeed on all the fundamental points, the test of truth, the nature of truth, the nature of reality, this theory is untenable. It must put the test of thought outside thought, in a relation of correspondence to something else, whereas we saw that even if this something existed, coherence within thought would be the only test of having reached it; 'truth has no criterion except the fuller truth'.[1] As for truth itself, it conceives this as a relation which, if it existed, would be unverifiable; and hence the theory makes knowledge impossible. And perhaps worst of all, it impoverishes reality for us by confining it in effect to an elusive and exiguous given,[2] whereas if we take the aim of thought seriously, reality is not poorer than thought but richer and more intelligible. All these points we have discussed. And if our conclusions have been accepted, 'more true' means not simply nearer truth, but also containing *more* truth. For thought in its very essence is the attempt to identify itself more and ever more fully with that system which is reality, and its truth means its success in its own characteristic enterprise.

[1] Bosanquet, *Science and Philosophy*, 70.
[2] It is assumed that the theory means by 'fact' the sort of fact that may be given in sense data. If 'fact' is otherwise defined the criticism would have to be somewhat modified.

'Truth', writes Bosanquet, 'I believe to be the degree in which the character of reality is present within a proposition or set of propositions.'[1] That is our view exactly.

6. Some logicians are repelled by such an account of thought and truth because they think it too metaphysical, others because they think it concedes too much to psychology. We who have insisted that no sharp lines can be drawn between these disciplines need not be greatly troubled by either criticism. However, while we are on the psychological ground of the theory of degrees, let us glance at the charge that a logician who is of our way of thinking is 'selling out' to the psychologist. The critic might say that after all this talk about mental growth the fact remains that Napoleon did lose Waterloo, and that whatever else may be in or before our minds, we are all referring to that same event. We do all manage to assert that the event occurred; there must, therefore, be a minimum proposition that is identical for all of us and unaffected by anything else that may be in our minds. We answer as follows: (*a*) it is not suggested for a moment that we are in no sense asserting the same thing; if we were so completely at cross purposes we should never in the least understand each other. But (*b*) 'to assert the same thing' is ambiguous. What it seems to mean here is that, despite the fact that our judgements vary, there is a little hard unvarying nucleus absolutely the same in all of them. And we saw long ago, in our criticism of the abstract universal, that this view of identity will not serve. If the common humanity of mankind, or the sameness between boy and man, or the identity of meaning in two minds really depended on this cast-iron capsule, movable like a domino from one environment to another, then our own identity from day to day would be unintelligible, still less our identity from

---

[1] *Implication and Linear Inference*, 102. Cf. Bradley, *Logic*, second ed., 620: 'Truth is reality taken as ideal, and that must mean reality taken as an intelligible system; and every judgement and inference therefore must be understood as directed and aimed at such reality.'

birth to age; nor would it ultimately be possible for anyone to understand anything said by anyone else. Minds are not mosaics, such that a piece can be taken out of one and found to fit exactly into a corresponding hole in another. Identity in thought is like identity in a growing plant or a growing man, and that is an identity of degree. Boy and man do make the 'same judgement'; granted. But that is not because the man retains in his mental organism an unassimilable pellet ingested in boyhood, but because his meaning is continuous with, because it carries on and fulfils, what the boy meant. (c) And finally we must insist that a logic that dispenses with the meanings of actual minds in settling the sense of its propositions is cutting its own root. *Words* are not true or false. Nor can we speak of *the* meaning of a verbal proposition as if it possessed one in its own right, apart from any investiture by thought. It is only as words are made the vehicle of meaning or asserted content that logic has any use for them. And this meaning, as asserted by actual minds, does clearly vary with its context.

7. 'But to force such meanings upon logic is to cut its root in another way. The thought that logic studies must assert something, to be sure; but this cannot be the fluctuating content of individual minds. The concepts and relations it deals with are not considered as in time at all. Though they may present themselves to an individual mind, they are considered in severe abstraction both from the other contents of such minds and even from the fact of being presented to any mind. For logic at least, they are fixed, identical concepts, which can be the objects of common study, which can be recurred to in the confidence that they are the same as before, which bear implications that can be settled once for all. If such entities are to be dissolved in the eddying streams of individual thought, logic must go also, for its prescriptions will be inapplicable. Its elementary rule that a term must retain the same sense throughout the course of an argument will be violated by

every argument. A middle term will have become different by the time the conclusion is reached, and hence will not be the conclusion of *these* premises, nor therefore a valid conclusion at all; every proposition one sets out to prove will be altered in the attempt to prove it; and since mental contexts are in continual flux, nothing will remain itself. In short the world will be mad.'

This is more than a piece of rhetoric. We concede at once that it is an argument of weight against the position here taken, and one that has not always been dealt with as fully and frankly as it deserves. Nor will any answer be adequate that does not admit that the world as we know it *is* a somewhat mad one and that traditional logic is no organ of final truth. But that we are fully prepared to make these admissions will surprise no one who has read the treatment in Chapter XVI of the abstract universal, or the discussion in Chapter XXV of the self-evidence of logical law. Still, a proposal that calls in question the established principles and practice of logic does obviously need further explanation.

8. That explanation, to which we now turn, gives us the distinctively *logical* ground of the doctrine of degrees. The *psychological* ground was that meanings as actually affirmed are organic to the mind of the thinker, and hence that the same words as uttered by different persons or by the same person at different times, bear contracted or expanded meanings which will therefore embody truth in varying degree. The logical ground is more subtle. Just as the asserted content is organic with the mind as a whole, so it is organic with a logical system whose influence permeates it through and through. This system may not be explicit, and it may vary immensely in scope and integration. But it is always there. Every attempt to cut concepts or judgements loose from it, however practically convenient or even necessary, is in strictness illegitimate. And since what is asserted takes its very nature from the system, to discuss its truth in abstraction from the system is idle.

9. There are two ways of showing this. It may be shown empirically, by running over a series of typical concepts; or a priori, by showing that the reference to system is involved in the very nature of definition, which is the process of making concepts clear. Let us apply each method briefly. Beginning with the empirical, let us consider first an instance where the implication of system is plain. Take the concept of any part of the body, e.g. stomach, aorta, fibula, pancreas; try to confine it strictly within its own limits, without any entanglements with other parts of the body; and see what you have left. The experiment need only be tried to convince anyone that what is left is not the original concept, but something unimaginably different. The concept of stomach *is* the concept of an organ of digestion in a living organism; its nature and essence are the performance of a certain function in the animal economy ; without playing that part it would not be a stomach, nor would the concept of it be the concept of a stomach. The attempt of a logician to isolate it from its matrix of connections and think it in abstraction is every bit as fatal to the concept as the excision of the living organ would be to the organ itself.

The concept of stomach is thus the concept of it as relative to a system. We may expect the reply here that our very language gives our case away, that unless there were an 'it' to stand in relations to the system, the relations would relate nothing, and that this 'it' is perfectly capable of being isolated. The answer does not seem difficult. (*a*) This 'it', supposing you arrive at it, is not what you meant by stomach, and no one would dream of saying so unless forced to fit the facts to a theory. (*b*) Even if all the relations of the 'it' to the bodily economy were blotted out, the remainder would still be in systematic connection. If it is conceived as organic matter, it is related within a system of classification to other kinds of matter; if it is conceived as barely matter, it is still placed in spatio-temporal relations. You may pursue the 'it' as far as you will, but you will never reach anything insular; what you get instead is something so integrated with a system that to think of it except in relation to this system is impossible.

Now if the concept of stomach takes an essential part of its nature from its relation to the bodily system, differences in the notion of that system itself should be reflected in the notions of its parts. And this is precisely what we find. Is the competent physiologist's concept of the stomach the same as the plain man's? Of course for practical purposes we may say it is, but practical purposes are not enough; we are aiming now at theoretical accuracy. And such accuracy reveals a difference. There are, if I am not mistaken, various functions of the stomach which the plain man has never heard of, but which are known by the physiologist to be so essential a part of its work that without them it would not be a stomach at all. Not that the physiologist's concept is the plain man's concept *plus* certain added bits of information. His fuller knowledge reflects itself in the thought of every part and function, so that, for example, everything he learns about the chemistry of the blood or capillary osmosis will affect his concept of familiar processes like digestion. He cannot understand this organ, he cannot see what it really is, without seeing it as an integral part of a more extended system.

10. It may be replied that this is a selected case and that there is no reason whatever to suppose that what holds of organic functions holds also of inanimate things. Let us see. Take any inanimate object at random, say a chair. Assume that our case is so far wrong that there are sensed patches which are known by acquaintance and without reference to anything else. Assume, then, that oneself or an animal is experiencing this acquaintance with the sense data of the chair, and let it be assumed, if one will, that all the data that in any way belong to the chair may be apprehended at once. Would the object so grasped be a chair? No. Why? Because a chair is not a group of sense data merely; it is not a physical object merely; it is not a piece of furniture merely. It is a special kind of such piece, distinguished from other kinds by possessing a special relation to human needs and purposes. A chair at the very least is an object so designed that it can be sat in. And such an object cannot be sensed, because to be apprehended at all it must be grasped in its relation to these needs and purposes. Take the relations away and what you have left, whatever it may be, is not a chair.

'But this loads the dice again. Naturally if you select an object expressly made as a means to an end, the thought of it will involve a reference to that end. But if your contention is that *everything* is to be thought of as part of a system going beyond it, then to be fair you must take examples from things that have not already been placed in systems by man's activity. Take a drop of water or a grain of sand; or better still, since these show a grouping of qualities that may be thought to express a subjective interest, take some abstraction whose independence is shown by the fact that it can change its context indefinitely without suffering the least alteration, for example, blue or the number three.'

We may do so, but the case will be the same. The very word 'abstraction' which we naturally use of such entities suggests that they have been 'dragged away from' their context, and the dragging has taken much of the context with them. Nor can we imagine what they would be like without this. Does the hen that has three eggs apprehend what we do when we conceive of three, i.e. of three as a member of the number system? What would three be like if *not* conceived as a number? I confess that I have not the remotest idea. What would blue be like if divorced in our thought from all the colours in the spectrum to which it is related by likeness and difference, all the shades within its own range, and all the definition it possesses in virtue of being thought as a quality rather than as a substance or a relation? Again I have no notion. The contention is not, of course, that a thing can be resolved away into its relations. The contention is that in every case there is a system of relations so essential to the thing that apart from them it cannot even be conceived. And if the reader doubts this, let him settle the matter empirically by continuing the search till he finds an exception. In our own search we have found none.[1]

11. There is another way, however, of satisfying oneself that to think of anything is to think of it in essential relations. The process of making clear to ourselves what it is that we are thinking about is the process of real definition. How does such definition proceed? Invariably by analysis and synthesis. 'Take, in arithmetic, the definition of "factor" or "multiple". We first construct a certain complex, involving integers illustratively symbolised by a, b, c; namely, the proposition $a \times b = c$; this complex, *being understood*, is used to define the terms that require definition, and the definition assumes the following form: a is said to be a factor of c, or c is said to be a multiple of a, when the relation expressed in the proposition $a \times b = c$ holds.' Here we define the terms 'by showing in what way they enter as components into the understood construct'.[2] The 'construct' is of course not always of this type; in the traditional 'logical' definition it is a hierarchy of genus and species. But in every case it involves a process which may be called analysis or synthesis, depending on one's point of view, either a process like the one described, which starts with some component and puts this together with others to make an intelligible whole, or one that starts with some whole imperfectly understood, for example linotype or helicopter, and, by exhibiting its parts in relation, at once constructs it and analyses it. Is our thought of *in*definables structurally different? It may be supposed that since defining relations cannot here be set out in words they do not exist. But this would be a mistake. I may be unable to put into useful words what distinguishes blue from other colours, but unless I can relate it by likeness and difference to these and to other qualities, I cannot, as we have seen, conceive it at all.

[1] For the completion of this argument see the discussion in Chap. XXXII of the internality of relations.
[2] Johnson, *Logic*, I, 108.

There is nothing new in all this. If I am not mistaken, it is what Bradley was saying when he held that every judgement, because selective, is conditional, and that its truth must be also conditional unless the judgement is so expanded as itself to include the conditions. In this he seems clearly right. In our ordinary thought of objects (and merely to think of them is always to judge), it does not occur to us that the characters they own are provisional and relative. But on reflection the conclusion that they are so is irresistible. The concept of the organ *is* the concept of a certain function in the bodily economy, and unless we have conceived this economy rightly, we cannot conceive the organ rightly. And by further reflection of the same sort we can see that this bodily economy falls itself in a wider economy with which its reciprocities are so intimate that if we misconceive them we shall misconceive it too. Nor is there in principle any end to these widening circles of dependence.

> 'Every judgement is relative to the whole of knowledge, and no judgement entirely escapes modification as this whole is modified.'[1] 'The growth of our knowledge consists in a widening and in an increase of systematic mediation. The more the conditions of the judgement are, or can be, included in the judgement, the truer and more real, the less condition*al* and the more condition*ed* does that judgement become. And the judgement that seeks to be at once true and at the same time a mere simple and unconditioned assertion of fact, implies the worship and the pursuit of an illusory abstraction. It involves the assumption of a false and perverted ideal of knowledge. Such a judgement, the more it attempts to assert itself as absolute, succeeds only the more in emphasizing itself as dependent on and subject to the unknown.'[2]

12. We have been setting out the logical ground for the doctrine of degrees of truth. Is its connection with the doctrine now clear? To make sure, let us briefly repeat: To think of any object whatever is to think of it in its relations to what is

---

[1] Bosanquet, *Logic*, II. 230.   [2] Bradley, *Logic*,[2] II, 639–40.

beyond it. There are always some of these relations (it is needless to maintain this at present of all of them) that are so vital to the thing's nature, and therefore to our concept of its nature, that neither could be what it is if cut off from them. Thus our concept can never be adequate till we have embraced these in our thought. And since we never do grasp them all, our thought remains inadequate. Not that as it stands it is worthless; to say that would be self-contradictory. It is plainly not wholly adequate; it is equally plainly not wholly worthless. Its adequacy is a matter of degree.

13. Now this simple and straightforward doctrine has had so much opprobrium as well as argument heaped upon it by those opposed to the type of philosophy with which it is allied that many students approach it with minds made up. Some of the criticisms are the merest confusions. For example, (i) the theory has been called 'absolutistic', presumably because it is commonly held by those who believe in an Absolute. Here the criticism presents a picture the reverse of the truth. It is the *critics* of the doctrine who are the absolutists in the only relevant sense, for it is they who lay down judgements as absolutely true, while the right to do this is just what the doctrine of degrees denies. But there are criticisms of far different value which we cannot dismiss so summarily.

14. (ii) Of these the most impressive is that we know many propositions already that we can see to be true without reserve. 'We seem clearly to know that $2 + 2 = 4$ is absolutely true if we know anything, and not merely to know that it is true under certain unknown conditions.'[1] The proposition that some judgements are *not* absolutely true would seem, even for the believer in degrees, to be true without qualification. Such a believer holds, again, that if two propositions do differ in their degrees of truth, one is more true than the other;

[1] Ewing, *Idealism*, 215.

and is not *this* proposition quite true? Is it not wholly true, once more, that if two propositions are in conflict they cannot both be true? Or consider Dr. McTaggart's statement: 'my knowledge that I am having the sensation which I am having is one of those ultimate certainties which it is impossible either to prove or deny';[1] is the statement that I am having this sensation really only partially true? Or take the following from Professor Laird: 'Logical monists . . . hold that there is no truth short of the whole truth, or, in other words, that every so-called truth is relative to its context, unless that context be The Whole. The major difficulty here is that "*x*-relatively-to-*y*" is an entire entity and therefore, that the-truth-of-something-particular-relative-to-its-partial-context is, according to the theory, true (i.e. absolutely true) and yet something that falls short of The Whole.'[2]

15. Now the claim to self-evident truth has been discussed, and we cannot go over the ground again. But since mathematical instances are so often produced as trump cards against belief in degrees, let us glance at the instance here given as typical of the rest. The first thing to realize is that the meaning or nature of any number involves a reference to the number system, and would not be what it is without relation to that system. I do not mean that in order to think of two or four we must think expressly of all its essential properties, in the sense of properties that could not consistently be thought different while it was conceived to remain the same. I do mean that we cannot think of it without an *implicit* reference to *some* such properties, e.g. that it falls in a number series formed in a certain way and composed of entities of a peculiar character which, however definite, is hard to define. The falling in such relations is part of what we *mean* by 2 or 4 or 39, as the being in space is part of what we mean by 'triangle'. Now since it is such meanings that are true or false, and these meanings

[1] *Some Dogmas of Religion*, 87.
[2] *Knowledge, Belief, and Opinion*, 205.

take their character so largely from the system, it is obvious that the truth of the meaning is bound up with the truth of the system; if *that* is true, the meanings, to the extent of their participation, will also be true; if it is illusion, they too will be infected.

> 'The judgement "2 + 3 = 6" is no more false as such, and in itself, than a road is wrong *per se* and without reference to the object of the traveller. There are no roads which are such that to take them is *eo ipso* to lose one's way; and there are no judgements so constituted that the person who makes them *must* be in error. The judgement "2 + 3 = 6" is false because its meaning is part of a context of meaning, and a part which collides with the other parts. The judgement is really "2 + 3 conceived under the conditions of the numerical system = 6"; and the collision, the falsity, and the error attach to the judgement *qua* brought into connexion with the system of judgements thus implied.'[1]

From all this two things follow: In the first place, if the system itself is wrongly conceived, its constituents also will be wrongly conceived; in the second place, so far as the system itself is an integral part of a wider system of nature, neither itself nor any component of it can be conceived with finality until this wider whole is achieved. Now it seems to me obvious that neither of these wholes *has* been achieved, and therefore that to claim an absolute finality even for the propositions of arithmetic is unwarranted. To say this is not, of course, to make the preposterous claim that one has found errors in the multiplication table. It is the very different and humble confession that one's concepts of number, quantity, and so on, and the judgements into which these enter, are not infallible and final. If the right to this sceptical attitude turned on special mathematical knowledge, the present writer would not venture upon it. But it is no presumption in the unlearned to point out that their betters fall short of Deity. And indeed it is needless, for history does it more tellingly. Not many years have gone by since men of science were using the Newtonian mechanics as an example of unshakable truth; if I am not

[1] Joachim, *The Nature of Truth*, 143.

mistaken, the later framework in which this mechanics has been placed by the theory of relativity has left not one of its propositions standing quite as before. And is it unreasonable to suppose that a science which in the last century has so largely transformed our concepts of, e.g., imaginary and infinite numbers, is capable of a progress which will affect the meaning of number itself, and therefore the propositions in which numbers are employed? To rule this out as impossible would appear at once dogmatic and unhistorical.

16. Dr. Ewing has made a distinction which he believes will blunt the edge of such criticism.

> ' "What is meant by two" may stand for (a) the number two as an objective characteristic. In that case it is plain that we shall never know fully what is meant by two, since we do not know the full nature of this characteristic. But it may also stand for (b) what I or most men intend to express when they say "two", and this is not the full objective nature of twoness, and therefore may be known by us.' 'I must admit indeed that, e.g., two presupposes the whole numerical system, and from this it follows that I do not know fully what is meant by "two" in the first sense. But it does not follow that we cannot know fully what is meant by "two" in the second sense.'[1]

This is a useful distinction, but I cannot think it of any particular value here. Granted the difference between 'two as an objective characteristic' and what we commonly have in mind when we talk of two, it is, I suppose, the former and not the latter that is the true concern of mathematical science. The primary aim of such science is to diminish the interval between these, to equate the immanent with the transcendent meaning of the idea,[2] to know 'objective characteristics' as they are. And when it is said that our knowledge requires revision, what we mean is precisely that our present concept would have to be changed if the 'objective characteristic' were ever known in its full setting. That it *would* thus have to be

---

[1] *Idealism*, 224–5.   [2] Chap. XIV, Secs. 11, 12.

changed Dr. Ewing admits. And in doing so he grants the point that we are chiefly concerned to maintain. He does hold, to be sure, that we possess final knowledge, namely, of 'what I or most men intend to express when they say "two" '. But this acquaintance with current meanings is not the knowledge here in question. When we say that mathematical knowledge is inadequate, we mean, for example, that our concept of two falls short of the real two, not that our concept of men's concept of two falls short of their actual concept. And to show that we have final knowledge of the latter is irrelevant to the question whether we have final knowledge of the former.

17. That even mathematical knowledge has only partial truth has proved so disturbing a suggestion that special efforts have been made to render it acceptable. Probably the favourite way is Bradley's, to admit that within the framework of its own assumptions, mathematics has final truth. Only when it is considered, Bradley would say, that this framework has been abstracted from an infinitely wider whole, i.e. only from the standpoint of metaphysics, do the propositions of mathematics require qualification. And thus, regarding $2 + 2 = 5$, he is able to say: 'I believe this to be sheer error. The world of mathematics, that is, I understand to rest upon certain conditions, and under these conditions there is within mathematics pure truth and utter error. It is only when you pass (to speak in general) beyond a special science, and it is only when you ask whether the very conditions of that science are absolutely true and real, that you are forced to reject this absolute view.'[1] The *unconditional* statement of a mathematical proposition is false, for 'so far as the condition of the judgement falls outside the judgement, we have error', 'the assertion of the unmediated as mediated'.[2] But the *conditional* statement of such a proposition may be 'pure truth'. We cannot in metaphysics say boldly, $2 + 2 = 4$, but we *can* say that if the postulates of arithmetic,

---

[1] *Essays on Truth and Reality*, 266. [2] *Ibid.*, 276.

the laws of deduction, etc., *were* true absolutely, then $2 + 2 = 4$ *would be* true absolutely, and *this* apparently is pure truth.

But there is an obvious objection to this. Granting that $2 + 2 = 4$ is only conditionally true, is the statement that it *is* true only conditionally *itself* true only conditionally? If so, what are the conditions? If not, have we not found a case of what the theory calls impossible, namely truth that is *un*conditional? Now I suspect that there really is here a crevice in Bradley's armour. He does hold that the judgement, 'assuming the postulates, laws, etc., of mathematics to be absolutely true, then its propositions are absolutely true', is an example of 'pure truth'. And for one who held that we never do get pure truth, that sounds odd. He was admitting that a contrary-to-fact hypothetical proposition could have absolute truth, whereas no one holding his views could consistently admit that in the long run such a proposition was either true or clearly conceivable. He was admitting into a proposition claiming absolute truth constituents, namely numbers as we now conceive them, which he held could *not* possess such truth. But probably this defection was largely verbal; in any case, if the defender of coherence will stick by his guns, the defence does not seem difficult. It lies in our old distinction between the immanent and transcendent meanings of an idea. Every judgement is an attempt on reality; thought in its very nature is an effort to lay hold of that. But the content we explicitly affirm in judgement can never *as such* be true. For it is always an abstraction, an abstraction made necessary by limited capacity and limited knowledge; and the absence of its context is bound, as we have seen, to affect its meaning and truth. Thus every judgement is conditional on what is perforce omitted from it, and this is as true of judgements conditional in form as of others. When I say that mathematical propositions are true under the conditions of a more inclusive system, or that they possess the degree of truth that such a system would allow them, there is clearly a conflict between what I conceive explicitly and what I really mean to assert. On the one hand, I cannot go beyond my knowledge; I cannot conceive of relations and numbers as I should conceive them if my knowledge were complete; I am confined to entities I can grasp. And yet I also know that my knowledge *is* thus limited. I am asserting the content I grasp subject to conditions I cannot grasp. If the reader points out the curious consequence that then we never know precisely what we mean, he is to be thanked for underlining one of the reiterated theses of this book, namely that thought is always a seeking for what will never be quite apparent till it has reached its journey's end. If it is objected, again, that my awareness of my judgement's limitations always comes after the act, and that at the moment of judging I do not intend a truth that is merely partial, the answer is that this, if true, is irrelevant. For the question now before us is not whether at the moment of judging we *take* our judgement as wholly true, but whether in fact it is so.

18. (iii) We have been dealing with a common and formidable criticism of the doctrine of degrees of truth, a criticism that relies on ultimacies within existing knowledge. There is another and similar criticism that can be met in a similar way. It is directed against that interpretation of the doctrine which holds that every judgement has partial truth because it has some part that is true absolutely. Dr. Ewing (if we may quote again from his excellent study of coherence) takes the judgement, 'I am in Australia now', and says:

> 'The proposition is not rendered even partially true by the fact that there is such a country as Australia, and such a person as myself, and that it would be physically possible for me to go there. It would not be in any degree partially true even if most of the conditions for my going there had been fulfilled and I had only been prevented from reaching my destination by now through what we may call the merest accident. The proposition as a whole is false, since what is asserted is not that Australia exists and that I exist and that I might be there, but that I am there.' He concludes: 'in the first place, a compound proposition which is analysable into simpler propositions one or more of which are false, is itself, strictly speaking, absolutely false,

even if some of these simpler propositions are absolutely true, since what it asserts is that they are all true, and this is false. And secondly, at least one of the propositions into which any compound proposition could be analysed would still be wholly false.'[1]

Now if the doctrine of degrees did mean that every judgement is thus a composite of which one part may be wholly true and another wholly false, this would be decisive criticism. But, as we have pointed out above,[2] the doctrine is so far from meaning this as to contradict it on a main point. If one judgement is truer than another, that does not mean that more of the parts are true, any more than if one patch is redder than another, that means that more of its parts are red. Increase, decrease, and degrees are not necessarily matters of partitive subtractions or additions. When we say that every proposition is true in some degree, we mean, not that certain pieces of it could be taken out whole and fitted into the mosaic of reality, but that in an insight that apprehended the system of truth in its entirety it would not be completely transformed (complete *not* meaning the sum of its parts) or dissolved wholly away. As of truth, so of falsity. Dr. Ewing says that the point of the judgement above is to assert a specific relation between me and Australia, which relation does not hold in fact, and that hence the assertion is false absolutely. But he has himself, I think, suggested the true answer. When discussing an arithmetical example, he says: 'whatever the truth as to the nature of two and the arithmetical system, it is quite clear that neither I nor any other human being understands this fully. . . Hence our cognitive attitude in judging that $2 + 2 = 4$ must be in part faulty . . . we could not say what the judgement really is for us, what the words really mean for us, without revealing views that are partly erroneous.' Why must we not say similarly of the judgement, 'I am in Australia now', or of any component judgement, that it is made with a similar partial understanding of the terms and relations involved, and that therefore it could not stand just as it is in a knowledge that was exhaustive?

[1] *Idealism*, 218–19.　　　　　　　　　　　　　　[2] Sec. 2.

If Dr. Ewing admits this in the arithmetical instance, he must admit it also, I think, in the Australia instance; and if he admits it in these, it is hard to see how he can reject it anywhere.[1]

It is needless to go over the various judgements for which absolute truth has been claimed and offer individual defences. In principle all are alike. And lest anyone point out that this doctrine is a sort of nihilism that leaves nothing in science standing, let us add that its acceptance would not change the procedures, nor would it even affect the conclusion, of any science whatever. Science does not defer its enterprise till it has elaborated a logic and theory of knowledge; if it did, it could not get forward; aware or unawares, it makes certain needed assumptions about the possibility and nature of knowledge and goes on its way. If these assumptions are successfully questioned by philosophical reflection, then the particular propositions of science may have a different ultimate value from what they were supposed to have. But that is not

---

[1] Dr. Ewing explains by a distinction an appraisal of Bradley's theory which looks dangerously like a simultaneous acceptance and rejection. The theory is essentially sound, he holds, if judgement is taken as the 'whole indivisible psychical event' or our whole cognitive attitude; it is not sound if 'judgement' means 'proposition'; and Bradley failed to distinguish these. Now I find it not easy to accept this last in view of Bradley's insistence on keeping the content logically asserted distinct both from the aspect of psychical event (see, e.g., Logic, II. 611 ff.) and from everything 'merely personal' defined as 'that which falls outside the matter here in hand'. (Essays, 328.) But apart from this, I cannot see how, in the light of his concessions to Bradley, Dr. Ewing can justify his sharp rejection of the doctrine of degrees. He concedes that our concept of two would have to be revised indefinitely to correspond to the real two, and yet holds that judgements containing this concept can possess truth absolute; this is part of his meaning, I think, when he says, 'Clearly 2 + 2 really is absolutely equal to 4' (217). But we read on the same page that, 'we can only see this through being aware of the nature of two and of the arithmetical system', and that these are fully known to nobody. How then can we be so confident of the absolute truth of our judgement? It may be replied that, though we do not fully know the nature of two and of the system, we do fully know those aspects of their nature that are involved in arithmetical processes. But these are just the essential aspects, and I suppose Dr. Ewing would agree that they cannot be conceived adequately in abstraction from the system.

to be remedied by science itself. In the attempt at such a remedy science would commit suicide, and reappear as speculative philosophy. The propositions of science will always have such truth as its assumptions and axioms allow to it, but precisely because it does and must proceed upon assumptions, the amount of that allowance is not in its own control.

19. (iv) Critics have complained that the doctrine of degrees of truth is inconsistent with the law of excluded middle. According to this law, as commonly interpreted, we may say of any subject A that it is either B or non-B, and of any proposition that it is either quite true or quite false. Now it is obvious that on the theory of degrees this cannot be accepted. 'The horse is a mammal'; on the degree theory, neither this nor its negation is true absolutely. That the theory is right about the affirmative judgement seems clear enough; in my mind there are certain conceptions of horse and mammal which are conditioned, in the way we have seen, by a limited experience and faculty. And there seems no good reason why the assertion of these meanings should bear an absolute truth. It may be said, however, that the limitation thus attaching to my affirmative judgement does not apply to the negative, since this denies simply and absolutely whatever the affirmative asserts. Either the judgement possesses truth (in any sense and degree you wish), or, if not, then its failure to possess such truth is no failure in degree, but *simple* failure, absence total and definitive; and this is what the negative asserts. But then is this doctrine of negation tenable? It implies that there can be a significant negative judgement which is confined to bare privation, and this sort of judgement seems to flourish only in the logic books of a certain tradition. The fact appears to be rather that every significant negative judgement is made from a positive base; it never simply denies P; it always says, 'S is such as to exclude P'. And whether the positive base is explicit or implicit, vague or definite, it inevitably shows the limitations already noted in affirmative judgements, and falls under the same restrictions as to absoluteness.

Thus we not only admit but maintain that the law of excluded middle cannot be accepted without reservation. But we add at once that the sort of reservation called for is so remote from ordinary thought as to have speculative significance only. For practical purposes, and even for the purposes of science, it is better to conform to a logic we can see to be imperfect than to apply a standard so far beyond us as to leave us confident of nothing. On the one hand it seems quite clear that when we say that the horse is a mammal, we have conceptions of horse and mammal and of their relation to each other that cannot be wholly true; and similarly when we deny the horse to be a mammal. On the other hand, the attempt to fix the final amount of truth would be futile in both cases. It is obviously far simpler, and for all ordinary ends it is justifiable, to take the first proposition as true, and the second as false, in both cases without qualification, and to say that we must choose between them. Nevertheless if reflection reveals that this position is not strictly sound, we should be very half-hearted philosophers to sacrifice such a result in the interest of convenience. And after all there is nothing astonishing in the fact that our reach exceeds our grasp. It is quite possible to use logical convention in the ordinary course of our thinking without worshipping it blindly, to render unto practice the things exacted by it without withholding from reason the things that are hers.

20. We have dealt at some length with the doctrine of degrees because the implications it carries are for many minds a principal obstacle to accepting the coherence theory. With the appraisal of these implications we have completed our task of reviewing the main objections to coherence. These have varied greatly in impressiveness. But none has appeared which can forbid our saying that we achieve and realize truth in the degree that experience is construed in a coherent system.

But of course this view is not adopted merely because of the failure of opposing considerations. To readers who have travelled the course of our preceding books, it will be evident that it is the consummation of a long argument. That truth consists in coherent system—absolute truth in a system from which nothing is excluded, relative truth in those comparatively chaotic and fragmentary systems to which a narrow capacity limits us—is precisely what our study, first of the nature of the idea, and now of the movement of reflection, has led us to expect. To entertain an idea at all, we saw, is to launch oneself on a course of defining one's object which, if allowed to complete itself, would make that object determinate, that is, fix its relations to everything else. And so far as thought remained true to its immanent end, it must take these relations, not as a disorderly litter, but as an intelligible system. In following, through the present book, the windings of the movement of reflection, we have found the movement dominated by that immanent ideal of system from beginning to end. It was a challenge to such system as we had already formed that set the movement going in the first place. It was by making explicit the point at which the system required expansion that the problem of reflection was specified. It was under the influence of system, both for ill and for good, that exploratory observation was conducted. When this observation had been made, it was again the dictate of a system, more or less logically ordered, and more or less deeply buried in the regions below explicit consciousness, that governed the leap of inventive suggestion. How was that suggestion appraised? Superficially by various means, by self-evidence, by correspondence with fact, by several other plausible tests. But every one of them, when examined, turned out to be either merely provisional, or to draw its validity from the unrealized operation of this same ideal of coherent system. But may it not be that while we must *measure* truth by internal coherence, this after all is not what it *means*? In the present chapter and its predecessor we have tried to consider all the main reasons which might be advanced in support of this view, and have found them wanting.

The only test of a proposition is trueness itself, and its trueness is indistinguishable from the amount of truth it contains. If the argument has been sound, the system which throughout the reflective movement has supplied the impetus and determined the direction of the advance is not merely an ideal of ours, nor merely a diagnostic of correspondence with the inaccessible. In the degree to which it embodies the end of thought it embodies truth itself.

But is that end clear? Is even the structure or framework of it clear? It is a system, we have said, whose parts or components are bound together by intelligible necessity. We have been assuming when we used such words that they conveyed an identical and accepted meaning. But even in the provisional sketch of understanding which prefaced our study of the movement of reflection, ambiguity began to appear. We said that understanding was always achieved by placing things in system; but when we began to illustrate what system meant, we found that there was an extraordinary variety of systems whose inner connections, though widely different in appearance, all confidently claimed necessity. There would seem to be a causal necessity that is a very staple of understanding. There are also spatial and temporal necessities. There are necessities of number and degree, necessities in moral judgement, even apparently necessities in the way the parts of a picture or poem may hang together. Is there something that all these necessities own in common? To make the matter more difficult, there are persons who would recognize some of these necessities, those of mathematics, for example, as genuine, and others, those of morals, perhaps, as spurious. And to make it worse, there are persons of weight who would say sweepingly that there are no necessities in experience at all, and that the impression of their presence is an easily explicable illusion. It is obvious, then, that when we say the system which would satisfy thought is such that its components are linked by necessity, we have not reached the end of our task. *What do we mean by necessity?* To this last and difficult question we now turn.

BOOK FOUR

THE GOAL OF THOUGHT

CHAPTER XXVIII

EMPIRICISM AND NECESSITY

1. Three principal views have been held of the nature of necessity. According to the first, necessity does not exist at all; it can be, and has been, explained away. According to the second, it plays a genuine and important part in experience, but is confined to certain regions; it is the characteristic of certain forms or relations connecting abstract elements. According to the third view it holds in degree everywhere; it is the characteristic, not of special forms, but of a whole or system into which everything apparently enters. The first is the traditional view of empiricism, represented with varying consistency by the early British empiricists, by Mill and Spencer, and in more recent and sophisticated form by Dr. F. R. Tennant. It is also the view of the logical positivists who reduce necessity to convention in the use of language. The second view can cite the authority of formal logic and of Kant; and it is held, though more apparently than really, and with important differences in the concept of implication, by present-day logisticians. The third view was suggested by Plato, brought to a little more explicitness in the "scientia intuitiva" of Spinoza, developed with vast power and obscurity by Hegel, stated brilliantly by Bradley and by the Royce of pre-logistical days, and given its most adequate, though hardly its most attractive, expression by Bosanquet. It will long ago have been obvious that the whole drift and pressure of our reflection on the nature of thought has been toward this third view of necessity. But since its advocacy has so often been charged, and not unjustly, with obscurity, it is of extreme importance that we get it clear. This will be achieved more readily if we set it in contrast with its chief rivals by preliminary studies of each. In the present chapter we shall examine the view of traditional empiricism, in the chapter that follows, the formalist theory; we shall then turn to logical positivism, which, though a form of empiricism, is so closely bound up with modern symbolic logic that it will be dealt with most advantageously after we have discussed the views of necessity entertained by that logic. In the two concluding chapters we shall set out the theory of concrete necessity advocated in this book.

2. On the face of things, necessity as clearly links some characters of experience as it is clearly absent between others. No one perhaps would claim to see not only that snow is white and leaves are green, but also that they *had* to have just these colours, and that their having any other is inconceivable. Yet such necessity does often seem to be present. If we start with two straight lines, arranged in any way we please, we can see that they not only do not, but cannot, enclose a space. If we start with a semi-circle and, using the diameter as a base, inscribe a triangle in it, we can see, if we attend carefully to the conditions, that the triangle *must* be right-angled. Between these two extremes, in one of which necessity seems clearly absent and in the other as clearly present, there are many intermediate cases. 'Matter gravitates'; 'while there is life there is hope': if it is difficult to say that either of these is self-evident, one also hesitates to say that they express nothing but bare conjunction; they fall somewhere between.

The empiricist agrees that we must start with such data as these, and he offers a theory which at first sight explains them with a persuasive neatness and completeness. Necessity, he says, is nothing whatever but habituation; and he shows this by pointing to a correlation between degree of certainty and degree of fixity in habit. Are leaves necessarily green? Of course not. How can we be so sure they are not? Because we have not uniformly seen them so: we have often seen them brown or red. Is snow necessarily white? We have never seen it any other colour, to be sure; but we have often seen things otherwise like it—powdery substances of various kinds—that were red or blue or yellow, and it is perfectly easy to imagine these colours as belonging to snow also. In neither of these propositions, then, is there any necessity. But it begins to awake as we approximate universality. Is hopefulness an attribute of human life? It usually is—so usually that we feel there is point in the proverb; yet we may have known in ourselves, or observed in others, some total eclipse of hope which left the saying forever less than certain. Does all matter gravitate? We may be pretty confident that it does; we have never, as in the previous case, known an exception; yet our notion of matter is somewhat foggy, and its kinds sharply limited in our experience; so it seems not inconceivable that somewhere and somehow the rule should be violated. Can two straight lines enclose a space? No, we say; the thing is impossible. We seem to reach here the ultimate in the way of certainty. But the empiricist points out that at the same time we reach the ultimate firmness in habitual connection. This statement about the lines 'receives confirmation in almost every instant of our lives, since we cannot look at any two straight lines which intersect one another without seeing that from that point they continue to diverge more and more. Experimental proof crowds in upon us in . . . endless profusion, without one instance in which there can be even a suspicion of an exception. . . .'[1] Thus, if we follow the varying degrees of apparent necessity, we find another variant that dogs them like a shadow. When A and B sometimes appear together and sometimes not, we say there is no necessity. When they appear together so constantly that exceptions are rare and doubtful, there is a proverbial or virtual necessity. When they are connected so uniformly that every waking moment exemplifies them anew without a single reported exception, their necessity is complete; we call the proposition certain or self-evident. But is it not plain to the reflective mind that this necessity is no iron linkage in the facts but simply a fixed association in us? A and B have come to us so regularly together that we can no longer think of them as separated; and because we cannot think them so, we say they cannot *be* so.

[1] Mill, *Logic*, Bk. II, Chap. V, Sec. 4.

3. To this, the central position of empiricism, an addition was made by Spencer that for many increased its plausibility. The experience that gave rise to certainty was not, he said, our own personal experience only, but the experience of the entire race. This immense extension of the learning period gives room for a far deeper and firmer fixity in habit. Behind those laws of logic that are the most transparent certainties we possess, there is now seen to be the unvarying experience of thousands of generations.

> 'The universal law that, other things equal, the cohesion of psychical states is proportionate to the frequency with which they have followed one another in experience, supplies an explanation for the so-called "forms of thought", as soon as it is supplemented by the law that habitual psychical successions entail some hereditary tendency to such successions, which, under persistent conditions, will become cumulative in generation after generation ... if there exist certain external relations which are experienced by all organisms at all instants of their waking lives—relations which are absolutely constant, absolutely universal—there will be established answering internal relations that are absolutely constant, absolutely universal.'[1]

The attempt of empiricism to do away with necessity has often been criticized, and I think decisively. Nevertheless it is a ghost that will not down. It is accepted, and will no doubt continue to be accepted, by many who, without formulating or examining it explicitly, feel that some such position is a plain dictate of common sense. It is well, therefore, to look into it again.

4. (1) The first remark that suggests itself is that the pretty parallel between habituation and apparent necessity will not stand. There are some connections that are common and unvarying, to which exceptions are conceived easily; on the other hand, certain connections that we have experienced

[1] *Principles of Psychology*, Sec. 207.

seldom, or perhaps only once, present themselves as completely necessary. Whenever we have put our hand in water or any other fluid, we may have experienced it as wet. Our ancestors for untold generations may similarly have experienced it as wet. Is it therefore inconceivable that when we put our hand in water, we should experience, not wetting, but a dry burn? The question is not, of course, one of probability, or even of practical possibility, but of conceivability. And the answer is that such a novelty is not even difficult to conceive. I can quite easily conceive that on some occasion burning rather than wetting should be conjoined with the other properties of water. On the other hand, a clever boy who is studying geometry for the first time and who comes to the proposition about the triangle inscribed in the semicircle may see at his very first reading, that, given these conditions, just this proposition *must* follow. All this is the opposite of what it should be if certainty rests on frequency.

It may be replied that although the demonstration as a whole is new to the schoolboy, the individual steps are not, and that each step is the sort of insight that, according to Mill and Spencer, is impressed upon our minds by almost every waking experience. But this defence is doubly inadequate. In the first place, even if the individual steps are familiar, the particular combination of them that now produces the certainty is new, and hence if certainty is a function of frequency, it is in this case unaccountable. Secondly, the individual steps are by no means all of the kind that are impressed at every glance. It is easy to draw figures which ordinary experience never presents, but which have relations among their parts—for example, equality in length or area—that are obvious at the first careful scrutiny. Draw a square with intersecting diagonals, and even the uninstructed can reel off propositions about it with a singularly complete confidence: the halves of the diagonals are equal; the central angles are equal; the triangles are equal; and so on. Is this confidence to be accounted for by the number of times oneself or one's ancestors—savages for the most part—have encountered such figures in the past, and, examing them, have seen these things to hold? That seems incredible.[1]

5. (2) Again, when an unbroken experience is claimed for the connections of greatest necessity, the claim runs far beyond verifiable fact. What ground have I, on empiricist principles, for supposing that, in respect to a geometrical figure, the experience of all my ancestors *has* been precisely like mine? I cannot enter into their experience; I cannot learn it by word of mouth; the vast majority of them have left no record of any kind. The answer, of course, is that I am assuming nature to be uniform; I am assuming that what happens to me under certain conditions is a safe guide to what happened to others under similar conditions. The question becomes, what is the ground of this assumption? What right have I to believe that what happens at one time is a guide to what happens at other times, that like conditions will give like results? To this the empiricist must answer that the belief in uniformity is itself a result of association. A has so constantly come along with B, C has so constantly come with D, E with F, and so on, that I am forced to believe that for everything there is a similar condition from which it invariably follows. It is evident that if the empiricist is to establish the long runs of experience required to show how any proposition came to be regarded as necessary, he must establish them, not directly, but through appeal to this law of uniformity. Has he a right to appeal to this law? Notoriously he has not.

It is an interesting exercise in logic to recount the ways in which the empiricist begs the question in his argument here. The point at issue is whether nature is uniform in the sense that would give one a right to hold that what is happening now would hold, under like conditions, everywhere and always. What precisely is under dispute is thus the right to use a limited experience as a guide to what holds generally. And

[1] Some of the steps through which Socrates led the illiterate slave boy, as described in Chap. XXII, Sec. 14, provide further examples.

the empiricist proposes to prove this right by arguing that since in his own limited experience, nature has proved uniform, therefore it must be so generally. But it is obvious that his argument holds only if the principle he is supposed to prove is used to prove itself. That principle must be somehow established, but consider his difficulties in establishing it.

(i) He is in a dilemma. If he claims that he has an inside track to the truth of the principle, then he is admitting that the empirical method is not the only means to certainty, and with this the empiricist view of necessity is abandoned. On the other hand, if he sticks to his guns and insists on an empirical proof of the principle, he can never prove it at all, for since it is itself the principle on which proof must proceed, whatever doubt attaches to it will attach equally to its proof. Thus in either case the attempt at proof fails.

(ii) It fails in another way. The argument starts by saying that uniformity has been found in one's own limited experience. But is this strictly true? 'There can be no doubt whatsoever that, while much in our experience suggests regularity of sequence, much suggests irregularity also. Unsupported apples fall regularly to the ground; but some sparks fly upwards. The seasons come and go in a stately, inevitable succession, but the wind (even now) appears to blow where it lists. The *prima facie* evidence is therefore conflicting.'[1] Of course we believe that when the sparks fly upward they are secretly obeying, not violating, the law of gravitation, and that even in the blowing of the winds there is order. But this is not what we ought to believe if our beliefs are compound photo-

---

[1] Laird, *Knowledge, Belief, and Opinion*, 434. Cf. Sigwart: 'Indubitable as it is that all men infer from known causes to unknown, it is equally certain that this procedure, if restricted to the phenomenal materials that spontaneously offer themselves, would never have led to the belief in a general uniformity, but only to the belief that law and lawlessness rule the world in motley alternations.'—*Logic* (Trans.), 381. And James: The fundamental laws of science 'are never matters of experience at all, but have to be disengaged from under experience by a process of elimination, that is, by ignoring conditions which are always present. The *elementary* laws of mechanics, physics, and chemistry are all of this sort.'—*Psychology*, II. 636.

graphs of what nature actually presents to us, for what it does present is something far more chaotic. Once the conviction of uniformity is present to guide our search and arouse suspicion of the outward show, we overlook these non-uniformities, or look beneath the surface till uniformity comes to light. But if, to get the conviction, we had to wait till nature forced it on us, we should never reach it at all.

(iii) And it is not only that we override non-uniformities in what, for the empiricist, is an unaccountably high-handed way; we also stretch absurdly the runs of uniformity. In arguing that nature is generally uniform we point to many particular sequences: when the heart stops beating, life invariably ceases; smallpox is invariably produced by a bacillus; the stars move day by day invariably in their orbits. On particular sequences of this sort, we found our general law. But how do we know that these sequences are uniform? What proportion of the cases in which stars have moved, or smallpox has broken out, or hearts have stopped, have we actually observed? Only a proportion microscopically small; yet we are confident that the sequence is regular. Why? Clearly because we have fallen back on the general law to help us establish the particular sequence. Our real argument is in two stages, and runs as follows: Since under the same conditions the same thing happens always, it is safe to say that all cases of smallpox follow the law of the relatively few cases actually observed; that is the first stage, which establishes the particular sequence. The second is: since smallpox shows a regular behaviour, and so also do stopping hearts and moving stars and all the rest, we must suppose that everything shows similarly regular behaviour. But what logic! We have established the general law by appealing to the particular sequences; but then to establish the particular sequences we have had to use the general law. The argument sums up to zero.

(iv) The vicious circularity of the argument may be brought out in yet another way. When the empiricist offers his argument for the law of uniformity, he commonly supposes that he is offering the same kind of argument that is offered for a law of science. He sees that scientists are continually establishing laws by citing particular cases, and to himself he seems to be doing the same thing when he uses these laws as a springboard for a further leap and, in the second stage of the argument, contends that since some events are governed by law, all are so governed. But the two arguments are not parallel. The argument of the scientist is: *assuming that there is some law governing the phenomenon I am studying*, the connection I have now uncovered must be it. The parallel argument in the second stage would be: assuming that all events occur lawfully, then from the lawful events I have observed I may infer that all events occur lawfully. That is nonsense, because the assumption one has to make is the conclusion one has to prove. The scientist, who is not raising ultimate questions, begins with the frank, unargued assumption of uniformity, and makes out his laws with the help of it. But the empiricist, who is not entitled to this same assumption, since it is the point he has to establish, finds himself checkmated from the start.[1]

6. (3) But apart from these circularities, the empiricist's case is fatally weak. He holds that in the widest generalizations, such as the law of uniformity and the laws of logic, we should have the highest degree of certainty; but if his account of how we reach such certainty is sound, these generalizations must possess, not more certainty than those they rest on, but less.

Consider the way in which we are supposed to arrive at them. We have found A accompanied by B a certain number of times, C by D, E by F, and so on. Now when we make the leap of thought from a few cases of A-B to the rule A-B, we are making a leap from something we are sure of to something we are by no means sure. of; for it must be remembered that in making the leap we cannot rely on the rule that what happens once will, in like conditions, happen always; that rule is still ahead. The only way in which the general rule A-B can really be established is by complete enumeration, and to leap to it

[1] Cf. Joseph, *Introduction to Logic*, 421 ff.

from an enumeration less than complete is to pass into the realm of conjecture. Now in reaching laws of wider generality, such as the uniformity of nature, which is really a law to the effect that everything is governed by law, we are making another leap, as we have seen; only this time it is not from particular events but from special laws. And just as the first leap was a leap into comparative uncertainty, so also is the second; but whereas the first was a leap from the certain to the uncertain, the second is a leap from a set of uncertainties to a still greater uncertainty. If the particular laws established by simple enumeration hold only doubtfully, is it not obvious that the more general law which says that *all* these laws hold without exception must be far more doubtful still? Yet it is precisely these laws of greatest generality, such as the law of uniformity and the laws of logic, which the empiricist says are the most certain of all. His scale of certainties is thus the opposite of what his method will justify.

The curious conclusion is thus forced upon us that every argument the empiricist uses is bound to be invalid. Mill saw that merely to assert what one has observed is not argument; argument must go beyond the premises to something new. But this something new can never be certain, since it has neither been given in experience already, nor is there any certain law which would enable us to go beyond experience. Thus in admitting inference at all, Mill is exceeding the bounds of empiricism, since this process

'involves a presupposition that he has not reflected upon; it implies that the new knowledge is not the result of experience, and must therefore be due to the inferring process itself. Thus the conclusion is unavoidable that in some important sense a mental process which is not experience can originate knowledge. It is futile to object that the mind merely works on the material which is given in experience, for this implies that we are able in the process to get on to new knowledge not in the material. This, then, must be due to the mental process which brings the new result. Such origination contradicts the very foundation of an empirical philosophy like that of Locke and Mill.'[1]

[1] Cook Wilson, *Statement and Inference*, II. 417; see also 609-10.

7. (4) We have already pointed out that what experience presses upon us is far from being the mass of orderly sequences which the empiricist nevertheless believes in. The half-conscious process by which he turns this raw material into grist for his mill illustrates again how impossible it is to square his theory with the actual procedure of thought.

According to the empiricist, when we find something holding of certain cases we normally reason that the same will hold in other cases resembling them in relevant respects. When he comes to examine the syllogistic classic—All men are mortal; Socrates is a man; therefore Socrates is mortal—he holds that the real argument is this: we have known many particular cases of men's dying; Socrates resembles these men in all essential respects; hence he resembles them in the liability to death. 'From instances which we have observed, we feel warranted in concluding that what we have found true in those instances holds *in all similar ones*, past, present, and future.'[1] If such similarity is to be of use, it must mean, not any similarity, but relevant similarity. Has the empiricist an adequate criterion for this? Unfortunately, no.

Suppose that a boy is learning to demonstrate some property of a circle. This property depends, of course, on the form of the figure, its circularity; and whether the circles he has observed are big or little, whether they are red or green, whether they are embodied in chalk or ink or barrel-hoops —such things he takes as making no difference. How, according to the empiricist, does he *know* that they make no difference, and that the property follows from the circularity alone? The only way is by a long-continued eliminatory experience of individual cases. If the circles he has worked with happen to be red circles, he will have no means of knowing that the redness is not essential to the property in question; indeed he will hold that it *is* essential until he finds that circles of other colours have this property too. If he has found a property to hold of a circle of a certain size, he has no reason to suppose it will hold of a circle of a larger size until he has found in

[1] Mill, *Logic*, II, III, 3; my italics.

particular cases that it does. Nothing that is presented along
with the property is irrelevant to it until he or nature has
contrived cases in which the two can be dissociated.

Now we are not nearly so stupid as this. A mind of normal
intelligence does not have to wait for experience of circles of
various sizes and colours in order to see that these things are
irrelevant; it penetrates straight through to the connection
between circularity and the property entailed. Grasping the
self-evident link between form and property, it is able to lop
off at a stroke the whole mass of attendant irrelevancies, actual
or possible. It does not have to try its conclusion with circles
of different sizes, because it sees that circularity is in the
nature of the case independent of change in size; it does not
have to exhaust the series of colours, because it can see that
colour as such has nothing to do with the figure. In short,
it does not have to stand and wait humbly for experiences to
supply it with standards, for it has standards of its own to which
it demands, and confidently expects, that nature will conform.
'Only in the light of ideals can we distinguish between what
is relevant and irrelevant to any natural transformation',[1]
and it is clear that the ideals of relevance we use are not
mere habits.[2]

8. Is the experience of conjunction, then, of no value in
revealing necessary connections? To say this would be going
much too far. The empiricist is right when he holds that
without the experience of particular cases we should have no
knowledge at all. If one were to take the keenest of mathematical minds, and by some unheard-of process imprison it
at the beginning within its own intelligence, cutting off all

[1] Cohen, *Reason and Nature*, 205.

[2] Cf. Bosanquet, *Implication and Linear Inference*, 55 ff.; and the
following: 'When the empiricist supposes that laws or principles can
be derived simply by generalization from experience, he *means* to
refer only to veridical experience, forgetting that without the criterion
of legislative principle, experience cannot first be sorted into veridical
and illusory.'—Lewis, *Mind and the World Order*, 28.

access to the world of sensible things, it would never arrive even at $2 + 2 = 4$. So much we may concede to the empiricist. We may concede more. Not only perceptual experience, but a repetition of experiences, is often required to bring a necessary connection to light. Frequently it is only after a long course of finding characters in conjunction that we come to see in their togetherness something more than conjunction; and similarly it may only be through finding that certain things never come together that we begin to realize that they *cannot* come together, because they are incompatible. And to the empiricist it has sometimes seemed perverse that one should admit so much, and yet refuse to go with him the whole way. But between the admissions we have made to him and the conclusion that we draw there is an immense interval that he is inclined to bridge by a confusion. He mistakes acquiring knowledge *through* experience for acquiring it *from* experience. The two are radically different. The child who learns that his puppy is pleased when its tail wags is learning something *from* experience. So far as we can see, there is no intrinsic necessity in a puppy's expressing his pleasure in this particular way, and if the child connects the two, it is simply and solely because the two happen to occur together. There is nothing in the conjunction to make him certain that it would repeat itself in another case; and of course when he comes to the cat, it conspicuously fails to repeat itself. All this is otherwise in learning *through* experience. When the child, in pushing the balls about on the rods of his counting-frame, first finds that two groups of three count up to six, the result may be as much a matter of mere conjunction as the pleasure and the wagging tail. He may need to see the truth illustrated in various other materials—apples, clothespins, and blocks—before he really seizes it. But could anyone say that when he does seize it, he finds it, like the other, a mere conjunction, and liable, like it, to breakage in the next case he comes to? Surely this is wide of the mark. In both, experience is admittedly equally necessary; but in the one, it furnishes the whole ground for the insight, in the other, the occasion only; in the one, sense experience is the source of the rule, in the other merely its vehicle; in the one, the number of cases observed is an essential point, in the other, it is unimportant; in the one, knowledge comes *from* experience; in the other, *through* it.

9. (5) We have seen that to make out his case the empiricist must assume the law of uniformity, and yet that he is not entitled on his principles to do so. This law, however, is not commonly included among the laws of logic, and there is a difference of opinion among logicians as to whether it is even implied in them.[1] We have now therefore to ask what is the position of the laws of logic themselves in the empiricists' scheme of things? This is of course a crucial point, for the laws of logic are commonly supposed to exhibit necessity in its purest and most perfect form, and if he could show that they were no more than firmly fixed habits, his case, by common agreement, would be made out.

Let us suppose for a moment that it is made out, and ask what the consequences would be.

(i) First, thoroughgoing scepticism. If the fundamental rules of our thinking, such as that a thing cannot both have and not have a certain character, are simply habits of ours, where is the guarantee that even our simplest judgements of perception hold of the real world? Ordinarily, if, starting from the admitted data, we can give a rigorously logical proof, we are confident that we have attained what is true. The inconceivability of any other conclusion from those premises seems to us a guarantee. To the empiricist such considerations signify little. For the very opposite of our conclusions would be thinkable and even necessary to a being differently conditioned. We ourselves, or our ancestors, were once free from the laws that now bind us; there may be beings now whose necessities are our impossibilities; hence to say that inevitability

---

[1] For an argument that it could not be denied without denying the law of identity, see Joseph, *Introduction to Logic*, 407-10; for an opposing view see Stebbing, *Modern Introduction to Logic*, 285 ff.

in reasoning or the inability to think otherwise proves anything about the nature of things is naïve. The laws of logic may be laws of thought without being laws of things. Our science and our philosophy may be nothing more than elaborate webs spun out of our own heads, with little or no correspondence to anything beyond.

It may be replied that the mode of origin of our knowledge is itself the guarantee of its correspondence, that the inner relations have become what they are precisely because the outer relations have pressed themselves for countless generations upon the plastic matter of our minds. But a little reflection on the methods of evolution makes this appear extremely dubious. For one thing, what in general determines the persistence of a habit is not its mirroring of reality, but its survival value, i.e., the aid it gives to the organism in the struggle for existence. Now the possession of survival value without any mirroring of nature is both possible and common. 'The burnt child dreads the fire'; it is of great importance that he should; unless he connected pain with touching the fire, he would probably be eliminated before he left any descendants to perpetuate his oddities. The connection he forms between a certain appearance on the one hand and pain or fearfulness on the other is of the very highest utility, but would the empiricist say that this connection mirrors anything in nature? Hardly. The sweet and bitter tastes of things, the attractive or repellent odours of things, are very important cues as to the food we should take or avoid; does this utility afford any proof that the tastes and odours exist independently? Evidently not. Survival value is clearly possible without resemblance, and hence the mere fact that certain rules and connections have come to prevail in our minds does not prove that they also prevail in nature. Such a supposition is not required by the argument, and unless the empiricist can offer proof, it must remain for him indefensible. And on his premise it is hard to see what special proof could be offered.

But even if correspondence were made out between the laws of logic and the structure of our immediate environment, we should still be left in scepticism. For compared with the universe at large, the corner in which we live may be an infinitesimal fragment, and for the empiricist there is no reason whatever to suppose that what holds in that fragment holds in the limitless unexplored areas. It would be vastly convenient if the empiricist could here fall back on uniformity, but from this resource, as we have seen, he is cut off. Hence the suspicion remains irremovable that his laws, even those he finds most constantly verified, are no secure indication of the laws of the real world. There is nothing in his system to forbid the view that in the greater part of the universe two and two equal seven, and that true propositions are also false.

10. (ii) Besides scepticism, the empiricist view of necessity has another interesting consequence, which, as Cook Wilson points out, has seldom been realized.[1] It implies that evolution is really devolution. According to it there is nothing in the native constitution of the mind requiring obedience to the laws of logic; the mind has been compelled to such obedience by the environment it chanced to have, but with another environment it might have followed laws unimaginably different. It is compelled to think that a thing cannot be both A and non-A, but this necessity is only a habit now firmly fixed, and with an environment that conditioned us otherwise, we could have seen that X was *both* A and non-A. Indeed, as we have just remarked, the potentiality, perhaps the actual practice, of so thinking was formerly present, since it is nothing but reiterated impressions from without that has made our logic what it is. But consider what this means. It means that instead of gaining powers as evolution has proceeded, we have lost them; our original capacities have been whittled down; whereas once we had it in us to think in terms of various logics, nature has stripped us of our powers and forced us, beyond escape, into the strait jacket of a single system. Why call this evolution? Evolution means development—the realization of present powers,

[1] *Statement and Inference*, II. 619.

and the gaining of new ones. But this is a process of taking away from us even those powers that we have.

To be sure, these consequences in the way of scepticism and loss of faculty are not decisive against the empiricist. He may agree that they are involved in his theory and that they are unfortunate in the extreme, and yet point out that a theory is not refuted by being shown to be disagreeable. This is true. Still the argument must weaken the confidence in empiricism of those who think that on some things certainty is possible, or who look to evolution, as Spencer did, to supply their theory of knowledge.

11. (6) We come now, however, to a consideration that *is* decisive, a consideration which, if need be, could stand alone. The empiricist theory of necessity is self-refuting. In explaining, or explaining away, the laws of logic, it is compelled to assign these laws a position incompatible with its own result. This may be shown in various ways.

(i) When the empiricist offers his account of how the laws of logic came to seem necessary, he offers it as itself the most logical account, i.e. the account which the data logically demand. And he obviously assumes that if his account is of this kind, it will be objectively true; the very fact that the data thus logically require his theory is the accepted guarantee of such truth. But the upshot of his theory is that this logically proves nothing, since logic itself is merely a set of habits. We have seen that conformity to these rules of habit cannot guarantee objective truth in the sense of conformity with the real world. What the necessity of a proposition shows is not that it *must* be true, but only that *we* must accept it. So far as the empiricist succeeds in showing that the laws of logic are mere habits, just so far does he increase our doubt whether the logic by which he shows this has any objective force. The very truth of his conclusion would render the proof he gives for it invalid.

12. (ii) Consider, again, whether his enterprise could in the nature of the case succeed. That enterprise is to explain, not merely how we come to think certain laws of logic valid, but how they came to *be* valid. If he began by assuming necessity to be objective, and contended simply that experience is required if we are to come to perceive this necessity, he would be urging only what is admitted by all his rationalist opponents. Very well; is there any sense in undertaking to show how, from a state in which logic had no validity, it went on to acquire this? None whatever. Every step of the explanation assumes that logic is valid already. Any intelligible explanation of anything must proceed in accordance with the law of identity, for example, and the law of non-contradiction; if these were suspended, no proposition would be true rather than its contradictory; indeed no proposition need be itself. These suppositions are of course meaningless; but that only shows that the laws of logic are the conditions of making any meaningful assertion. You cannot explain how logic came to be valid; for any state other than one in which logic is already valid turns out to be strictly unthinkable. You cannot explain the laws of logic, in the sense of showing how they follow from something else which is their warrant, for they are themselves the principles of explanation and are inevitably assumed in any attempt to derive them

13. (iii) But suppose propositions were found that did seem to warrant logical laws, what would this mean? It would mean, presumably, that these propositions possessed greater simplicity, clarity, and certainty than those derived from them, and that the derivative propositions gained force through being linked with them. But the difficulty here is that the ultimate laws of logic are already the clearest, simplest, and most certain principles we have. They are the trump cards always produced when certainties are called for; and while we have agreed that in a special sense they have their warrant,[1]

[1] Chap. XXV, Secs. 34–8.

that warrant cannot possibly lie in propositions more primitive
or simple or certain. If they are held obscure, at least the
explanation of them must be of the *obscurum per obscurius*
type, and thus really no explanation at all. And it is particularly
fantastic to derive their certainty from a theory as complex
and conjectural as a theory of habit-formation among the
savages of pre-history.

14. (iv) Indeed it is fantastic even on the empiricist's own
assumptions. For the laws of logic are principles, indeed the
only principles, that are exemplified in our every thought, no
matter what the subject. They are principles of which, as
Mill would say, 'experimental proof crowds in upon us in
endless profusion, without one instance in which there can
be even a suspicion of an exception'. But if so, they must possess
already, and in the highest measure, the only kind of necessity
that the empiricist recognizes. The attempt either to explain
them or to explain them away must on his assumptions be
misguided—to explain them, because there can be nothing
clearer; to explain them away, because, by his own account,
they have the firmest empirical warrant that anything ever had.

15. (v) There is substance in Lotze's remark that in dealing
with the first principles of knowledge, we only 'increase our
difficulties if, instead of regarding those principles themselves
as the one element of certainty in our knowledge, from the
vantage-ground of which we may go on to take possession of
the rest of the domain, we explicitly attribute this certainty,
not to those principles themselves, but to a particular unanalysed application of them, viz., to our supposed insight
into the *origin* of our knowledge'.[1] In knowledge there is a
hierarchy of principles: the laws of physiology imply the
general laws of biology, and those of biology imply the laws of
logic; but, at least to our present insight, the line of implication

[1] *Logic*, Sec. 322; see also Cook Wilson, *op. cit.*, II. 627.

does not run in the reverse direction. Physiology is dependent on the laws of logic, in the sense that none of its laws would hold unless the laws of logic held; but logic is not similarly dependent on the special laws of the sciences. The empiricist forgets this. He tries to take a special theory—the theory of association—from one of the special sciences—psychology—and make it the foundation of knowledge generally. The result is not only a hysteron-proteron in proof, but a distortion in logical perspective in which the true relations of subordination are wildly disarranged.

16. (vi) There is still another way of showing that the empiricist begs the question when he comes to deal with the laws of logic. This is suggested simply by the fact that he is offering an argument. For the present purpose it makes no difference what that argument is. An argument must always proceed upon a principle which it does not itself establish, and this is true of the argument designed to account for the origin of logic as well as of other arguments. But where, upon empiricist premises, does the principle of that argument come from? The empiricist is here in a dilemma which has been so well put by Mr. Joseph that I transcribe his statement of it:

'The Empiricist . . . holds that the proposition, "$3 + 4 = 5 + 2$" is a mere generalization from experience, entertained so confidently not because it is seen to be necessary, but because it is verified in so many instances. He is, however, herein using an argument—"*Because* this equation holds good in so large a number of examined instances, *therefore* it holds good in the unexamined". Either the conclusion of this argument follows necessarily from the premise, or it does not. If it does not (and in fact it does not), he cannot justify our confidence in any process of arithmetical thinking; if we have put three shillings into an empty purse, and then four, and have taken out two, we ought not to say that there are five left until we look, or be surprised if we find more or fewer. If, on the other hand, the conclusion does follow necessarily from the premise, then here at least is an instance of our discovering by thinking a fact about things which we have not learnt by experience. Empiricism breaks down over the validity of inference; if it allows that, it gives away its case; if it disallows it, it cannot argue.'[1]

If we were examining empiricism generally, we should have to point to many shortcomings besides those we have reviewed, and particularly to what Professor Cohen has described as 'the fundamental paralogism of empiricistic systems',[2] namely that because one cannot discover through sensation any rational structure of things, there is no such structure to be discovered. But we are concerned with the empiricist view of necessity alone, and more than enough has now been said to show that that view will not hold. We are surely justified in concluding that necessity does not reduce to association, even if the period of its formation is taken to cover the whole natural history of mind.

Of late years another kind of empiricism has appeared, which would make logical laws not the expression of fixed associations, but tautologies, statements of what is contained in the meaning of our words. This theory of 'logical positivism' is so closely linked, however, with views of necessity developed by recent formal logicians that we shall study it to better advantage after we have examined these views in the chapter that follows.

[1] *Logic*, 194. [2] *Reason and Nature*, 197.

CHAPTER XXIX

FORMALISM AND NECESSITY

1. The understanding that thought seeks is not to be found in empirical conjunctions, however regularly repeated or firmly fixed. That is the conclusion we carry forward from the last chapter. To understand anything is to see not merely *that* it is thus and so, which is the only kind of grasp empiricism recognizes, but also *why* it is thus and so; and *why* involves necessity. What is the nature of this necessity? The question is still unanswered. For anyone who has been tempted by empiricism, and tried it and found it wanting, the natural recoil will be into formalism. If necessity is not to be found among the sensible elements of things, if it is not a sight or sound or taste or odour or any congeries or succession of such as these, where else could it lie than in their arrangement or structure? In the disposition of things we can note certain patterns or forms, inapprehensible by sense, and so constantly recurrent that we have come to take them for granted and can isolate and attend to them only with some effort; these, when once we have distinguished them, we can see to be the skeleton supporting all experience. It is to this abstract, non-sensible, unchanging framework of things that necessity belongs. This was essentially the answer given by Kant to empiricism, and in one form or another it is probably the most popular answer still. Its contrast with empiricism is clean-cut. The empiricist fastens his eye upon the sensible matter of experience, dealing with relations uncomfortably and as an afterthought; the formalist makes it his chief concern to single out and study these relations. The empiricist holds that what is called necessity is a function of repetition; the formalist holds that, though repetition may aid us in grasping necessity, it has nothing to do with necessity itself. The empiricist holds that there is really no such thing as necessity, what is taken for this being regularity of experienced conjunction; the formalist holds that there *is* such a thing as necessity, and that it is a property of those invariant forms that constitute the bony structure of experience.

2. Take any case where what is commonly meant by necessity is present, says the formalist, and you will find that the necessity lies in the form. 'That dog must have a black tongue, for he is a chow.' This is a syllogism which tells us an interesting fact about this particular dog; but what makes the conclusion follow from the premises, what gives the reasoning its necessity, has nothing specially to do with dogs or tongues or chows; it is simply the *form* of the argument; and this form could be exemplified equally well in any other kind of matter. The argument is of course a syllogism in Barbara: All chows have black tongues; this dog is a chow; so he has a black tongue. Strip off from the argument everything that has to do with the particular case; in place of its three terms write symbols, S, M, P, which have no specific reference and could stand for anything; and you find, says the formalist, that the argument loses none of its cogency. If M is P, and S is M, then S is P. You do not need to fill in the blanks to see that this argument is valid; you can see that it holds whatever the symbols may stand for; the naked form has all the necessity that the flesh-and-blood argument had. Hence it cannot be the matter that gives the argument its necessity, but the form alone. Take another instance. 'The stove is warmer than my hand, and my hand than this bowl; therefore the stove is warmer than the bowl.' It is obvious that for stove, hand, and bowl, we could substitute anything else that had the same temperatures; the objects we happen to use do not themselves carry the necessity. We can even strip off the temperatures, and instead of making the objects differ in degree of heat, make them differ in degree of something-we-know-not-what, and it will still follow with unabated necessity that if A is higher on the scale than B, and B than C, then A is higher than C. Here again we have a form consisting of mere blanks that could be filled in with anything one chooses; yet the

necessity is there unimpaired. And so, says the formalist, of all other reasonings in which necessity is present. It is a characteristic that inheres in the form of the proposition or argument that owns it, as distinct from the matter.

There is a possible misunderstanding here that should be cut off at once. The formalist may be supposed to hold that necessity is *coextensive* with logical form. But he neither says this nor implies it. To hold that necessity, where it occurs, lies in the form of the argument is not to hold that all form, even all logical form, exhibits such necessity. It would hardly be held by the Kantian that the various categories, which he considers equally necessary in the sense 'indispensable to experience' are also equally necessary in the sense 'intelligible', that we possess the same insight, for example, into the sequence of cause and effect as into the sequence of axioms and theorems in geometry. Indeed there are many formal logicians today who would hold that, tautology apart, even the forms of logic have no necessity. If necessity appears anywhere, one would expect it to appear in logical implication, yet in such implication, as studied for example in Messrs. Whitehead and Russell's *Principia Mathematica*, necessity plays no part. Any proposition p is said to imply another q when either p is false or q is true; to put it in another way, if there are no cases of p's being true while q is false, then p implies q. From which it follows that all true propositions imply each other, whatever they are about, and all false propositions also imply each other, and every false proposition implies every true proposition; statements may imply each other whose contents have no bearing on each other whatever. Implication is regarded as a relation which, though logical and purely formal, is not necessary. It is thus evident that while for the formalist necessity must reside if anywhere in logical forms, logical forms do not always convey necessity.

3. What then is logical form? It is safest to take the words of formal logicians themselves. 'The "form" of a proposition is that, in it, that remains unchanged when every constituent of the proposition is replaced by another.'[1] 'The form of a proposition is what remains unchanged although all the constituents of the proposition are altered. The form is the way in which the constituents are put together.' 'When there is complete abstraction from all material constituents the proposition is completely formal.'[2] 'Logical implication is formal in the sense that it holds between all propositions, no matter how diverse, provided they stand to each other in certain relations.'[3] 'If, in the apprehension of a fact, everything is disregarded excepting the numerical identity and diversity of its elements, and their grouping into wholes, what remains will be the logical form.'[4] 'Logical form is the least common factor of all objects.'[5] The emphasis in all these statements is the same. Form is the element that is relatively invariant in facts, propositions, and inferences. There is wide difference of opinion among formal logicians as to what forms should receive most study, which are most fundamental, how they should be symbolized, and whether they are expressible;[6] but happily we may avoid these controversies. What we are alone concerned with is the doctrine that where necessity exists, it is a characteristic of logical form, in the sense of something independent of the matter in which it is embodied.

But what does 'independent' mean? Here is a second danger in the interpretation of formalism. The doctrine may be taken to mean that form can exist in separation from matter, or can be conceived without reference to matter. Such formalism is untenable. Form exists only as it imposes itself upon matter. Though it is distinguishable from matter, it can

[1] Russell, *Introduction to Mathematical Philosophy*, 199.

[2] Stebbing, *Modern Introduction to Logic*, 126, 445–6.

[3] Cohen and Nagel, *Logic and Scientific Method*, 11.

[4] Eaton, *Symbolism and Truth*, 47.   [5] *Ibid.*, 43.

[6] It is contended by Professor Wittgenstein, for example, that logical forms cannot be expressed at all. A true proposition can exhibit in its own structure the structure of the fact it asserts, but can never report this in words. That is why most philosophy, attempting a verbal report of such structures, is considered by this writer to be meaningless.

neither be nor be conceived in isolation. A skeleton with the flesh removed is as self-subsistent and clear in outline as the figure it once supported; and some have been led to think, perhaps through analogy, that the form of an argument, with the matter removed, could similarly stand or be conceived by itself. This is a mistake. Even in those propositions and inferences in which the form seems most sharply marked, and freest from entanglements with matter, this notion is still a mistake. '$3 + 3 = 6$.' Is this pure form? If such can anywhere exist apart from relation or reference to matter, it should be in propositions like this. Yet we fail to find it even here. We not only arrive at number through numbering *objects*; number is such as to involve in its very nature the reference to objects. Numerical abstraction, as Jevons says, 'consists in abstracting the character of the difference from which plurality arises, retaining merely the fact. . . . Abstract number, then, is *the empty form of difference*; the abstract number *three* asserts the existence of marks without specifying their kind.'[1] Clearly in a world in which there was nothing to differ, number, as the abstraction of difference, would be not only practically beyond achievement, but theoretically meaningless. Difference, and therefore number, could not *be* unless there were entities to differ. So also of the laws of logic. 'If formal reasoning means reasoning with a naked form, then it has no existence. It is sheer illusion and impossibility.' 'For we have no bare forms we can so take in hand. The principles of Identity, of Contradiction, and of Excluded Middle, are every one material. Matter is implied in their very essence. For without a difference, such as that between the letters A and B, or again between the A in two several positions, you can not state or think of these principles. And the nature of these differences is clearly material.'[2]

Now as against the formalism that they attack, these considerations are decisive. But we should add at once that the day of this kind of formalism has gone by. Few if any logicians would now maintain, as Kant did occasionally, that form

[1] *Principles of Science*, 158.   [2] Bradley, *Logic*, 520, 519.

can be studied in abstraction from all matter whatsoever. The present-day formal logicians would grant to form an independence of matter that is not absolute, but relative; their contention is that while the form must be embodied in *some matter or other*, it need not be embodied in *this matter or that*. Their position is clearly put by Professor Cohen:

'The notion that formal propositions are empty of meaning is a persistent radical confusion. It is true in a sense that every form is independent of its matter. But a formal act is one that is the same for all, regardless of the individual differences in the class to which it applies; and so the rules of logic or pure mathematics universally apply to all propositions irrespective of differences of their material content. But this does not mean that logical or mathematical forms can exist apart from all reference to any possible content. On the contrary the most formal propositions are those which apply to all kinds of entities, and reference to such possible application is essential to their meaning.'[1]

If we are to do the formalists justice, it is this critical and guarded formalism that we must consider. And, as in the case of empiricism, we must confine ourselves to one question about it: does the necessity of a proposition or an argument lie exclusively in its form, defined as thus independent, not of all matter, but of the particular matter involved?

Such formalism is an immense advance beyond empiricism. But it still falls short of the goal. It is too sweeping and un-qualified a doctrine to do justice to the complex facts. Let us look at some of these facts.

4. (1) In a useful review of the meanings of 'necessary',[2] Dr. Tennant remarks that 'intuitive inductions have better claim than any other judgements to be called necessary truths of reason or, at least, of understanding. . . . These intuitive inductions are instanced by the judgement, based on a single case, that red differs from yellow, and differs from yellow

---

[1] *Reason and Nature*, 196. [2] *Philosophical Theology*, I. 404-7.

more than from orange.' Dr. Tennant is surely right that
necessity is present here.[1] If the formalist view is correct,
this necessity should as truly lie in some form, independent
of the special matter, as it seems to do in '3 + 3 = 6'. Is
any such form to be found? It is not. The difference seen as
necessary is a difference in and of these specific colours, and
could not be seen or intelligibly asserted except from the
basis of these; the necessity is so bound up with the concrete
matter perceived that if any other matter were substituted,
the necessity that is actually seen would be there no longer.
The view of the consistent formalist that the difference seen
as necessary has nothing specially to do with the colours
perceived is therefore incredible. To be sure, he may reply
that if what was presented had been two soldiers or two sounds,
or a sound and a colour, difference, and necessary difference,
would equally have been seen, that these differences are all
the same, and hence that what is now apprehended is not a
specific difference of colour but difference as such. But this
will not serve. (i) It is simply untrue that I am perceiving
just the same thing when I perceive the difference between
two sounds as when I perceive the difference between two
colours. In these instances at least the characters of the things
that differ affect the nature of the difference. (ii) The theory
relies on the abstract universal which we have weighed and
found wanting long ago.[2] It says that what we perceive is a
difference that is no *kind* of difference, and this is something
that can neither exist nor be definitely thought. When we
perceive things to differ, what we perceive is *this* difference,
and this, and this; and after we have perceived a number of
these, we use the general idea of difference. But if we are

---

[1] Cf. the following from McTaggart: 'That what is red cannot be
blue is a universal proposition which is not proved by induction, but
is evident to anyone who knows what red and blue mean. And therefore
it is not empirical. It is true that we should never have had the concepts of red and blue without sense-perception. But without sense-
perception we should never have had the idea of a straight line, and
this does not make geometry empirical.'—*Nature of Existence*, I. 62,
note.   [2] Chap. XVI.

referring to anything actual, the true object of this idea is the range of varying differences, not Difference with a big D, the abstraction supposed to be left when we have omitted all that differentiates the varying differences. When treating of the general idea we dealt at length with this idol of the market-place, and cannot here reopen the argument. (iii) If any doubt remains that the character of the terms affects the relation, and therefore the form and the necessity, it should be removed by Dr. Tennant's second instance, 'red differs from yellow more than from orange'. Here the terms between which the difference holds are differences themselves, and what is seen as necessary is that these differences differ. To say then that the difference apprehended is purely formal, and identical wherever difference appears, is merely to contradict oneself; differences cannot differ if difference is always the same. And when we ask where lies precisely the difference between these two differences, we find that we can answer only through specifying their terms. The difference between red and yellow differs from the difference between red and orange in a way which, with the colours before us, is perfectly evident, and with anything else before us, is lost.

5. Let it not be supposed that we are working here with an out-of-the-way case. There are hosts of similar judgements in which the necessity is so immersed in the matter that the extraction of a form to serve as a carrier is palpably artificial. 'Pleasure is better than pain.' Substitute for these terms any other terms whatever, and the necessity vanishes. If necessity resides only in logical form, and logical form resides only in complete generality, it ought to be possible to substitute here any other terms at random, for example elephants and quadrangles. In the light of an instance like this, such a doctrine is so obviously unlicensed that we prefer not to impute it to the formalists, though they use language that seems to imply it. It is impossible even to substitute other terms that, like the originals, are intelligibly related by 'better than', such as beauty and ugliness; when one sees that pleasure is better than pain, one is not merely seeing what is *common* to this relation and to beauty's being better than ugliness; one is grasping a relation which is what it is because of the character of its terms. 'I ought in these particular circumstances to tell the truth.' 'The laws of harmony demand that this note should be natural and not sharp.' We hold that it would be mere pedantry to deny that these are cases of necessity. But the necessity arises from the concrete circumstances of the case, not from some form indifferent to them.

Such cases, it may be replied, are not of the kind contemplated by the formalist. Perhaps not, we reply, but they ought to be. If the case is to be made out that necessity lies in a form indifferent to its matter, the existence of a great class of common instances to the contrary can hardly be ignored. But if the formalist is reluctant to discuss the issue on this ground, we are ready to turn to the sort of instance he prefers.

6. (2) '$(a + b)^2 = a^2 + 2ab + b^2$.' '$3 + 4 = 5 + 2$.' 'The area of a sphere $= 4\pi r^2$.' 'If A precedes B, and B is contemporaneous with C, A precedes C.' When these, either in their own right, or linked to a simple demonstration, are offered as necessary,[1] the necessity seems clearly to lie in the form. *What* numbers a and b stand for does not matter, any more than *what* things we count; *what* sphere is taken is indifferent; *what* events we think of may be left to our own choice. The vehicle of the necessity is apparently the abstract form of quantity, number, space, or time.

Let us meditate on this a little. And let us begin our meditation by recalling a succinct definition just supplied us by a formal logician: 'logical form is the least common factor of all objects.'[2] It would not do to say that there were any objects, at least any objects of thought, to which logic did not apply,

[1] The sort of formalism that would make them necessary but tautologous we shall examine in the next chapter.
[2] Above, p. 359.

since it is this very universality of application that is supposed
to supply the difference between logical and other abstractions.
Hence, if the necessity of the above propositions lies in their
logical form, it should lie in something which, at the least,
is shared by every object of thought. Now *is* the relation that
carries the necessity a relation shared by all such objects?
The relation in the first of our cases is one of pure quantity,
in the second case one of number, in the third one of space,
in the fourth one of time. What about the form of the first?
Do all objects of thought possess quantity? The question is
a nice one. What is the magnitude of my concept of honesty?
Presumably quantity itself is an object, since formalists talk
about it; what is the quantity of quantity? But it is needless
to puzzle ourselves; we may admit for argument's sake that
every thinkable object does possess quantity, and numerical
quantity, and still point out to the formalist that necessity
does not always lie in the purely formal as here defined. In
the last two instances it lies clearly in something else, namely
in temporal and spatial relations; and these relations are
certainly not 'common factors of all objects'. Take, for example,
the equations that formed our first two cases; it would be
meaningless to ask Where? or When? of either of them, though
such questions might have point as applied to the *event* of their
appearance to us. Spatial and temporal forms do plainly carry
necessity, though they are not logical forms in the sense defined.
And if not, necessity and logical form again fall asunder.

7. (3) It is possible that when this is pointed out to the
formalist, he will reply that the distinction of form from
matter is one of degree.

> 'The distinction between form and matter may as it were be
> taken at different levels. This is plain in a science that deals
> with some order of sensible things, like zoology. We may say
> of all men and all horses that they have severally a common
> form, that as compared to a man a horse is formally different,
> but as compared to one another all horses are formally the same,
> though each horse in his body is materially different from every

other. Or we may consider not the form of horse common to Black Bess and Bucephalus and Rosinante, but the form of vertebrate common to man, horse, eagle, crocodile, etc.; and now man and horse (as compared with oysters for example) are formally alike. Or we may take the four orders in Cuvier's now obsolete division of the animal kingdom, vertebrata, coelenterata, radiata, and annulosa, and regard them as only different examples of the common form of animal; and from this point of view, a horse and an oyster differ materially, but not formally.'[1]

Here what is form at one level is matter for the next higher level, and it is only at the top of the hierarchy and in something possessed equally by every member of all the lower levels, that we arrive at pure form. And it might be held that even if necessity does not always reside in pure form, it always resides in the general, in that which relatively to *some* distinguishable matter, may still be regarded as formal.

But (i) to say this is to abandon formalism in the sense in which we have been discussing it. Such formalism placed the necessary in the logical and the logical in that which was general completely; the doctrine loses what was chiefly distinctive of it if it holds that necessity may be found all the way down the scale. (ii) The term might be worth retaining, however, in a modified sense if it could be shown that as we go up the scale to forms that are more and more general, the necessity grows more and more rigorous. But no such concomitance is to be found. Necessity and generality are not only different things; they do not vary together. The proposition, 'Given all the circumstances of this case, I ought to repay this debt', is a singular proposition, but it is also a necessary proposition. 'Matter moves' and 'water wets' are propositions of very high generality, but the formalist would hardly call them necessary. Thus necessity and generality do not go hand in hand. (iii) Take an argument whose generality is certainly less than absolute: 'If B and C lie east and west on the equator, and A is a mile north of B, C is southwest of A.' Suppose that, following the present proposal, we were to make this a degree

[1] Joseph, *Logic*, 5–6. Of course Mr. Joseph is not a formalist in the sense discussed in this chapter.

more formal by leaving out, as non-general, the spatial construction involved. On the absolutist theory of formalism, the necessity should be unaffected; on the relativist theory, it should actually be increased. In point of fact it is neither; it is simply abolished. It is so bound up with the spatial construction that it cannot survive apart from this. (iv) Here we have destroyed necessity by making the argument more formal. We may similarly increase necessity by making it less so. Take such a proposition as 'lying is wrong'. The troubles Kant fell into when he tried to find in such propositions a formal abstract necessity which held independently of circumstances are too well known to call for rehearsal. Moralists seem now agreed that what he sought is not there. Does this mean that necessity in ethics is to be abandoned? By no means. If we fail to find it by going up the scale to the barest abstractions, we may still find it—and the significant thing is that we do actually find it—by going down. And the certainty is commonly greatest when we reach the concrete circumstances of the individual case. Indeed it is only when the circumstances and consequences of lying in a particular case are known to us, and the consequences of alternative actions can be seen in some detail, that the evidence fully warrants 'lying would here be wrong'. It is not the omission of concrete detail, as it ought to be on formalist principles, but on the contrary the inclusion of it that renders certainty possible.

One may reply that 'necessity' of this kind is not necessity at all. Whether we can accept that depends on how we conceive our inquiry. If it is a search for a merely nominal definition we can of course end it at any moment by defining the term as we please. But we are engaged in nothing so frivolous. We are not concerned about verbal usage; we are trying to find the nature of a certain relation that in point of fact keeps cropping out among the objects of thought, and, as we have seen, in the most diverse quarters. In all these quarters we discover that certain data are so connected with others that if we accept the first we *must* accept the second. And it is the character of this 'must' that we are investigating. Our account of it should be adjusted, not to convenience or pre-conception, but to its own nature, wherever it appears. And we can only say that to us it seems a plain fact, verifiable by anyone for himself, that it appears as truly in morals and in art and in the commonest and most concrete of perceptual experiences as in pure logic or mathematics.

8. The formalist may admit this, however, and yet insist that it in no way weakens his case. 'I have not denied', he may say, 'that necessity is to be found in the concrete; indeed, holding as I do the temperate kind of formalism which considers form to exist only as embodied in matter, I should even be willing to say that necessity exists *only* in what is more or less concrete. What I do hold is that if a concrete case is analysed, the necessity will be found to belong, not to the experienced mass as a whole, but to a thread of connection within it, that this thread can be dissected out and studied, that when it is so studied, it will be found to have a certain pattern which may be repeated indefinitely elsewhere, and that it provides, wherever it appears, the nerve of the argument and the sole locus of necessity. Form appears in matter, and only in matter; granted; but it is not merged or lost in matter; it stands out in sharp distinction from it. One may compare various arguments, note in all of them the same structure, for example that of syllogism, observe that in each case it is in virtue of this form that the conclusion follows, and then by abstracting the form get a genuine logical law which at once exhausts the necessity found in the varying cases and owes to them not one jot of its own necessity. Surely it is undeniable that this is constantly done. The whole work of one special science, the science of logic, consists in investigating laws so derived. If it is denied that they exist, "the only alternative is a totally lawless intuitionism which can give no account of its arguments and relies simply and solely on a unique and equally inexplicable intuition in each instance".'[1]

[1] A. C. Ewing, *Proc. Arist. Soc.*, Sup. Vol. X (1931), 9–10.

It is hard to see how anyone could regard this case as un-reasonable. What is insisted on chiefly is that there *are* universal elements in experience; and we have of course agreed long ago that this is true. But much depends on how one conceives of the universal. The theory that there is a little, hard, abstract, unchanging essence of colour or triangularity or humanity, absolutely identical in all colours, triangles, or men, absolutely unaffected by its context, and capable of being compounded with foreign elements into a mosaic, which is then describable as a species of it—this was a theory that we found unverifi-able. We found that humanity, as realized in Socrates, was not a naked essence identical with that of Adam and *Pithe-canthropus*, only juxtaposed in this instance to assorted irre-levancies; the species bites into the genus; humanity itself is modified as it is realized in different types; universals are incompletely themselves when undeveloped into their species, and their species likewise so long as they are withheld from embodiment in the concrete. Our position is the same here. We do not deny that there are universals; we deny that the true universal is an atomic abstract whose relation to the matter of its own species is that of two marbles in a box. We deny that from a flesh and blood argument you can cut away everything but a skeleton, so little characteristic of this argument that it could belong equally to countless others, and still leave the argument all the cogency it had. We are not holding that logic is useless; we are holding that it is not enough. Matter invades form. And therefore necessity cannot be secluded in the abstraction of pure form. It cannot be lifted from concrete argument by clean excision and without remainder.

9. (4) We have seen this already of certain 'inductive intuitions' where necessity was clearly present but incapable of being extracted and nakedly displayed. But it may be said that in fixing our eye on such arguments, or even in dealing with temporal or spatial necessity, we are evading the sort of argument that traditional logic would take as typical. Can our contention be shown to hold of perfectly regular and formally valid reasoning?

Yes, without difficulty, I think. The reader should bear in mind, however, that the kind of examples used in logic books, and even those that might here be introduced for the special purpose of illustration, are not quite fair. They are inevitably divorced from that context with which their meaning and, we should hold, their necessity are bound up; as in the old stock instance, 'All men are mortal, Socrates is a man, therefore Socrates is mortal', the special meaning has been so dried out of them that they are rather symbols or paradigms themselves than cases of actual thinking. Yet even here our thesis plainly holds. If pure formalism is true, then, so far as *argument* is concerned, there is nothing more in the syllogism given above than in 'M is P, S is M, therefore S is P'. The special natures of the terms do not enter into the logical structure at all. The S, M, and P of the structure are any terms whatever; anything, then, in the special case that goes beyond what terms as such have in common is to be taken as falling outside the object of logical perception. And the moment we begin to think about this we see that it is absurd. When we grasp that Socrates, being human, must die, it is ridiculous to say that the subject of which we see this is not Socrates at all, but Sness, or the abstract property of being a term. That which we are thinking about, that of which we assert the property of being human and the connected property of being mortal, is not some impossible abstraction possessed in common by Socrates and everything else, but *Socrates*. To insist that what intelligence is grasping is a mere skeleton into which the characters of the terms do not enter is to say that when I reason thus about Socrates, I am grasping precisely the same thing as when I say 'eels die, since they are organisms', and even when I say 'all geese are swans, and since all wishes are geese, they too are swans'. We are not concerned, of course, to deny that in this last example, or in what is presented through bare symbols, necessity is in no degree present; our contention is the modest one that the form does not exhaust the content of the individual intellectual insight. The special natures of the terms *are* involved in the thought.

10. (5) This will become clearer if we consider another implication of formalism. If the theory is to work, a term must be unaffected by its position. If the terms are not units freely movable from place to place and capable of unlimited substitution for each other, they are suffering from adhesions of matter which must be removed if one is to abide by the rules. The P that goes into the major premise must be exactly the P, no more and no less, that comes out as qualifying S in the conclusion. If it is not, there will be four terms, and both form and necessity will be destroyed. But the verifiable fact is that in actual reasoning the P *is* modified, the meaning of the terms *is* qualified by their being placed within a structure, and the argument, far from losing its validity as a result, only gains in richness and force. This is of course concealed in the syllogistic formula, but it already begins to be apparent in an argument so little removed from formality as the syllogism about Socrates. The mortality that we think of as belonging to Socrates is not precisely that which we think of as belonging to an eel, a bacillus, or a daisy, or even to every form of human life, for it takes its meaning in some measure from the nature that dies. This influence of the context becomes clearer as we move away from the relatively formal into closer contact with actual thought.

> 'If you say, "Oxygenated blood is bright; the blood in the arteries is oxygenated blood; therefore the blood in the arteries is bright", you have brought together your terms in the conception of the circulation of the blood, and your conclusion, although it exemplifies a rule, shows also a system in which the terms are factors, their union is rationally explained, and their meaning developed. Such a term as "bright" acquires a new meaning in the construction, and it is a mere matter of convenience whether this demands a modification of expression. If it

does not, it is only because general language enables us to understand such a change of meaning without altering the word. But a rule which is aimed, like that of the syllogism, at excluding in principle all modification, would really destroy the vital essence of reasoning.'[1]

That terms are thus modified in their meaning through being placed in relation to each other, and that this modification strengthens rather than weakens the web in which they are related seems to us plain fact. What line is the formalist to take about it? He may stoutly insist that with this modification in the meaning of terms the argument has lost its form and hence its validity. It *has* lost its form, to be sure, but that it has lost its validity is merely untrue. He may say that while it has lost one form, it has acquired a new one, and that it is in this new one that the validity really lies. But apart from the difficulty of extracting any such form, consider what this leads to. If the sense of a term has been affected through its entry into *this* structure, that sense may be further affected through its entry into other structures, and to the series of such structures there is in principle no end. If formalism is to complete its work, it must therefore exhaust a series of forms which is inexhaustible. The theory is thus trapped in an alternative. If it abstracts from matter sufficiently to reach a form that will be universal, or even one, like the syllogism, that will apply to any considerable range of argument, it omits what is used by thought as intrinsic to the argument. On the other hand, if it includes all that is intrinsic, its attempt to set out *the* forms of reasoning is an impossible programme, since the forms are infinite.[2]

11. It would not be difficult to continue this criticism of formalism. It would be easy to show, for example, that the traditional doctrine of reduction, sometimes regarded as a

[1] Bosanquet, *Implication and Linear Inference*, 27.
[2] Cf. Bradley, *Logic*, Bk. III, Pt. II, Chap. I, and Terminal Essay I. If Bradley's strictures on formalism, first offered sixty years ago, have been effectively met, I do not know where.

triumph of formalism, is really mortal to it, since it implies that arguments of genuinely different types may be expressed through a single form, and arguments of approximately the same type may be expressed through differing forms. If this is true, the adjustment of form to argument must be very loose indeed. But we shall not continue this commentary on traditional formalism because in recent decades formal logic has undergone an immense development, and if we are to show that necessity eludes form, our discussion would no doubt be more convincing if conducted in terms of this newer logic. There is no doubt that this logic is far more sensitive to differences in form than the older one. For example, the old rough formal logic would lump together under the blanket heading, S is P, every variety of categorical proposition; 'John is a sophomore', 'some criminals are intelligent', 'the internal angles of a triangle equal 180 degrees', would all be set down as statements of the same form. Symbolic logic would recognize in each a different form, and attach to it a symbol of its own.[1] And this logic is far more cautious about claiming necessity for its forms. It would freely admit that in the universality of a logical form there was nothing whatever to render it necessary, and would say that to determine this, one must examine the forms themselves; some may be necessary, some not; the most popular doctrine indeed is that none of them are, except in the sense that tautologies are necessary. Of the three propositions just stated, it would seem antecedently possible that one or more should be necessary, but not all; the third, which assigns a property to a triangle, looks like a clear case of necessity. To those trained in intensional analysis, there is something a little shocking in the discovery that symbolic logic would not so regard it, nor do they find the explanation offered wholly reassuring. The explanation is that this logic takes propositions exclusively in their extensional

---

[1] In the symbolism of *Principia Mathematica*, for example, the first would be of the form, '$xe\,a$', i.e. 'x is a member of the class a'; the second of the form '$(\exists x)\,.\,\phi x$', i.e. 'there is an x such that ϕx is true'; the third of the form '$(x)\,.\,\phi x$', i.e. 'for all values of x, ϕx is true'.

reading; it takes them as asserting, not a connection of content which might or might not be necessary, but the *fact*, in which necessity plays no part, of inclusion within or exclusion from a class. The statement about triangles would not be interpreted as meaning 'S is such as necessarily to be P', but 'All S's are in fact P's'. Thus if we are to find necessity in symbolic logic, we must not look for it in the relation of subject and predicate *within* propositions. We must find it, if at all, in a relation *between* propositions. But in what relation? for of course there are many of these. Obviously, if anywhere, in the relation of implication, by which one proposition necessitates, if it ever does, another. A great deal of study, happily, has been devoted to defining and investigating this immensely important relation.

Formal logicians would agree that propositions may be so related that one can be deduced from the other. The relation that then unites them is one of implication. Mr. Russell writes: 'in order that one proposition may be inferred from another, it is necessary that the two should have that relation which makes the one a consequence of the other. When a proposition *q* is a consequence of a proposition *p*, we say that *p implies q*. Thus deduction depends upon the relation of *implication* . . .'[1] To understand what, if anything, the newer formal logician would accept as necessity, we must fix our eye on this relation of implication. What does he mean by it? Unfortunately, he means various things. But with his admirable regard for precision he has carefully distinguished and defined these. The chief of them are (1) material implication, (2) formal implication, and (3) strict implication.

12. (1) There is no doubt that in the development of modern logistic systems by far the most important part has been played by material implication, and hence it calls for fuller notice than the passing mention we have given it.[2] Perhaps the clearest way of conceiving it is as follows: take two

[1] *Principia Mathematica*, I. 90. Cf. Stebbing, *A Modern Introduction to Logic*, 221.   [2] p. 358.

propositions at random, *p* and *q*. Obviously each of them may be either true or false, and thus four combinations are possible. Both may be true: that is the first possibility. Both may be false; that is the second. The third is that the first proposition may be false and the second true. The fourth is the opposite of this, namely that the first may be true while the second is false. Now in the usage of the formal logicians one proposition is said to imply another materially when *any one* of the first three possibilities holds. If two propositions are both true, then they imply each other, even though one of them is the proposition that snow is cold and the other the proposition that grass is green. If two propositions are both false, again they imply each other, regardless of what they assert; 'Darwin discovered gravitation' implies that Benedict Arnold wrote *Jerusalem Delivered*. Finally, if the first proposition is false and the second true, once more the first implies the second; 'Darwin discovered gravitation' implies that Roosevelt was re-elected in 1936. It will be noted that our false proposition about Darwin has been used twice and that it implies not only every false proposition that can be made, but all true propositions as well; 'a false proposition implies all propositions'. In sum: *p always* implies *q* except when *p* is true and *q* is false.

13. What are we to say of implication so defined? Does it describe or define the element of necessity we are seeking? On the contrary, necessity does not enter into it at all.

(i) We shall see this more clearly if we ask whether it provides a basis for inference. For it will be admitted that in inference, if anywhere, we are genuinely using necessity, and that any satisfactory account of necessity must accord with the use we make of it there. Now it is plain that in the actual work of inference we constantly succeed in passing from one proposition to another *without knowing the second independently*. What sort of relation must hold between them to make this possible? It must be one in which the second is the *consequence* of the first. Mr. Russell writes, as we have seen, 'in order that one proposition may be inferred from another, it is necessary that the two should have that relation which makes the one a consequence of the other'. Now take two propositions of which the first materially implies the other: 'snow is cold' implies 'grass is green'. *Is* the second a consequence of the first in any sense which would render possible that without knowing it independently, I should reach it from the first? Obviously not. There is nothing in the mere facts that *a* is *b* and *c* is *d* to provide a basis for passage from one to the other. Inference in the logical sense begins when I perceive that from the truth of '*a* is *b*' there *follows* the truth of '*c* is *d*'. And nothing is clearer than that 'grass is green' does not follow from 'snow is cold'. If, when the logistician says that, both being true, the one implies the other, he meant that in the ultimate nature of things the coldness of snow is so related to the greenness of grass that neither could be what it is without the other, he would at least find us listening with interest. But of course nothing is farther from his mind. He would admit that in the proposition 'snow is cold' there is not the slightest hint that grass is green, but would add that that is quite irrelevant to whether one implies the other.

Indeed his very definition of material implication precludes its being a general basis for inference. For according to this definition $[p \supset q. = .\sim (p. \sim q)$ i.e., p implies q means that the truth of p is not combined with the falsity of $q]$, 'logical necessity is the necessity for asserting what one has already asserted';[1] no proposition can ever be known to be implied by another until *after* its truth or falsity is known, whereas, as Professor Cohen has pointed out, 'in all sciences the consequences of rival hypotheses, such as those concerning the ether, must be deduced irrespective of their material truth, and indeed as a necessary condition before their material truth can be determined'.[2] Thus 'no relation of truth-implication has any possible use in the investigation of hypotheses. For example,

[1] D. W. Prall, 'Implication', *Univ. of California Pub. in Philosophy*, Vol. XIII. 142.

[2] *Journal of Philosophy*, XV (1918), 684.

in terms of material implication any known fact is implied equally by *all* hypotheses'.[1] The fact that we are able to make inferences to propositions not yet known is, for such a logic, inexplicable, and shows that in actual inference we have command of a relation of which that logic knows nothing. In sum: if, with p before us, we can gain no hint as to whether q follows; if, with both p and q before us, we can discern no relation between them except that both are true, then to say that they still imply each other is to introduce a sharp divorce between implication and necessity. A logic whose propositions are bound together only by this sort of implication is a logic in which, strictly speaking, nothing *follows* from anything else.

14. (ii) How far material implication is from the necessary implication commonly used will be made clear by looking at some of the paradoxes to which it admittedly leads. Thus $\sim p \supset p$; any false proposition implies its own truth. Or $\sim (p \supset q). \supset .q \supset p$, if one of two propositions does not imply the other, then the other implies the one; if 'the day is rainy' does not imply 'Caesar was a man of letters', at least 'Caesar was a man of letters' implies that it is a rainy day. Or $\sim (p \supset q). \supset .p \supset \sim q$; if p does not imply q, it implies the falsity of q; if 'the day is rainy' does not imply 'Caesar was a man of letters', it implies that he was not a man of letters. Consider even some more obvious consequents of the definition of material implication. Take any false proposition at random, and it will be found to imply every other proposition, true and false; '$2 + 2 = 5$ implies that Saccho and Vanzetti were executed for murder'.[2] Take any true proposition at random and it will be found to imply every other true proposition; ' "Paris is the capital of France" materially implies "the sun sets in the west" '.[3] Take any true proposition at random and it will be found to be implied by every proposition, either

---

[1] C. I. Lewis, in Lewis and Langford, *Symbolic Logic*, 261–2.
[2] Cohen and Nagel, *op. cit.*, 127.
[3] Eaton, *General Logic*, 228.

true or false. How loose the tie of material implication is is shown vividly in the following passage from Professor Lewis:

> 'Let an equal number of true and false statements—chosen at random, and regardless of their subject-matter—be written on slips of paper and put in a hat. Let two of these then be drawn at random. The chance that the first drawn will materially imply the second is $\frac{3}{4}$. The chance that the second will materially imply the first is $\frac{3}{4}$. The chance that each will materially imply the other is $\frac{1}{2}$. And the chance that neither will materially imply the other is 0.'[1]

That is, it is impossible to find two propositions between which, in one direction or the other, the relation of implication does not hold. Now we should not for a moment deny the utility of this relation in building up certain types of system. But to say that this is what we mean when we say that the premises of a syllogism imply its conclusion, or that selfishness implies injustice, or when, in the language of common thought, we say that anything implies anything else, is merely grotesque.[2]

[1] *Symbolic Logic*, 145.

[2] Another very curious property of material implication has been pointed out by Dr. D. J. Bronstein, namely that a proposition may be inconsistent with all the propositions which it itself implies. This is shown as follows: 'Two propositions are inconsistent when and only when one implies the contradictory of the other. Therefore, two propositions p and q are consistent when and only when it is false that p implies the contradictory of q. Using "$p \circ q$" to symbolize "p is consistent with q" we have the following definition:

$$p \circ q \overset{df}{=} \sim (p \supset \sim q).$$

The proposition "$p \supset \sim q$" is false only when p and q are both true. Therefore $p \circ q$ is true only when p and q are both true. That is to say,

$$p \circ q = pq,$$

i.e. to assert that two propositions are consistent is equivalent to asserting that both are true. Thus, if two propositions are consistent, they must imply each other. But it is possible for two propositions to imply one another and be inconsistent with one another at the same time; this is the case whenever both propositions are false. For example:

$$2 + 2 = 5$$
and
$$2 + 3 = 6$$

are equivalent, that is, they imply one another. Yet they are incon-

15. (iii) Material implication itself is not, we have seen, a necessary relation. But we can go farther; it is not a relation at all.[1] To say that it holds between *p* and *q* is to say that either (*a*) both are alike in being true, or (*b*) both are alike in being false, or (*c*) they are unlike in that the first is false and the second true. Now likeness is undoubtedly a relation, and so is unlikeness; but *disjunction* is not something else of the same kind. To be sure, it is based on difference, and difference is a relation, but that does not make disjunction itself a relation. 'A man at forty is either a fool or a physician.' Does this intend some special relationship between the classes of fools and physicians? If so, what? Again, we are told that the relation which provides the basis of inference must lie among the facts related, and have whatever objectivity those facts themselves possess. But 'how in the world can a *fact* exist as that strange ambiguity "*b* or *c*"? We shall hardly find the flesh and blood alternative which answers to our "or". '[2] And once more, even if disjunction *were* a relation and *did* lie among the facts, it would still not relate *p* and *q*. What it would relate are the three propositions given above as (*a*), (*b*), and (*c*). '*P* implies *q*' is thus really a proposition stating a disjunction between three propositions *about p* and *q*. Far from stating a necessary relation between *p* and *q*, it does not assert any relation between them at all.

16. 'What an extraordinary performance', it may be said, 'to elaborate a system of logic from which all necessity is excluded!' If this means that it is a curious way to invest so

---

sistent because they are not both true. Thus, although a false proposition implies every proposition, it is also inconsistent with every proposition.'—'The Meaning of Implication,' *Mind*, XLV (1936), 159–60.

[1] Cf. Joseph, *Mind*, XLI (1932), 430; XLII (1933), 435 ff.; XLIII (1934), 318 ff. In these three articles Mr. Joseph has subjected to criticism some of the fundamental ideas of symbolic logic. Competent answers have been offered, but though I have studied these carefully, I cannot find that his strictures have been met.

[2] Bradley, *Logic*, I. 46–7.

much ingenuity, we shall offer no comment. But if it means that this or any other logic has been devised in which necessity *has* been wholly excluded, we should perhaps point out that this feat has still to be done. With whatever deliberateness and ceremony necessity is driven from the front door, it is bound to appear again at the back. In the system before us, implication is defined in terms of combinations of truth and falsity in propositions. But how are truth and falsity themselves to be determined? It is assumed that into their determination necessity in no way enters. But we have already considered this assumption,[1] and found reason to think it unsound; and we shall have more to say of it later. *No* propositions can be seen to be true in and through themselves alone; if a proposition is to be taken as true, it must be in virtue of a systematic necessitation for which this logic does not provide. The assumption that truth can be determined through some special insight into correspondence with fact or through immediate self-evidence turned out to be an illusion. What sort of necessity it is to which appeal must be taken we shall further inquire in the final chapter.

Moreover, actual systems of symbolic logic, even in their explicit development, are by no means as lacking in 'logic' as is often claimed for them. Their authors, while professing to develop a system solely by material implication, sometimes leap within a single statement from a meaning of implication in which necessity is not involved to another in which it plainly is involved. Thus, as Mr. Joseph has pointed out, 'when they write $p . p \supset q . \supset . q$ the symbol $\supset$ is not used in the same sense each time. That p implies q means merely that in fact it does not happen both that p is true and q false. . . On the other hand, that p and $p \supset q$ together imply q is true necessarily . . . Thus the relation, if any, intended by $p \supset q$ is one, a knowledge of which requires knowledge of particular fact. . . To know that $p . p \supset q . \supset . q$ I need only know the law of contradiction'.[2]

[1] Chaps. XXV and XXVI.
[2] *Mind*, XLIII (1934), 319. In the article the propositional functions given above are converted into propositions and worked out in

This tendency to shift from a looser to a stricter meaning of implication is worth noting because of its source. The source lies pretty clearly in the disparity between the highly artificial implication we have been describing and the implication of ordinary thought. The tendency to fall back on an implication that is necessary is so strong, the indulgence of this tendency so common, and the notice of this indulgence so difficult, precisely because in returning to the notion of necessity one is returning to what everyone ordinarily means by implication. If logicians do not keep to the orbit of material implication, it is because they are deflected by a steady gravitational pull towards a different kind of nexus. And the existence of this pull only serves to confirm our conviction that to gain an account of the sort of necessity that is really important, namely, the sort that makes things intelligible, we shall have to look elsewhere than to material implication.

17. (2) We turn, then, to formal implication. Our hopes rise as we do so, for Mr. Russell describes it as 'a much more familiar notion' which as a rule is really in mind even when material implication is mentioned. But these hopes sink again as we learn what formal implication means. 'Formal implication is a class of material implications; it asserts that in *every* case of a certain set of cases material implication holds. "If anything has S, then that thing has M" states a formal implication.'[1]

more detail. Cf. the following as another instance of this shift in the meaning of implication: 'Mr. Russell, in explaining "Descriptions" in his *Introduction to Mathematical Philosophy*, p. 177, uses a form of implication not material when he says of the three propositions, "at least one person wrote *Waverley*", "at most one person wrote *Waverley*", "whoever wrote *Waverley* was Scotch", that "the three *together* (but no two of them) imply that the author of *Waverley* was Scotch". Since according to material implication true propositions imply each other, either two of the first three, or any one of them alone, materially implies the conclusion! In this case the notion of implication Mr. Russell has in mind appears to be similar to entailment.'—E. J. Nelson, *Mind*, XXXIX (1930), 445, note.

[1] Stebbing, *A Modern Introduction to Logic*, 224.

In the statement 'Socrates is a man implies Socrates is mortal' we have the expression of a material implication. In the statement 'If *anything* is a man then it is mortal' we have the expression of a formal implication. The customary formula for this, $(x) . \phi x \supset \psi x$, i.e. 'for all values of x, ϕx implies ψx', is nothing more than a summary, stating that in all cases where ϕ occurs, it implies ψ. ϕ and ψ are blanks which may be filled in in countless ways. If for ϕ we substitute 'triangle', and for ψ 'having internal angles equal to 180°', then the statement would mean that in all cases where the character of being a triangle appears, this character implies the further character of having angles equal to 180°. Now as an account of necessity do we find here any advance?

Certainly not so far as concerns the items summarized. Each statement of ϕa implying ψa, ϕb implying ψb, etc., is merely a factual statement that ϕa and $\sim \psi a$ (the truth of ϕa and the falsity of ψa), etc. do not occur together. And we have seen that there is no necessity there. Does it appear then in the review by which we take in all the items at a glance? No again. If the connection of p with q in some one case falls short of being necessary, that same connection does not become so merely through holding in all cases. And even if, *per impossibile*, it did, its necessity would be beyond the reach of a logic of this type. For extensional logics, generality means the exhaustion of a set of particulars. And how are you to exhaust all triangles to see whether the equality of their angles to two right ones always holds? Of course, one can find by 'perfect induction' that in all the members of an audience or all the players of a team a certain conjunction of attributes holds. But by universal truths we do not mean that kind of thing.

We begin to see, then, in what such logic involves us. It cuts us off altogether from the knowledge of universal truth. The very logic that was supposed in virtue of its formal character to hold of all actual or possible objects turns out to be incapable of any general propositions or any inference universally valid. The laws of logic themselves are merely statements of empirically found dissociations. The principle of the syllogism in Barbara, for example, $(x) . \phi x \supset \psi x : (x) . \psi x \supset \theta x : . \supset : (x) . \phi x \supset \theta x$, has no *must* about it; it is simply a statement that the first two premises never in fact hold true *along with* the falsity of the conclusion. There is no necessity in this; nor can we be sure, since exhaustion of cases is impossible, that the principle generally holds.

18. This ignoring of necessity on the part of what is offered as *logic*, where if anywhere one would expect to find necessary connections, is a legitimate ground of dissatisfaction with the newer logistic disciplines. The doctrine that $p \supset q . = . \sim (p . \sim q)$, i.e. that '$p$ implies q' *means* only that p's truth is never to be found along with q's falsity, that the truth of p is always in fact *accompanied* by that of q, strikes the reflective reader as eccentric if offered as a verbal definition, and not only false but irresponsible if offered as a 'real' one. Furthermore, it stirs uneasy memories of 'far-off things and battles long ago'. One seems to have heard this sort of thing before. Gradually the memory comes back. Stripped of its symbolism and regarded in bare logical essentials, this is the well worn atomism of Hume and Mill. There are no necessary propositions, only statements of class inclusion. There are no necessary inferences; what look like these are statements of exceptionless conjunction. Of course, the elaborate techniques and the esoteric virtuosity of the new performers make them outwardly very remote from these simple elders, but as our ears become more attuned, we recognize that they are playing the old metaphysical instrument with something like the old scale of atomically discrete notes. And as we reflect further, the question obtrudes itself, Is this new logic, philosophically speaking, an advance at all, or is it an elaborately masked retreat? Are we to admit that in logical essentials, Mill and Hume still hold the field? Is synthetic a priori knowledge, in spite of the *Critique*, a myth? Was the examination by Green and Bradley of logical and metaphysical atomism, which seemed so decisive a generation ago, merely an over-publicized futility? The substance of our own answer has been offered and defended in the last chapter. It sums up to this, that if Hume and Mill were really right, and implication is only the conjunction or disjunction of 'truth-values', then the attempt to *understand* is hopeless from the beginning. And that inadequacy to actual thought which we found so marked in the earlier atomism has, so far, only been repeated under technical disguise by the theory that is before us.

We are not raising at the moment the question whether, if there is a 'must' in our thinking, it can legislate for reality; our question is the prior one whether there *is* any 'must' in our thinking at all. Now we have admitted that there is no sharp line between empirical and necessary propositions; and certainly, such distinction as can be made does not turn on mere number of cases, a proposition becoming necessary when for 'some' we are able to write 'all'. It is needless to go back to earlier arguments to prove this. We shall merely ask the reader whether, when the proposition about the angles of a triangle is put to him, the logistic statement expresses what he really sees or intends. When he says 'triangles have internal angles equal to 180 degrees', does he mean 'no triangles do in fact lack this characteristic'? If this is all he means, he has no reason to be surprised if he finds a triangle tomorrow with half or twice that number; there never was any *must* in the case; the new fact is merely one to be noted, and added to his collection. But surely we do *not* mean this when we assert about the triangle; we are saying something about its nature, about the sort of thing it is and what this sort involves. Indeed extensional logic has here reversed the true order of priority; it is only because we have a prior insight into the nature of the triangle and what this nature involves that we can be so sure about particular cases. When we say *a* implies *b*, we surely mean that *a in virtue of being a* rather than *c* or *d*, implies *b*; the implication is bound up with intension. And we are clear that in the intension or content upon which thought is directed, we find connections far more intimate than the *de facto* togetherness to which material and formal implication are both restricted.

19. (3) It was to remedy this deficiency in these two types of implication that Professor Lewis devised his system of 'strict implication'. He would agree that when p implies q materially or formally this gives us no assurance that q is deducible from p, nor does it give us what we usually mean by implication. He believes that his own 'strict implication' gives us both.[1] This relation he defines as follows (the symbol $\prec$ stands for 'strictly implies' and $\Diamond$ for 'possible' or 'self-consistent'): $p \prec q . = . \sim \Diamond (p \sim q)$; that is, ' "$p$ strictly implies q" is to mean "It is false that it is possible that p should be true and q false" or "The statement 'p is true and q false' is not self-consistent." When q is deducible from p, to say "p is true and q is false" is to assert, implicitly, a contradiction.'[2] An alternative definition, in which the symbol o stands for 'consistent', runs as follows: $p \prec q . = . \sim (p \text{ o} \sim q)$; i.e. 'that p strictly implies q means that p is inconsistent with the denial of q'.[3] What do we mean here by consistent? 'When we speak of two propositions as "consistent" ', Professor Lewis answers, 'we mean that it is not possible, with either of them as premise, to deduce the falsity of the other.'[4] Thus when 'p strictly implies q' is defined as meaning that p is *in*consistent with the denial of q, what is meant is that from the assertion of p the falsity of that denial *can* be deduced. It can be deduced because to assert p and deny q would amount to self-contradiction.

There is no doubt that this sense of 'implies' is far nearer to the ordinary meaning than the previous senses. It no longer asks us to say anything so alien to common usage as that every true proposition implies every other, or that every false proposition implies all conceivable propositions; it is far more critical and selective. To be sure, whenever p implies q strictly, it

[1] Lewis and Langford, *Symbolic Logic*, 122.   [2] *Ibid.*, 124.
[3] *Ibid.*, 154.   [4] *Ibid.*, 153.

implies it also materially; but one cannot reverse the statement; not all material implications are also strict implications. 'Roses are green', for example, implies materially 'sugar is sweet', but it does not imply this strictly. It would do so only if the denial that sugar is sweet contradicted 'roses are green', and this it does not do.[1] In material implication logical necessity simply disappears; there is no distinction between the necessary and the true, between the self-contradictory or absurd and the false. In strict implication necessity and impossibility as well as mere truth and falsity are explicitly recognized.[2] Material implication says that one proposition implies another if in point of *truth* we cannot affirm the first and deny the second; strict implication says that one proposition implies another when we cannot in point of *consistency* affirm the first and deny the second. Is *this* what we mean when we speak of necessitation? In spite of my admiration for the care and competence of Professor Lewis's work, I am afraid the answer must be No, again.

20. (i) Take an instance. 'If anything is red, then it is extended.' This, I think, is a fair example of implication in its ordinary sense. Now when we say that anything's being red implies that it is extended, is our meaning this, that if we denied that it was extended we should also have to deny that it was red? I do not think so. I agree, of course, that when p implies q, to deny q does commit us to denying p also; I agree that in such a case to affirm p and deny q would be inconsistent; I agree that such inconsistency is a negative test of implication. But to say that because all these things are true, therefore they give us what we *mean* by implication would be a *non sequitur*. X may be an infallible test of the presence of y without being y. And that the two are not in this case the same is evident from inspection. When I say that p implies q, I am saying that a certain relation holds between them. The inability to insert *not-q* consistently instead of q is not the *same* as that relation

[1] Lewis and Langford, *Symbolic Logic*, 154.   [2] *Ibid.*, 143.

but something that holds *in virtue of it*. Similarly of the inconsistency that would be revealed if I did insert *not-q*. If we see in this case that *p* and the denial of *q* are not consistent, it is because we see that between *p* and *q* there holds a special and intimate relation exclusive of that consistency. That there really is a distinction between implication and the inconsistency that would follow on a denial of the implicate may be clearer in an example. Can we not think of redness's implying extension without thinking of the inconsistency that *would* be involved *if* we affirmed the one and denied the other? If we can, '*p* implies *q*' does not *mean* '*p* is inconsistent with the denial of *q*'. To say that it does is to confuse essence with property, and a *ratio essendi* with a *ratio cognoscendi*.

21. (ii) We have seen that material implication carried with it certain paradoxes revealing how far it was from the common meaning, such as that every true proposition implies every other. Now the presence of such paradoxes does not necessarily condemn the system that involves them; if one starts by defining implication in certain terms, there is nothing paradoxical in remaining true to those terms. The paradoxes arise only when the results of the definition are contemplated from a point outside the system. But this does not destroy their significance. For if a view of implication has results that sharply conflict with common thought, it can hardly be the view that common thought accepts. Of course it may have made no claim to present that view, and if so, the paradoxes will not disturb it. But Professor Lewis does offer his theory of implication as a statement of what we commonly mean by the term; he thinks that 'it expresses precisely that relation which holds when valid deduction is possible, and fails to hold when valid deduction is not possible'.[1] The presence or absence of paradoxes is therefore of importance in estimating the success of his theory.

Unfortunately, in the system he proposes paradoxes are

[1] Lewis and Langford, *Symbolic Logic*, 247.

numerous. Indeed they are as numerous in the system of strict implication as in that of material implication, though they are perhaps less obvious and distressing.[1] Consider the following proposition, of which Lewis supplies the demonstration: $\sim \Diamond p . \prec . p \prec q$, 'a proposition which is self-contradictory or impossible implies any proposition'.[2] An example of this would be: 'a triangle is not a figure' implies 'grass is green'. Does this exhibit what we ordinarily mean by implication? On the contrary, so far as common insight will take us, neither the assertion nor the denial that a triangle is a figure has anything to do with the greenness of grass, and to say that either of them strictly implies this is only to show that the word 'implies' is being used in a foreign sense. Or consider the following: $\sim \Diamond \sim p . \prec . q \prec p$, 'a proposition which is necessarily true is implied by any proposition'.[3] An example would be '$9 \times 7 = 63$' is implied by 'Justice Taney wrote the Dred Scott decision'. Does the second of these propositions imply the first in the ordinary sense, the sense, for example, in which the premises of a syllogism imply the conclusion? Surely to say so is paradoxical in the extreme.

22. Professor Lewis is of course alive to such objections and has his defence. His defence is that such propositions are paradoxes only in an innocent sense; they are not so much violations of implication in its ordinary meaning as curious consequences of it, which, though seldom reflected upon, are clearly involved. It may be well to look at his proof of the first paradox given above, namely, that an impossible proposition strictly implies every other proposition, meaning that every other proposition is in the ordinary sense deducible from it. To begin with, we assume that every impossible proposition can be expressed by $p \sim p$, that is, p is at once true and false. We then proceed as follows:

[1] See Bronstein, *Mind*, XLV (1936), 165, for a parallel listing of some of these paradoxes.
[2] *Symbolic Logic*, 174, 248.
[3] *Ibid.*

Step 1: assume $p \sim p$.

Step 2: assert that step 1 strictly implies p, since if p is true and also false, then it is true.

Step 3: assert that step 1 also strictly implies that p is false, since if p is both true and false, then it is false.

Step 4: assert that step 2 strictly implies $p \lor q$ i.e either p or q, since if p is true, at least one of the two, p and q, is true.

Step 5: assert that steps 3 and 4 together strictly imply q, since if by 3 p is false, and by 4 either p or q must be true, q must be true.

This deduction is offered as proof that any proposition is implied by an impossible proposition, 'implied by' meaning 'deducible from'.[1] There are several points to remark here.

(a) The demonstration is effected by the initial assumption that every impossible proposition can be expressed by $p \sim p$. This has been questioned.[2] If 'what is red is extended' is a necessary proposition, 'what is red is not extended' is an impossible proposition. But it is hard to see how this can be expressed in the form $p \sim p$. And if such an expression were offered us and the proposition then deduced from it, 'Charlemagne was crowned in 800', we should at once surmise either that the original proposition had been altered in the attempt to force it into a form, or else that some unheard-of process had usurped the name of deduction. In either case the proof would have lost its cogency.

(b) Or consider any step in the demonstration. From the conjunctive proposition 'p is true and p is false' it is 'deduced' in step 2 that p is true, and in step 3 that p is false. In step 4, from the proposition that p is true, it is 'deduced' that either p or q is true. Why should we suppose these to be genuine cases of deduction? If appeal is made to the system of strict implication and it is argued that according to its terms the propositions $p \sim p \prec p$, $p \sim p \prec \sim p$, and $p \prec p \lor q$, state implications that are valid, the question at issue is being

---

[1] *Symbolic Logic*, 250.

[2] Cf. Dr. A. F. Emch, 'Implication and Deducibility," *Journal of Symbolic Logic*, I (1936), 27. For a criticism of Dr. Emch's alternative view of implication, see Lewis, *ibid.*, 77–86.

begged, for that question is whether conformity to strict implication does give us genuine deduction.[1] On the other hand if appeal is made to intuition, the answer again seems clear: these are not cases of deduction at all. Take the man whose mind is intelligent, but as yet unenlightened by symbolic logic; start with the statement that p is at once true and false, and try to exhibit what 'follows' from it; how far will you go before he protests that he does not know what you are about, that your very first statement, p is true and also false, seems senseless to him, and that the drawing of deductions from the senseless seems equally senseless? This, one suspects, is the line he would take; and in this respect he stands for the rest of us. What we commonly mean by 'deducible' and what is here meant by 'strictly implied' are not the same.

23. (c) No doubt what lies at the root of the common man's objection is the stubborn feeling that implication has something to do with the *meaning* of propositions, and that any mode of connecting them which disregards this meaning and ties them together in despite of it is too artificial to satisfy the demand of thought. As Morris Cohen puts it, 'a proposition devoid of all meaning would be just nonsense from which nothing could possibly be deduced. The particular logical consequences of any proposition surely do not follow from the mere sounds or marks on paper, but from the nature of the objects asserted in the proposition.'[2] Implication is commonly supposed to link the natures or characters of things; logistic method ignores these characters in order to relate propositions extensionally; hence to the thinker whose prime concern is to understand, i.e., to discern the web of necessity on which the nature of things seems to be woven, that method is a clumsy and almost useless tool.

Unfortunately, this seems to hold of both strict and material implication. And since it is a point of importance, let us try to

---

[1] Cf. Bronstein, *op. cit.*, 163, and *Philosophical Review*, XLIII (1934), 308.   [2] *Journal of Philosophy*, XV (1918), 675.

see it in both cases, taking the latter and easier case first. We saw that material implication would make any proposition p imply any other proposition q except when p was true and q false. Consider the propositions 'Berkeley was a devotee of tar-water' and 'pain is better than pleasure'. Here the first does not 'materially' imply the second. Why? Is it, as we should naturally say, because Berkeley's tar-water has nothing to do with the superiority of pain to pleasure? Not at all. It is merely because the first proposition happens to be true and the second false. That *what* is asserted is irrelevant is shown by the fact that if the first proposition should turn out to be false, or the second true, or if we merely changed their order, we should have a genuine case of material implication. In short, p and q are two blanks which we may fill in any way we like so long as we avoid the one combination, p true and q false. Implication is not a relation of meanings; it is a relation of truth-values. This is what is meant when it is said that symbolic logic is extensional. 'When we take the extensional approach, we are interested in knowing what can be necessarily concluded from the knowledge of the truth-values of a proposition or set of propositions, without any consideration of the meanings of the propositions.'[1]

Once meaning has been discarded, there is no longer any motive for trying to conform to common thought, and the definition of implication becomes arbitrary. The definition is limited only by the mechanical possibilities in the combination of truth-values. Thus, to take the simplest case, if p's implying q is a relation not between their meanings but between their truth-values, and each such proposition has two such values, truth and falsity, the four following combinations are possible:

p true, q true,
p true, q false,
p false, q true,
p false, q false,

and any of these could be used as the defining relation. Indeed there are more than four, since we might define implication

[1] Paul Weiss, 'On Alternative Logics,' *Phil. Rev.*, XLII (1933), 521.

as any one of a *set* of these, as did *Principia Mathematica* when it selected three of the four and said that implication was present if *any* of these was present. Thus the *Principia* is only one of a great variety of two-valued 'logics' that might have been elaborated. But why confine ourselves to two values? Why not three, or four, or a hundred? The answer is that there is no reason in the world. When the control that is exercised by meaning has disappeared, the number and kind of truth-values become as arbitrary as their combinations, and they may be multiplied indefinitely. By adding a category that may be called 'doubtful' to 'true' and 'false', Professor Lukasiewicz has devised a three-valued system; Dr. W. T. Parry has worked out a four-valued system; and there is no reason for stopping there except the contracted boundaries of human wit. The possibilities for 'free-thinking in logistics' are without end. We could add ninety-nine new categories at a stroke by recognizing the 1 per cent probable, the 2 per cent probable, and so on; and remembering that definitions here are arbitrary, we might if we chose become imaginative and announce as categories the real, the ribald, and the revolutionary. We should thus found systems whose originality would remain permanently unchallenged.

24. It is this loss of any lodestar for the thinker, this sense that one could 'go on doing that sort of thing' indefinitely without being any nearer to what it really concerns us to know, that for the serious mind makes logistic literature so largely an arid waste. Professor Lewis himself is apparently not untouched by this feeling. He has said expressly that 'inference depends upon meaning, logical import, intension',[1] and has endeavoured, as we have seen, to equate his logic with that of actual thought. If one proposition is to imply another, he would say, more is needed than their joint truth; that in itself can give no 'must'; *p* implies *q* strictly only when it is *impossible* for it to be true while *q* is false. Now 'impossible'

---

[1] *Survey of Symbolic Logic*, 328.

is an intensional word. It goes beyond mere truth-values; if a proposition is impossible, you know that it is false, but if it is false, you do not always know that it is impossible. When Professor Lewis introduces this notion into his concept of implication, it appears therefore as if he had freed himself from the extensional strait-jacket. But let us look at the matter more closely. 'Impossible' means inconsistent with self. Now when Professor Lewis takes as the earmark of implication that it should be impossible for p to be true while q is false, in the sense that this would involve internal inconsistency, his view is no doubt sound. To affirm something and then deny what it implies *is* always inconsistent. But when he goes on to say that in precisely the same sense an impossible proposition implies every proposition, that is, that if we affirm it we cannot consistently deny anything at all, we are at a loss; where is the inconsistency between 'a circle can be squared' and 'Miles Standish did not love Priscilla'? Indeed if we cannot consistently deny anything, then we cannot consistently deny the proposition's own contradictory, and '$2 + 2 = 5$' will be consistent with '$2 + 2$ is greater or less than 5'. Surely there is something wrong here. That disregard of content which made material implication so futile seems to have returned with its attendant blight. What is the trouble?

The trouble is that Professor Lewis has relapsed from intension into extension, from a use of 'impossible' and 'consistent' based on meaning to a use that again ignores it, after the manner of the 'material' logics. When he says that p's implying q means that p-true-and-q-false is an inconsistency, we understand; the two meanings are so linked that to try to combine the first with the denial of the second would produce a collision within the content. But when he says that an impossible proposition is inconsistent with every one, 'inconsistent' has a new sense; it means not 'discrepant in respect to meaning' but 'not conjointly assertable according to arbitrary rule'. That rule declares it impossible to assert an impossible proposition along with any denial. But the first 'impossible' here is not the impossible used in defining implication; if the joint assertion is here impossible, it is not in virtue of a collision of content, but simply because, the first proposition being impossible, the double assertion containing it is likewise impossible. Technically, the condition of strict implication, that it should be impossible to affirm p and deny q, is fulfilled. But the impossibility is not an inconsistency between the meanings of p and *not-q*; it is an impossibility that attaches to p alone. Against this we might protest that *no* proposition is impossible in itself, that possibility always has reference to a system; but let that pass. The present criticism is this: when it is said that an impossible proposition implies any proposition, implication has become as truly a relation holding between values rather than meanings as it is in systems that are purely extensional. When material implication tells us that to be sure of p's implying q all we need know is that both are true, common thought rebels; extensional knowledge is not enough; some knowledge of meaning is needed. Similarly when strict implication tells us that all we need to know is that p is impossible, common thought rebels; this is to treat implication extensionally once again; and it will not do. *No* logic can do justice to such thought which holds that we can determine what propositions imply each other without knowing what they assert.[1]

25. We have been discussing the appearance in the system of strict implication of *paradoxes*, that is, propositions which, though an integral part of the system, constitute an affront to our natural ways of thinking. We have held that these paradoxes cannot be made plausible, and that the only way to eliminate them is to break more completely with that extensional logic from which strict implication is a partial escape. Before we leave the paradoxes, it may be well to point

[1] Cf. with the above criticism the article, 'Intensional Relations', by Professor E. J. Nelson in *Mind*, XXXIX (1930), 440 ff., to which I am on several points indebted.

out some others which are not counted as such in either the strict or the material system, but which plainly fall under the description given above. In both systems there are many expressions like the following: $p \prec p$; $pp . \prec p$; $p . \prec .pp$: $pp . \prec .p$:. $\prec .p \prec p$; $p = p. = : p \prec p.p \prec p$; $pq. \prec .q$; i.e., p implies p; p and p imply p; if p implies p and p, and p and p imply p, then p implies p; the assertion that p is equivalent to p is equivalent to the assertions that p implies p and that p implies p; finally, p and q imply q. To say that these propositions express what we commonly mean by implication or deducibility is scarcely less paradoxical than the admitted paradoxes themselves. 'Strictly implies', we are told, means 'deducible' in the ordinary sense, and hence $p \prec p$ indicates that between the first p and the second a genuine process of deduction is possible. It is hard to make sense of this. If strict implication links meanings, as we are sometimes told it does, there are no two things here to link, since in respect to meaning the first p is identical with the second. If, again, it links truth-values, again there are no two things to link; the truth-value of p means the truth or falsity of the asserted meaning; and out of the truth of a single meaning you cannot extract more than one truth-value. It would scarcely be contended that implication is a nexus between acts of assertion or between marks on paper; but it is hard to think what else the two p's could stand for. One may put the difficulty thus: if the p's symbolize distinguishable propositions, then the possibility of deducing one from the other at least has meaning, but the symbolism is misleading. On the other hand, if the two p's stand for the same proposition, it is meaningless to say that one can be deduced from the other, for there are no 'one' and 'other' to be found. It may be said that within the system, at least, a perfectly intelligible meaning can be assigned; 'one proposition implies another' means only that one cannot be affirmed while the other is denied; and thus in the present instance p cannot be affirmed while p is denied. But the difficulty persists. The p that is affirmed is either different from the p that is denied or it is the same. If it is different, the statement $p \prec p$ is a deception, for it does not record the difference. If it is the same, then the gap between implication as here defined and as ordinarily meant becomes palpable. Everyone would admit that you cannot intelligibly both affirm p and deny it. But it is a shock to be told that in that admission one is *deducing* p from p. For ordinary thought the very least that will give you deduction is a distinguishable premise and conclusion; but here the p that you affirm and the p that you cannot deny are one and the same. And to *deduce* a thing from itself is, for common thought, nonsense.

Now if one can be quite clear what strict implication means, and be quite clear at the same time that in a particular case of it what one means by deducibility is not there, then what one means by deducibility is not strict implication. And if most men would reject $p \prec p$ as a case of possible deduction, still more emphatically, I suspect, would they reject such a formula as $p . \prec . pp : pp . \prec . p : . \prec . p \prec p$, 'if p implies p and p, and p and p imply p, then p implies p'.

No doubt to most men such propositions would seem to say precisely nothing. What is significant is that the formal logicians would themselves admit this; such propositions make no assertion of the actual world; they are not true or false at all; they are mere tautologies. Yet it is tautologies of this kind, they hold, that make up the whole of logic and provide the exclusive locus of necessity. There is thus no reason to think that necessity belongs to the nature of things. So far as we know, or can know, it is a relation which nowhere obtains except among our own meanings, and which holds, even so, only in propositions where we assert in the predicate something that is already contained in the subject. It is clear that the truth or falsity of this view of necessity is of the first importance for our study, and demands careful examination. As it happens, it forms a central thesis of the new and interesting school called logical positivists, whose doctrines at many points have been suggested by symbolic logic, and whose views on necessity are interesting enough to merit a chapter by themselves. The element of tautology, then, which enters into the notion of necessity as construed by both material and strict implication, is reserved for treatment in the next chapter.

26. Before proceeding, let us be clear where we are. The aim of thought is at understanding; and understanding, we saw, was only achieved in terms of a system in which the parts necessitated each other. But what does this necessitation mean? It means, replies the empiricist, only that certain parts have been presented together with such unfailing regularity that we have become unable to dissociate them. We found this theory so riddled with difficulties that we abandoned it unhesitatingly. Formalism we have found more plausible. It admits the element of necessity which empiricism denies; its peculiarity is that it confines the necessity within certain highly general forms, excluding this from the matter in which, at its best, it agrees that those forms must be embodied. But we found that necessity was much too lively a spirit to remain pent up in these tidy bottles; it burst them and flowed out on every side; it appeared in the most concrete sort of aesthetic and moral perceptions, in judgements about space and time, in the commonest inductive 'intuitions'; and even when the reasoning was of the most conventional syllogistic pattern, a little scrutiny revealed that the terms and structure which in actual thought possessed the necessity bulged at every point beyond the framework provided for them. As for symbolic logic, we found it, for our special purpose, less helpful than the older logic, primarily because with its decision to ignore intension, it had abandoned interest in necessity. Of its three principal ways of conceiving implication, material, formal, and strict, we recognized in the last a marked advance over the others, but could find in none of them a definition of implication that would cover, even approximately, the necessity actually used in inference and understanding. We are left then with these conclusions: necessity is not habit, induced in us by an inexplicable regularity of presentation. Necessity is not a form or skeleton which, while sustaining the fleshy matter of the world, is sharply distinct from it. These dismissals bring us nearer to our goal. Apparently the one suggestion of great importance that remains to be examined is the suggestion that necessity is not something enforced on us at all, but an arbitrary convention of our own. To this theory we now turn.

CHAPTER XXX

LOGICAL POSITIVISM AND NECESSITY

1. Logical positivism is a blend of the older empiricism with the newer formal logic. It holds that all propositions can be divided into two classes, the necessary and the factual. Its theory of necessary propositions derives from the symbolic logic with which we were concerned in the last chapter; as for factual propositions, it sides, roughly speaking, with the empiricism discussed in the last chapter but one. We must try to understand these two positions; and in doing so we shall follow a text which, if not the most authoritative, is I think the most intelligible, exposition of the theory, that of Mr. A. J. Ayer.

According to Mr. Ayer, no necessary proposition says anything about the world of fact at all.[1] The only propositions that do so are empirical ones, and many, even of those that seem empirical, turn out on examination to have no 'factual content', and therefore, strictly, no meaning. The test whether a proposition does have meaning is to ask whether it could conceivably be verified, and the only terms in which it can be verified are those of sense experience. This does not mean that all statements are meaningless that cannot in fact be so verified; a statement about the mountains on the other side of the moon is a case in point; but here I know the sort of sense impressions that would verify it if I could get them; 'therefore I say that the proposition is verifiable in principle if not in practice, and is accordingly significant'.[2] But if one cannot imagine *any* sense experience that would refute it or bear it out, then the statement is meaningless and not really a statement at all. Furthermore even when such statements are meaningful, they are never certain. Sense contents themselves are never connected necessarily. If statements about them are not expressions of the meaning of words, like

[1] *Language, Truth and Logic*, 104.   [2] *Ibid.*, 21.

'red is a colour', they report mere empirical conjunctions; such propositions as 'man is mortal' are no more necessary than 'crows are black', and since if the latter is to be a certainty we must exhaust the whole tribe of crows in our observations, it is and must remain merely probable.

So much for empirical propositions; now for the other, and in the present context more important, class of necessary propositions. These it is, and particularly the logico-mathematical type of them, that have been the perpetual thorn in the empiricist side. And 'the empiricist', says Mr. Ayer, 'must deal with the truths of logic and mathematics in one of the two following ways: he must say either that they are not necessary truths, in which case he must account for the universal conviction that they are; or he must say that they have no factual content, and then he must explain how a proposition which is empty of all factual content can be true and useful and surprising'.[1] Traditional empiricism has taken the former of these two lines and tried to explain necessity away as nothing but high probability; it failed, and in a recent chapter we saw why. The novelty of logical positivism is that, with the aid of the new techniques of symbolic logic, it resolutely takes the second line. It seeks, like the older empiricism, to explain necessary knowledge away; but instead of reducing the necessary to the empirical, it reduces it to empty form. This it does in two distinguishable ways, which amount in its estimation to the same thing, but are outwardly different enough to merit separate statement. Necessary propositions are explained sometimes as (1) tautologies, sometimes as (2) conventions of language.

2. (1) Logical propositions 'tell us only what we may be said to know already'.[2] According to the material logic that the positivists generally follow, the statement 'p implies q' is simply a reminder that p does not in fact occur in the absence of q, that one or other of the three remaining combinations

[1] *Language, Truth and Logic*, 91–2.   [2] *Ibid.*, 105.

is the case, i.e., either both present, both absent, or the first absent and the second present. Such a statement is not properly a logical statement at all, but a disjunctive report of empirical facts. Suppose, however, that we wish to proceed from one proposition to another by means of logical deduction. We know, for example, that p is true; then if we know also that p implies q, we can perform an act of inference and say that q is true. It looks at first glance as if, in saying this, we had arrived at something new. But the positivists insist that this is an illusion. In stating our conclusion we are only putting in a different form what has already been stated in our premises. This will be clearer, perhaps, from a simple use of what symbolic logicians call 'the matrix method'. Consider this table:

	p	q	$p \supset q$	$p \cdot p \supset q \cdot \supset q$
(1)	1	1	1	1
(2)	1	0	0	0
(3)	0	1	1	0
(4)	0	0	1	0

Here '1' means true, and '0' means false. In the first two columns are given all the possible combinations of truth and falsity for p and q. In column 3 is given, on each line, a statement of whether $p \supset q$ holds in the light of the values for p and q just given on that line. This column is thus a definition of what we mean by $p \supset q$; it tells us that we mean one or other of the pairs of truth-values given on lines (1), (3), and (4). Let us now inspect the statement $p \cdot p \supset q \cdot \supset q$, i.e., 'if p is true, and p implies q, then q is true'. When, to begin with, we say 'p is true', we rule out the combinations given on lines (3) and (4), for in both of these p is false. When we go on to say that p implies q, we rule out line (2), since that particular combination is no part, as we have just seen, of what we mean by 'p implies q'. There remains only line (1), and on inspecting it we find that q is actually given along with 'p' and 'p implies q'. This conjunction is recorded in the 1 of column (4). But that column adds nothing new; it summarizes statements already made. A little reflection, without the matrix, will show us that if we define '$p \supset q$' in material terms, then the assertion of p together with 'p implies q' *includes* the assertion of q. The final statement only unfolds explicitly what we have said before. And that is all there is to our deduction. That is all there ever is to any statement of necessity. 'To find that a proposition is necessarily to be asserted only means to find that it has already been asserted'.[1]

3. (2) Since all necessary propositions are tautologies, i.e. explicit statements of what is already contained in the meaning of our terms, they are not assertions about the world of fact but illustrations of our use of language.[2] 'The principles of logic and mathematics are true universally simply because we never allow them to be anything else. And the reason for this is that we cannot abandon them without contradicting ourselves, without sinning against the rules which govern our use of language, and so making our utterances self-stultifying.'[3] In the absurdity of this alternative, indeed, we find 'the sole ground of their necessity'.[4] When we say that p is true and that it implies q, the assertion of q is contained, as has been said, in the meaning of our words; to assert it explicitly is merely to illustrate or confirm that we are using words in one sense rather than another. Of course we could adopt different conventions if we wished; 'modern' logic has thrown open to us innumerable definitions of 'implication'. 'But whatever these conventions might be, the tautologies in which we recorded them would always be necessary. For any denial of them would be self-stultifying.'[5]

If one puts together the two main doctrines of the positivists, that all necessary propositions are tautologies, and that other propositions have meaning only if they are sensibly verifiable, it is clear that what is proposed is a philosophical revolution.

[1] D. W. Prall, 'Implication', *Univ. of California Publications in Philosophy*, Vol. XIII (1930), 155. This essay is a clear and uncompromising statement of the positivist point of view.

[2] Ayer, *Language, Truth and Logic*, 114.   [3] *Ibid.*, 99–100.
[4] *Ibid.*, 114.   [5] *Ibid.*, 114.

The 'high priori road' travelled by so many classic philosophers is now seen to lead nowhere. The very statements in which they offered their views about God, the Absolute, the soul, freedom, good and evil, an independent material world, are meaningless because incapable of sensory verification. Metaphysics in its old ambitious· sense goes overboard. Indeed philosophy generally goes overboard as a discipline engaged in the search for truth. 'Philosophy is a department of logic',[1] and its business henceforth is that of logical lexicographer and grammarian. It lays down the conditions under which propositions have meaning, lists the more useful of the arbitrary definitions that people employ· in their thinking, and exhibits, through the newer techniques, what these definitions formally imply.

While it is naturally the wholesale destructiveness of this philosophic bombshell that has aroused most interest in it, this is not the point of our direct concern. The one question we can ask about the doctrine is whether it is right about necessity. And if we review the account just given, we shall find that three points of vital importance emerge from it. All necessary propositions are said (1) to be tautologies, hence (2) to express only linguistic conventions, and therefore (3) to say nothing of fact. These views call for comment.

4. (1) The positivist view on tautologies is admitted to rest on the analysis of necessity made by symbolic logic. And within this logic it takes its guidance, not from any intensional theory, or from any partly intensional theory like that of Professor Lewis, but from the thoroughgoing logical atomism of Messrs. Russell and Wittgenstein. This theory would make logic purely extensional. According to it, a statement of material implication is, as we have seen, a disjunctive statement of fact; a formal implication is the same statement generalized.[2] ' "Socrates is a man" implies "Socrates is mortal" ' is a material implication;

---

[1] *Language, Truth and Logic*, 62.
[2] Above, Chap. XXIX, Secs. 12, 17.

'if *anything* is a man, that thing is mortal' is a formal implication. Now it is of the first importance to remember that this statement is purely extensional; it does not mean 'the attribute "being human" necessitates the attribute "being mortal" '; it means that the attribute of being a man and that of not being mortal are never in fact conjoined; this is the sense of 'for all values of x, x is a man implies x is mortal'. When, with this majoɪ, I say 'Socrates is a man and therefore mortal', I am clearly tautologizing, since Socrates is one of the values I must have considered in laying down my major. We thus go back to the *dictum de omni* as the true principle of the syllogism and indeed of reasoning generally. And not only is every syllogism a tautology; the principle of syllogism is itself a tautology. If we put it in its usual form, $p \supset q . q \supset r : \supset . p \supset r$, we could easily show by the matrix method that this merely illustrates in a new form what we take implication to mean.

Is this sound? I am convinced that it is not. Indeed the answer to it is as old as Aristotle, namely that when we think about implications, or about one thing's implying another, we are not thinking in extensional terms. When we say that being human implies being mortal, we do not have in mind an enormous class of rational bipeds past, present, and future, with each and every one of whom death, by the purest accident, is conjoined. We mean, foggily without doubt, and if you will, unjustifiably, but still beyond all question, that the *character* of being human has some special and intimate connection with liability to die. And when we say that if p implies q, and q, r, then p implies r, what are we trying to say? The extensional logicians tell us that what we really mean is this (I expand the above formula to give its exact import): no case in which it is conjointly the case that p is not the case conjointly with a case of the falsity of q, and also that q is not the case conjointly with a case of the falsity of r, is the case conjointly with a case which conjoins p's truth with q's falsity. Now if anyone charges me with meaning this when I state the principle of syllogism, I can only plead not guilty. I do not deny that I am asserting the kind of connection between three terms which would carry with them all the conjunctions of truth and falsity here set down. But if the conjunctions held, it would be in virtue of something else, a connection of content. It is this connection of content that I directly mean. And it is just this that extensional logic disregards.

5. Thus the view that necessary propositions are tautologies is achieved by squeezing out of them what they primarily mean. It may be replied, however, that one cannot escape tautology simply by abandoning the extensional reading, for tautology may belong to intensional readings too. Kant's analytic propositions, for example, were all intensional tautologies; they were propositions in which the subject concept contained the predicate concept; 'body is extended', he said, only makes explicit in the predicate an element that is contained in the thought of body and is a part of its definition. And it may be held that necessary propositions, if not tautologous extensionally, are at least tautologous intensionally.

But that will not do either. For in the first place, a proposition that is tautologous in this sense is not a proposition at all. A proposition must make an assertion; but if by 'body' you *mean* an extended something, then your proposition is 'something that is extended is extended' ; and just what does this assert ? Nothing, if only for the reason that it offers nothing that could intelligibly be denied.

Positivists like Mr. Ayer, however, would not only accept this, but would turn it instantly against us. 'Abandon if you will, they would say, the extensional interpretation, and fall back on necessity as a nexus of meanings; you will find it a worthless refuge. Take any proposition you now regard as necessary, examine it, and you will see that it owes its necessity to its being analytic, that is, to the predicate's being contained in the subject in such a way that to deny it would be self-contradictory. We should agree with you that such a statement is not a meaningful assertion at all. Indeed that is just what we are saying when we call it a tautology. Tautology is equally tautology, whether the predicate states part of the extensional range or part of the intensional content of the subject.'

Where, then, do we part from the positivist? It is here: we hold that there are necessary propositions that are *not* analytic, even in this intensional sense. Indeed we should hold that many of the propositions Kant would have described as analytic express, in actual use, a non-analytic necessity. Take the proposition 'red is a colour'. If by 'red' I mean a conjunction of certain elements of which colour is one, then to say that red is a colour would, no doubt, be as truly tautology, and its denial as truly self-stultifying, as if I had said 'red is red'. But if I mean that within what I call 'red' there are distinguishable aspects, such that one involves the other in the peculiarly intimate relation of genus and species, then my assertion does say something. It may be replied that red could not be red without being of the genus colour, that being a colour is part of what I mean by red, and that I could not withhold it without absurdity. Granted. But it does not follow that my subject is a conjunction of attributes, externally related, of which in my predicate I restate one; and if a so-called logical analysis forces me to say this, then there is something wrong with the analysis. I certainly may, and I often do, mean by statements of this kind, not that SP is P, but that within the whole SP, S is related to P in that manner which we call necessary. And the relation of species to genus is an example of such necessity.[1]

6. But we are understating our case. To show that there are intensional necessities that are non-analytic in Kant's sense, we have taken an example that he himself would have called analytic. But he recognized also a class of *synthetic* necessary judgements; indeed it was they that set the problem of the *Critique*; and though he said much that was questionable about them, we hold that at least he was right that there are

[1] For a good account of the 'analytic' judgement, see Joseph's *Introduction to Logic*, 207, 212 (second ed.).

such things. Nor do we think there is any difficulty in finding examples; there follows a considerable list of them. Of each of the propositions below we should hold (*a*) that at least two characters or contents are involved which are qualitatively distinct; (*b*) that neither is contained in the other, nor asserted to be so contained; (*c*) that therefore the proposition is not, or at least need not be, tautologous; (*d*) that the primary meaning asserted is a connection of content; (*e*) that the connection is not simply conjunction, but a far more intimate one for which, in logical positivism, there is no place.

> Whatever is coloured must be extended.
> Whatever has shape has size.
> Whatever is an integer is odd or even.
> Pleasure is good.
> The infliction of needless pain is evil.
> If I ought to do something I can do it.
> Of all plane figures whose perimeters are of a given length, the circle encloses the largest area.
> Any quantity is divisible without limit.
> In Euclidean space a straight line is the shortest line between two points.
> If A is hotter than B, and B than C, then A is hotter than C.
> If A precedes B in time, and B, C, then A precedes C.
> If A is north of B in a plane, and B west of C, C is southeast of A.

Everyone of these, we should hold, is at once synthetic and necessary. 'Yes', it may be said, 'synthetic in the psychological sense, in the sense that the subject, or antecedent, can in fact be thought of without referring to the predicate or consequent. But still analytic and tautologous by the only sound criterion, namely, whether the predicate or the consequent could be denied without contradiction.'[1] No, we reply, but synthetic even by that test.

The positivist is here confusing contradiction with self-contradiction. Fairly interpreted the test says, 'a proposition is analytic when to deny the predicate would contradict the

[1] Cf. Ayer, *op. cit.*, 102.

subject'. Now when you deny that what is red is extended, you are not saying 'what is red is not red'; extension is not one element in the quality red, which you first accept and then deny. What you are rejecting is a web or scheme which embraces both red and extension in one small system and which is so articulated that if one of these is replaced by its negative the scheme falls into incoherence. And there is an immense difference between saying 'This proposition is true on pain of S's not being S', and 'This proposition is true on pain of S—P's incoherence'. For the first guarantee is based simply on the law of contradiction, that the same cannot be different; the second is based on the insight that where diverse elements are linked by necessity, to deny either disrupts the system. The first ignores the possibility that elements really different may be intelligibly connected; the second allows for it and uses it. And for every one of the propositions just listed it is the second that is the actual warrant. Consider the final example: 'If A is north of B in a plane, and B west of C, then C is south-east of A.' No doubt with a little manipulating we could get this into the form of an analytic proposition in which the subject could not meaningfully be denied. But it is clear that what really guarantees the statement is the construction of a system within which we see that if one set of relations holds, another must hold.

7. (2) Positivists like Mr. Ayer, however, would say that all these propositions, unless indeed they state empirical probabilities, are statements of convention in language. They 'enlighten us by illustrating the way in which we use certain symbols. Thus if I say, "Nothing can be coloured in different ways at the same time with respect to the same part of itself", I am not saying anything about the properties of any actual thing; but I am not talking nonsense. I am expressing an analytic proposition, which records our determination to call a colour expanse which differs in quality from a neighbouring colour expanse a different part of a given thing. In other words, I am simply calling attention to the implications of a certain linguistic usage.'[1]

The first thing to notice about this theory is that if it is taken at its face value, it contradicts itself. No analytic propositions, we are told, say anything about empirical fact. What they really do is to 'record our determination' to use words in a certain way; or, as is said on the next page, their work is that of 'indicating the convention which governs our usage' of words. But if to 'record our determination' means to state that we are so determined, if to indicate conventions of usage means, as one would naturally take it to mean, that such conventions are actually in use, then analytic propositions do report empirical facts;[2] the very propositions that were said never to report such facts are defined in such a way that they must. But it would be unfair to make much of this. In spite of such statements as these, other expressions of Mr. Ayer's and the general tenor of the positivists' writing make it sufficiently clear that they do not mean by 'conventions of usage' the sort of facts that are reported in dictionaries.

What, then, do they mean? It is brought out in another statement of Mr. Ayer's, that 'a proposition is analytic when its validity depends solely on the definitions of the symbols it contains'.[3] Now definitions, we are told, are arbitrary. You may define implication, for example, in an endless variety of ways, but in whatever way you define it, your assertion that p implies q will merely illustrate that definition; to say that it does anything more is to forget that your definition is optional, that you might have chosen any one among countless others and your statement might still have been valid. This, then, is what the positivists apparently mean. When they say that 'necessary' propositions express conventions of language, they mean that the logical constants involved (for example, 'if', 'not', 'or', 'implies') have all of them arbitrary meanings which, so far as validity is concerned, might equally well have been

---

[1] *Language, Truth and Logic*, 104.
[2] Cf. C. D. Broad, *Arist. Soc. Proc.*, Sup. Vol. XV (1936), 107.
[3] *Op. cit.*, 103.

otherwise, just as the words in our language might all have had different meanings from those that are actually attached to them.

8. We may well attend to this with some care, for it is the sort of reasoning by which metaphysics generally is to be ruled out of court. Once we understand this matter of conventions, we are expected to see that what Plato and Plotinus, Spinoza and Hegel, Bradley and Royce, considered the most important part of their thought is literally nonsense, and that traditional ethics, aesthetics and theology have all been following will-o'-the-wisps. I have no doubt there is more in the argument than I have succeeded in seeing, but I can only record that all I do see is a quibble, a bad analogy or two, and an implicit self-contradiction.

(i) The quibble is about definition. 'Definitions, of course, are arbitrary.' How many an argument of pith and moment has had its current turned awry by that tiresome remark! There is an air of sophistication about it, as though one had seen how idle it is to ask *the* truth about anything; 'it's all a matter of definition, you see; start with a different set of definitions and you can prove anything'. I say the remark is tiresome because in spite of its many repetitions there is far more falsity than truth in it. That there is *some* truth in it is obvious. There is no word in our language that might not have meant something else if its users had so chosen. And at the present time I can agree with myself or others that whenever I make a certain noise, say 'Popocatepetl', I shall be referring to a certain mountain, and not, as I might, to justice or the north star. This free choice is always open to us, and in technical discussions it is sometimes of advantage to use it, though in ninety-nine cases out of a hundred of ordinary speech, to do so would be foolish. But in the commoner and more important cases of definition to call the process arbitrary is plainly false. When someone asks me the meaning of 'right' or 'the equator' or 'necessary', am I free to offer anything I

please? By no means. It is assumed that in my answer I will
not tie meanings to words at random, but that I will carefully
suit words to what is antecedently meant, that my interest is
not in how a word is used but in what an object is. Now when
I am called on to define such constants of logic as 'and', 'not',
and 'implies', which kind of definition is in order? Both are
open to me. But if I adopt the first kind of definition, there
would be no conceivable interest in what I might say, except
to someone silly enough to want to study my whims. If I adopt
the second, I may bring to explicit awareness a relation constantly used but dimly apprehended. Surely in logical matters
this second kind alone has any importance or interest; and
there is nothing arbitrary about it.[1] It is hard to resist the
conclusion that some persons have confused the two senses of
definition. Realizing that definition in the first sense is arbitrary,
and being called on to define certain logical terms, they have
supposed that definition there too is arbitrary. Unknowingly
they are quibbling.

9. (ii) When we say that one definition is better than another,
however, we are introducing a distinction that the positivist
looks at askance. The fact that one definition of implication,
one system of logic, is more generally meant or more widely
used or more practically helpful than another has nothing to
do, he would say, with its validity as logic. Granted that we do
mean by implication a certain kind of connection, that does
not prove that we *might* not and *can* not mean something else
which, in spite of its unfamiliarity, would, solely as logic, have
all the validity of the first. *Practically* we are justified in using
one rather than the others. Practically, we are justified in using
one form of language rather than another. Practically, the man
laying out a tennis court will be well advised to use Euclidean
geometry. But it would be absurd for anyone to argue that
because he found one language so useful, no other language

[1] There are some good remarks on this head by Mr. A. J. D.
Porteous in *Arist. Soc. Proc.*, Sup. Vol. XV (1936), 133–4.

existed, and because Euclid gave such valued aid with his tennis court, every deduction in non-Euclidean systems is invalid. Yet that is the burden of our case, we are told, if we insist that there is but one necessity and one logic.

But the analogies are not sound. In choosing vocables, any one of an indefinite number would do equally well as a means to the ends of speech. But it is not similarly true that varying definitions of implication will equally well serve the end of thought. The end of thought, as we have seen, is to understand; and to understand is to lay hold of necessity. We have seen, furthermore, that implication is so defined in the logic most commonly followed by the positivists as to contain no trace of necessity; for that reason we were forced to reject it, together with all other definitions which make it a disjunction of truth-values. 'But what right have you thus to pick and choose among logics? In doing so you are yourself imposing a standard that is purely arbitrary because it comes from outside logic.' Such an objection would only betray the extent to which the study of logic has been perverted from its natural office and made into an idle game. Logic was originally, it has been historically, and in our judgement it ought to remain, a discipline that has some connection with the enterprise of thought, that is, with the attempt to understand. It is the discipline that seeks the conditions under which reasoning is cogent, and ultimately there is just one way to tell whether reasoning is cogent, namely, whether it satisfies the logical sense, whether it fulfils the impulse of intelligence toward understanding. Cut the nerve of connection between logic and actual thinking, and the study resolves itself into an enormous sprawling mass of anarchic inquiries in which each ant-like investigator involves himself more and more deeply in ingenious but aimless intric-acies, while the spectator who is still naïve enough to have an interest in understanding his world looks on at first with bewilderment and then with an invincible growing repugnance. He has regarded philosophic reflection as 'an unusually stubborn effort to think clearly' about *the* ultimate nature of things, to lay bare *the* interconnections which would render these things intelligible; and this end, immanent in his thought, not explicitly discerned by it, yet as unmistakable in its influence as the pull of an unseen planet, would assure him when he was nearing the intelligible, and warn him when he was falling away into inconsequence. We think he was right. This immanent end of thought is really a bar to which all logics must submit themselves, and if a system presents itself in which the implicatory relation is defined as some random combination of truth values, it says, 'Does this satisfy the demand of thought for a connection that is intelligible and necessary? If not, out it goes.' Thus we are by no means free to choose conventions in logic as we are in language. Any word we happen to fix upon will carry a meaning, but it is not true that any logic we happen to fix upon will satisfy the need for necessity.[1]

If I am not mistaken, our case would hold even without appeal to this standard. For the supposed alternative logics turn out upon examination not to be substitutes for the familiar logic, but supplements to it. An adequate defence of this statement would require much space and technicality; fortunately it has been worked out already by more competent hands.[2] But technicality is not needed to show that there is at least an impassable limit to the substitution of new logics for old. Remove the law of contradiction from your system and replace it with a substitute, and what do you get? Some bizarre

[1] Cf. the following from Professor Nelson: the claim to alternative logics amounts only to the statement 'that we may, for aught anyone can stop us, give to the word "implies" different meanings—now it is to mean one thing, now another. A mere misuse of words appears to be the magic wand for bringing forth alternative logics. . . . Indisputably true it is that if I decide to use the word "women" now for females, and at another time for males, then, if I keep my mind sufficiently muddled, I may be able to delude myself into thinking that there are alternative systems of sex. But what we are interested in is logical structure—not words, but their meanings. Anyone can write a fake dictionary; but not even God Himself can make men into women by shifting words, or make what we call "implies" symmetric by changing names'.—*Mind*, XLII (1933), 34.

[2] See the article of Nelson's just cited, on 'Deductive Systems and the Absoluteness of Logic," and Paul Weiss, 'On Alternative Logics.' *Phil. Rev.*, XLII (1933), 520–5.

alternative system? No. You get no system at all, and no assertion at all, for you have removed the condition of intelligible statement in any system whatever. It is odd to call such a law a 'linguistic convention'. A convention can be exchanged for something else. But when you changed the law of contradiction, what would you change *to*? Such laws cannot be abandoned, nor are they in fact abandoned by any of the so-called alternative logics; they provide an *ur*-logic or proto-logic which conditions assertion in all systems. In this sense, as Dr. Bronstein has recently pointed out, one may accept Professor Lewis's dictum that a necessary proposition is implied by any proposition. For 'necessary propositions state the formal conditions which anything that we call a fact must satisfy. They prescribe the necessary conditions of sense in assertions that such and such is or is not the case. Necessary propositions are, thus, second-order propositions, which implicitly define "proposition" by stating the properties of anything that is a proposition. They are not pictures of reality, but the canvas on which all pictures of reality are drawn.'[1]

10. Thus the analogy of logical with linguistic convention fails. So also does the analogy with the alternative systems of geometry. There is no real contradiction between Euclidean and non-Euclidean systems; it is true they start with differing postulates about parallels, but one no more contradicts the other than the proposition 'If A is not B, it is D' contradicts 'If A *is* B, it is C'. The conflict arises when the geometer seeks to interpret his system in terms of some actual given space. To this space he finds that one or other of the rival systems will not apply, and thus that the propositions 'This space is Euclidean' and 'This space is non-Euclidean' conflict.

'Hence he might be led to conclude that the propositions of these systems of geometry are not necessarily true. But there is a confusion here, due to the geometer's taking, e.g., "triangle" as generic, whereas *in the system* it is a species of triangle. The

[1] The 'Meaning of Implication,' *Mind*, XLV (1936), 170.

proposition he finds to be false will be one like this, "The sum of the angles of this real triangle in real space equals two right angles." But the proposition in the system of Euclidean geometry is, "The sum of the angles of an Euclidean triangle equals two right angles", which two propositions are not at all one and the same. Had the system of geometry been generic, this situation would never have arisen. . . . Hence geometries are alternative only in the sense that some exemplification of one of them is not an exemphfication of another, and these two possible exemplifications are not identical."[1]

Even this kind of alternativeness is not to be found in logic, since logic is completely general and a system of geometry is not. There is a logic that holds alike of every proposition, but no geometry which, if its variables are interpreted, i.e. not left in the bare abstractness of a 'system-form', will hold alike for all triangles. The 'alternative' systems of geometry, like the alternative conventions of language, provide no real analogy to the canons of logic.

11. (iii) We have owned to the suspicion that in his doctrine of conventions the positivist is not consistent with himself. What we mean is this: in spite of holding that logical laws are conventions and arbitrary, he seems careful in his own practice to follow one kind of logic rather than others, a course which needs a justification it does not get. In defining implication, for example, he starts with a simple matrix consisting of the four combinations of truth and falsity in p and q. These four he declares to be the only ones possible. But how does he know that they are the only ones possible? He may say we arrive at it by experience, by finding of every experienced character that it is either present or absent, with no co-ordinate third state occurring.[2] But it is not clear how an impossibility can be established by experience, however protracted. If not based on experience, the assertion that the matrix gives the only

---

[1] Nelson, *ibid.*, 39.
[2] This is apparently the position of Mr. Prall; see *Univ. of California Pub. in Phil.*, XIII (1930), 142.

possibilities must be a convention, and therefore arbitrary, and therefore not, on simply logical grounds, preferable to another. But when it is said that the statement 'these are the only possibilities' is arbitrary, that can only mean that one is free, if one wishes, to replace it by an alternative, such as that there *are* other possibilities. Why, in the light of this alternative, positivist logicians should lay so much stress on the matrix method, should cling so pertinaciously to a view of implication based on it, and should pride themselves as they do on their logical rigour, is somewhat puzzling. It would almost seem as if they thought their logic *the* right one.

Necessary propositions, says Mr. Ayer, 'simply record our determination to use words in a certain fashion. We cannot deny them without infringing the conventions that are presupposed by our very denial, and so falling into self-contradiction. And this is the sole ground of their necessity . . . any denial of them would be self-stultifying'.[1] But why should we not stultify ourselves? To be sure, the denial of a necessary proposition would mean 'infringing conventions', but if they really are only conventions, why may we not adopt the infringing of conventions as our particular pet convention? If you say that is the one thing that is *streng verboten*, it is idle to say also that you are putting conventions on the same level, for you are elevating one to a position of primacy; you are not only taking it for your own, but are saying that anyone who fails to follow it is ruled out of court. Now we have not the least objection to anyone's saying this, for to us it seems perfectly sound. What does seem unacceptable, because inconsistent, is to say, first, that all necessary propositions are conventions with alternatives, and then, in the case of one of these, to accuse anyone of talking nonsense who tries to avail himself of an alternative. Is not that equivalent to the admission that here there *is* no alternative and hence that the rule is *not* mere convention?

And what of the proposition itself that all necessary propositions are conventions? Which of the two classes does it fall in,

[1] *Op. cit.*, 114.

the class of empirical probabilities or the class of tautologies? If in the former, then at any moment a necessary proposition may turn up that is not tautology, and hence the sweeping statement above is illegitimate. If in the latter, the theory is self-contradictory again, for having laid it down that no necessary proposition says anything about facts, it lays down a necessary proposition about propositions; and since a proposition is described as 'a class of sentences',[1] and sentences are facts, we have a necessary statement about facts after all. And apart from that, it is hard to believe that this theory about conventions figures in the minds of its advocates as just another convention which 'records our determination to use words in a certain fashion'. It does not seem, in their discussion of it, to be that kind of proposition, yet it will fit nowhere else in their system.

12. (3) Of the three positivist contentions about necessity, we have now commented on two, namely, that assertions of it are tautologies and that they are linguistic conventions. There remains the third, that they say nothing about fact. 'They none of them provide any information about any matter of fact. In other words they are entirely devoid of factual content.'[2]

Now by 'factual content' the logical positivist means something extremely narrow. According to his principle of verifiability, the meaning of a statement is yielded by the method of its verification; a statement *means* the set of observations that would verify it. And by 'observations' he means sensations; an empirical proposition is really 'a forecast of our sensation'.[3] It follows that only those propositions that refer to our own

---

[1] Ayer, *op. cit.*, 121.   [2] Ayer, *op. cit.*, 104.
[3] *Ibid.*, 144. In *Mind*, XLV (1936), 201, Mr. Ayer says in reply to criticism, that the positivists do not rule out non-sensuous experience as impossible; what they say is that if we speak about entities knowable only in such terms, our statement will mean only that we have this sort of experience. But Mr. Ayer and his fellow-positivists evidently do not believe that anyone does have such experiences.

future sensations have any factual content. From this it follows again that many statements that are constantly made without a doubt of their being significant must be set down as un-meaning. Most persons, perhaps, would contemplate serenely enough that elimination of metaphysics which is a main article in the positivist creed. But even they must grow uneasy as they consider the following developments: All statements about the consciousness of other people are meaningless, since none of our own sensations can verify its existence; the best we can do is to observe their bodily behaviour; and hence when we speak of their experience, it is their behaviour that we mean. As regards everyone but himself, the positivist is therefore a behaviourist.[1] Every statement about the past must be unmeaning, or at least if it does have a meaning, that is utterly different from anything we had supposed we meant; if we judge that the Greeks won at Marathon, we are really laying down 'a rule for the anticipation of future experience'.[2] As for ethical judgements, 'they have no objective validity whatsoever'.[3] If they are not 'pure expressions of feeling' they are statements of how I or other people feel.[4] Now when we are called upon to say whether necessary propositions are factual, is it this sense of 'factual' that we shall find most useful? No doubt it is, if our interest is solely in contriving a polemic against positivism. But our interest goes beyond that; we are trying to find whether necessary judgements in any important sense say something about the real world. And we must confess

[1] As regards the self, it has been remarked by Dr. Weinberg that positivism is 'a solipsism without a subject'.—*An Examination of Logical Positivism*, 68.

[2] *Language, Truth and Logic*, 146; this is applied, indeed, to 'every synthetic proposition'.

[3] *Ibid.*, 161.

[4] Mr. Ayer, *Mind*, XLV (1936), 201, says that positivism is 'plainly compatible' with utilitarianism. This is a surprising statement. One would have supposed that utilitarianism involved reference to other people's pleasures and pains in a sense that the 'methodological solipsism' of the positivists would not allow. But for a criticism (decisive, I think) of this view of moral judgements, see E. F. Carritt, 'Moral Positivism and Moral Aestheticism,' *Philosophy*, XIII (1938), 131 ff.

that the positivist interpretation of 'factual' seems so im-
plausible, so evidently at variance with the plain meaning
with which people commonly use words, that we should prefer
not to forfeit a wider interest in our discussion by conducting
it in these terms.[1] The question whether necessary propositions
are factual or not in the restricted positivist sense is not the
question of first importance. That question is whether or not
they can be *true*, in the sense, whatever that is, in which other
propositions are true. And since the positivist claim that they
are not factual statements, but merely linguistic conventions,
carries with it the further claim that they are neither true nor
false, we have here a real issue. It seems to us clear that some
necessary propositions are meant to state what holds of the
real world, and are true or false in the same sense as other
propositions.

13. (i) An example already given by Mr. Ayer is worth
meditating on. 'If I say, "Nothing can be coloured in different
ways at the same time with respect to the same part of itself",
I am not saying anything about the properties of any actual
thing; but I am not talking nonsense. I am expressing an
analytic proposition, which records our determination to call
a colour expanse which differs in quality from a neighbouring
colour expanse a different part of a given thing.'[2] If the reader
is like the present writer, he will have, on reading this, a
curious sense that the cart has got before the horse and is
pulling it energetically around. It is very much like saying that
when, with Smith and Jones before me, I remark that they
cannot be the same, what I really mean to say is that I am
determined to call Smith Smith and not Jones, and Jones
Jones and not Smith. Surely if my statement does record such

---

[1] For criticism of the positivist view of meaning, see, e.g., W. T.
Stace, 'Metaphysics and Meaning,' *Mind*, XLIV (1935), 417 ff.;
A. C. Ewing, 'Meaninglessness,' *Mind*, XLVI (1937), 347 ff.; and C. I.
Lewis, 'Experience and Meaning,' *Phil. Rev.*, XLIII (1934), 125 ff. I
think that Professor Lewis, however, is too generous to the positivists.

[2] *Language, Truth and Logic*, 104.

a determination, it is in virtue of my seeing in the facts something that calls for this difference of names, to wit that Smith and Jones are exclusive of each other. And if I assign to differently coloured parts of the same thing the *names* of different parts, my naming is surely based on the insight that, *being* qualitatively different, they *are* not the same. Again, why should I 'determine' not to describe the same spot, seen under the same conditions, by the names of different colours? To do so would of course be easy enough. Is it replied that it would also be extremely inconvenient? Yes, it would, but why? Because the plurality of my words would be in constant conflict with the singleness of fact; I should be using two names when I could see from the nature of the case that one of them would always be impertinent. Thus our determination or convention is anything but arbitrary; it is an attempt to conform our speech to the apprehended character of fact. And even if we were entirely mistaken about this character of fact, the positivist theory would still be wrong. For it says we do not *mean* to assert a character of fact. And whether the character is there or not, it is clear that we do mean to assert it. We mean that nature itself, at this particular point, and under these conditions, will not admit two colours at once. We are asserting a necessity understood to be imposed on us by the real world.[1]

14. (ii) Indeed it is hard to see how an assertion could be made without being made of the real world; what else is there to assert it of? We are told, of course, by some logicians that propositions are *Zwischendinge* which occupy a realm of sub-

[1] Cf. the following from Mr. Reginald Jackson: 'The very consideration which may drive a philosopher who rejects intuition to say that a priori propositions are commands must drive him, if he is consistent, to say that they are aimless commands. It is only because the sum of two and two is four that it is worth while to issue or to obey a command to call the sum of two and two "four". . . . What is stated is the fact that saves the command from futility.'—*Proc. Arist. Soc.*, Sup. Vol. XV (1936), 143, note.

sistence where they may be neither asserted nor denied. We are told by the positivists that necessary propositions are not really asserted at all, since they are expressions of 'determination'. We have seen, however, that they may be more than this, and may affirm connections. both synthetic and necessary. Now when we affirm such connections generally, are we affirming anything true or false about the real world? If we say that the real world is wholly made up of sense data, undoubtedly not, for logical relations are not the sort of things that can be touched or heard or tasted. But however hard it may be to see what region of reality we are asserting of, to hold that we are not asserting of it at all is inconsistent with the evident intent of assertion as such. When we say, 'what is red must be extended', are we saying anything we mean to be true? Of course we are. Is it *capable* of truth or falsity? Yes, again, unless either we call our assertion a convention, which we have seen it is not, or confine reality to sensation, which nobody really does. Is what is thus meant to be true, and is capable of truth, also *actually* true or false? I do not know how to deny it. Must there be a region which what is true is true *of*? Obviously again. Is this region an integral part of the world we take as real? Yes; if not, it is nothing. Just how it is related to the rest may be hard to say; we should not care to be called on at the moment to say what the connection is between Shakespeare's world of fancy and the Shakespeare who drank at the 'Mermaid'. But that we include even this world in the reality which is independent of our thought and demands conformity from it, is shown by our recognition that it would be as genuinely false to say 'Hamlet was Prince of India' as to say 'Shakespeare was a Lord High Admiral'. Similarly, in '*p* implies *q*' we bow to the exactions of a something not ourselves, independent of our thought and will, which makes our statement true or false. It is, happily, needless at this point to undertake the difficult metaphysical business of defining that reality. For it is perfectly possible without this to see that the acceptance of some such reality belongs to the very heart of assertion; it is what we mean when we say that to assert is to assert *of* something, and that *of* that something the assertion is true or false.

15. (iii) Consider the following argument of Mr. Joseph's regarding the so-called 'laws of thought':

> 'Though these are called laws of thought, and in fact we cannot think except in accordance with them, yet they are really statements which we cannot but hold true about things. *We cannot think* contradictory propositions, because we see that a thing *cannot have* at once and not have the same character; and the so-called necessity of thought is really the apprehension of a necessity in the being of things. This we may see if we ask what would follow, were it a necessity of thought only; for then, while, e.g., I could not think at once that this page is and is not white, the page itself might at once be white and not be white. But to admit this is to admit that I can think the page to have and not have the same character, in the very act of saying that I cannot think it; and this is self-contradictory. The Law of Contradiction then is metaphysical or ontological.'[1]

Does this argument *prove* that logical law holds in 'the being of things'? I do not suppose Mr. Joseph would claim that. But it does show that when questions arise as to the character of the world which we assume to exist apart from our thought of it, the laws of logic are in a peculiar position. As regards such qualities as colour and sound and odour, there is no difficulty in conceiving that they do not exist in that world. But regarding the laws of logic we can neither prove that they hold there nor intelligibly deny that they do. Any 'proof' would be circular. For the demonstration would have to accord with the laws it was 'proving', and unless these already held for the world in question, the argument would have no standing. On the other hand, the suspicion that they do not hold turns out, as Mr. Joseph says, to be self-destructive. We may sometimes ask ourselves, 'Why, after all, may there not be some islet among the Pleiades where everything is different, and even the tiresome law of contradiction gets a holiday?' But

[1] *Introduction to Logic*, 13.

the instant we try to attach definite meaning to our words we find ourselves beaten. To assert that the law was suspended would 'mean', for example, that there might both be and not be such an idyllic islet; and that, we see, is nonsense. 'But this only shows the more clearly', may come the retort, 'how firmly confined we are to our "logico-centric predicament"; it does not show that beyond the horizon of our logic is nothing.' But is confinement really confinement when there is no desire or thought of escape? Is there sense in saying we are 'in a predicament' if we can attach no sense to being out of it? Our situation, in short, seems to be this: We find it assumed in every judgement that the laws of logic are valid of the world with which thought is concerned, a world independent of present assertion. And this assumption is compulsory, since without it thought cannot take a step. Is it also true? That we cannot prove. But the contrary suggestion is meaningless. And thus the alternative actually before us is to accept these laws as independently valid or to cease thinking altogether.[1]

16. (iv) The positivist's doctrine about necessity involves the sharpest sort of severance between propositions that are a priori and tautologous on the one hand, and those that are empirical or factual on the other. The only necessity he recognizes is either absent entirely, as in empirical propositions, or present in a form absolute and unqualified. But we have seen long ago that one cannot force the delicate gradations of actually perceived necessity into any such black-and-white dichotomy.[2] If, instead of peering at thought through heavy

---

[1] 'In thought the standard, you may say, amounts merely to "act so"; but then "act so" means "think so", and "think so" means "it is". . . . Thinking is the attempt to satisfy a special impulse, and the attempt implies an assumption about reality. You may avoid the assumption so far as you decline to think, but, if you sit down to the game, there is only one way of playing. In order to think at all you must subject yourself to a standard, a standard which implies an absolute knowledge of reality; and while you doubt this, you accept it, and obey while you rebel.'—Bradley, *Appearance and Reality*, 152–3.   [2] Chap. XXV, Sec. 33.

lenses of mathematical preconception, we look directly at what is there, we shall find that the necessity actually used is a matter of degree. How this may vary has been illustrated earlier in our discussion of degrees of self-evidence. The perception that necessitation is thus a matter of degree is inconsistent with the sharp line between a priori and empirical which the positivists are wont to draw. In the face of such insights as that anything red must be coloured and extended, or that orange falls in the colour-series between red and yellow, it is idle to say that judgements about empirical fact are *completely* without necessity. It is also idle to say that any judgement whatever possesses, with exactly its present meaning, so absolute a necessity as to be incapable of modification by any extension of knowledge. But we have argued this matter before, and shall refer to it again. It will suffice here, perhaps, to say that if our contention is true, if necessity has begun to appear even in a posteriori judgements, if it is less than complete even in a priori judgements, then a conception of necessity that would convert these two into watertight compartments does not answer to what thought finds. And from a division so artificial it is impossible to draw any presumption as to whether necessity holds in empirical fact or not.

17. (v) There is still another consideration that may help us to see how assertions of necessity may be assertions about the real world. The traditional form in which such judgements are expressed is hypothetical: *if p*, then *q*; and naturally so, for what is directly stated is that a consequent depends on a condition. Now we have seen that even this is an assertion about reality; no judgement is a pure hypothetical; the categorical element, the assertion that something is true, invariably enters in. But certain logicians who, unlike some others, have kept their interest alive in the actual intent and content of thought, have pointed out that in such judgements there is a further categorical element. 'Trespassers will be prosecuted', may be stated with equal propriety as, '*If* anyone trespasses, he will be prosecuted'; but when we so judge are we merely declaring the linkage of abstractions? Clearly we mean to say more. But how much more? We do not always mean to assert the antecedent as a fact; we see that our judgement might still be true even if no trespasser ever appeared: it still holds, we say, that if a trespasser *had* appeared, he *would* have been prosecuted. Similarly of the consequent: the absence of prosecutions would not of itself refute our judgement. But when neither antecedent nor consequent is fact, the link between them will not be fact, and it begins to look as if reference to fact had been omitted wholly.

That would be an error. The best clue to the *point d'appui* of such a judgement is the question what would directly deny it. If some actual state of affairs would contradict it, then an assertion about a state of affairs is being made. Very well; could anything in the world of fact conflict with 'trespassers will be prosecuted'? Yes, obviously; many things. The owner of the property may have a disposition as unpugnacious as a rabbit's; the warning sign may be a jest; there may be, in that locality, no system of law enforcement; and so on. One who cited any of these facts would at once be understood as taking exception to the judgement, and this seems inexplicable if the judgement says nothing about them. To be sure, the reference to them is not direct, and the speaker himself might not find it easy to drag them fully to light. But whoever denies that one is here going beyond the explicit terms of one's judgement and making an assertion about facts will, if it please him, begin by explaining how otherwise these facts could be so pat in refutation.

There is of course nothing new in this doctrine; it comes straight from Bradley. 'The relation of the elements in a hypothetical judgement is not an actual attribute of the real. . . It need not be true outside the experiment. The fact which existed before the experiment, and remains true after it, and in no way depends on it, is neither the elements, nor the relation between them, but it is a quality. It is the ground of the sequence that *is* true of the real, and it is this ground which exerts compulsion.'[1]

Now the illustration we have chosen, and all the examples used by Bradley, are of hypotheticals that are far short of necessity. On our own part this is deliberate, for the existence of an ulterior ground is in such cases easier to see. In the ordinary examples of 'necessary judgement' the content explicitly offered is supposed to supply all the warrant that is needed; it is self-enclosed; nothing beyond it is asserted whose presence could condition the necessity, or whose failure diminish it. Is this supposition correct? Or do hypotheticals that are 'necessary' assert, like those that are less stringent, an ulterior ground and condition? We think they do; and in spite of his illustrations, there is no doubt that Bradley thought they did. But his conception of this ground wavered curiously. Sometimes, as in the passage quoted, the ground is a 'quality', more or less occult and mysterious, a brute fact to which thought must conform if it would be true. But this is not his final view. He used it in his *Logic*, because he sought in that work to retain, so far as possible, the metaphysic of common thought; but before the work reached its end he had frankly abandoned the attempt,[2] and throughout his *Appearance* and *Essays* he holds a more defensible theory. One would not expect a thinker like Bradley to cling with particular affection to 'brute fact'. He held, and rightly we think, that no such fact can stand as ultimate before a fully critical scrutiny; any attempt to say what it is reveals that it is relative to a context on which its very nature depends.[3] What the fact really is you cannot say till you have exhausted that context, and there is no reason to suppose that you will exhaust it till you have fixed the place of the 'fact' in the universe as a whole. Bradley maintained to the end, as did Bosanquet from the beginning, that hypothetical judgements affirm something of reality;

[1] *Principles of Logic*, I. 88.
[2] See the second edition notes appended to the last chapter.
[3] See above, Chap. XXVII, Sec. 9 ff., and the discussion of internal relations in Chap. XXXII.

but it was only as a metaphysic was slowly wrought out in the course of his logical struggles that he came to see quite clearly that this reality could not be identified with phenomenal fact, since such fact is itself contingent. And if we are to get beyond the contingent we must follow the radiating lines of necessity beyond all present horizons until we arrive at a system which, because subject to no further conditions, can alone be self-subsistently real. What qualifies the truth of our judgement is thus not brute fact with which thought must correspond, but a presumably intelligible system with which thought must cohere. No judgement can lay hold of 'fact' as it really is unless it seizes the conditions of the fact, and its degree of truth will be measured by the extent to which, so to speak, it includes these conditions in itself. Hence if every judgement is categorical, in the sense that it asserts of reality, it is also hypothetical, since it is made subject to a mass of conditions that are not specified or even known.

Now hypothetical judgements that claim necessity are in this respect like the rest. They too assert of reality, and are subject to conditions outside their own content. We sometimes say, to be sure, that $7 + 5 = 12$ is necessary in itself, absolutely and unconditionally; but would it hold if, for example, 2 and 3 did not make five? and if not, is there any sense in saying it has *no* conditions? Quite obviously it belongs to a system, and is conditioned by that system. And the system of number is itself but an abstraction from a wider and concrete whole; what reason have we for saying that it gives us unqualified necessity unless indeed we can see that in this wider whole it somehow lives upon an island and has no commerce with anything outside that might affect it? *Are* there such insular judgements or insular systems? Or is all necessity relative to a whole which in the end is *the* whole? With the answer to this question we shall have reached our journey's end.

CHAPTER XXXI

CONCRETE NECESSITY AND EXTERNAL RELATIONS

1. We are now nearly in sight of our goal. But to ensure no loss of direction as we approach it, let us look back along the line of conclusions that have appeared in our advance. Here are some of the more conspicuous ones:

Thought is a purposive activity, to be distinguished from other activities by the character of its goal.

So intimately are end and process bound up with each other that thought can be defined only with reference to its end; indeed it *is* that end in course of realization.

Knowledge is impossible unless the inner end of thought, i.e. intellectual satisfaction, coincides with the outer end, the revelation of its object. There is only one hypothesis that would make such coincidence other than miracle, namely, that an idea is a potentiality which, if fulfilled, would *be* its object.

What is that end upon which the inner and outer aims of thought converge? Our answer here has been confident and emphatic. Throughout the career of thought, from its first tentative appearance in perception to the flights of speculative reason, there is a single continuous drive toward intelligible system, a system which, as all-comprehensive, is logically stable, and, as perfectly integrated, leaves no loose ends.

The mainspring of reflection is the impulse to bring within the system of experience some isolated fact that challenges it.

What controls the process of reflection and provides the key to invention is the operation within the mind of that system which forms its end, an operation that may be none the less effective because it works below the level of explicit consciousness.

The test of any conclusion is whether or not it coheres with such system as we have; but that system itself must be revised,

and revised perpetually, under the correction of the immanent
end that is working through it.

What do we mean by coherence? We mean far more than
consistency. Perfect coherence would mean the necessitation
of each part by each and all of the others.

What then does necessitation mean? This is our final question,
with which we have been indulging in preliminary struggles
throughout Book IV. We have seen that necessity does not
mean what the empiricists think it does, mere strength of old
association. Nor does it mean what the formalists think it does,
a necessity that may be complete in an abstract system or an
isolated judgement. Nor yet does it mean what the newer
positivists think it does, tautology and linguistic convention.
What then does it mean? That is where we are now.

2. It will be well to fix at once upon the point where our
view of necessity comes into clearest and sharpest conflict
with the views we have been discussing. According to those
views, necessity, if there is such a thing, invariably links two
terms or two propositions; and between these two, it is as
simply present or absent as a tow-chain is simply present or
absent between two motor-cars. C. I. Lewis has put clearly
the contrast between such theories and ours. After explaining
his own absolutist theory, he says:

> 'A second—and colloquially more frequent—meaning of
> "possible", "impossible", and "necessary" has reference to the
> relation which the proposition or thing considered has to some
> state of affairs, such as given data, or to our knowledge as a
> whole. In this second sense, "possible" means "consistent with
> the data" or "consistent with everything known"; "impossible"
> means "not consistent with the data, or with what is known";
> and "necessary" means "implied by what is given or known".
> Such meaning of "impossible", etc., is *relative*—"possible in
> relation to——": by contrast, the meanings which we symbolize
> are *absolute*; they concern only the relation which the fact or
> proposition has to itself or to its negative. . . .'[1]

[1] *Symbolic Logic*, 161.

We take the relativist view. We hold that one cannot define implication in terms of p and q, because more is always involved. If one is said to imply the other, it is because both belong to a wider system and to grasp the implication between them *is* to grasp them as members of that system. Implication is systematic interdependence. It is a relation between parts of a whole imposed on them by the nature of the whole itself. Since there are many kinds of whole, there are many varieties of implication. Since wholes, again, have many degrees of unity, there are many degrees of necessity with which one proposition may imply another. The points of most conspicuous challenge in such a view of implication would appear to be three: (1) it maintains that implication is never a function of one proposition alone, or of two propositions alone, but always of a system partially revealed in the terms as related. It holds that implication is (2) various in kind and (3) various in degree. All these points have been touched upon earlier, but the view of necessity here advocated will become far clearer if we set them out in connected fashion.

3. (1) On the question whether necessary propositions derive their necessity wholly from themselves, little more need be said. When we were discussing self-evidence as a test of truth, we took the two types of proposition whose necessity has been regarded as clearest, namely, axioms and logical laws, and asked how they were validated. If they were called in question, could we do anything but repeat them, insisting that their validation lay in themselves and must be found there or nowhere? The answer was that no proposition was self-contained in either its necessity or its meaning. 'The angles of a triangle equal two right angles'; yes, but here our triangles are obviously conceived as in Euclidian space, and our proposition is warranted by the collapse of the Euclidian system that would follow on its denial. 'Cruelty is wrong'; yes; but, to say nothing of the complicated texture from which each of the concepts involved is abstracted, would not the statement be defended by pointing out to any questioner that a justification of wanton pain would send a shudder, so to speak, throughout his system of moral judgement?[1] Even the law of contradiction, we saw, is most effectively supported neither by an appeal to its inner necessity, nor by showing that it cannot consistently be denied, but by showing that its fall would carry down with it the intelligible world.

Now what holds in this respect of single propositions holds of pairs of propositions. When p implies q, it is not mere p that does the implying nor mere q that is implied; nor does the implication exhaust itself in the linkage of this pair. The point may be illustrated by a memorable difference of opinion that arose between Messrs. Russell and Bosanquet over a very odd proposition, 'If a donkey is Plato, it is a great philosopher.' Does the antecedent here imply the consequent? According to Mr. Russell's 'material implication' it does; so far as meaning is concerned, antecedent and consequent are capsules whose relation to each other and to everything else is without bearing on whether either implies the other. To settle that point all one need know is their truth or falsity. And since a false antecedent implies any consequent, the above is a genuine case of implication. To Bosanquet this seemed wildly at odds with the actual intention of thought. Implication was for him a relation between meanings; these meanings were themselves integral with a wider context; and it was within that context alone that implication could be discerned. Hypothetical judgement was typically of the following form: Suppose A is B, then (*reality in other respects being what it is*) C is D. The fact that the parenthesis is a silent partner should not lead us to forget that it is there. For 'you cannot draw a conclusion from a mere and pure supposition';[2] 'absolutely pure hypothetical judgement, an assertion of implications following upon a supposition which is in no way attached to an underlying real system, I

---

[1] See the discussion in Chap. XXV, Sec. 33, and the appended note from Professor Paton.

[2] *Implication and Linear Inference*, 4–5; see also *ibid.*, Chap. VIII.

do not believe to have a meaning'.[1] It is involved in this view that if the antecedent destroys the system within which the consequent normally follows, then the implication itself disappears. Of this we have an instance in the case above. Suppose a donkey to be Plato, what can you derive from that? Bosanquet answers, Nothing at all. You cannot responsibly suppose such a thing, in the sense of really grasping its meaning, and still leave unaffected that world of co-operating conditions on which, in part, the consequent depends. 'The hypothesis scatters your underlying reality to the winds, and what I should call the basis of implication is gone.'[2] In a world so different from ours as one would be in which a donkey could be Plato, we should be helpless to say what followed.

4. Which of these views is right? 'Both or neither', it may be replied; 'for the definition of implication is arbitrary.' We answer: The question what verbal tag to attach to a given meaning is a question that anyone may amuse himself with if he wishes. We are *not* amused by it; the problem here is different and serious.[3] When we commonly say that one statement or character implies another we presumably mean something by it, and Bosanquet at least was trying to find what this was. As for ourselves, we can only say that his answer does fit what we mean. If the reader is in doubt whether it fits his own meaning, we suggest a test. Let him take what he would ordinarily recognize as an instance of implication from any department of experience, let him make quite clear to himself what is contained in the explicit content of his judgement, and let him then ask himself whether there is no set of conditions, taken for granted by the judgement yet falling outside its explicit content, whose denial would put the implication in jeopardy. If he reports that there is such a set, then to say also that the consequent follows from the antecedent taken alone is self-contradiction; it is to say that these

[1] *Logic*, II. 41.   [2] *Ibid.*, note *c*.
[3] For a more formal answer, see above, Chap. XXX, Sec. 8.

conditions both do and do not contribute to the result. And we hold that such a set will in every case be discovered. 'If I leap from the top of the Empire State Building, I shall be a sorry mess at the bottom'. Why yes, *if* I carry no parachute, *if* my body retains its mass, *if* the law of gravitation continues, and so on. It never occurs to us to state such conditions expressly, because that is unnecessary; we know that they will be taken for granted without reminder. But conditions merely assumed to exist are as truly conditions as those expressly stated. 'If a beam of light is reflected from a surface, the angle of reflection equals the angle of incidence.' Yes, *if* the space is Euclidean, *if* the influence of gravitation on the beam is discounted, *if* no other distorting factors enter in. Would your consequent hold if these tacit conditions did *not* hold? And if it would not, can you call them irrelevant? 'If Marathon came before Thermopylae, and Thermopylae before Salamis, then Marathon came before Salamis.' It may seem here at first sight that nothing is needed to warrant the inference but the two temporal relations, taken in bare abstraction. But consider first, that the implication is only seen as the result of a construction in which the three terms are placed in an arrangement and the relation between the extremes is read off from that. And consider, secondly, that every temporal connection is asserted subject to the laws of identity and contradiction, which get their warrant in turn from the whole of experience.[1]

There may be those who are willing to admit that every hypothetical judgement is thus subject to tacit conditions, and that the implication holds only within a system that includes them, but would still say that in assuming these conditions they were not asserting about reality. They do not like the view that the validity of an inference, even an inference from a mere supposal, is conditional upon the nature of things, or upon a true apprehension of that nature. The whole complex, they say, composed of the antecedents, the consequent, and the relations that bind them together, might remain in the world of supposition. But in effect this is to deny the difference

[1] Above, Chap. XXV, Sec. 34 ff.

between supposition and judgement; and obviously there is such a difference. To judge is to assert that something is true, i.e., true of the real world; it is responsible and 'means business' in a way that supposition does not; it recognizes that the consequent it draws may be blocked by conditions unforeseen; but it commits itself nevertheless and ventures to hold that what is unknown is not unfavourable.[1] And of the attempt to get all relevant conditions within the antecedent, we must remark, in the first place, that, on grounds not yet fully stated, you could never exhaust the series; and, in the second place, that if you try to do that, it is hardly possible to play fair. You start with a supposition which, as supposition, is arbitrary; you find that, taken alone, it will not give you the consequent; so you set out to amend and expand it till it will. Where do you get the matter for this process? By parthenogenesis from the initial abstraction? Not at all. You get it by observing the further conditions that have been actually imposed by nature. That is, in the very attempt to mould your supposition so as to avoid appeal to reality, you find yourself making the appeal [2]

Statements of implication, then, are not statements of connection between bare abstractions. There is always a reference to further conditions which, together with those that are explicit, form a system; and it is within this system that the implication holds. This is true, we have found, of propositions that assert categorically an implication between terms; it is equally true of hypotheticals, which assert an implication between propositions; and if we cared to make the inquiry, we should find that it holds more plainly still of trains of inference. As for the degree of abstractness in terms or propositions, that makes in principle no difference.

[1] 'When conditions are specified and conclusions drawn from them, the resulting affirmation presupposes *all* conditions, known or unknown, indispensable to its truth, and therefore claims a support from the real universe which cannot be measured or limited.'—Bosanquet, *Implication*, etc., 169.

[2] Bosanquet, *ibid.*, 170 ff. Cf. Bradley, *Appearance*, 365–70; *Essays on Truth and Reality*, Chap. III.

5. (2) Does necessity have *kinds*? We have described it as a relation between parts of a whole imposed by the nature of that whole. But of course there are all sorts and dimensions of whole. A steam engine is a whole; so is a poem; so is a house, a horse, a flower, a century, a mind. Our remark, at its face value, would mean that the parts of any of these wholes were related to the other parts necessarily, and might even be said to imply them. And this seems odd. Is there any sense in saying that in a given engine the valves imply the drive-shaft, or that in a given painting one figure necessitates another?

There is a great deal of sense in it. Indeed, if one looks at these wholes from the inside, as the mechanic or painter does, such language is natural enough. For the mechanic surveying the engine, the valves in their very essence are means by which power is transmitted to the drive-shaft, and the drive-shaft *is* a means by which power is transmitted from valves to wheels. Apart from its office in the whole, and therefore apart from each other, neither would be what it is; to say the same thing slightly otherwise, the parts take their function, and therefore their relevant nature, from their place in the engine as a whole; and so regarded, it is not apparent why the scheme of the engine should not present as genuine a necessity as anything in Euclid. (We are not raising at the moment the question whether necessity is involved in causality;[1] what has been said, so far as we can see, may be said without that.) Similarly of the relation between parts of the picture. Responsible painters, when they paint, do not surrender to uninstructed, wayward impulse; even when they work effortlessly they are under constraint by their subject-matter, or, more strictly, by the requirements of the aesthetic whole they want to embody. A remark that Bosanquet quotes from Whistler illustrates the point. A visitor to the painter's studio 'remarked that the upright line in the panelling of the wall was wrong . . . adding, "of course, it's a matter of taste". To which Whistler replied . . . "remember, so that you may not make the mistake again,

[1] See below, Chap. XXXII, Sec. 10 ff.

it's not a matter of taste at all, it's a matter of knowledge".[1] To suppose that a painter who says this can only be declaring dogmatically the superiority of his own taste is to miss the point completely. The remark may consort with a genuine humility, whether it did in Whistler's case or not. For the artist may be saying that so far as his work is sound, it is precisely because he has *prevented* his self from intruding, because he has managed to keep what is merely subjective and personal in abeyance, in short, because his brush has been under dictation from his subject. But this has been illustrated before from art,[2] and it is perhaps needless to insist on it further.

6. Now there are difficulties in holding to kinds of implication. What are they kinds *of*? According to traditional logical theory, a kind is constituted by a nuclear identity, owned in common with other kinds, plus an addendum that serves to distinguish it. It should therefore be possible, on a review of these kinds, to elicit the identity that runs unaltered through them all; and when we have found this in the present case, we should have the essence of implication. Can we discover such an identity? Is there some relation between part and part within a whole that appears with unaffected sameness in systems as extremely different as the multiplication table, a sonnet, a starfish, and the science of modern physics? If there is such a thing, it is of course important for us to find it, for it will provide us the definition that is the goal of our present inquiry.

But whoever goes quarrying for this hidden identity will find himself curiously baffled. He can say, as has been said already, that in all these cases there is some kind or other of whole, and that within it each part takes its special character from the others within that whole. And to say this is not simply useless. On the other hand, it must be admitted to be singularly unenlightening. One had probably hoped for some

[1] *Principle of Individuality and Value*, 62, note, from Whistler's *Life*, I. 185.

[2] Chap. XXIII, Sec. 13; for further illustrations of the subconscious working of necessity see Chap. XXIV.

neat, compact master-key that would unlock all the locks of system, a sort of 'open sesame' that would show us how systems as such and everywhere hold themselves together. But with this meagre result before us, are we a whit more able than we were to complete the Venus de Milo, or follow the quantum theory, or explain the drunken porter in Macbeth? It must be admitted that we are not. But then it is an ancient mistake, which we tried to expose long ago, to expect much use or light from such formulas. The expectation plainly rests on belief in the abstract universal, a little hard nugget of qualities that enter like an iron pellet into all the species of a genus; and this universal we had to reject as an illusion. There is no colour or colouredness, different from red and blue and the rest, which yet is the same in all of them; no figure or figurehood from which the various figures are manufactured by grafting upon them adjuncts from without.[1] Not, of course, that when we speak of colour or figure we are thinking of nothing; on the contrary, we should hold that the object of the thought is far richer than has been supposed. Instead of dealing with a mere extract or abstract from the species, the thought of a genus is essentially a purpose whose end could only be realized in compassing the range of the species; they are not addenda to the genus but developments of it; hence what we mean when we think of the genus can only be fully seen through its forms of realization.[2] Now all this holds of the thought of necessity. There is no single abstract relation that relates in precisely the same fashion the parts in a machine, the propositions of Euclid and the notes in a song. The necessity of Euclid belongs inextricably to a kind of space; the necessity of music belongs inextricably to the world of sound; omit space from the one and sound from the other, and it is idle to say that what you have left is somehow the essence of the matter. The idea of necessity does of course have meaning, and one is certainly not saying nothing in describing it as the

[1] Chap. XVI.
[2] Chaps. XVI and XVII; on the relation of idea and object, see Chap. XIV.

interdependence of parts in a whole. But we can now perhaps see why the description says so little. It is because necessity is not a single golden thread that in all fabrics remains the same. Rather, it is like the famous chameleon on a Scotch plaid. It takes its character from its context, that is, from the wholes it appears in, and these wholes are extremely various. To exhaust the meaning of necessity we should have to exhaust the varieties of whole which imposed upon their parts any sort of interdependence.

7. To recognize kinds of necessity, that is, varieties of implication corresponding to differing subject-matters, may be thought to carry with it an awkward consequence. We have made system the goal of thought and the test of truth. If we now recognize that system may be as genuinely present in a painting as in a science, are we not committed to the view that a painting is true, and likewise a sonnet and a sonata? And is not that absurd?

Evidently a further distinction is called for. We can hardly withdraw what we have said about varieties of system; their existence is too indisputable a fact. What needs to be added is that the interest that leads to the constructing of systems is itself various. There is clearly distinguishable in the mind, though intimately bound up with other functions, a theoretic or logical impulse; the whole course of our study has been concerned with its manifestations. Its end is understanding; and understanding, we have seen, is always in terms of system. But there is this peculiarity about the theoretic as opposed, for example, to the aesthetic impulse, that its satisfaction is always and in the nature of the case incomplete. Any partial system, just because partial, must be rejected and transcended; the impulse to expansion will tolerate no arbitrary arrests; its goal is nothing short of a system perfect and all-embracing. The end of the theoretic impulse may thus be said to be system as such, or better perhaps, a system that would include and order all lesser systems.

Now it cannot be said in the same way that the impulse toward beauty, or pleasure, or goodness, is the impulse to system as such. Take the interest in system of the painter. It is, as we have said, a genuine one; given a painting nearing completion, he may be so bound by the necessities of the case as to feel that there is only one right way to complete it. But is it not clear that system for him is not, as for the theorist, an end in itself, but rather a means to something else? For the theorist it would be pointless to ask, *why* be consistent? since the achievement of consistency is for him a self-justifying end. But the question does have meaning for an artist, and this in itself is enough to show that his end is different from the thinker's. His end is to satisfy, not the logical sense, but the aesthetic. The 'must' that is implicit in his painting is the must that says, In this particular context, this particular line or colour is imperative if aesthetic *feeling* is to be satisfied; it is not the must of the thinker which says, Such and such evidence is still needed if one is to meet the demand of the sceptical intellect for *proof*. What aesthetic satisfaction consists in is of course a question of much difficulty, to which an abstract answer, we suspect, would be as uninstructive as to the parallel question about thought. Fortunately we are not called on to deal with it further than is needed to distinguish aesthetic from theoretic satisfaction. And for this it is enough to say that aesthetic satisfaction does *not* lie in the grasp of system as such, while theoretic satisfaction does. And since it is only the latter that gives truth, there is nothing in our view that would identify the aim of the artist with that of the thinker, or confound the truth of art with its beauty.

Thus the logical and aesthetic impulses require for their satisfaction different types of whole. The unity of a philosopnic system is not that of a poem. It is true that these wholes may have much in common. There is philosophy in the *Prelude*, and there is not a little poetry in Plato. But as many a critic has pointed out, when the speculative interest dominates in the *Prelude*, the poem ceases to be primarily poetry; and similarly when a philosopher writes to please, his success in that irrelevant enterprise cannot save him as a philosopher. It is a somewhat subtler question whether the introduction into an aesthetic whole of a larger element of truth may increase the value of that whole *as* a thing of beauty, and whether a finer feeling for beauty may carry a philosopher nearer truth. We should not hesitate to answer Yes to both these questions. A. C. Bradley once inquired whether the fall of man does not offer the poet, as a poet, a better subject than a pin-head;[1] and there are persons so sure that intellectual content has nothing to do with aesthetic possibilities that they are ready to brand as a philistine anyone who would answer 'Yes, it does'. 'So you think, do you, that it is the business of poetry to instruct!' Of course we think nothing of the sort. What we are saying is that the aesthetic impulse, like others, must have matter to work with, that the intellect may, and often does, supply such matter, and that when it offers a theme of such vast dimensions as the fall of man, the artist finds more matter that is appropriable than he could in a pin-head or a point. If art attains its fullest flower in tragedy, as Aristotle thought, that is not exactly an accident. Sweep of intellectual vision, while of course not the end of art, may enter into it so essentially and effectively as to augment its power as art. Conversely, aesthetic sensibility, like moral, may enhance the value of a philosopher's work. Indeed, for a rounded philosophy he would find it indispensable. An important part of his business is intellectual synthesis, and when he tries to construe the ultimate nature of things without being able to draw on these major realms of experience, he is trying to make bricks without straw.

8. However, though aesthetic and theoretic wholes may each be involved in the other, there is no great danger of confusion between the immanent ends at work in them. What is really dangerous is that the theoretic end should be identified with some partial system which, informed by the genuine

[1] *Oxford Lectures on Poetry*, I.

theoretic aim, still falls so far short of the end as to present
this only in abortive form. It was the invaluable service of
Hegel to show once for all that these hasty rationalisms would
not do, that the momentum of a freely expanding thought
carried one inevitably beyond them. If you take mechanism,
for example, as your key to the universe, you are locked out
when you come to the understanding of persons or values. A
very great part of nature can, no doubt, be brought within
the scope of the theory; but to try to force the whole universe
into it, to seek within a system of interacting particles a place
for colour and sound, right and wrong, the beautiful, the
comic, and the ugly, is either blind or very naïve. The same
holds of the traditional teleology. There is plainly much in
human experience that can be brought under the idea of the
good, in the sense of being taken as means to a special and
limited end. But sooner or later the attempt to work this scheme
over the whole field of experience breaks down, and to persist
in it is fanaticism. Intellectualism is another such fanaticism;
pragmatism still another. The intellectualist is the man who
would explain everything in terms of the kind of necessity found
in the systems of greatest abstractness, such as traditional or
symbolic logic, or mathematics, forgetting that these are not
the only necessities, and forgetting likewise that, as Hegel
showed, one cannot get explanations that are anything but
formal and tangential from applying the categories of abstract
quantity, or mechanism, or 'chemism', to experience in the
concrete. Explanations do not explain when they leave out
nine tenths of the matter to be explained. The pragmatist
would, in the same one-sided fashion, bring all truth and reality
within the bounds of practice, which, as a bed of Procrustes,
is as bad as the others. Such one-sidedness is usually due to
one or other of two parallel errors, specialism and abstractionism. Specialism takes a system that applies to a limited
range of fact and tries to stretch it over the whole of experience.
Abstractionism takes forms of colourless generality, like those
of traditional logic, and tries to convince itself that they will
illumine the tropical jungle of the concrete. A system that is in

the long run to satisfy the immanent demand of thought must be one that is neither based on some bare category, alleged to be common to all the minor wholes of experience, nor extended by provincial enthusiasm from one's own bailiwick to the universe, but one that is a genuine system of systems, which unites the lesser wholes into an intelligible structure without omitting what is distinctive in each.

We can see, with this in mind, that what presents itself to common sense as differences between kinds of necessity would probably appear to the more sophisticated eye as differences in degree. The various wholes within which explanation and proof are offered—that system of pure quantity which is algebra, and of numerical quantity which is arithmetic, the systems of time and of geometry, of cause and effect, means and end, organism, and the rest—these are not so many separate blind alleys with no common direction or terminus. If they are really systems within a system—and this, as we have seen, is the 'invincible surmise' of thought—we should expect to find in them embodiments in differing degree of that whole which, so far as they represent efforts to understand at all, is the immanent end of each of them. To that difference in degree we now turn.

9. (3) There is something paradoxical in 'degrees of necessity'. When we solve a problem in arithmetic or algebra, it seems clear that the right answer is necessitated absolutely, and all others absolutely excluded. It sounds absurd to say that a demonstration in geometry *more or less* implies its result. Necessity in its very essence seems to preclude degrees, and a necessary conclusion to be one that follows without escape or abatement. To be sure, there are often cases in which the conditions that would, if given, determine a result completely are not all of them present, and then we may say that as the missing conditions are added we come nearer and nearer to necessity. A detective on the track of a criminal may weave very slowly and painstakingly his net of incriminating evidence, becoming 'more and more certain' of his man, until finally it is 'complete', and he springs. But even here the plain man would probably say on a little reflection that 'degrees of necessity' puts the case badly. As the evidence accumulated, piece by piece, the guilt of one suspect became more *probable*; but it is loose thinking to call it more *necessary*; necessity came at the end when the evidence was all in; before that, strictly speaking, it was not there at all, while from then on it was present absolutely. Necessity is a limit, and a limit does not increase as it is approached. To say that necessity itself increases would be like saying that in a series with zero as a limit one gets more and more of zero.

This is a very plausible view, and for practical purposes it may be better than anything that can be put in its place. Nevertheless in the end it will not stand. It rests on two assumptions, both of which are questionable, one of them regarding the *extent* of the system within which necessity holds, the other regarding its *structure*.

10. (i) The first assumption is that necessity is complete within an arbitrarily limited system. Consider the case of the detective. He approaches his problem with many presumptions which it hardly occurs to him to question, presumptions that limit suspicion to a certain range of persons. Whoever committed the crime must have been on the spot at the time; he must have had a motive, a weapon, and a certain amount of physical strength; he must have entered and left by certain windows or doors, and so on. Only persons who meet these requirements are considered as possible culprits. Among these persons, it may then be found that all but one can be eliminated, since there are certain facts about each which (again on the basis of certain presumptions) are inconsistent with his having done it. In the case of one of these persons, however, there are no such incompatible facts, while there are positive indications which (if once more we are allowed to assume various things, including that nature is uniform) assure us of his guilt. It is then said that he 'must' have committed the crime. And very well he may; one can conceive that a jury, on such evidence, might be justified in a verdict of guilty. But is it not clear that the evidence is taken as complete only because a mass of outlying conditions is taken for granted, and the problem confined to a few points in an inner circle? These points alone are taken as doubtful, and when they are settled the case itself is considered settled. But whatever will do for a juror, it surely will not do for a logician, to say that a conclusion has been made out completely, i.e., through exhaustion of the relevant evidence, when it is based on a dozen assumptions any one of which might conceivably turn out false. It is as unlikely as you please that the criminal killed his victim by using ectoplasm or telepathy or what not, and that nature had ceased to be uniform over night, but until you can rule these out as impossible, it is surely inaccurate to say that you have arrived at *complete* necessity.

The opponent of degrees in necessity has his reply to this. He would agree that necessity is not achieved so long as some relevant evidence remains unexamined, and that the plain man had mistaken for necessity what was only high probability. But he would contend that a mistake as to when necessity has been achieved has no bearing on the question what necessity really is. Granting that many instances, possibly even all instances, of what we had supposed to be necessity are only cases of probability, still it does not follow that necessity *when* achieved is less than absolute. And if the conditions which the plain man, rightly or wrongly, assumes to be fulfilled were really fulfilled, then the necessity *would* be absolute. The conditions of the conclusion, however hard in practice to exhaust, are still limited in number and quite definite in character; they are hence capable of complete fulfilment, and the conclusion of complete necessity.

But it is clear that this reply assumes the point it was supposed to disprove, namely, that necessity *can* be complete within a limited system of conditions. It assumes that it is possible to gain an absolute knowledge of the conditions of some proposition, so as to grasp its absolute necessity; and since this necessity is then complete, it could not, of course, be added to by any subsequent extension of knowledge. Now we have just suggested, and have argued at some length earlier[1] that the necessities of actual knowledge are not of this kind, that th systems within which they immediately hold are not, as they appear to be, self-enclosed. But further consideration of this point belongs to the second assumption we have referred to in the common view of necessity.

11. (ii) That assumption is that propositions and the evidence for them constitute a sort of mosaic of which, in respect to meaning, all the pieces are independent of each other. We start with a certain proposition whose meaning is supposedly fixed, we study the system of which it is a member, and little by little we bring to light the mass of further propositions which, if we rejected it, we should have to deny; these form the context within which our proposition is necessitated. Now (this is the point), the expansion of this context before our eyes is simply the addition of piece to piece in a mosaic, the central piece and all the others retaining their meaning unaffected as the expansion goes on. As a picture-puzzle leaps to completion when the last piece is inserted, so probability gives way to necessity when the last piece of evidence is gained. If a proposition is to be made out completely, there are certain other propositions, implying it and implied by it, whose truth must be established. Other things equal, its probability increases by discontinuous leaps as these are shown to be true, and when the last of them is established, the ring of evidence snaps shut with finality.

This view of a system as a mosaic is natural enough. It has spatial analogy in its favour, and to a certain extent also mechanical analogy; and these exert a powerful influence on speculative thought. But the influence may be unfortunate, and it is so here. Perhaps the most useful thing we can do at

[1] See Secs. 3, 4, above, and Chap. XXV, Secs. 31–33.

the moment is to replace these false analogies by others that are better, even though the system that would wholly satisfy is unique and therefore beyond adequate presentation through any analogy.

Consider the growth of a flower. Within the bud there is a certain pattern or arrangement of parts; a week later when the bud has burst into bloom, the arrangement is very different; sepals, petals, and stamens are now developed and distinct. Here the first system has evolved into the other, but it is evident that the process is not one of adding part to part while the original nucleus is untouched. It is general and correlated change. Every change among the stamens is balanced by one in the sepals and petals, so that a botanist who was expert enough could tell from the stage of development of any of these precisely what to expect in all the others. At every stage in the process the parts are so related that a change in any one of them is reflected throughout the whole. Here is a type of system whose development clearly proceeds by degrees. Its growth can be measured by its approximation to the pattern of its maturity; but it would be absurd to measure this interval by the number of pieces that had still to be added, as in the case of a picture puzzle. The measure is the degree of approximation achieved by an actual system to that other and ideal system which it is tending to become.

A still better analogy is one we have already used, the growth of a mind. In the case of the school-boy who becomes a historian we saw that the meaning of his judgement, the very substance of what he asserts when he says 'Napoleon lost at Waterloo', is different in his maturity from what he meant by these words in his youth. And the change has consisted, not in an addition of certain elements to an unchanging core of meaning, still less in a subtraction from it, but in a complete pervasion or permeation of the earlier meaning by the influence of a wider knowledge.[1] Accessions from without involve transformation of what is there already. One can no more enlarge the horizons of a mind without reordering it internally

[1] Chap. XXVII, Secs. 4, 5.

than a state can double its territory and leave the old govern-mental arrangements exactly what they were.

It is this sort of analogy, if any, that will convey what is meant by degrees of necessity. Such degrees are exhibited whenever one passes from systems where the parts are relatively external to each other to those where there is completer inter-dependence, from a machine to a plant, for example, or a plant to a mind. They are revealed again in any process of growth through which an immanent end is realized, since as the process goes on and the parts become more determinate, they take their character increasingly from the whole to which they belong.

12. Now the use of such analogies is sure to provoke an objection. It will be said that they are irrelevant as illustrations and question-begging as arguments, for they use relations that hold within knowledge as guides to what holds outside it. Even if it is admitted that a state of mind or an individual's system of knowledge has some such pattern as the above, and that its growth is in some sense total rather than piecemeal, it does not follow that anything similar holds in the real world. Suppose it granted that as one's geometric or philosophic grasp increases, one achieves a system that is better and better articulated, it does not follow that there are corresponding changes or degrees in the nature one is seeking to know. The geometric or causal system is what it is irrespective of our fluctuating knowledge of it; its links are fixed and unchanging; within its web, one element A either does or does not necessitate another element B; degrees are in no way involved. The fact that in the system as apprehended by us, i.e., in our knowledge of the system, A and B are conceived as linked in some other fashion and perhaps with varying degrees of intimacy is beside the point. For the question is not whether there are degrees of intimacy among our ideas, but degrees in real necessity, in the necessity that links elements or propositions apart from our knowledge of them.

Now (i) this objection may mean different things; for the denial that we can identify what we find in present knowledge with absolute reality may have differing grounds which affect its sense. If the objector means that since what is real can be nothing less than systematic and coherent utterly, our own confused and partial systems cannot, *as such*, have a place in this, we shall at once admit its force. Indeed it is a major part of our contention that the chaotic and fragmentary character of experience belongs not to the nature of things but to our knowledge in a transitional stage, and that our knowledge loses this character precisely in the degree to which it approximates, or rather achieves and embodies, the real. But the objector is probably standing on other ground. He is not thinking, one suspects, of the real as the remote fulfilment of the ideal of knowledge; he probably believes that things and systems are quite capable of real existence independently of experience precisely as we experience them, and is only holding that partial necessities are *not* among these. But if this truly is his position, there is little in it. When he has abandoned the criterion of system for the presence in knowledge of the real, he has also abandoned the ground for denying to partial necessities independent reality, and in lieu of any other criterion we can only suppose he is falling back on what he would call presented fact. But with this his case evaporates. For when we examine the necessities actually presented in experience, we find that they do evince degrees. They invariably hold within systems, and these systems show degrees of integration and necessity is a function of such degree. Of these experienced partial necessities we have in various places given many examples, which we might here call in evidence as facts. Of course if he insists that there is no meaning in the partial realization of a system except the realization of part of the system, he may deny that these are facts. We would ask him in that case how he conceives the relation, let us say, between bud and flower, or between the minds of youth and maturity. Can he suggest a more accurate way of describing this than as the relation between a system partially realized and the same system realized more completely? If not, why object to degrees of necessity? There is nothing occult in the notion. It stands for one of the commonest of facts.

(ii) The inference from degrees of knowledge to degrees of reality may be objected to on other grounds. It may be taken as implying that, since there is no absolute necessity in knowledge, there is none in reality. But there is no force in the alleged implication. The immanent end of thought is a system at once perfect and all-embracing; in such a system necessity would be complete; and it is the working assumption of thought that reality *is* such a system. For the aim of thought is to explain things; its assumption is that things are explicable; and explicability *means* full systematic necessity.

(iii) Finally, to accept a discrepancy between the structure of reality on the one hand and the ideal of thought on the other is to commit thought to defeat. Suppose reflection to pursue its enterprise until it reaches the intelligibility in which it finds rest. Dealing with the commission of a crime, or a problem in arithmetic, or the causation of some disease, it presses its inquiry till, in the light of all the relevant evidence, it sees the solution standing before it clear as noon. And suppose it is then informed that all it has gained is a subjective satisfaction which no more reveals the facts than does the quenching of a casual thirst; what this does reveal is that we happen to have a liking for working up our experience into a special kind of pattern; that is all. Is this a sensible or tenable view? We have seen that you cannot *prove* it wrong,[1] since such proof would assume as independently valid the very structure which is here claimed to be not so. But one thing is plain. If the view is accepted, the claim to knowledge is an idle one. If what satisfies intelligence does not also report the real, then there is nothing whatever that thought can affirm as true, not even the present statement. Its only recourse is to relapse into a silence that certainly cannot claim to be wise.

13. We must admit, then, that there is no direct road by which we can prove that the intellectual ideal is applicable

[1] Chap. XXX, Sec. 15.

to the real world. There are those, however, who would attempt to extract from us a far larger admission, namely, that this ideal is *in*applicable, that there is conclusive evidence to show that the world is *not* the sort of system which, according to our account, intelligence demands. They say that in the sort of system we have in mind all relations are internal, whereas many of the relations we find in experience are obviously and irremediably external. And they would hold that this discovery is significant for the ideal of thought itself. For if an ideal is known to be incapable of being realized, it is disqualified even as an ideal. If the matter with which thought has to do is such that it could not possibly be moulded or forced into the transparently intelligible system we have been speaking of, then it is fatuous for thought to retain this as an end. Or, to put it in our own earlier terms, when there is a conflict between the immanent end of thought (to gain intellectual satisfaction) and the transcendent end (to see things as they are), the first must always give way. We must suit our ideals to the facts, for we can no more suit the facts to our ideals than Canute could stop the sea.

This question whether there are in fact irreducibly external relations, or whether, for a full understanding, the world would be a system bound together by internal relations only, is an extremely thorny one which we would avoid if we could. But it lies directly in our path, and threatens the success of our whole endeavour. For of what use is it to prove that the ideal of thought is thus and so, if that ideal is irrelevant to the world that is to be known? Those who hold to external relations believe that some at least of the objects found in nature are so deeply indifferent to each other that by no extension of our understanding could we hope to discern between them the kind of connection that would satisfy intelligence. So far from being mutually implicatory and interdependent, each could perfectly well be different without entailing any sort of difference for the other. We do not need to wait indefinitely to find out whether nature is rational and intelligible or not. We know that it is not already. Hence the attempt to construe reality as the fulfilment of thought is merely wasted effort.

Such a challenge cannot and will not be ignored. Indeed, since it is the last obstacle of major importance in our path, we propose to devote to it the rest of this work. Even so, it will be impossible to canvass the issue thoroughly. But it may be possible to present to the reader a few of the leading considerations on each side, and the reasons which incline us to the more hopeful view of the capacity and promise of thought. The procedure will be as follows: in the remainder of the present chapter we shall consider what appear to be the strongest arguments for conceiving of certain relations as irreducibly external. In the chapter that follows we shall present certain grounds for holding that, appearances and these reasons to the contrary, all things are related internally, and that the transcendent and immanent end of thought coincide.

14. What precisely is the issue over internal and external relations? It is simply whether a term could be what it is apart from the relations it bears to others. A relation is internal to a term when in its absence the term would be different; it is external when its addition or withdrawal would make *no* difference to the term. Those who believe in external relations usually hold a qualified position, saying that some things are related externally, others not. Those who accept the theory of internal relations are usually more uncompromising, and hold that everything, if we knew enough, would turn out to be internally related to everything else. Let us get each contention a little more fully before us. Professor Spaulding, who defends the theory of external relations, says he means by it '(1) that, if two terms are related, neither term influences the other, (2) that the absence of either term would be *without effect* on the other, (3) that either term may come into being and into relation with the other term without affecting it, (4) that, accordingly, no term is *complex* by virtue of being related, and (5) that no third term, *u* underlying *aRb* . . . is necessary. . . Briefly, the theory of external relations is that *relatedness and* *independence are quite compatible*'.[1] The theory of internal relations has not, as a rule, been so unequivocally formulated; Dr. Ewing enumerates ten distinct meanings to which the name has been attached.[2] But there can be little doubt, after all, as to the principal meaning. It is the position we have already described as the logical ground for the belief in degrees of truth, namely, that everything is so integral a part of a context that it can neither be nor be truly conceived apart from that context. Put more formally, the theory is this: (1) that every term, i.e. every possible object of thought, is what it is in virtue of relations to what is other than itself; (2) that its nature is affected thus not by some of its relations only, but in differing degrees by all of them, no matter how external they may seem; (3) that in consequence of (2) and of the further obvious fact that everything is related in *some* way to everything else, no knowledge will reveal completely the nature of any term until it has exhausted that term's relations to everything else.

Of these two theories there is no doubt that the external relations theory is closer to common sense. That *some* relations are internal would be generally admitted; if middle C on the musical scale were to lose its relations of higher and lower to the other notes, would it still be the note it is? Clearly not. But to say that *all* a term's relations are internal commits us to saying that if anything anywhere were different, the term itself would have to be different; and that seems absurd. The plain man finds it hard to take seriously the contention that a motor accident in China has something to do with the weather in Philadelphia, or that the pleasure he takes in his own breakfast would be different if Genghis Khan had not, as an infant, had the croup. The theory seems preposterous on its face. To be sure, reflection often domesticates theories that to common sense are very wild, and in our own view the present theory is one of them. But our first task must be to take stock of those glaring difficulties which, so long as they remain, make it all but impossible for the theory to get a serious hearing.

[1] *The New Rationalism*, 177; italics in original.
[2] *Idealism*, 199 ff.

We hold that the ultimate object of thought, in both senses of the word, is an all-inclusive system in which everything is related internally to everything else. The most probable objections fall into two groups corresponding to the two senses of 'object'. On the one hand, it will be said, 'If by "ultimate object of thought" you mean what thought is trying to know, i.e., the real world, to say that *that* is any such system as you suggest is palpably contrary to fact'. On the other hand, it will be said, 'If by "ultimate object of thought" you mean ideal of thought, i.e. that which would in the end be satisfactory, then you are offering as the pattern of intelligibility something that is unintelligible itself'. On the one hand, relations that are obviously not internal are found in fact. On the other hand, the very concept of internal relations is illegitimate. Taking these contentions in turn, we shall examine what appear to be the two most striking arguments for each of them.

15. (1) Perhaps the objection that leaps first to mind when it is said that everything is connected internally with everything else is that in nature as we already know it all sorts of discontinuities have been actually found. Take the odd fact that puzzled Darwin, that tom-cats that were white and blue-eyed were also deaf. Although these characteristics accompany each other in the same cat, their connection seems purely contingent; we cannot see the smallest reason *why* they should go together in this way. Again, certain changes in the brain are the concomitants of certain sensations; yet not only do these things differ as widely as any two things in the universe; no special bond between them that would go beyond mere concomitance has ever been discovered.

Still, no one after reflection is likely to attach much weight to this argument, least of all, perhaps, the scientists most directly concerned. Far from resting satisfied with such concomitance, they regard it as at once a challenge and an assurance, the sign of a more intimate connection which they must bring to light if they can. We may recall Bosanquet's question, 'Is there any man of science who in his daily work and apart from philosophic controversy, will accept a bare given conjunction as conceivably ultimate truth?' Behind such concomitance he would surely divine an intrinsic connection, whether he could isolate it at the time or not; and an intrinsic connection, we shall presently see,[1] involves necessity. What he would never naturally do is to suppose the characters conjoined by miracle or luck; he would agree that in such cases at least 'the merely external is, in short, our ignorance set up as reality'.[2] And here the history of science would support him. 'No one before the end of the eighteenth century could have seen any connection between propositions about thunder and lightning, the colour of mother of pearl, and the attractive power of a lodestone. Now they are all part of electro-magnetic theory.'[3] One cannot argue plausibly from our inability to see such connections that the connections are not there.

16. (2) The next objection is far more serious. What about characters between which the independence is not a matter of our ignorance, but demonstrable by experiment? An 'undoubted result of experience pointed out by Newton is that the weight of a body does not in the least depend upon its form or texture. It may be added that the temperature, electric condition, pressure, state of motion, chemical qualities, and all other circumstances concerning matter, except its mass, are indifferent as regards its gravitating power.'[4] Such results could no doubt be duplicated thousands of times over. Indeed is not scientific method as truly a means of dissociating things that are not relevant as of connecting those that are? Every one of the experimental canons, for example, does its work by elimination, that is, by showing that all but certain factors are *un*connected with a given result, either because they are present when it is absent, or absent when it is present, or independently

---

[1] Chap. XXXII, Sec. 20.   [2] Bradley, *Appearance*, 577.
[3] Cohen and Nagel, *Logic and Scientific Method*, 56.
[4] Jevons, *Principles of Science*, 422.

variable. If there is now to be no such thing as irrelevance, if everything is to be dependent on *everything* else, not on certain factors selectively and to the exclusion of others, science would seem to be one great blunder.

This sounds like annihilation. And we confess that we should have little sympathy for the defender of internal relations who, on the strength of his speculative theory, should seek to disparage science. He would be soon swept away in any case. At the same time, no self-respecting metaphysician could be asked to accept without criticism the rules of current scientific method as ultimate arbiters of truth within his own province. We believe that he has a province of his own, and that this issue falls squarely within it. It is part of his business to ask whether the notion of relevance that is applied, and successfully applied, in inductive inquiry can be carried over into the determination of ultimate truth. And we conceive that when he raises this question, two points of importance will require to be made.

17. (i) The first is that every investigation is carried on within a restricted universe of discourse which prescribes what shall be relevant. Reflection, as we saw long ago, is the attempt to answer a question whose character is set by the system requiring completion. The engineer who is studying a gully that he must bridge ignores facts about the geological succession of strata as falling outside his province. The historian who is dealing with Napoleon as a strategist does not feel called upon to discuss Napoleon's aesthetic tastes or domestic affections. Indeed unless it were practicable to specify our problem thus and confine it to one universe of discourse, our feeble wits would be overwhelmed; the range of factors to take account of would be hopelessly beyond the scope of our consciousness or subconsciousness. But it would be a curious kind of anthropomorphism to fix the range of relevance in nature by the span of our own grasp. For the special purpose of the engineer the order of succession of the strata *is* irrelevant, no doubt; but then the universe of discourse demarcated by his purpose is as arbitrary as a circle drawn in water, and quite without binding force on nature. The instant he takes a larger view, he may see that the succession of strata is of prime relevance to his concerns, for example as determining the terrain with which he must work. Still more obvious is it that there is no such thing as military genius *in vacuo* and that however necessary it may be for the biographer to abstract, the concrete person he deals with is one whose tastes and affections *are* bound up in extremely intimate fashion with his character as a soldier. To suppose that because thought, through practical necessity, must move within limited fields, these fields are geographical divisions in nature, is an illusion.

18. (ii) The second point is more important, namely that relevance has degrees. It is a mistake exposed long ago to imagine that what the inductive methods approve as *the* cause is the only relevant circumstance, or that the factors 'eliminated' are revealed as irrelevant absolutely. In scientific inquiry, *the* cause usually means the efficient or precipitating cause. But in no case is this the *only* condition of the result. Indeed conditions that are eliminated by the inductive canons may be as essential to the result as those selected. Take the first method on the list, which in this respect is typical, the method of agreement. It would reject as irrelevant any circumstance that is not present with the result uniformly. A series of typhoid cases is examined; the water supply is declared to be the only constant factor; it is therefore pronounced guilty, and the variable supplies of milk and what-not are exonerated. But if a factor may be accounted relevant when it affects the result, then, judged as a measure of relevance, this method will not stand a moment's examination. There are two types of factor it eliminates. It eliminates, first, factors which, though present throughout the series, are also present constantly outside it, such as fixed conditions of climate, gravitational pull, the existence of the sun and fixed stars, the solidity of the earth's surface. *Are* these irrelevant? Obviously Yes, if you rule out, to begin with, everything but the efficient or precipitating cause. But just as obviously No, if you attach to 'relevant' what in a discussion like this is the only appropriate meaning, namely affecting the result. For it is at least as certain that the non-existence of the sun and gravitation would have made a difference to the result as would the absence of a particular water system. If so, then in the required sense these factors are plainly relevant. Secondly, the method eliminates all factors that are *not* present throughout the series. Patient A has just recovered from diphtheria, B has tuberculosis, and C is a centenarian; but because these conditions do not repeat themselves in all the cases, they are pronounced to be in no case relevant to the result. Now whatever 'logic' may tell us, we know better than that. To typhoid fever as it appears in any actual patient, Jones, there is no one factor that is relevant to the exclusion of all else; we know perfectly well that his general state of health, his age, even his disposition, his philosophy, and his religion, may exercise their influence, each in its appropriate and perhaps minor degree, upon the complexion his disease assumes. To say that relevance must be present absolutely and in perfection or else in zero quantity, that the presence of a certain bacillus is everything, and all else shall count as nothing, is merely arbitrary. Innumerable conditions contribute in innumerable degrees.

The objection to internality that we have been considering began with a quotation from Jevons intimating as 'the undoubted result of experience' that the gravitational pull upon a body was totally indifferent to its form, its texture, its temperature, electric condition, pressure, state of motion, and chemical qualities. This was presumably unquestioned when he wrote. But it is suggestive of the danger of any dogmatic statements of indifference to reflect on how the same statement would be received today. It is to be doubted whether any one of the factors named would be taken by the present-day physicist as totally indifferent to gravitation, or indeed to any of the other factors. The discoveries of the electronic composition of matter, the affinity of gravitation with the action of electricity and light, and the apparent contraction of bodies in the line of motion (to name but a few of many) have transformed the confident absolutism of a generation ago. Perhaps there was no relation which would then have been pronounced with more confidence to be absolutely external than that of spatial properties to temporal. Whoever accepts the theory of relativity can no longer believe that even these are externally connected. One lesson of the extraordinary development of physical science in the present century is that *any* assertion of pure externality is to be received with suspicion.

So much for the externalities reported empirically. Considerations drawn from causality join with those from the history of science to induce a sceptical mood about them. But we have suggested that there is a quite different type of objection to the internal relations theory. It is a more formidable sort of objection because it is based on considerations of logic and affects not only the applicability but also the intrinsic validity of what we have taken as the ideal of reason. Both the character of the objection, however, and the inevitable line of our answer will be clearer if prefaced by the reply which would no doubt be given to our last point by the defender of traditional scientific method.

19. He would say that we have misconceived the aim of science. Science is not interested in John Jones's typhoid fever. It is not interested in this particular plant, or the contents of this particular test-tube, or in particulars at all; it is interested only in a type or universal that particular cases may exhibit. What it studies, for example, is typhoid fever *as such*; and in view of this, its dismissal as irrelevant of Jones's age and general health and disposition is perfectly sound. What science is looking for is laws. And laws do not link individuals as wholes; they link states or attributes of wholes, abstracted from their setting. Thus pathology as a science (which is distinct, of course, from medicine as an art) would isolate one feature in John Jones, namely a special diseased condition, and then inquire for *the* factor, likewise abstract, which in every variety of environment is found in company with this. It would be absurd to deny that law of this sort has actually been discovered. To deny that, when found, it has a high explanatory value would be equally absurd. But such law is attainable only if abstraction in a two-fold sense is allowed. We must be allowed to break Jones up ideally into factors that can be studied in isolation, and we must be allowed to throw aside as irrelevant all factors in Jones's nature that are not found with typhoid-as-such in other natures. Thus the existence and discovery of laws turn on the real irrelevance of many of the circumstances in which they appear.

We must own that this is an effective reply. Nevertheless, the position it attacks seems valid also. The fact is that we are caught here between two profoundly different ways of conceiving the end of thought; and if we can be clear what the issue is and the right way of escape, we shall have gone far toward understanding and answering the second set of objections mentioned above.

20. The issue is really between the abstract and the concrete universal. Traditional logic and traditional science have held —to stick to our example—that if John Jones, Jenny Brown and others all suffer from typhoid fever, there is a state or condition which is exactly the same in each, which by a mental act of abstraction can be lifted out of its matrix in the individual, which can be held there and scrutinized in its sharply delimited nakedness, and which then can be linked to some twin or companion in the form of another *abstractum*. To this abstract universal, which is what 'universal' means in traditional logic, everything is declared accidental except the other universals that are found invariably in its company. There is thus the most intimate connection between the doctrine of abstract universals and the doctrine that things may be related externally. Suspicious of this whole way of thinking is a group of philosophers who are sceptical of the sort of logic that must assume to begin with that every whole is of one general type, a mosaic of independent pieces, each of which remains in abstraction precisely what it was in union. They would ask if this is in fact the only sort of whole we find? Look at the case before us. John Jones's typhoid fever is a complex state of body and mind. Is it or is it not true that from this condition of Jones you can excise a universal portion, as at breakfast you slice off the top of an egg, and then, dealing with it apart, can go on to discover a similarly isolated cause that will be necessary and sufficient? For our own part we disbelieve this, and for the fairly obvious reason that Jones is not an egg. Typhoid fever, as suffered by Jones, is coloured, tinctured, pervaded, permeated to its last and least detail by Jones *ipso*. Lassitude, we are told, is one mark of the disease; it is one of the abstract universals that has always been found in this; and in Jones it appears again. For ordinary purposes it would be tiresome to take exception to language of this kind. But there can be little doubt that if we want to speak correctly, we must say that lassitude *à la* Jones is not quite like anything else on earth, for it is a feeling so complexly and delicately determined by Jones's special fears and anxieties, past experiences and nervous character, which neither singly nor in union are the same as anyone else's, that to deal with it as a little detachable lump, precisely the same as one we may have detached yesterday from a different individual, is to assume what is incredible. Lassitude or typhoid fever, taken as an abstraction from various contexts, is a typical abstract universal which wears the defects of such universals upon its head.[1] Taken as an inseparable part of the context that makes it what it is, it is a concrete universal. And it is evident that just as the abstract universal and external relations are natural allies, so are the concrete universal and internal relations.

21. Are these two conceptions of the task of thought irreconcilable enemies whose feud can be settled only when one

[1] Above, Chap. XVI.

or the other is dragged out? That is not our own position. Our position may be put as follows: The breaking up of wholes into *abstracta* which, when seen as identities, are abstract universals, and the linking of these with like *abstracta*, play an inevitable and indispensable part in the pursuit of under-standing. Thought can proceed in no other way. But to say this is not to say that the distinctions so made exist in the nature of things. The adequacy of the method varies with its subject-matter. Sometimes, at least at first glance, the existence of abstract identities independent of their differing environ-ments is so obvious that to question it seems captious. It seems absurd to say that the colour of a particular dress is so insepar-ably bound up with its context that it could not appear in another dress, or that the number three as contemplated by two minds could not be absolutely the same for both. In other cases, e.g. a specific disease in John Jones, such abstrac-tion is clearly more questionable; to demarcate within Jones a little area which could be translated intact into someone else's constitution begins to seem like magic. And as we saw long ago, the abstraction becomes incredible when it pretends to extract from a snail and Socrates a little pellet of animality, precisely the same in each, or from the mind of a school-boy and himself when become a historian a chunk of unchanging meaning called 'Waterloo'.

What is it, now, that accounts for the decreasing adequacy of such abstract analysis? At the bottom of the scale are cases where it seems unexceptionable; at the top are cases in which it must clearly 'murder to dissect', since the parts of the wholes it would analyse resist abstraction and isolated study. What is it in the subject-matter that makes the method more or less applicable? The only sound answer is an obvious and all but circular one, namely, the degree of unity in the whole that is analysed. The unity we find in a 'thing', for example, is loose; we saw in Chapter III that our grouping of qualities into a thing, while not exactly capricious, had curiously little regard for any intrinsic affinities among them. The colour of a red dress or the feel of a cold poker seems to belong to its group only with the sort of attachment possessed by elements that happen to exist and move together, and conjointly to serve a purpose. And where we find this loose sort of unity, the method that turns on abstract universals and external relations will be comparatively adequate, because there its assumption is comparatively true, namely that many of the attributes with which a given one is conjoined are irrelevant to it. But this all but rubbish-heap type of unity has clearly been left behind when we turn to a plant, a disease, a state of mind, a legal system, a scientific or philosophic theory, a sonnet, or a symphony. A legal system is not a heap of laws, nor a sonnet a heap of words, nor a symphony a heap of notes, and we should feel it a bore to argue such a point. These things have a unity that is obviously of a different kind, in which each part is what it is in virtue of its office in the whole. There is nothing especially obscure or mysterious in this conception. Everyone uses it constantly, whether he has thought about it or not. Even those who shake their heads over it would no doubt object if anyone were to attack a statement of theirs torn completely out of its context, or interpret a sentence in conversation as an attempt to juxtapose a set of dictionary definitions. The unity here in mind is only what they themselves insist on, and what all of us insist on except when we are dealing with the most loosely organized wholes.

Now it is our contention that between these loosely and closely organized wholes there is, for all their seeming disparity, only a difference in degree. They are at different points on one scale. In the wholes at the top, where the unity is greatest, the relations are never completely internal, for the dependence of terms on the system is never absolute; these terms always bear in abstraction some semblance of their former selves. Again, in the wholes at the bottom (and this is the point we would emphasize) there is never mere externality or aggregation. Not that in the whole presented to us a closer relation is always apparent or can even be readily discerned on reflection, but that if one penetrates deeply enough, and is willing to follow circuitous threads, it is always there. The red of the dress has, after all, a connection with the other qualities that is not bare and pure accident; its conjunction with them was no doubt appointed by someone's taste; and aesthetic requiredness, as we have seen long ago, is genuine necessity, which not even stupidity in these matters can dissipate altogether. Is the conjunction of coldness with the other qualities of the poker *mere* conjunction? Nobody can believe this who, like ourselves, would find in the causal action by which the metallic properties produce the sense datum of cold a trace of necessity.[1] But these connections, or rather disconnections, are empirical, and in insisting that they present us nothing that is unalterably and hopelessly external we are only reaffirming what has been said about empirical conjunctions generally. There is another type of aggregative whole that cannot so easily be dismissed.

22. Here appears the second type of objection mentioned above to the internal relations theory. It suggests the existence of wholes whose parts are external to each other, not empirically only, or even merely by inductive proof, but a priori, necessarily, and demonstratively. The argument may take various forms. We shall put it briefly in what are probably its two most effective forms, one drawn from logic, the other from mathematics. (1) In its logical form, it runs as follows: All reasoning proceeds through universals, that is, through the use of what remains the same through various contexts. The syllogism, for example, depends on an identical middle; unless the M in the two premises is the same, no conclusion will follow; and indeed this holds of all the terms. All organisms are mortal, Socrates is an organism, etc. Unless the character of being an organism to which mortality is attached, is precisely the same as that which appears in Socrates, unless the mortality that appears in the conclusion is without excess or defect, the mortality of the major premise, unless Socrates after the ascription is identical absolutely with himself before it, there is no middle term, there is no continuity of argument,

[1] Chap. XXXII, Sec. 16 ff.

and the reasoning disintegrates into a row of unrelated terms. Strict identity is essential. But if relations are to be internal, this identity is destroyed. The 'organism' of the major premise will become something different when it assumes its Socratic setting. The minor term, Socrates, will be altered by the predication of mortality, and the mortality you ascribe at the end will itself not be the mortality you started with, because it has gained a new connection. And with this, all fixities in discourse vanish; no word means quite the same thing to any two persons, or to the same person through successive uses. This is not logic but chaos or madness, and not even madness with any fixed method.

(2) Let us now put the objection in its simplest mathematical form. On the theory of internal relations no character of an object is indifferent wholly to the other characters of that object. Very well; I consider a collection first of three apples, then of three philosophers, and then of three empires. Surely the threeness is completely and equally irrelevant to the other qualities in each, and is not in the least affected by acquiring a further exemplification. Likewise in arithmetical calculations three is always the same, no matter what the variety or complexity of the processes into which it enters.

For anyone whose peace of mind has been given as a hostage to formal logic, such considerations will close the discussion. And it is perhaps true of most of us that this tradition has subtly worked itself into our intellectual bones. Nevertheless even cases like these, if attentively considered, appear to provide no ultimate exception to the reign of internal relations and the concrete universal. They must be dealt with, however, somewhat differently from the cases of empirical externality. In those cases the externality rested on ignorance. In these cases it rests on strongly established convention which, by reason of a measure of truth and an immense utility, has fixed itself as unexceptionable. The issue is somewhat similar to that between Newtonian and relativity physics. The Newtonian principles, with their neater and simpler formulas, were so adequate to all ordinary problems that they came to seem obviously true, and many physicists refused to abandon them even after they had proved inapplicable in crucial cases. We believe that, for all its impressive history, the conventions of formal logic *have* proved inapplicable, not merely in out-of-the-way cases, but most conspicuously of all in the cases that are most important.

23. (1) Formal logic insists that reasoning proceeds through a universal. So it does. The question, of course, is what sort of universal. The older logic has its answer ready. The universal must be an identity that in its various contexts admits no diversity whatever. This view is regarded as indispensable to the unity of inference. But the curious thing about it is that it destroys the unity of inference, dissolving it away into a set of unrelated terms.

Consider the syllogism just given, and take first the middle term. Unless this middle term, organism, as it appears in Socrates, is the same absolutely as it is in all the organisms of the major premise, i.e. all there are, the reasoning is declared to be worthless. Good; let us make it thus the same, and see what happens. In order to get the organismic character pure, you must leave out everything whatever which might distinguish this character as realized in a polyp or a paramoecium from what it is in a lion or in Leonardo. Now we have argued long ago that this is something you will never get.[1] There is no such thing in nature. Leave out everything into which organism differentiates itself and you will find that the identity has vanished also; pure organismicity, unsullied and uninfected by the characters of its species, is a myth. But suppose it did exist and that you could intellectually isolate and play with it. It will then supposedly supply the link between Socrates on the one side and mortality on the other. What do you mean by these terms? If you are consistent, you will have arrived at their meaning as you did at that of the middle, by the path of abstraction. Socrates will not be the flesh-and-blood man of

[1] Chap. XVI.

any particular moment, but a set of characters possessed by all the members of a long series of extremely different objects all called by this name. And what you assert when you assert mortality is of course likewise a universal, which will consist similarly of the common characters, and these alone, possessed by all cases of mortality, from cabbage to Goethe. The two *abstracta* forming the extremes are then linked by the third *abstractum* which forms the middle. Now what do you mean by *linked*? Your major premise says that all organisms are mortal. If that means what it says, simply that each and every organism is mortal, then besides being unwarranted in fact (the future is unknown) it reduces the syllogism to tautology, the argument for this being too familiar to repeat. If the statement means that organism-as-such is mortal or mortality, it is nonsense. Does it mean, then, that the character of being an organism entails that of mortality? This would be by far the most important sense if it were true, but, unfortunately, from that sense your convention cuts you off. For the two contents, assuming that they are discernible at all, are so pared away, withered, and desiccated, as to have lost the base required for such entailment. There may be something in this or that organism that necessitates its death, but there is nothing in the abstraction, organic-character-as-such, that entails the abstraction, ceasing-to-be. Let us turn to the minor premise. It 'links' Socrates to organism; how? Recall that Socrates' character as an organism is not now something that pervades his nature, but is an abstraction arrived at by that process of omission which assumes at every step the externality of the severed relations. When we say, therefore, in the present case that Socrates is an organism, what we mean is that to his other characters this abstraction is externally conjoined. And the whole syllogism will amount to the statement that a conjunction of *abstracta* previously found in other contexts is now repeated exactly in this one.

24. This is the sort of account we shall give of reasoning if we are faithful to the S-M-P tradition. The letters we use to stand for our meanings are freely and independently movable, and keep their identity as they move; why should not the meanings also? The suggestion is natural, but it has done untold harm. It has distorted, by over-simplifying and mechanizing, our conception of the way thought works. The bare identities it points to are not the counters used in reasoning, and if they were they would render genuine reasoning impossible. When we say Socrates is an organism, our two terms are not external to each other as are the letters S and M; if Socrates were not an organism, he would not be Socrates at all; the organic character is no attribute somehow associated with his other attributes; he is what he is only through realizing or embodying this. When we turn from symbol to fact, we find that 'S' is related to 'M' internally. So is 'M' to 'P' if the insight involved in inference is really present. If mortality is entailed at all, it is entailed in the special form that is prescribed by the special embodiment of the organic character in Socrates. And the inference will thus be a passage from one 'difference' to another within a concrete universal, from one point to another within a little system whose points are so linked together that each can be itself only as belonging to the system. In short, as regards the middle we are confronting a clear alternative. If you take the middle, organism, to be a bare abstraction, you get no *common* term at all; you get only an attribute, or set of attributes found *along with* the extremes, a middle term only in the sense that it is somehow between them, the middle domino, so to speak, of three dominoes in a box. And we hold it absurd to say that this serial arrangement is what is meant by implication, or that the passage along it is inference. There is no entailment, no necessity, anywhere. The minor is related externally to the middle, the middle to the major, and how are you to conjure necessity out of two contingencies? Suppose that, seeing this, you take the other horn of the alternative. You bring the middle out of its abstraction and expand it to the dimensions used in actual thought. The moment you do so, you find its relations to the other terms transformed. The organic character is no longer something tacked on to Socrates from the outside, but something that permeates him and makes him what he is;

it is his nature regarded in one aspect, a nature that on the one hand manifests itself in the special nature of Socrates and on the other appoints the form of his mortality. The argument is then a passage from one point in this nature to another.

How exactly does this meet the criticism of the internal relations theory? That criticism was that unless the universals used by thought remained absolutely the same through their diverse contexts and these contexts were therefore indifferent to them, and related to them only externally, there would be no middle term in reasoning, and no fixities in thought anywhere. Our reply has been that this sort of abstract identity is not what we use in reasoning, and that if we did use it, we should never get to our conclusions. The middle actually used is one that, far from being indifferent to the terms it links, always in some degree takes its character from them, just as organic structure, as realized in Socrates and used in our thought of him is different from what it is in the amoeba.[1] The impulse of thought, on this theory, will be perpetually away from the abstract and toward the concrete. It will seek to do away with middle terms altogether, and even with the traditional independent extremes, and will find its ideal inference in the passage from point to point within a system so closely organized that, as in a work of art, every part takes its character from every other and from the whole. If it is said that such a theory would leave no terms of absolute fixity in discourse, we not merely accept this conclusion but add that it is the only conclusion that can in the end be made to accord with the facts. It is simply not the case that as the school-boy learns more of Waterloo, the term as used in his thinking remains the same;[2] nor is it the case, as we saw in our study of formalism, and have just been seeing again, that the terms of a syllogism remain wholly unaffected by being shown in connection with each other.[3] Objects as dealt with by thought are never fixed piles of hard round shot.

[1] Where the difference in organic character has its counterpart in a different sort of death; does an amoeba die when it propagates by fission?   [2] Chap. XXVII, Secs. 4, 5.   [3] Chap. XXIX, Sec. 10.

25. It is difficult, with the best of intentions, for minds trained in the formalist tradition to do justice to such a view. They have been habituated to think of logical distinctions as flat either-or's, whereas in the logic of concrete necessity most distinctions, and perhaps all, are matters of degree. Hence the opponents of concrete necessity are inclined to level a pistol at its proponents and say, Do you accept abstract universals, external relations, and the inductive method, Yes or No! And at this abrupt demand, the thinkers who have struggled to keep their logic close to the facts and aims of knowledge are likely to hesitate, and answer finally Yes *and* No, where upon they are promptly charged with equivocation. The truth is that they have given the only sound answer. What it means is that the method of abstract analysis *is* applicable to wholes in the degree to which their parts are ununified (in the sense of being related externally), and *not* applicable in the degree to which they are unified; that since none of the wholes of actual experience are mere and pure aggregates, it is *perfectly* applicable nowhere, but since none of them are ideal unities either, it is *in some measure* applicable everywhere; finally, that since the ideal of thought is a system completely unified it will hold *nowhere in the end*. To be sure this answer is less simple and downright than Yes or No. But where is the equivocation?

The believer in concrete necessity does not simply dismiss the logic of abstraction. He is thoroughly well aware that he cannot in practice do without it. But its theoretical position will be that of a propaedeutic. We may want to know what it is in the concrete nature of Socrates that makes him die, and since in these matters we can hardly rely on mystic divination, there is no alternative to the laborious route through the comparison of likenesses and differences, in a word, the route of analysis. It is only through analysis that we can single out constituent elements. And everybody knows that to a considerable and practically all-important extent we can actually do this. We can discuss a man's kindliness or courage; we can say, and to some extent see, that it entails this and excludes that; it would be absurd to deny, because necessity is ultimately concrete and not abstract, that these insights give us knowledge. Certainly there is no such denial in this book. On the other hand there is surely nothing arbitrary or cryptic in saying that while analysis is necessary, what it leaves us with at any given stage is less than ultimate truth. Analysis, we said, singles out. Unhappily, our powers being what they are, in the process of singling out we invariably shut out of our vision some of the relations our term possessed while still embedded in nature. Any atomic element we may bring to light when we try to isolate within Socrates that which is exclusively and precisely relevant to his death, is seen to be inadequate; to make it adequate we begin to extend it; as the extension goes on we realize that there is no attainable end to this process, and we hasten fearfully back again to the comfortable refuge of abstraction. But it is then no longer the refuge that it was. We have been abroad and seen enough to shake our confidence in its authority. We see that we cannot quarry a term out of the continuum of nature, put it in the different and limited context of our own experience, and expect it to be unchanged. We can still talk about someone's kindliness, or courage, or humanity, and very usefully too, but we realize, or ought to realize, that what is there and at work in his constitution is not the poor rag or shred that thought has succeeded in tearing off, but living tissue. *His* humanity, *his* courage, are not these bits and pieces. As they really are, they are elements or moments in the concrete universal of his mind.

'Moments' we say advisedly. In such a context as this, the hard, sharp disparateness of 'terms' does not correspond to what we find. As thought turns itself to, or achieves, more closely integrated systems, it finds itself increasingly unable to draw the clean boundaries that divided abstract universals. Socrates, being what he is, is of necessity an organism; but try to mark the line where Socrates leaves off and the organic character begins, and you cannot do it. You can even see that to do it would be meaningless. The two terms, so to speak, flow into each other; to set them up like posts in a plain, and then formally chain them together, is a process that, however useful, still mutilates the face of nature. If you keep to what is presented there, you find the truth about it two-sided. On the one hand, there *is* a difference; you cannot resolve organism away into Socrates, or Socrates into organism. On the other hand, when you try to mark the difference, it eludes you, not because of the vagueness of what is before you, or merely its continuity, but because of an intimate unity or wholeness which, while familiar enough to everyone, is impossible to describe or analyse in any satisfactory way, since description and analysis commonly proceed on lower levels of organization. This is the sort of identity which concrete logicians have called 'identity in difference'. Existing in and through its differences, it resists abstraction from them.

26. (2) We are now ready for the last step. We have considered two forms of empirical argument against internal relations, and we set out to consider the two most effective forms of the a priori argument. We have just finished with the first of these forms. It was to the effect that internal relations would not permit of the identity required in reasoning. Our answer has been that the identity really required was of another type, in which identity and difference entered into, informed, and determined each other. Once we have grasped the notion of such an identity, we are in possession of the principle needed to deal with the second a priori objection, on which we shall now comment very briefly. The objection was, it will be recalled, that certain abstractions in the field of quantity, for example the number three, remain the same and unaffected through every possible embodiment, and in every possible context, in which calculation could place them. Without pretending to deal adequately with a point that raises the whole problem of the nature of mathematics, we shall confine ourselves to three comments.

First, this independence of context does not hold, and perhaps would not even be claimed, for the number three in all *its* aspects. Indeed this or any number might be cited as an example of extreme relativity. For it is so intimately bound up with the other members of the number series that if its relations to any one of them were altered, if three were no longer to be greater than two, for example, or less than four, it would simply vanish. Secondly, even in arithmetical analysis and equation, identity in difference creeps in. Three is said to be abstractly identical in all its forms and appearances. Are we saying nothing, then, when we say $3 = 2 + 1$? This equation asserts that in some respect or other the two sides are the same. Now if they are merely and abstractly the same, i.e., the same with no difference at all, the distinction of two sides is a cheat, because it is admitted to be a distinction without a difference. On the other hand, if they are merely different, then the equation is again a cheat, for it expressly declares that they are *not* different wholly. The problem here is essentially that of Kant when he inquired into the sense of '$7 + 5 = 12$' and denied that the statement was mere tautology. We must certainly follow him to the extent of saying that the two sides are neither merely the same nor merely different; and we do not see how the assertion that a quantity is the same through its various analysed forms could be given any meaning except through the concrete universal.

Both the comments so far made have concerned the relation of abstracted quantities to each other; but what about their relation to concrete things? Are they not in *this* respect utterly indifferent? The answer to this is our third comment. And the answer is, Yes: they are thus indifferent because made so by definition. The concept of abstract number was presumably arrived at in the course of efforts to enumerate. And enumeration, to begin with, is always a process of constituting a concrete whole made up of specifically differing parts. There would be point, for example, in counting one's fingers or toes, or the sheep in a flock, because one would gain thereby an analysed grasp of a whole; but to enumerate when no such whole was involved, e.g. to start out and count things in general—fingers, stars, emotions, drops in the sea—would have been thought mad. Similarly, the units distinguished always differed in some special way; if one egg in a nest was distinguished from another, it was in virtue of its different place or colour; things were considered different only because their characters differed. Now suppose that both these controls which govern the process of actual enumeration are dropped out of sight. On the one hand, there will no longer be any kind of thing that is being enumerated, hence no whole that the process can exhaust, and hence again nothing at any point that could arrest it. On the other hand, everything that could distinguish qualitatively one embodiment of a kind from another will likewise be dropped out.[1] The units then will not be units *of* anything, nor in respect to character will they differ among themselves; the unit will be an abstract difference as such, what is called a purely numerical difference. Now when it is asked whether such purely numerical differences, or the assemblies of them of which the several numbers are composed, depend on the special differences of the terms, the answer presumably is No. But does that prove that there are purely numerical differences in nature? It is hard to see that it does. All that it shows is that if one *defines* one's units as independent of special differences, then they will be independent of special differences. It does not show that one's definition corresponds to anything in reality. And however useful the notion of a purely numerical difference may be, the attempt to attach any clearly conceivable meaning to it is likely to be so frustrated as to leave the question of its existence without further interest.

27. Of course a great many arguments have been offered for external relations besides the few that have been considered. But so far as we know, these arguments contain nothing stronger than those we have studied; we have selected considerations which, though few, seemed to present the most effective and representative case for externality. But neither on the empirical nor on the a priori side has anything come to light that offered an insuperable barrier to the belief that the

[1] Cf. Bosanquet, *Logic*, I. 144 ff. (2nd ed.).

world which thought must deal with may be construed in accordance with its implicit ideal.

Our goal, however, is not yet reached, though this chapter has brought us nearer to it. We have seen that understanding —the ideal of thought—involves the grasp of necessity; in the present chapter we have further defined that ideal by showing that it invariably involves a system taken as warranted by the nature of things, and that systematic necessity may vary both in type and degree. But it must be realized in the very highest degree if the end of intelligence is to be attained; and that means, we saw, that the world which thought is called on to construe must be a system of parts related internally. At first glance the hypothesis that it could be such a system seemed merely absurd. But the sort of objection that made it appear so has now been examined and has been found far from decisive. Still, this is not enough. Are there any sufficient reasons for taking the hypothesis as *true*? If it can be shown that there are, our task will be done. For it will then have been shown that with the achievement of the immanent end of thought, we shall also have achieved the transcendent end, the apprehension of things as they are. Let us turn to the evidence.

CHAPTER XXXII

CONCRETE NECESSITY
AND INTERNAL RELATIONS

1. Is there any positive reason for believing that the nature of things is intelligible? We have seen that the world could be accounted intelligible only if it were a system, all-inclusive and perfectly integrated, and that such integration would be achieved only if the parts were internally related. By an internal relation between two parts we mean a relation such that neither could be different without entailing a difference in the other. We have agreed that first appearances impose an all but overwhelming veto upon belief in such interdependence; and if it were not for the pressure of the implicit ideal of thought, making itself insistently felt in the scientific search for connection behind apparent irrelevance, and surging up continually in the long line of speculative thinkers who have held to the unity of things, the belief would probably have been discarded long ago as fanaticism or perversity. This verdict *may* be the right one. We have said repeatedly that *proof* of the rationality of things was not logically possible, since it would assume validity for a supposedly independent world of the very canons whose applicability was at issue.

But if the question is not whether logic is applicable to some unexperienced *Welt-an-sich*, but whether our known world of persons and things might with a keener wit be understood or intelligibly construed, we have suggested that an affirmative answer can be established as at least probable. That such an answer would also be desirable need hardly be pointed out. An answer in the negative would mean that the enterprise of thought was doomed from the outset, since the conditions of understanding could not be fulfilled; of some arrangements in the system the question why? would have no answer. Even uncertainty about the answer, if genuine, would leave us perpetually in the dark, not only as to whether we could find answers to our questions, but whether there were any answers to be found. We have seen that scientific and speculative practice has assumed a reply in the affirmative; not that scientific men, for example, can be put down as speculative rationalists, but that at each successive step, when they have asked the question Why? have assumed an intelligible answer to be waiting, whether they found it or not, and that rationalism is only a generalization of this assumption. Unhappily the desirability of anything hardly proves that it exists. If evidence is to be offered that the world thought is seeking to construe is a whole of internally related parts, it must be drawn from other and more difficult sources. Some of these sources we now propose to explore.

2. (1) Consider, first, an argument of Hegel's, which derives perhaps from Plato. It is an argument designed to show that the internal relation of each to each is a condition implicit in the very being of anything at all. For if a thing is to be at all, says Hegel, it must be this *rather than that*, and the 'rather than that' belongs as truly to its essence as the 'this'. 'Something is in this relation to Other from its own nature and because otherness is posited in it as its own movement: its Being-in-Self comprehends negation, through which alone it now has its affirmative existence . . . it is just as this cancellation of its Other that it is Something.'[1] This is Hegel's forbidding way of making a comparatively simple point. To use an illustration of his, a meadow is clearly *not* a wood or a pond; on that all would agree. But few reflect on what, nevertheless, is a fact, that 'not to be a wood is a part, and an essential part, of the nature of the meadow'.[2] Putting it generally, everything is related to everything else by the relation of difference at least. If it were not so related, it would clearly not be the thing it is, since then it would not differ from that which is admittedly other than itself. But a relation that could not be theoretically changed

[1] *Science of Logic*, 1. 138 (Johnston and Struthers' trans.).
[2] McTaggart, *Commentary on Hegel's Logic*, 29–30.

without changing the thing itself is precisely what we mean
by an internal relation. Whence it follows that everything is
related internally to everything else.

Common sense will no doubt be unmoved by this argument.
But if so, this is not, so far as one can see, because the argument
is unsound, but because common sense is unaccustomed to
moving among considerations so abstract. If it could do so,
what would it say? It might contend that difference is not a
relation. The natural reply to this would be a definition of
relation such that, while including difference, it obviously
answered to men's common thought of relation; but from this
reply we are cut off, since 'relation' is indefinable. But of course
the indefinability of a term does not mean that there is anything
either arbitrary or indefinite in our thought of it. And I think
that on careful inspection we shall see that difference does fall
within the common meaning of relation. Likeness and difference
go together in our thought as having the same sort of being;
but likeness is plainly a relation, and it would be odd if difference
were not. And if it really is not, what else can it be? To call
it a substance, or a quality, or an event, or a way of behaving,
or indeed anything *except* a relation seems forced and unnatural.
We must conclude that it is either a relation or some form of
being that is unique; and this it clearly is not.

It may be replied, again, that to take as part of what a thing
is its not being something else is merely capricious. This
objection has been so well handled by Dr. McTaggart that we
shall borrow his reply:

> 'It may be objected that it is paradoxical and wilful to treat
> it as part of the nature of a table that it is not a phoenix, or,
> again, not a prime number, and to place such characteristics on
> a level with its characteristic of being a table, or even with its
> negative characteristic of not being a chair. And it is true, no
> doubt, that from any practical point of view it is much more
> important to believe about any substance which is, in fact, a
> table, that it possesses the characteristics of being a table, or
> of not being a chair, than that it possesses the characteristics
> of not being a phoenix or a prime number. And even apart
> from all practical considerations, we shall gain more knowledge

of the nature of the substance by realizing that it possesses the first two characteristics than we shall by realizing that it possesses the other two. But it remains the fact, nevertheless, that the last two characteristics are as truly and objectively characteristics of the substance as the first two are.

'For it cannot be denied that any person who should assert that the table was not a prime number would be asserting something that was true. The assertion may be unimportant, foolish, a waste of time. But it is not false, and it must be true. And it cannot be true unless it is made true by the nature of that thing about which the assertion is made.'[1]

If all this is true, as I think it is; if a thing is as truly (though perhaps not as usefully) characterized by *not* being *x* as by *being y*, then clearly a change in its relations of difference would mean a change in itself. It is thus internally related to everything else in the universe.

3. (2) Consideration shows that what holds in this respect of the relation of difference holds of other relations also. The nature of any term, unless the term is itself a relation, consists of attributes or properties (in the non-technical sense); by the nature of an apple we mean its roundness, its redness, its juiciness, and so on. Thus a change in any of the properties would be a change in the apple's nature. Now is a relation a property? No. Nevertheless it seems clear that whenever a term does have a relation of any kind to anything else, it also has a property in virtue of that relation—what Dr. Moore calls a 'relational property'—and that this property belongs to its nature as truly as does any other. 'If A is father of B, then what you assert of A when you say that he is so is a *relational property*—namely the property of being father of B; and it is quite clear that this property is not itself a *relation*, in the same fundamental sense in which the relation of fatherhood is so. . .'[2] A relation, then, though not a property, gives rise to a property. And these properties are part of the nature

[1] *The Nature of Existence*, I. 29–30.
[2] G. E. Moore, *Philosophical Studies*, 281; his italics.

of that which has them; the properties of being 'above the beasts of the field', 'a little lower than the angels', and 'the father of B', belong to A as part of his nature. Now could the relations be different without the properties also being different? Obviously not. Could they be different without a difference in the nature of their terms? Obviously not, again; for the properties *are* part of the nature of the terms. Thus it holds of all relations that if they were different, their terms would also be different. But this means that all relations are internal.

4. No doubt the reply will come that it is absurd to include *all* relational properties in the nature of a thing; some belong there, others do not. A boy has an 'I.Q.' of 120; he also wears Arrow collars. It will be said that the first characteristic is genuinely essential to him, since his intellectual superiority in certain respects to others of his age could not be removed without a significant difference in his own nature. On the other hand, there is nothing essential in his wearing a certain brand of collar, for he could perfectly well wear another while remaining precisely the person he is. Though both relational properties thus belong in a sense to his nature, the first belongs essentially, the second only loosely and accidentally. There are internal and external properties, just as there are internal and external relations.

Now this reply may mean either of two things. First, it may mean that between the alleged classes of internal and external properties a sharp line can be drawn; and if it does mean this, we have seen that it will not do.[1] The problem of demarcating essences is notoriously insoluble. If the term is an individual, the characteristics that make up its nature are inexhaustible; that is why an individual is not logically definable; technically speaking, its differentia is infinite. If the term is general, we shall find, in any attempt to state the essence, either that some

[1] Chap. XXVI, Secs. 27, 28.

constant characters have been taken for granted and left out, or that some have been elected to the essence for irrelevant reasons, such as serving most conveniently to set a figure before us, or that essence and properties (in the logical sense) are interchangeable, or, as in the case of organic kinds, that different characters have differing importance in the determination of other characters, suggesting that essentiality is a matter of degree. So also of accidents. It is impossible to mark them off sharply from either essence or property. What is blackness in the crow? Is it a separable accident, an inseparable accident (whatever that means), a property, or part of what crows are essentially? Any answer that would fit this question will pretty certainly be wrong. Crow nature is an immensely complicated thing, and blackness may be intimately connected with many features of it, themselves of varying importance and connected with varying degrees of intimacy. In all probability the colour is neither a mere accident, nor yet as indispenable a part of crow nature as certain other attributes; it lies in what, for traditional logic, is a no-man's land between pure accident and pure necessity. These old sharp lines of mutual exclusion between essence, property, and accident are like the lines of a surveyor, of great convenience, no doubt, to ourselves, but misleading when taken as divisions marked out by nature.

What, then, about the other meaning of the distinction? This would admit that the division between internal and external characteristics is one of degree only. Thus the characteristic of being intellectually in advance of others of one's age would be a *relatively* essential one, and the characteristic of being the wearer of a certain sort of collar a *relatively* unessential one, since the difference in the boy's nature involved in the absence of the first characteristic would be far more pervasive than that involved in the absence of the second. To call the first characteristic internal absolutely would, on this theory, be a mistake, since its removal would not leave the subject simply and totally other than he was, but only partially so. Nor is the second characteristic absolutely external.

Being the wearer of one sort of collar rather than another does seem an extremely trivial characteristic of anyone; but if we bear in mind that we are dealing, not with the prepared abstractions of logic books, but with attributes in their concrete setting, if we recall that this characteristic reveals the wearer's choice, and thus is bound up in intimate fashion with his standards of taste, his proneness to imitate, his openness to suggestion, can we say quite confidently that in its absence he would be precisely the same? To the believer in degrees, such an assertion would be ill judged. It would be harking back to the view that persons or minds are mosaics. And we can see here again how false that is. Hard as it may be to say what the other characters are with which the collar-wearing is connected, or precisely how it is linked to them, we are clear that the relation is not that of one marble to others in a box, that this particular trait could not be different unless the wearer's choice had been different, and that his choice could not have been different without *his* being different. The characteristic may not be an important part of his nature, but it is a part nevertheless. It is not merely external; it is internal, even though internal only in degree.[1]

This line of thought we accept. But note that it is merely a refinement of the internal relations theory. It offered itself as a reply to one argument for that theory, namely, that all of a thing's relations give rise to properties, and that these properties belong to its nature. The reply was: even if that is true, they do not belong to its nature equally; some are irrelevant, some essential. But what this really means, we suggest, is that their removal would involve the alteration of the thing in very different degrees. And this is precisely the doctrine of internal relations again, appearing now as a doctrine of internal characteristics. It is not an answer to our last argument for such relations, but an acceptance and development of it.

[1] It may be said that 'make a difference to' is used ambiguously to mean both 'logically determine' and 'causally determine'. From our point of view this does not matter, since causal determination always contains an element of logical necessity. See below, Sec. 24 ff.

5. (3) We have been contending that if the relations of a term were different, it would itself be different. But since our aim is to show that a term and its context are interdependent, we could argue just as well that if the term were different, its relations would be different. This contention is often put in the form that 'relations are grounded in the nature of their terms', which means that the relation can be what it is only on condition that the terms are what they are, that the character of the terms appoints and limits the relations in which they stand. Thus if a thing is spatial, it may, and does, have spatial relations, but it would be absurd to say of justice that it was north-west of courage, for the natures of these two preclude that sort of connection. It will repay us to look more closely at the extent and manner in which terms may thus determine their relations.

Dr. Ewing has pointed out that 'most, if not all, kinds of relation presuppose a specific common character, usually or always of the type called by Mr. Johnson a determinable, in the related terms, without which the assertion of the specific relation would be not merely false but absurd. . . .'[1] If one picture is more beautiful than another, they cannot differ in nature absolutely; there must be something common in respect to which they can be compared. Things temporally related must both be in time; things spatially related must both be in space; if one man is the uncle of another, both must at least be organisms. It is clear that such relations are 'grounded in the nature of their terms', for if the common nature shared by the terms were to disappear, the relations would go too. Still, the extent of this determination by a common nature is easily overstated. If one knows only that a thing is spatial, one knows that it will have spatial relations, but *what* relations in particular, whether it is north or west or to the left of any particular other thing, remains in darkness. The influence of the common nature would appear not to extend so far.

Are such relations determined, then, not by some universal character possessed in common, but by the concrete and

[1] *Idealism,* 128.

specific natures of the terms? The White House at Washington is a mile or so north-west of the Capitol. You could not infer that particular relation simply from the fact that the two buildings were spatial. Could you derive it from anything else in the nature of either or both? Yes, I think you could. The argument is indirect, but it is perhaps none the worse for that, since it involves showing *both* that the terms depend on their relations and the relations on the terms. You proceed through denial of the consequent. If you can show first that *unless* the terms were thus related, they could *not* be what they are, you can then argue that their being what they are requires their being so related. Very well, *can* you show that without standing in these relations the Capitol would not be the Capitol or the White House the White House? One's first impulse is to call the suggestion absurd. *Of course* the Capitol might have been elsewhere; it might have been placed in New York, or St. Louis, or at the geographical centre of the country; and as for the White House, it might either have been placed there too, or set up in another state. But the trouble with this is that, instead of answering our question, it answers another of its own devising. It assumes that we mean by 'Capitol' simply the chief legislative building of the country, and by 'White House' the official home of the president, and it points out, rightly enough, that there is nothing about a chief legislative seat *as such* or a president's house *as such*, to require that they be at one place rather than another. But as an answer to the question before us, that is both irrelevant and question-begging. It is irrelevant because we are not talking about *as such's* or abstractions, but about wholly specific, concrete things, this unique building, and this. It is question-begging because it assumes that what holds of these abstractions must hold also of the concrete things that embody them. And surely there is no sort of reason to believe this. 'Chief legislative building' and 'president's residence' are not actual parts of nature; they are mere abstract universals; they are arrived at by cutting the connections which their originals had with their context; they are *disjecta membra* of nature, withered now and mummified. Whether a character can be thus carved from the body of nature without being affected we must soon inquire; meanwhile it is not to be simply assumed. A human heart in a bottle of alcohol does not even appear to be the thing it was; nor is it permissible anywhere to take abstractions without further ado for realities.

With this we have made some advance. The terms we are discussing are not abstractions, but terms in the concrete. The question then is whether these terms, as they exist in nature, dictate their relations or no. Could this specific Capitol building, as distinct from mere 'capitolness', have different spatial relations and yet be what it is? Well, what *is* it? We seem to have come round again to the old problem of isolating the essence, and we might fall back on the sound enough doctrine that, the differentia of an individual being infinite, any restriction of the essence must be arbitrary. But we have already discussed that point. Here we should like to show that if we mean by individual things what the plain man means by them, then they do dictate their terms, since their having the relations they have is part of the very meaning of their being what they are.

Certainly for common sense 'the Capitol' does not mean merely a building of a certain design. If one were to stumble, by some miracle, upon a building of the same size and proportions in the jungles of Uganda, it would not be what we mean when we speak of *the* Capitol. Its being at Washington rather than somewhere else is one of those relational properties that fall within the nature or character of the thing we mean. But so also are hosts of others. To those at least who know it best, the Capitol is inseparable from its functions, and even the layman can see that these connect it in the most complex and intimate fashion with the treasury, the department of state, the army and navy headquarters, and all the other departments of government with which the city is dotted; it is a building that is and must be accessible to some hundreds of legislators who live around it at all points of the compass; it is run by a staff whose roots are similarly wide-spread; it is surrounded by certain parks and approachable by certain avenues; it maintains the closest contacts with railway station and post-office, through which it has further contacts, all but infinite in number, with the various parts of the country. Now consider: if these functions and relations were removed, would what the plain man means by 'the Capitol' remain? It would not. They are part of what he means by the term, and when this is seen, it is also seen that to call them external is absurd. To be sure, particular spatial distances, such as that from Capitol to White House, or the functions subserved by these, may be unimportant; still, they belong to that set of connections without which, in the mass, what we mean by the Capitol would not be itself. We must thus say that they are internal, even while admitting, and indeed insisting, that they are internal only in degree.

6. It may be said that by introducing these functions and relations into the essence we beg the question for internal relations just as do the abstractionists for external relations. We reply that, on the contrary, it is impossible *not* to introduce them if we are to deal with the objects of actual thought. But we should go further. Even if we were to cut off from what is meant by 'the Capitol' all these entangling alliances, the conclusion would still be the same. Let us try (what is not strictly possible) to strip away from the object before us all its associations and offices, and leave only an arrangement of stones and mortar. It is, of course, this specific arrangement and these particular stones that are in question. Now it is worth while to note in passing, since the point is typical of what we should often find elsewhere, that this specific arrangement and location were by no means an accident, but part of the larger Washington-Jefferson plan for the city. (The writer did not know this; he looked it up, and was warmed to find even the encyclopaedias rallying to his support.) And if this arrangement of the stones and their relations to their nearer surroundings are part of this larger design, selected with reference to its aesthetic qualities as a whole, could the lesser arrangement either be or be perceived apart from its place in the larger? To ask an analogous question, would a person who saw a carburettor lying about grasp what it really was if he had no idea that it was part of an engine? We think not. But we have no desire to take advantage of what would perhaps be called coincidence, or to raise at this point the question whether teleological properties really belong to nature. Let us get back to the stones themselves.

They are these unique and particular stones, and what do we mean by that? Our answer has been given, with reasons, long ago.[1] We mean the stones that are *related* in certain ways to other things, and ultimately to all other things. We showed how in the case of another natural object, a mountain, the question 'What mountain?' was always and inevitably answered by such specification. We must give a similar answer here. What makes these stones *these* stones is an infinity of relations, temporal, spatial, and other. Nor are the relations mere *rationes cognoscendi.* They are part of that which individuates; they are part of what goes to make the specific differences of the terms. Two stones that were exactly alike not only in quality, but in these relations as well would not be two stones but one. The qualities of what we call a single stone, if they had two differing sets of relations, would not make one stone, but two. We must either admit that the relations are essential to a thing's being what it is, or exclude from its nature what is indispensable if it is to be *this* thing at all. The second course does not make sense. We accept the first.

We say that this view on the whole is in line with common sense. Consider the manner in which, for the plain man, temporal and spatial relations eat their way into the essence of things. The Capitol is built partly of sandstone from Virginia, partly of marble from Massachusetts. Would the plain man say that the stones would be what they are apart from their relations to their past? No, he would not; these *are* the stones, they are *the* stones, that came from Massa-

[1] Chap. XIV, Sec. 19.

chusetts and Virginia; and if they had come from somewhere else, they would not be the stones they are. To be sure, he would probably falter when pressed; for if asked whether they could not still have been the same if shipped by a different route or quarried somewhat later, he would no doubt say they could. Similarly of spatial and other relations; part of what differentiates these stones from others is their being here rather than there; yet the plain man would probably admit that they *might* have been elsewhere. But when he thus vacillates between saying that the same thing might and might not have had different relations, he is vacillating between two notions of the thing. The thing that might have had different relations is a pattern of qualities artificially abstracted already; start by assuming that a stone *is* merely a certain shape, size, hardness, and weight, and there seems to be nothing requiring that it should be here rather than there. But of course this group of qualities is not what makes *this* stone what it is. A quality or set of qualities thus abstracted has had its lines of attachment cut; it could theoretically be repeated anywhere, and therefore is the reverse of unique. This stone *is* unique. What makes it so is a set of relations that fix its connection with everything else in the universe. Omit these relations, all of them or indeed any of them, and you omit some part of that which makes this stone what it is. And with this you have admitted that it is related internally to everything else.

It may be replied that this is again prejudging the case. We secure the admission that existent things are unique, and then define uniqueness in such a way as to involve internal relations. But as to the uniqueness of the existent, it is to be doubted whether anyone would deny it. And as to the definition of uniqueness, we have been at pains before to show that there is nothing arbitrary about this; it is the only definition that accords with our actual meaning.

7. (4) The argument just offered, however, has been applied only to the unique, and we shall at once be reminded that even

if it holds of the unique, it may not hold of universals. And the case for internal relations must, if complete, apply to both. For the doctrine means that terms *as such or generally*, and not merely concrete existing things, are what they are in virtue of their relations. Now is there any reason to think that an abstract character or attribute is so connected with others, and ultimately with all others, that none of its relations to these could be different without involving a difference in itself? This is harder to believe. There are probably many persons who would admit that in order to say fully what this unique thing is, one must exhaust its relations to other things, but would draw back from the same suggestion as applied to a universal. Thus red-headedness may appear in a great variety of persons who have different temperaments, antecedents, and states of health. It therefore bears relations to all these characters, as it does indeed to countless others. Can one seriously say that red-headedness would not be red-headedness *unless* it were thus related? If this were true, we should have to hold that no one could know what red-headedness was without knowing all its relations to the mental and bodily traits of the people who had it. And is not that preposterous? For surely we do *not* know all these relations while we *do* know perfectly well what red-headedness is. That is, we actually possess knowledge which, on the theory, would be impossible. Hence the theory must be wrong.

But, for all its plausibility, this argument does not prove what it seeks to prove. What it proves is that we can have *some* knowledge of red-headedness without knowing all the relations of red-headedness. What it ought to prove is that we can know red-headedness *fully and as it really is* without such knowledge. And between these two there is an enormous difference. We admit that if the theory of internal relations asked us to deny the first, it would be asking something absurd. For it is obvious that we do attach some meaning to red-headedness even though we do not know all its relations. But what defender of internal relations has ever denied this? To deny it would be to take the self-destructive position that every bit of knowledge that we possess is equally and utterly illusion, since nothing ever comes before us whose relations we know exhaustively. And why anyone who holds, as do believers in internal relations, that all knowledge is a matter of degree, should be supposed to accept also this nihilism in knowledge is very far from apparent. Indeed it is the essence of the doctrine of degrees to hold that we *can* have *some* knowledge without an exhaustive grasp of relations. Between us and our critics, then, there is important common ground. It is agreed that when we use the term 'red-headedness' we do use it with a meaning, we do have some knowledge of the attribute it names, even though we do not know all the relations of that attribute.

But is this equivalent to saying that the red-headedness now explicitly presented in thought is all there is to that attribute as it exists in the nature of things? That is what is implied in the criticism just offered us; for unless this criticism means that we can know the real nature of an attribute without knowing its relations, it is saying nothing from which we should differ. But to assume that what is now presented in idea does give the whole nature of what is referred to is not only to beg the question; it is to adopt a position that we have already examined and found false. An idea always points beyond itself; it always means more than it is; it always refers to more than it includes within the circle of its explicit content. Indeed that is what makes it an idea. This difference we have carefully studied under the head of immanent and transcendent meaning.[1] That there is such a difference is undeniable; it is the difference exemplified (though of course not perfectly, since transcendent meaning can never be captured wholly) by the interval between what presents itself to the schoolboy when he thinks of Napoleon's loss of Waterloo and what presents itself to the historian; both refer to the same thing, but by general admission the historian's explicit grasp is nearer to the fact than the school-boy's.[2] *What makes the second grasp better than the first?* We have seen that it is the fuller grasp

[1] Chap. XIV.   [2] Chap. XXVII, Secs. 4, 5.

of context, that is, of the antecedents, methods and bearings of the engagement. The school-boy must lay hold of these things if he is to see the defeat as it really was, and as he apprehends the context more fully his thought at once remoulds itself internally and approximates to the fact without. Similarly of the more trivial thought we have taken in illustration. For purposes of everyday intercourse on the level of common sense, the ordinary notion of it suffices. Does our notion at this level therefore exhaust the nature of the object? There is no more reason for thinking so than that our ideas of anything else on this level are truly adequate to their objects. Little, perhaps, as would be the point of reflecting on it ordinarily, it still remains the fact that red-headedness is an integral part of an organism, and indeed is so bound up, for example, with the structure of hair-fibres, and this in turn with all manner of constitutional factors determining racial and individual differences that our common notion of it supplies scarcely more than a sign-post to its real or ultimate nature, i.e. to what it is as embedded in its own context. As we grasp these further relations, our explicit thought of the attribute is modified while our reference remains the same; we see that we are advancing toward the character as it really is. Our contention, in sum, is this: (1) in such a series of ideas, our reference is the same throughout; (2) our comprehension of what we refer to changes throughout; (3) the changes in comprehension arise from the grasping of our original content in a fuller context of relevant relations; (4) our comprehension at the end of the series is a closer approach to the real character than our comprehension at the beginning; (5) further advance must be assumed to lie along the same line; (6) no limit can be set beforehand to the context that complete comprehension would demand. Do these propositions seem rash and irresponsible? To us they seem scarcely more than a report of what can be verified as fact in any process of improving knowledge.

8. They provide our comment on a suggestion made by some contemporary writers as to the limits of the internal relations theory. The theory, according to these writers, 'cannot be applied to relations between abstract universals, e.g. the relation of equality between the pure number 4 and 2 + 2, because we cannot speak of the possibility of an abstract universal being different from what it is, but only to relations between concrete terms'.[1] Plainly there is a sense in which this is true. If an abstract universal means an *abstracted* universal, i.e. a universal considered by itself and apart from its context in nature, then it will not depend on its relations because we have expressly defined it as the sort of thing that does not. But the practice of using universals *as if* they were thus independent proves nothing as to whether they *are* so; and our argument is of course to the effect that they are *not* so as they exist in nature. In a sense, then, we hold, with these writers, that the doctrine of internal relations applies only to concrete terms. It applies only to things, attributes and relations taken *in situ*, though this does not necessarily mean that the *whole* of their concrete context must be exhausted before the internality is apparent. The doctrine does not apply to objects taken in that abstraction which would plainly beg the question, but in their real or natural habitat.

We have laboured the trivial case of red-headedness because of its very triviality; the attribute seems at first so plainly 'external' to its subject as to afford an instance of extreme difficulty, and hence a crucial instance, for one who believes in internal relations. There is this further advantage in using it, that it happens to have been used by Bradley, and made the occasion of a general statement which is happily less dark than his pronouncements on this problem usually are.

'If you could have a perfect relational knowledge of the world, you could go from the nature of red-hairedness to these other characters which qualify it, and you could from the nature of red-hairedness reconstruct all the red-haired men. In such perfect knowledge you could start internally from any one character in the Universe, and you could from that pass to the rest. You would go in each case more or less directly or indi-

[1] Ewing, *Idealism*, 130–1, where the same view is attributed to Dr. Moore.

rectly, and with unimportant characters the amount of indirect-
ness would be enormous, but no passage would be external.
Such knowledge is out of our reach, and it is perhaps out of the
reach of any mind that has to think relationally. But if in the
Absolute knowledge is perfected, as we conclude it is, then in
a higher form the end of such knowledge is actually realized,
and with ignorance and chance the last show of externality has
vanished.'[1]

9. (5) Further evidence for internal relations is to be found
in the nature of causality. There are two propositions about
causality which, if made out, would establish that everything
in the universe is related internally to everything else. These
propositions are, (i) that all things are *causally* related, directly
or indirectly; (ii) that being causally related involves being
logically related. We believe that there are sound reasons for
accepting both propositions; and since the conclusion they
carry with them is so important for our position, we must
examine them, particularly the second, in some detail.

(i) First, is everything related causally to everything else? If
anyone denies this, it is pretty certain to be on one or other of
two grounds, either (*a*) that some events are not caused at all,
or (*b*) that if all events are caused, at least they are not each
of them related causally to all of the others. (*a*) Until lately,
the first of these grounds would have been considered almost
absurd. The universality of the law of causation was generally
accepted without question. But recent work in quantum
physics has raised grave doubts about it. At least two independent lines of reflection have converged to suggest that the
ultimate components of matter are not governed in every
detail by causal law. On the one hand is the 'indeterminacy
principle' of Heisenberg, that 'a particle may have position or
it may have velocity, but it cannot in any exact sense have both'.
On the other hand is the view made familiar by Eddington
that the macroscopic objects whose behaviour science is able
to observe are all enormous aggregates of sub-atomic particles,

[1] *Appearance and Reality*, Appendix, note B.

that the regularity of their behaviour is merely the statistical stability displayed by other large aggregates, and that this regularity is as consistent in the one case as in the others with caprice among the ultimate components. The theory that there is something in the situation of a particular radium atom determining it to break up at one time rather than another 'is just like a multitude of other speculations which have at one time or another been put forward without evidence'.[1] An adequate discussion of these views would demand more space and far more knowledge of physics than the present writer has at his disposal. Two remarks will have to suffice. (α) Some physicists of the first competence in this realm have not been persuaded that the new results point validly to any suspension of causality, for example Einstein and Planck, Lodge and Rutherford. Thus, whichever side the layman takes, he will at least have high authority with him. (β) Some competent writers who have examined the Heisenberg principle are clear that it confuses indeterminacy in our knowledge with indeterminism in fact. Mr. Russell writes:

'As J. E. Turner has pointed out (*Nature*, December 27. 1930), "The use to which the Principle of Indeterminacy has been put is largely due to an ambiguity in the word 'determined'." In one sense a quantity is determined when it is measured, in the other sense an event is determined when it is caused. The Principle of Indeterminacy has to do with measurement, not with causation. The velocity and position of a particle are declared by the Principle to be undetermined in the sense that they cannot be accurately measured. This is a physical fact causally connected with the fact that the measuring is a physical process which has a physical effect upon what is measured. There is nothing whatever in the Principle of Indeterminacy to show that any physical event is uncaused.'[2]

In view of such opinions, it would be precipitate to assume that the principle of causality has finally been exploded. Of course one does not prove it true by showing that certain objections to it are questionable. But since, apart from such

[1] Eddington, *Arist. Soc. Proc.*, Sup. Vol. X (1931), 173.
[2] *The Scientific Outlook*, 109–110.

objections, the principle so clearly holds the field, a constructive argument for it is perhaps here uncalled for.

(*b*) But there is another ground of objection to the view that everything is causally related to everything else, a ground that does not lie in any doubt whether causation is universal, but in the belief that, granting its universality, there are spheres of causal influence that are closed to each other. Thus, what is happening now in the sun can be neither cause nor effect of anything now happening on earth; for no causal agency, not even gravitation, can travel faster than light, and it takes light an appreciable time, about eight minutes, to make the journey from sun to earth. But there is nothing in such facts to disturb us. We should not contend that everything is connected *directly* with everything else, i.e. that one could pass from any event to any other by following a single line of causation forward or backward. Obviously one could not. What does seem extremely probable, however, is that everything is connected directly *or* indirectly with everything else. Events now happening in the sun are traceable to causes occurring only a few minutes ago which in turn did affect the course of events on earth. Thus events in the two regions, even when neither is the cause of the other, are connected through *common* causes. Nor, if this mode of connection is recognized, does there seem to be any region or any event that is cut off from any other. There is of course nothing startling in this to the contemporary scientist. It is almost certain, writes Sir James Jeans, that 'every body pulls every other towards it, no matter how distant it may be. Newton's apple not only exerted its pull on the earth, but every star in the sky, and the motion of every star was affected by its fall. We cannot move a finger without disturbing all the stars'.[1]

Our first proposition about causality was that every existent is causally related to every other. If the causal relation is really

[1] *The Stars in Their Courses*, 74. I owe notice of the passage to Ewing, *Idealism*, 185. Cf. Francis Thompson:

'Thou canst not stir a flower
Without troubling of a star.'

universal, which we saw no compelling reason to deny, and 'causal relation' is interpreted to include indirect causal relation, this proposition has an excellent claim to be believed.

10. (ii) What about the other proposition? That proposition was that causality involves an element of necessity in the logical sense. This is far less likely to be accepted without protest than the first. Time was when it was accepted as evident by thinkers of the first rank, but this confidence was destroyed by Hume, and the prevailing tendency at present is to follow writers like Mach, Pearson and Russell in holding that there is nothing in causal law but regular antecedence and consequence. According to this view, all we are justified in meaning when we say that *a* causes *b* is that neither is ever found without the other. But it has become reasonably clear that this notion will not serve. There can be no doubt that we *mean* more than this by causality, and it can be established pretty certainly that there *is* more in it. We have not the space either for a complete discussion of the regularity theory or for an analysis of causality into its factors; but our purpose will be served if we show that among these factors logical necessity is one.

11. (*a*) That necessity does thus enter into causality is easier to see in some cases than in others, so we shall take at once the case in which its presence seems to us clearest. Consider any instance of reasoning, for example our old case of the abbé and the squire. 'Ladies', says the abbé, 'do you know that my first penitent was a murderer'? 'Ladies', says the squire, entering shortly afterward, 'do you know that I was the abbé's first penitent?' A conclusion was of course produced in the ladies' minds, and our question is as to the nature of the causation that produced it. It would be agreed between holders of the regularity theory and ourselves that the ladies' entertainment of the premises had something causally to do with the emergence in their minds of the conclusion. The question is whether, when we say that the one contributed causally to the other, our only proper meaning is that whenever the first appears the second does, or whether we must say also this, that the special logical relation in which the content of the premises stands to the content of the conclusion had something to do with the appearance of that conclusion. To us it seems plain that it had. According to the regularity theory our only ground for expecting the judgement that arose rather than some other quite different one, e.g. that Florida raises grapefruit, is that thoughts of the first kind have regularly been followed by thoughts of the second; the question *why* what followed did follow is one on which we are, and must remain, in total darkness; the connection between the events is no more intelligible than the connection of lightning and thunder for a savage. We must confess to feeling that there is something perverse in talk of this kind. If the ladies were asked how they came to have the belief with which they ended, they would say that it was because this belief was obviously implied by what they were thinking the moment before; and we are convinced that this answer, which is the natural one, is also substantially the right one. Not that no other causes contributed to the result; we are not suggesting, of course, that causality *reduces* to logical necessity. What we hold is that when one passes in reasoning from ground to consequent the fact that the ground entails the consequent is one of the conditions determining the appearance of this consequent rather than something else in the thinker's mind.

12. It has been held that this confuses two different kinds of relation. Logical relations are timeless, connecting essences or characters; causal relations are temporal, and connect events. Hence in reasoning '*logic* is not the *cause* of the outcome. Logic itself is not a series of causes and effects, whether physiological or psychological. Logic is simply the fact of the consistency of one proposition with another. It is the *knowledge* of these consistencies and inconsistencies which is (to some slight extent) the cause. . . .'[1] Causality links events; and the events in the case we have been considering are, first, my *acceptance* of the premises, then my *apprehension* that the premises entail the conclusion, and finally my *acceptance* of that conclusion. It is between these events, or psychical facts, that the causality holds, and it would be as meaningless to say that one such event *entails* another as to say the premises *cause* the conclusion.

This view is attractive for the moment, but it will not stand criticism. It attempts to draw a line horizontally through a train of events, and to say that above that line are characters or universals, the domain of logic, and below it existences or occurrences, the domain of causality. But we have seen long ago that no such line can be drawn,[2] and that if it could, causality would be deprived, not of necessity only, but of all meaning. The characters dealt with by logic do enter into the causal process; an event that was a mere event, endowed with no sort of character, would not even be an event; if *what* happens is nothing, then nothing happens. When a hammer drives a nail, the cause (in part) is the motion of a certain mass at a certain velocity. These characters are an integral part of the cause; it is in virtue of their presence that this effect rather than some other is produced, and no statement of what caused the effect could disregard them. Similarly the psychical event called the occurrence of a judgement in a mind is not a naked act or event; it is always a presentation of this rather than that; and the character of this content enters vitally into the causation.

Now if we go so far, we must go farther. If we say that the contents or characters of the events enter into the process, can we say that the relations between these characters are wholly irrelevant to it? Plainly we cannot and do not. Perhaps no one would deny that there is such a fact as association by similarity; and however hard it may be to construe the mechanism at work, it would be idle to deny that the similarity of content

---

[1] Durant Drake, *Invitation to Philosophy*, 372; italics in original.
[2] Chap. XII, Secs. 11, 12.

does at times have something to do with the appearance of an associate. That relations within the content thus play a part in causation is clearer still when the relation is one of logical necessity. In explicit inference we have a process in which we can directly see not only *that* one event succeeds another, but in large measure *why* it succeeds. Surely it would be absurd if, after the presence in our minds of the judgements, 'the squire was the abbé's first penitent' and 'that first penitent was a murderer', and the ensuing conclusion, 'the squire is a murderer', we should say we had not the faintest notion why this conclusion emerged rather than a judgement about Florida grapefruit. The fact that this was the logical conclusion to draw is clearly not irrelevant to its appearance as an event. This does not in the least commit us to saying that our thought processes are always logical, or that logical relations are temporal, or that they do not link timeless contents. It does commit us to saying that relations of necessity, connecting the content now before us with something else that is not before us, have something to do with the development of this content in one direction rather than another, that necessities within the subject-matter lay under some degree of compulsion the temporal course of thought. One may or may not accept the metaphysical theory we have offered earlier to explain this compulsion, but that it is a fact seems to us undeniable.

13. However, if direct inspection does not convince, there is another consideration that will perhaps fare better. It is this, that unless necessity does play a part in the movement of inference, no argument will establish anything. When one reaches a conclusion from evidence, one commonly assumes that one has been moved by the special character of this evidence, that the relevance of the evidence and the cogency of the argument had something to do with one's concluding as one did. If they did not and never do, then no conclusions are ever arrived at *because* the evidence requires them. The supposition that one has been moved by reasons is an illusion; one has been moved only by causes, between which and their effects there is no rational connection. The fact, then, that a conclusion is reached at the end of a course of argument, however rigidly each judgement may seem necessitated by the judgement that preceded it, has no bearing on its validity whatever, since in the actual causation of the judgement logical factors had no part. Now it is difficult to see how the advocate of such a position can even argue for it consistently. If he does argue for it, he assumes that his own belief and that of those he is trying to convince may be affected by his argument, and that the more reasonable or logically compelling he can make his case, the better his prospects of carrying conviction to 'reasonable' minds. If he were to act consistently with his theory, he would abandon reasoning himself and never seek to reason with others, since no one is really moved by such means to the adoption of any conclusion.

14. (*b*) But inference is of course only one of many mental processes. Can the influence of necessity which is displayed in it so plainly be traced in others also? We think it can. Not that its presence in those other processes is equally plain; nor would it be fair to expect this, since inference is concerned with necessity in a special manner. But we must remember what we have found earlier, that necessity, whatever our first impressions, is a matter of more and less, and that between a complete demonstration and a mere accidental conjunction it may be present in very many degrees. A process of rigorous inference approximates to the first of these extremes; association by mere contiguity approximates to the second; and between them are numerous processes in which there is more contingency than in inference, but more necessity than in association. Consider some examples. A painter is painting a landscape that is half completed, and he finds himself moved to put a tree in the foreground. Is such a development normally quite unintelligible? Certainly most painters would not say so. Is it then an example of pure necessity? No again; it clearly falls somewhere between. Or let us say that a man is intensely afraid of dogs. With the help of psycho-analysis he discovers that at an early age he was badly injured by the attack of a dog; it may come to him as a quasi-intuitive insight that it was this that caused his fear; and let us suppose that in this belief he is right. Can one say in such a case that it remains absolutely unintelligible to him how the fear arose? We do not think so Again, 'why are modest men grateful? Because they think lightly of their own deserts. This implies a syllogism in Barbara. All who think lightly of their own deserts are grateful, and modest men think lightly of their own deserts.'[1] Does the major premise here, 'All who think lightly of their own deserts are grateful', express a causal or a logical connection? We suggest that it expresses both. If a man whom we know to think little of himself proves grateful for another's esteem, is that, apart from inductions made on such people in the past, as start ing a development, as unpredictable and unintelligible, as if he had begun talking in a Sumerian tongue or had run murderously amuck? Surely that is an odd view. We are not contending that between thinking lightly of oneself and being grateful there is the same simple abstract connection that one finds in geometry; it is true that one cannot isolate in human nature the precise reciprocating conditions of gratitude, or formulate one's law in anything better than a statement of tendency; but that, after all, is not utter darkness; we do have *some* insight into why the man of low self-esteem should be grateful for the esteem of others. And so of numberless other processes of the mind.

Dr. Ewing puts the case well:

'It seems to me that we can see and to some extent really understand why an insult should tend to give rise to anger, why love should lead to grief if the object of one's love die or prove thoroughly unworthy, why a success should give pleasure, why the anticipation of physical pain should arouse fear. It does seem more reasonable on *other than inductive* grounds to sup-

[1] Joseph, *Logic*, 306.

pose that if A loves B that will tend to make him sorry when B dies than to suppose that it will make him intensely glad. . . . At any rate anybody who denies altogether the insight for which I am contending will have to hold that it is just as reasonable to think of love as causing intense joy at the death of the person loved, except that this does not happen in fact.'[1]

Indeed, Ewing would go farther. He would hold that

'if the regularity view were the whole truth, all practical life would become sheer nonsense. For all practical life presupposes that we can "do things" and are moved by motives and desires. . . . To say that such and such an action is due, e.g., to desire for power as a motive is more than to say that such actions generally are preceded by desire for power. . . . It is to say that in this particular case it does not merely follow on but is determined by the desire in question.' And this view accepts 'causation in the sense not of regular sequence, but of genuine intrinsic connection.'[2]

15. Those who are determined to reduce necessity to tautology will have a ready answer to all such arguments: the consequent that seems to be entailed by love, or low self-esteem, or the incomplete work of the painter, is not a predicate distinct from the subject and necessitated by it, but part of the subject itself; to feel gratitude when praised by others, for example, is part of the meaning of low self-esteem; the judgement is analytic. But this will not stand inspection. An analytic judgement is one in which the predicate forms part of the subject *concept*, that is, part of the subject as thought of. 'A circle is round' is analytic if to think of a circle *is* to think of a round figure; 'a circle is that plane figure which encloses the largest area with the smallest perimeter' is not analytic, because, though it is as necessary as the first, the predicate need form no part of the subject concept; one can think of a circle without thinking of this property of it. To say that a judgement is still analytic when the predicate is part of the subject, not as thought of, but as existent *in rerum natura*,

[1] *Idealism*, 176–8.　　　　　　　　[2] *Ibid.*, 161–2.

would make the drawing of the distinction impossible in the larger number of our judgements. Very well; *is* the feeling of gratitude part of what we mean by low self-esteem, in the sense that we cannot think of the latter without thinking of the former? The answer is clearly No. I can perfectly well think of low self-esteem without any reference whatever to gratitude, and yet see when it is pointed out to me that there is more than an accidental connection between them.

Again, it may be said that to call such propositions necessary is to take them as a priori, and to take them as a priori is to say that they are not dependent on experience, and to say that propositions about special types of emotion and desire are not dependent on experience is preposterous. But once more the answer is plain. The earmark of a priori connections is not our ability to conceive them before they are presented in fact, but simply their necessity; and necessary connections are as truly presented in and through the given as any other connections. That whatever is red is extended is obviously learned *through* experience, though this does not involve saying that, like the proposition 'red coals burn', it is a mere empirical conjunction. It may be said, still again, that necessity holds only among formal characteristics, such as those studied in arithmetic and geometry, not among such qualitative characters as love, hate, and desire. But this is mere superstition. The propositions 'what is red is extended' and 'pleasure is a good' are every whit as a priori as '2 + 2 = 4'. We are not suggesting that in the instances mentioned of mental causality the factors connected and the connections between them can be isolated as they can in these simpler instances. It seems probable that the causal relation is everywhere complex, and that the relation of necessity is but one of its strands. It is probable, too, that when we speak of low self-esteem producing gratitude, our two terms are themselves far vaguer and more complex than we realize, so that if they were fully analysed we should see that we had included something in each which was not intimately connected with the other, and omitted from each something that was so connected. And any law that we attempted to formulate would no doubt be of the roughest kind. But what does that prove? Only that in these cases no necessary nexus has as yet been analysed out. Such failure to discern connections has been too frequent in the past to weigh decisively against the almost certain conviction that in these cases we do have insight into *why* the result arises.

16. (c) There is thus good reason to think that not only in inference but also in many other mental processes the causal relation involves necessity. But what of causation in physical nature? This is the field in which most cases of causation are considered to fall, yet current philosophies of science are disposed to agree that no relation whatever is discoverable between physical cause and effect but one of regular conjunction. Certain it is that between the blow of a hammer and the sinking of a nail, or between the motion of one billiard-ball and that of a second, no one has shown the same transparent relation that appears in a course of inference and may be recognized under veils of varying depth in other processes of the mind. The challenge laid down by Hume to show *why* any particular physical event was followed by any other has not been met. Nor do we propose to add one more to the list of futile attempts to meet it. But we should be clear as to what is implied in the failure to meet it. Does such failure in particular cases show that causality generally is nothing but regular sequence? Very far from it. Indeed I think it can be shown that regular sequence is not enough, that there must be some intrinsic connection between cause and effect, and that this intrinsic connection probably is, or includes, one of logical necessity. We must dwell on this a little, since it is important for our position that it should be seen.

In order to overthrow the regular-sequence theory, nothing more, strictly speaking, need be shown than what has been contended for already. It will hardly be denied that mental processes supply genuine cases of causality, and any case at all in which the relation involves necessity is enough to invalidate an account which asserts that it never does. But we are dealing now with causality in physical nature. It seems to me that even there the theory has been disposed of by certain criticisms that have recently been made of it.

17. One of the most persuasive of these has been offered by Professor Montague. It is substantially as follows. How do we proceed when in ordinary life we must calculate the probability of finding a sequence repeated, where the events that are conjoined are not known to be connected otherwise? Suppose we throw a die and get a six. The chances that six will be given in a single throw, we say, are one in six, or $1/6$. Assuming that there is nothing, to our knowledge, in the manner of throwing the die that will secure one side rather than another, what are the chances that a second throw will bring a like result? They will be $1/6 \times 1/6$ or $1/36$. What are the chances of getting three sixes in a row? They will be $(1/6)^3$ or $1/216$. The likelihood of getting six sixes in a row would be one in a little less than 50,000, and if we carried the repetitions to ten or more, the figures would become astronomical. Now if we found that anyone, in throwing a die, kept getting sixes regularly, we should soon begin to harbour suspicions. We should accept his results tolerantly perhaps through two or three repetitions, or if we were extremely charitable, perhaps a few more; but there would soon come a time for the most naïve of us when the hypothesis of mere luck would impose such a strain on our belief as compared with the hypothesis of some sort of control, that we should think anyone a dupe who went on crediting it.

Now, says Mr. Montague, suppose that we throw water on fire. We cannot say what the chances are of getting any one result, say quenching the fire, because we can set no limit to the number of possible alternatives.[1] But we *can* say something, he thinks, if one of these results goes on repeating itself to the

---

[1] Strictly speaking, we cannot set such a limit in the other case either. We cannot a priori rule out the possibility that the die should stand on one of its corners and spin there permanently.

exclusion of all others. If there is really nothing in event *a* that would compel or require event *b* to follow, then it is antecedently as likely, indeed enormously more likely, that *a* would be followed in a second case by something other than *b* than by *b* itself. And if, in spite of this, *b*, and *b* alone, continues to appear with *a*, is it not as naïve to suppose them unconnected by anything but chance as would be the like supposition about unfailing wins at dice? Yet that is essentially what the regularity theory, with its denial of intrinsic relation, commits us to. It says in effect that if water continues to quench fire, that is only 'an outrageous run of luck'.

Unfortunately, as Mr. Montague recognizes, the case is not quite so simple. For if you take seriously the hypothesis of merely chance conjunctions, then among the possibilities covered by that hypothesis is not only repetition of *a* with varying consequents but also its repetition with the same consequent. This will be less surprising if we reflect on the literal truth of the old adage that it is always the improbable that happens. Whatever side of a die comes up, the chances against it before it happened were five to one; yet it happened for all that. The simultaneous occurrence of the events composing the present universe is only one out of an infinite number of possibilities, and hence was all but infinitely improbable a moment ago; yet here it is. Similarly the repetition of *a* and *b* together a dozen times, or a hundred, or a thousand, is most unlikely beforehand, but still it is one of the possibilities conceivable under the reign of chance. And therefore it is absurd to offer it as evidence against the reign of chance.

Is there any effective rejoinder to this reply? On its own grounds I do not think there is.[1] Of an infinite number of chance combinations, the known history of the world may present one, and it might fairly be argued that any extension of that history, with any multiplication of its uniformities, could only produce another. Nevertheless, as a reply to the

---

[1] I say 'not on its own grounds' because I think there are other ways in which the theory that all succession is chance succession can be attacked, e.g. through the direct exhibition of necessity in inference.

case just presented, the argument commits the fallacy of inexhaustive division. The question at issue is how the successions we actually find are to be interpreted or accounted for, and the original argument proceeded by offering the alternative of chance or some form of necessity, and then eliminating the first. The alternatives considered in the reply are not these at all; they are all of them combinations that would be possible under *one* of these, namely, the hypothesis of chance. The exponent of the view has been so eager to show that the hypothesis he prefers will cover the facts that he has forgotten that to the hypothesis under which all his combinations fall there is a further alternative which may cover the facts equally well. And when we turn from chance hypothesis to the hypothesis of an intrinsic connection, we find that it not only covers the facts equally well; it covers them vastly better. For on the chance hypothesis every successive repetition of a conjunction given in the past is the occurrence of the progressively more improbable,[1] while on the hypothesis of intrinsic connection, it is only a confirmation, more impressive at each recurrence, of what the hypothesis predicted. So far, neither theory can absolutely exclude its rival. But the chance hypothesis, while according with the known arrangement, would accord equally with any other. The hypothesis of connection accords selectively with the arrangement actually found.[2]

18. The view that cause and effect are connected by more than conjunctions, even in the physical realm, would thus appear more reasonable than its opposite. But further, even those who accept the regularity view are compelled, sometimes in

[1] Not, to be sure, if every length of run were to be counted as equally probable; but in that case, the hypothesis, as according equally with every conceivable arrangement, could neither be compared with any other, nor, therefore, urged in preference.

[2] This reply is stated a little differently from Professor Montague's but I think it is in substance the same. For his discussions of the point see *Proceedings of the Seventh International Congress of Philosophy*, 198 ff., and the somewhat fuller account in *Ways of Knowing*, 199 ff.

the statement of this view itself, to assume that it is false. When they say that events have causes in the sense of regular and special antecedents, they intend this to apply to the future as well as to the past. But they have not experienced the future, and hence they must be using an *argument*: *Because b* has followed *a* in the past, it will continue to do so. Now unless *a* is connected with *b* by something more than mere conjunction, there is no ground for this argument whatever. What, apart from such connection, could be our reason for saying that uniform sequence in the past would carry with it uniform sequence in the future? We may say of course that when we have argued from such uniformities in the past to their continuance in the future, we have found our expectations verified, but plainly this will not do, for the uniform sequence of verification upon expectation is only another sequence, on a par with the original ones, and is entitled to no special privileges when the question is as to our right to argue from *any* past sequence to others. Again, if we make it a matter of probability, and say that a conjunction frequently recurrent is more likely to be maintained than broken, this either repeats the old assumption whose basis is in question, that the past is a guide to the future, or else is clearly false, since if *a* and *b* are really unconnected, there is no more reason to expect them to continue together than there is to expect an unloaded penny to go on giving heads because it has just done so ten times running. When this old puzzle about induction is raised, the answer usually given is that we 'postulate' the uniformity of nature, viz., that the same cause is always followed by the same effect. But what is the status of this postulate? Is it merely an arbitrary assumption? Clearly not; in some sense it arises out of experience. Is it then a conclusion derived from experience? No, for, as has been pointed out times without number, the argument would be circular; unless we assumed 'same cause, same effect', we could not argue that the same cause as in the past would be followed by the same effect. But then the question arises, what part *does* this assumption play in the argument? And the answer is that it is the *principle* of the inference, just as the principle of syllogism is the canon involved in any syllogistic reasoning. Now can the principle of an argument or inference be totally without necessity? We can only say that, if so, the 'inference' to which it applies is no inference at all, and quite without cogency. We are not maintaining, of course, that the principle of uniformity has the clear and definite necessity of geometric demonstration, nor is that to be expected while the terms that pass muster as causes and effects remain so loose and vague. We do maintain, however, that the passage from past to future sequences is clearly an argument, that the principle of the argument, as of inferences generally, must be more than a chance conjunction of symbols or characters, and hence that the linkage between cause and effect in virtue of which we predict their future sequence is always implicitly taken as intrinsic.[1]

19. Indeed, whatever the difficulties of finding the true connection between cause and effect, the difficulties of holding that they are not connected at all except by *de facto* conjunction is far greater. We have no room here to develop these in full, but by way of rounding out our brief case against this theory, we may set down the following paradoxes. (1) If causality *means* regularity of sequence, every unique event must be regarded as uncaused. An unexampled biological sport could not even be set down as miracle since miracles are supposed to be caused; it would have to be an explosion of chance.[2] (2) No human action would ever spring from a self or from a motive; there is

---

[1] Cf. Mill's definition of cause as *unconditional* antecedent. On the argument involved in induction, see Ewing, *Idealism*, 151 ff.; for the difficulties of the regular-sequence view, see Ewing, *ibid.*, and Ducasse, *Causation and Types of Necessity*, Chaps. I, II, V.

[2] The converse criticism is also sometimes urged, that there are regular sequences where there is no causal or other intrinsic connection; day follows night, ruminants are cloven-footed, white tom-cats that have blue eyes are deaf. The argument is unconvincing. For there is usually, if not always, the suspicion that if the terms are not themselves connected intrinsically, they are both so connected with a third term.

no intrinsic connection between volition and behaviour, character and conduct, motive and performance. Strictly speaking, no one murders anyone, though in some cases homicide has unhappily and quite inexplicably associated itself with certain elements of a person's constitution. This association is the more unfortunate because, though wholly irrational, it is also permanent. Such a view conflicts at a thousand points with our everyday judgements about practical action and moral accountability; and though all these judgements may be mistaken, the fact that the sequence view would *require* that they be mistaken is enough to impose on it a heavy burden of proof.[1] (3) Note that we used the word 'require'. It was natural to use it, and those who hold the regularity view do frequently use it. Yet, as we have seen, if they hold any belief that is said to be required by their theory, its being required can have nothing to do with their holding it. (4) Nor is their explanation of how we came to suppose that causality involved more than association at all convincing. The usual explanation is Hume's, that the regular repetition of *a* and *b* together produced a habit of conjoining them in thought. But apart from the difficulty that a habit or even a thought of uniform conjunction is clearly different from the thought of necessity, what is meant here by 'produced'? When one says that regular repetition produces a habit, does one mean only that there is a regular repetition of regular-repetition's-being-followed-by-a-habit? It does not seem likely. (5) Hume's confident denial that we could perceive anything more than sequence in the connection of particular events becomes more doubtful the more one thinks about it. Mr. Montague has pointed out that though the way the body acts upon the mind remains in darkness, still, when we resolve to attend to something more closely and 'in consequence' succeed in doing so, we have a sense of 'enforcement' that does not leave us wholly blank as to the mode of connection; and Mr. Whitehead has urged that in particular cases of perception we are immediately aware of being causally acted upon by some external agency.

[1] See Ewing, *op. cit.*, 162.

(6) The position would guarantee a scepticism that may be unavoidable, but is not to be accepted till necessary. It says that between the percept and its cause there is no intrinsic connection. Now since we have no access to nature except through impressions that are presumably produced in us causally, we must depend for knowledge of nature on an argument from the character of the impressions to the character of their source. Such argument would be rendered impossible by the sort of causation before us. (7) Stout and Ewing have held, rightly I think, that the memory of our own experiences would be rendered impossible by it. When I recall a particular event that happened yesterday, one of the factors that led to the recall was the occurrence of the past event itself. And when we say that this event 'conditioned' this recall, we do not mean that all similar events are followed by such recalls, for we plainly have in mind one particular event happening at a point in past time. (8) Finally, to say that causality involves nothing but regular sequence brings one into sharp conflict with both common sense and science. The plain man has undoubtedly got it fixed in his head that when he drives a nail with a blow of his hammer, there is an inner connection between these events which is not to be found between either of them and, say, a storm in the Antilles. If it is objected that his views are worthless, it may be pointed out that science from its birth has suffered from the same obsession. To be sure, in some manuals like Mill's and Pearson's the uniformity view is insisted on, and Mr. Russell has even suggested that the name and notion of causality should be dropped by science.[1] But we do not believe that scientific thought, even in physics, on which he too exclusively relies,[2] really has succeeded, or will succeed, in dispensing with it. The reason is that behind the scientist's desire to unbare the causes of things is his desire to understand, and his intuition that in mastering the cause of something he *has* to some extent understood it. We do not believe that the *only* reason why the scientific mind has rejected

---

[1] *Mysticism and Logic*, 180.
[2] Cf. Stebbing, *Modern Introduction to Logic*, 289.

astrology is that the correlation between positions of the stars and the ups and downs of human fortune has been imperfectly made out. We do not believe that when the connection was revealed between tuberculosis and bacilli, physicians would have admitted that it gave no further understanding of the disease, but only a new fact, concomitant though wholly external. It is notorious that the physical scientist finds his ideal in mathematics; and if he continues to refine and purify his statements of abstract connection, it is surely because in doing so he feels himself approaching not only the precision but also the necessity of mathematical relations. Of course his conviction may have been a delusion from the beginning. But whoever says so assumes the burden of proof.[1]

20. For all these reasons we believe that the view which would deny to causality any intrinsic connection and reduce it to conjunction may be dismissed. *Some* intrinsic connection there must be. But of what sort? Does the insight that between cause and effect there is an intrinsic connection suffice to show that this is also a *necessary* connection? We believe that it does.

Consider the meaning of 'same cause, same effect', which we have seen to be the principle of all inductive causal argument. Why do we accept it? We have seen that if it is taken as expressive of conjunction only, no evidence for it and no argument under it are possible; and we have suggested that if it is accepted nevertheless, that is because we have an insight that is felt as justifying it. The nature of this insight will become clearer if we try for a moment to conceive the connection to be

[1] We may repeat Bosanquet's question: 'Is there any man of science who in his daily work, and apart from philosophic controversy, will accept a bare given conjunction as conceivably ultimate truth?' (*Distinction between Mind and its Objects*, 59–60); and Ewing: 'Thinkers and scientists looked for causes because they wished to *explain* events, and if they had seriously held from the beginning the views of causation which most realist philosophers hold to-day, half the inspiration of the scientific search for causes would have been missing and induction would never have been trusted at all.'—*Op. cit.*, 176.

otherwise. Conceive a state of affairs in which there is causation but no uniformity; everything now has a cause, but the causes vary; everything produces effects, but the effects vary; the blow of the hammer sinks the nail today, but tomorrow under precisely the same conditions it fails to do so, and produces instead the *Melody in F* or a case of measles in Novgorod. We can talk thus, since we have just done it, but can we think thus? We cannot. For as Mr. Joseph says, 'to say that anything may produce anything is to empty the word "produce" of all its meaning'.[1] Why? Because it implies that when *a* produces *x*, the *nature* of *a* had nothing to do with the result; that result could equally have appeared if nothing resembling *a* had been on the scene. But if *a*, in virtue of its nature, exercised no constraining influence at all, why say *it* produced something? *It* is a thing of special character; this character makes it what it is; and we should be talking idly if we said that *it* produced something when this character was in no way engaged.

> 'To assert a causal connexion between *a* and *x* implies that *a* acts as it does because it is what it is. . . . For the causal relation which connects *a* with *x* connects a cause of the *nature a* with an effect of the *nature x*. The connexion is between them *as a* and *x*, and therefore must hold between any *a* and any *x* . . .'[2]

Now we suggest that when *a* is said to produce *x* in virtue of its nature as *a*, the connection referred to is not only an intrinsic relation but a necessary relation. There are two considerations that make us think so. (1) Reflection seems to show that necessity is part of our *meaning* when we call such relations intrinsic. If we lay down a yellow card, then to the right of it an orange card, and to the right of that a red one, they have spatial relations to each other, but those relations are not *prima facie* intrinsic, for so far as we can see there is nothing about a card of one colour *as such* to demand particular space relations to cards of other colours. Now consider the relations, not of the cards, but of the colours themselves. Regarded merely

---

[1] *Logic*, 407.　　　　　　　　　[2] Joseph, *ibid.*, 408–9.

as colour, orange comes between red and yellow. And that relation is intrinsic in the present sense, since it is obviously determined by the natures of the three colours. But note that it is also necessary; we see that, yellow, orange and red being what they are, orange *must* come between the other two, and could not possibly fall elsewhere. Is this not the case with all relations that turn on the oontent or character of the terms? It seems to us that it is. Not that the necessity is seen with equal purity or clearness in all such cases, but that whenever we see that a relation depends on *a*'s being what it is, we see *that* the relation is necessary whether we can isolate the nexus or not. Whether the tendency to gratitude, for example, follows from the nature of modesty we may not be quite sure, but *if* we are, we are sure that modesty *must* carry with it this tendency. Indeed to say that something follows from the nature of *a*, but not necessarily, seems meaningless.

But is this necessity in the logical sense, or have we smuggled into the term some meaning that is allied, perhaps, but distinct? That the necessity is genuinely logical will be clearer from our second point. (2) To say that *a* produces *x* in virtue of being *a* and yet that, given *a*, *x* might not follow, is inconsistent with the laws of identity and contradiction. Of course if *a* were a cluster of qualities abstracted from their relations, and its modes of causal behaviour were another set conjoined with the former externally, then one could deny the latter and retain the former with perfect consistency. But we have seen that when we say *a* causes *x*, we do *not* mean that sort of conjunction; we mean an intrinsic relation, i.e. a relation in which *a*'s behaviour is the outgrowth or expression of *a*'s nature. And to assert that *a*'s behaviour, so conceived, could be different while *a* was the same would be to assert that something both did and did not issue from the nature of *a*. And that is self-contradiction. The statement would also, though perhaps not so apparently, conflict with the law of identity. It implies that a thing may remain itself when you have stripped from it everything which it is *such as* to be and do. To strip it of these things would be to strip it, so to speak, of the suchness that makes it what it is, i.e., to say that it is other than it is.[1]

21. We are now in a position to see the upshot of our long argument about causality. There were two propositions, we said, which if established would carry with them the conclusion that everything that exists is related internally to

[1] Against a similar position as advanced by Mr. Joseph (*Logic*, 406 ff.), an acute critic (Professor L. S. Stebbing, *A Modern Introduction to Logic*, 286) has urged that 'Mr. Joseph at least appears to be confusing two different propositions which it is of the utmost importance to distinguish. The two propositions are: (1) A has the causal property P because it in fact has it; (2) A must have the causal property P because nothing which had not P could be A. Whilst the first of these propositions is a truism, the second is by no means obviously true'; indeed Miss Stebbing, following Dr. Moore's well-known essay on external relations (*Philosophical Studies*), thinks it frequently untrue. Without presuming to know what Mr. Joseph's reply would be, I must own that I cannot see the confusion here. The charge is that Mr. Joseph must be saying either (1), which is trivial, or (2), which is a *petitio*. He is evidently not saying (1), for he holds that in 'A causes B' we do not assert merely that B accompanies A, but that it does so in virtue of A's nature. Is he then asserting (2)? I do not see he is, nor that if he were, any *petitio* would be involved. What (2) asserts, we are told, is a material implication: 'proposition (2) above is equivalent to the assertion that it is not the case that "A has the causal property P" is true whilst "anything that had not P must be other than A" is false.' But Mr. Joseph is not saying, as I read him, merely that A has P *and* that X's not having P entails its not being A; he is saying that A has P in such a sense, i.e. in virtue of its nature as A, as to *entail*, and not merely to be accompanied by, the truth of this second assertion. But even if he were saying what is attributed to him, where is the *petitio*? To say that A produces something in virtue of its nature as A does surely entail the proposition that X's not having P entails its not being A; to deny this would be absurd. The objection then must be that the very statement that anything produces anything in virtue of its nature must be question-begging. But if so, it would appear to be question-begging to adopt any position on any controversial issue. Mr. Joseph contends, I take it, that when we attentively consider what we mean by saying A causes B (or has the property P of causing it) we find that part of our meaning is that A acts in this way (or has this property) in virtue of its special nature. I do not myself see that this assertion is either question-begging or untrue.

everything else, i.e., is so related that without this relation it would not be what it is. These propositions were that everything is *causally* connected with everything else, directly or indirectly, and that being causally connected involved being connected by a relation of logical *necessity*. The first proposition, while perhaps undemonstrable, we found probable enough to commend itself to most philosophers and scientists, and the arguments against it were unconvincing. The second proposition has given us far more trouble. Does causality involve intelligible necessity? We have seen that in some cases it does unquestionably, for it does in every case of genuine inference. But can we say the same of causality generally? We saw that the principle could be extended to a great many other mental processes, though the presence of necessity was here less clearly discernible. But what about the enormous range of causal processes in physical nature? Was any hint or trace of really intelligible connection to be found among them? Many writers on scientific method have denied this and have sought to commit science to the view that there is nothing in causality but regularity of sequence or functional dependence. This view we have found so full of paradoxical consequences as to be incredible. Its rejection left us with the result that between cause and effect there is some sort of intrinsic connection, a result confirmed by considering that ordinary inductive procedure involves an argument which without this would be invalid. But is this intrinsic connection necessary? Yes, for when anything is said to have a consequent or a consequence in virtue of its special nature, necessity is part of our meaning, and what follows can not be denied except on pain of self-contradiction. Note that in this we have made no such unredeemable claim as that we can see *why* a particular hammer-stroke should drive a particular nail. Despite all the changes in physics since the turn of the century, we are very far from the sort of insight into physical things that would enable us to isolate the nerve of a given physical interaction. But unless there is such a nerve, the principle is illusory on which all practice is conducted and all causal argument is based.

22. Now if all this is true, it is hard to see how the conclusion is to be resisted that the universe of existing things is a system in which all things are related internally. Let *a* and *x* be *any* two things in the universe. They are then related to each other causally. But if causally, then also intrinsically, and if intrinsically then also necessarily, in the sense that they causally act as they do in virtue of their nature or character, and that to deny such activity would entail denying them to be what they are. And to have this sort of relation to all other things is precisely what we mean by being related to them internally.

From this there is another important conclusion that in turn will follow: the immanent end of thought is no will-o'-the-wisp; it is relevant to the experienced nature of things; to the best of our knowledge the immanent and transcendent ends coincide. The aim of thought from its very beginning, we saw, was at understanding. To understand anything meant to apprehend it in a system that rendered it necessary. The ideal of complete understanding would be achieved only when this system that rendered it necessary was not a system that itself was fragmentary and therefore contingent, but one that was all-inclusive and so organized internally that every part was linked to every other by intelligible necessity. But was this *more* than an ideal? Was there any reason to suppose that by its attainment thought would be nearer to its second end, the apprehension of things as they are? Such an ideal, as we have said, appears ludicrously remote from the world of actual experience, where we are met at every turn by seeming contingency and unintelligibility. At least it is thus remote at the first glance, and perhaps also at the second and third. But we have seen that in the very nature of terms in relation, and in the nature of causality, there is ground for believing that such contingency is apparent only. In what we take as the real world we can see the outlines of a necessary structure that is the counterpart of thought's ideal. There is nothing to stay our conclusion that with approximation to its immanent end, the achievement of systematic necessity, thought is also approximating its transcendent end, the apprehension of the real.

With this result we have reached the natural end of our inquiry. We have sketched the ideal of thought, and shown, so far as we could, that it is applicable to the real. If any reader is disposed to complain that the idea of a completely coherent system is still obscure, we may point out that in our present position there are two kinds of obscurity. One is the kind that comes of relaxing logical tension in the face of ultimate difficulty, of letting all holds go, surrendering to 'wishful thinking', and plunging blindly into the mist. As one nears so high a conclusion, and one so much to be desired, as the intelligibility of the world, the temptation to relapse into a milky mysticism is strong. If there has been any compromise with this sort of thing, we are culpable; we hope there has not. On the other hand, there is a kind of vagueness whose condemnation, on such an issue, would be far less reasonable. If thought is what we hold it is, namely the pursuit of an end whose character can be realized only as the pursuit advances, a full and clear account of that end must in the nature of the case be impossible at any point along the journey. An account that was really adequate would not now be intelligible; an account that was quite simple, neat and plain could only be suspicious. The tale we have told of the concrete universal, and concrete necessity, and a system of parts such that none can be or be known without the others, cannot be rendered entirely clear from the level of a logic of mosaics. And of this particular kind of obscurity we trust we have been adequately guilty.

23. If our account of the end is accepted, it will be found to throw light backward along the whole course of the inquiry. For it presents the goal which thought, from its first stirrings in perception, has more or less unknowingly been seeking, the end potential in every idea, the whole implicitly at work at every stage of the movement of reflection, exercising its

steady pressure against irrelevant excursions and toward the completion of fragmentary knowledge into stable system. The farther thought progresses, the more clearly does its system, as now attained, reveal the character of the system that lies beyond. When we began our study of the movement of reflection, we gave examples of the sort of whole that governed the movement at the level of ordinary thought. We said at the time that they were only provisional, that if the impulse of thought toward self-revision was a fact, they would inevitably be superseded by systems more satisfactory. What in detail lies at the end of this process of continual self-revision we do not know, nor ever can know till we have attained it. But at least we can see the direction in which we must move if we wish to attain it. Thought is seeking to supersede all partial systems by a further system that will not so much nullify its earlier gains as absorb and extend them, and it can come finally to rest only when this process is incapable of further continuance. And if we are right in our contention that thought is the potentiality of the object it seeks to know, then what brings fulfilment to the theoretic impulse must bring also the most complete and immediate experience of the real.

24. We have not of course *proved* our view regarding the end of thought. There can be no question of proof where the very nature of proof is at stake. In the last resort, all we can say to the doubter is, Here is the standard and ideal that for our own part we seem to be using in the practice of thought; is it not yours also? When you have seemed to understand, has it not always been through system? As your understanding grows more complete, is it not always through a system of greater unity, in the sense explained? And if the ideal seems unconvincing and artificial, consider its alternatives. Do they formulate better or worse what you mean by understanding? When we read a famous book called *Ethics Geometrically Demonstrated*, most of us feel that we are getting light. The empiricist would say that in the end this illumination consists in following association, that and nothing else; can you verify such an account of your own understanding? We read *The Origin of Species*, and man's place in nature is transformed for us. We have gained a flood of light, of indubitable intellectual light. How much of it would be left as light if, following the lead of formalism, we denied all degrees to necessity, and confined it to a nexus of the barest abstractions? Again, speaking for ourselves, we get light from *Principia Mathematica*, less perhaps than we should, but some. Does its genuineness depend on ensuing changes in practice, as the pragmatists would have us believe? Or perhaps in a poem, or a piece of music, or one of the varieties of religious experience, an insight is gained that one hesitates to call understanding, because understanding has come to be thought so abstractly intellectual an affair. On our view it *is* understanding, special in kind, to be sure, and limited in degree, but still with rights of its own; and to reject it as understanding on the ground of its concreteness is perverse. If you accept the ideal of concrete necessity, these varying insights are legitimized, ordered, and appraised. Accept any other whatever, and, against what seems to us your better judgement, some must be excluded.

25. It is perhaps not for a speculative writer to speak of the utility of his doctrines, still less to commend them on grounds of their utility. But one may be forgiven a final word on the contemporary pertinence of a theory that has been laboured through so many pages. That theory, as any informed reader will have seen, only restates with variations an ancient doctrine of 'the great tradition', of what Professor Urban has been persuasively urging as *philosophia perpetua* or *perennis*, the doctrine of the autonomy and objectivity of reason, the doctrine that through different minds one intelligible world is in course of construction or reconstruction. This holds quite simply that the secret of sound thinking is the surrender of individual will to an immanent and common reason. Of the value of such an attitude in art and letters, where present standards of

THE NATURE OF THOUGHT

criticism are not perhaps conspicuous for either unity or freedom from caprice, we shall not speak. But there is another field where self-will and the repudiation of a common standard of judgement and obligation threaten to extinguish the life of reason altogether. We conclude this book at a time when the recognition of such a standard, set by a common intelligence, and adequate as a court of appeal to the settlement of even national differences, is receding into the distance. The philosopher's way of protesting is perhaps too qualified and muffled to be heard; certainly it is when the drift toward chaos once gains momentum. But the writer would like to think that the insistent and reiterated emphasis, maintained throughout this work, on the membership of minds in one intelligible order may serve, however minutely, to confirm the belief in a common reason, and the hope and faith that in the end it will prevail.

INDEX

[*For a full synopsis of the argument, see the Analytical Table of Contents.*]